BOOKS

BOOKS

The Culture and Commerce of Publishing

LEWIS A. COSER
CHARLES KADUSHIN
WALTER W. POWELL

Basic Books, Inc., Publishers

NEW YORK

The authors gratefully acknowledge permission to use, in chapter 6, excerpts from Beulah W. Hagen's Oral History, Oral History Research Office, Columbia University, 1976; and information provided by Elizabeth Geiser in an interview with Michele Caplette in May 1978.

Excerpts from *Publishers Weekly* reprinted by permission from R. R. Bowker Company, a Xerox company. Copyright © by Xerox Corporation.

Portions of the manuscript draw upon the following previously published articles:

Lewis A. Coser, "Publishers as Gatekeepers of Ideas," *Annals* of the American Academy of Political and Social Science, vol. 421, September 1975, pp. 14–22; "Asymmetries in Author-Publisher Relations," *Society* 17 (1 [November/December 1979]), pp. 34–37; "The Private and Public Responsibilities of the American Publisher," 4 April 1979, Library of Congress seminar reprinted in John Y. Cole, *Responsibilities of the American Book Community* (Washington, D.C.: Library of Congress), pp. 14–19.
Charles Kadushin, "Managed Texts: Prose and Qualms," *Change*, March 1979, pp. 30–35, 64.
Walter W. Powell, "Publisher's Decision-Making: What Criteria Do They Use in Deciding Which Books to Publish?" *Social Research* 45 (2 [summer 1978]), pp. 227–52; "The Blockbuster Decade: The Media as Big Business," *Working Papers for a New Society*, July/August 1979, pp. 26–36; "Control and Conflict in Publishing," *Society* 17 (1 [November/December 1979]), pp. 48–54; "Competition versus Concentration in the Book Trade," *Journal of Communication* 30 (2 [spring 1980]), pp. 89–97.

Library of Congress Cataloging in Publication Data

Coser, Lewis A., 1913–
  Books : the culture and commerce of publishing.

  Includes bibliographical references and index.
  1. Publishers and publishing—United States. 2. Books industries and trade—United States. I. Kadushin, Charles. II. Powell, Walter W.
  Z471.C69   070.5´0973   81–66100
  ISBN 0–465–00745–7   AACR2

Contents

Contents

PART II

The People Who Make Books

Contents

PART III

Key Outsiders in the Book Trade

Contents

Preface

A S IN any collaborative project, the authors come from different backgrounds. Two of us had done previous work in what may loosely be called the "sociology of intellectual life." Lewis A. Coser, in *Men of Ideas* (Free Press, 1965) had attempted to throw light on such settings as coffee-houses, salons, academies, and bohemian communities as backgrounds for the emergence of professional writers since the eighteenth century. Charles Kadushin, in *The American Intellectual Elite* (Little, Brown, 1974), had analyzed the networks of social relations, the circles in which contemporary intellectuals move, in an effort to elucidate the shape of intellectual life in America and its impact on the world of politics and social issues. Walter W. Powell had, at an early stage of his career as a graduate student, developed a strong interest in the sociology of knowledge and in organizations and occupations involved in the production of culture.

When we joined our efforts, we were moved to study the publishing industry because we considered it a vivid nodal point in the production and dissemination of ideas. We began the study at a moment when a variety of voices were beginning to question whether recent developments in the publishing industry—mergers, takeovers, and bureaucratization—might not endanger the key cultural functions of publishing. These voices wondered whether the precarious balance between commerce and culture that had characterized the industry since its inception might not be fatefully tilted in favor of commerce. We paid attention to these critical voices but were equally attentive to the somewhat Panglossian defenders of the industry who were inclined to claim that there was no reason to get upset—that, in fact, all was for the best in all possible publishing worlds. What struck us, however, was that attackers and defenders alike tended to reason from a flimsy factual base. It appeared to us that we could offer an analysis of book publishing that was based on more than opinion. This book is the result.

Our research consisted of interviews and observations of people in the publishing industry. Since our respondents have been promised anonymity, we cannot thank them publicly; but we owe a very great debt to all those who actively assisted our research by allowing us to interrupt their work. These people took time from busy lives to explain the operation of their publishing houses and their places in them. Without the help of many individuals in the book trade, this project could never have been successfully completed. We doubt that any one person will appprove fully of the final text; but we hope that those who recognize their comments in the text will feel they have been accurately quoted.

The division of labor among the three of us was neither hierarchical nor fixed. This was very much a collaborative project. Although we did divide up the work load, we freely poached on each other's tasks. The initial idea was Coser's; both Kadushin and Coser applied for research support; soon thereafter Powell joined the team and contributed to the research design. Coser was responsible for negotiating access to the various publishing houses. He and Kadushin interviewed most of the top-level publishing executives. Powell was project director and supervised the interviewing of editors and the participant observations of the publishing houses. Kadushin was primarily responsible for the analysis of the quantitative data, while Powell analyzed the qualitative materials. The writing load was similarly shared. The introduction was written by Coser and Powell. Chapter 1 was done by Powell with Coser's assistance. Chapter 2 was written by Powell and Kadushin. Chapter 3 was Kadushin's responsibility, and he and Powell jointly wrote chapters 4 and 5. Michele Caplette contributed chapter 6. Powell wrote chapter 7. Chapter 8 was done by Kadushin and Coser. Each of us had a hand in chapters 9 and 10, although the lion's share was written by Kadushin. Chapters 11 and 12 were written by Coser with Powell's assistance. Chapter 13 was done by Powell, and all of us wrote the epilogue. Kadushin wrote the appendix.

We used a number of different methods to study the world of book publishing: we interviewed, both with a formal interview schedule and informally over lunch, in hallways, at trade booths, and whenever and wherever we could; we sent out written questionnaires; and we watched—that

Preface

special kind of watching that anthropologists call "participant observation." The study is a blend of the results of all these data-gathering techniques. As social scientists we know that a single method and approach will never do. We must observe, listen, count, sample, query, collate, and tabulate. We quickly learned that people in different positions have very different points of view, and that no account given us by an informant is valid in itself. Opinions had to be weighed and compared against the opinions of other informants and respondents. Only by utilizing a variety of research methods could we gain an adequate picture of this complex industry.

The formal interviews were developed from a sample of scholarly and text editors in the social sciences as well as from trade editors and publishers whom these editors suggested we interview. Eighty-five editors from 56 houses—mainly in the New York metropolitan area but also on the West Coast—gave complete interviews. Another 13 gave partial interviews, and an additional 35 were interviewed informally. We systematically observed 10 houses, of varying size and with different forms of ownership, which included trade, college text, scholarly, and university presses. Two hundred and nine recent authors responded to questionnaires dealing with their experiences with the various houses we had studied. Additional interviews with agents, reviewers, booksellers, and specialists in the production of managed texts, together with 317 returned questionnaires dealing with the career patterns of men and women, comprise the data that were gathered for this study. All of our respondents were promised strict confidentiality, and we have held closely to that. In the text, when we identify individuals, we do so only when their statements are a matter of public record.

We have not attempted to cover the entire publishing industry. For the most part, we have studied the publishing of nonfiction; although when we looked at houses that publish both literature and social science, we collected information on both. While we spoke with people in a variety of non-editorial positions, our focus is largely on the editorial process. We did not pursue topics such as book manufacturing, copyright, computer technology, or international sales. We were also unable to secure access to a major book club, so we do not discuss book clubs in detail. More information on sampling and other methodological matters can be found in the appendix and in the chapters that use specific material.

The data from the formal interviews and the questionnaires were coded, tabulated, and analyzed using the standard methods of survey analysis. In an effort to make our study more accessible, the tables upon which the analyses are based are not reported in full but are verbally summarized. In most cases, no more than two or, at the most, three variables are analyzed in any one table, and the results seemed easily stated in words. By the standards of survey research, the number of cases in most of the tables is small, but the tabular analysis is always supported by qualitative field observation and qualitative material in the interviews. Details on statistical significance can be found in the appendix.

In the end, the main difference between social science and journalism is not so much in the data-gathering techniques but in the social scientist's self-conscious attention to the details of sampling, observation, tabulation, and interpretation. At times, this attention results in detail that the journalist seldom reports but that we believe is essential to developing a verifiable analysis of social institutions that goes beyond a collection of startling stories.

Many individuals, at one point or another, worked on our project and assisted us in data collection and transcription. Interviews and field work were done by Michele Caplette, Ingrid May, Laurie Michael Roth, Arthur Samuelson, and Frank Sirianni. Additional research assistance was provided by Mary Anne Devanna, Sanford Miller, Robert Smith, and Annabelle Srebeny. Peter Abrams contributed expert computer services, and Laurie Michael Roth also helped with data analysis. Michele Ethier undertook the arduous task of coding all the interviews.

We regret that acknowledgments will fail to do justice to the many people who gave us help over the years of our work on this study. Colleagues clipped articles on book publishing in obscure journals for us, introduced us to their friends in publishing, and pointed us to useful references we had overlooked. For detailed reading and critical comments on parts of the manuscript, we particularly want to thank Michele Caplette, Paul DiMaggio, Richard Elman, and Irving Howe.

At Basic Books, Margaret Steinfels has been a model editor; we are extremely grateful for her considerable assistance. Without her aid we would undoubtedly still be working on the manuscript. Erwin Glikes initially approached us about publishing our study with Basic Books, and we agreed to work with Basic only after our interviewing and field work were completed. We did not want to be placed in the unethical position of discovering trade secrets at one house while we were under contract to another. Our original notes and interviews remain with us and have never been seen by anyone at Basic Books. After Glikes's departure from Basic, Martin Kessler supervised our manuscript, and both he and Jane Isay provided us with detailed comments on our various drafts. Bart de Castro commented on chapter 13; and Phoebe Hoss, our copy editor, did an excellent job of blending the writing styles of three very different people and took care of all the details. We are most appreciative of the work of the entire staff at Basic Books.

We are particularly indebted to Denise Fennelly for her superb services in typing and steadily moving the manuscript forward to readiness for publication. The knowledge that we could depend on her to translate successive drafts, however illegible, into a readable manuscript was most comforting. We also want to thank Barbara Brieman for helping type the final manuscript. During the data-collection phase of our project, Selma Lenihan, Anna Arnheim, and Ellen Beebe ably served, at various points, as our administrative assistants.

Financial support for the project was provided by a grant from the National Institute of Mental Health, "Publishers as Gatekeepers of Ideas" (MH–26746). At NIMH, our grant officers were Howard Davis and Susan Salasin. We are grateful to them for their support. Lewis Coser spent a year as a fellow at Clare Hall, Cambridge University, courtesy of a Guggenheim Foundation fellowship; he is most grateful to both institutions. During this time, he interviewed a number of British publishers. The administration of our grant was facilitated by the Center for Policy Research, New York, N.Y., and the Research Foundation at the State University of New York at Stony Brook. At Stony Brook, both Kitty Rockett and Robert Schneider were particularly helpful in assisting us in the execution of our research. Selma Lenihan, Sophie Sa, and Clara Shapiro provided administrative help for us at the Center for Policy Research.

New Haven, Connecticut
Fishers Island, New York
Wellfleet, Massachusetts
June 1981

BOOKS

Introduction

GUSTAVE FLAUBERT remarked more than a century ago that it was high time to get rid of the absurd notion that "books dropped like meteorites from the sky." He made this remark in connection with the publication of Hippolyte Taine's *History of English Literature* (1871), one of the early self-conscious efforts to see literature as rooted within a social context and as the expression of a specific society. Since Flaubert's day, literary critics and sociological analysts have further developed the approach that Taine adumbrated. Yet very few of them have attempted to look carefully at the organizational setting in which books are produced.

Ideas are the brain children of individuals; but books, in which ideas are given concrete shape so as to be conveyed to their intended audience, are the products of the collective work of members of publishing firms that specialize in the production and distribution of books. Thus, publishing houses are indispensable intermediary points in the diffusion of ideas. If the marketplace of ideas is to allow the blooming of many flowers, it is of the essence that there exist a publishing industry capable of fostering diverse intellectual and literary products that can compete for the attention of the public.

The roughly forty thousand books annually produced in America are not created in a vacuum. Instead, after a manuscript has been delivered to a publisher, an arduous process involving many people and lasting at least

3

nine months, is required before a book can be sold in a bookstore. "Between the idea and the reality, between the notion and the act"—as T. S. Eliot put it in *The Hollow Men*—"falls the shadow." This book is designed to shed some light on the shadow between the moment the author types the last page of a manuscript and his or her book's appearance in the bookstores many months later. We aim to elucidate the various facets of the publishing industry, but we will also pay attention to many professions and organizations—from book reviewers and literary agents to booksellers, from the mass media to the world of large corporations—that influence the making and selling of books.

The relations between creators of ideas and their publics are typically mediated through a variety of social mechanisms that provide institutional channels for the flow of ideas. When we began this study, the notion of "gatekeepers of ideas" seemed apt: that is, people who, by virtue of their position in an organization, operate sluice gates for ideas, deciding which will be offered and what will be excluded. Such gatekeepers can be found in a variety of settings. Editors in newsrooms, for example, function as gatekeepers in so far as they select for their readers a small minority of news stories from the many events around the world.[1] Gallery owners function in similar ways, as crucial filtering agents screening and selectively choosing those works of art that they deem the public will buy.[2] Educational institutions, academies and learned societies, salons, coffee houses, learned journals, the modern mass media, and many other institutions occupy central positions that allow them to select among intellectual products, sifting the chaff from the wheat and making authoritative decisions about which deserve sponsorship for distribution and which are to be kept out of circulation.[3] We felt that prominent among these gatekeepers were publishers, with their product—books.

Although we now realize that the metaphor does not fully convey the complexity of the publishing industry—since publishers not only sift ideas but give them shape—the image of channels and floodgates remains useful: people and organizations in, but also outside, the publishing industry function as gatekeepers of ideas insofar as they make decisions about what to "let in" and what to "keep out." Book reviewers, booksellers, and literary agents can also be seen as gatekeepers.

We are aiming here at a full-scale study of the modern publishing industry, a project that has never before been attempted. Even though one could argue that, in an age of modern electronic media, book publishing no longer occupies the pre-eminent cultural position it enjoyed until the Second World War, books are still a central—though by no means the only—medium for the dissemination of myriads of ideas—be they mediocre or

4

sublime—that shape the public mind. A study of the book industry hence seems to us of crucial significance for any assessment of the contemporary world of ideas.

Our approach in this book is sociological: that is, we are largely concerned with the rich context of human relations, within and outside the publishing industry, that shapes the production and distribution of books. Economists approach the analysis of their data in terms of price, cost, market relations, and the like and hence pay little attention to the human relations that are at the very center of decision making in the publishing industry and elsewhere. Literary critics concentrate on the merits of a particular book and are only marginally interested in the process and the social context of the selection and subsequent shaping of a book prior to publication. Sociologists, on the other hand, are peculiarly attentive to both the texture and the networks of personal and organizational relations that nourish books. Thus, while we describe the structural conditions influencing the decisions of men and women in the book trade, and profit from the findings of economists, we will, above all, show that books are seldom produced by impersonal factors. A published book is very much the product of a chain of a great many individual decisions made by people inteconnected within the various niches in the publishing industry.

Until the rise of the mass market for books in the late eighteenth and early nineteenth centuries, book publishing was a simple cottage industry. An author would approach a bookseller-printer—these two roles were not yet differentiated—and contract for the printing and selling of his book. Frequently the costs were borne, wholly or in part, by a patron of the author, who thus ensured that the book would reach its intended audience among the cultural and social élite of the day.

Conditions changed drastically in the latter part of the eighteenth century and after. Rising literacy widened the reading public and hence enlarged the market for books. With the social ascent of the middle class came the emergence of a new stratum of people with enough leisure and education to develop a taste for reading books. Up until the eighteenth century the middle classes, if they read at all, read mainly religious tracts and political broadsheets. Only in the eighteenth century did they broaden their concerns and evince wider interest in other types of literature. Furthermore, while in preceding centuries the audience for books was almost exclusively male, in the eighteenth and nineteenth centuries women became major consumers of books. This change must, in turn, be accounted for by a marked change in the role of middle-class women who, at that time, gained leisure as they were relieved of the habitual drudgery of household routines.

5

Introduction

The increase in number of printing houses and in sales of books serves to indicate the increase in readership. In England the process started somewhat earlier than in America. At the Restoration, in 1660, there were 60 printing houses in London; by 1757 there were already between 150 and 200; and the number increased even more rapidly in the next hundred years. In America, as we shall show in chapter 1, the process was similar. The number of books sold tell a similar story. *Paradise Lost* (1667) sold only 1,300 copies in two years. But five editions of *Pamela* (1740–41) sold in a single year, and the British edition of Thomas Paine's *Rights of Man* (1791, 1792) sold more than 50,000 copies within a few weeks.

With the widening market for books—which, by the way, was due not only to higher levels of literacy but also to a decline of the price of books as a result of economies of scale and improved production methods—the printer-bookseller gradually disappeared and was replaced by modern publishing houses. As we shall show in some detail in chapter 1, the early publishing houses in both the United States and in England had still fairly simple organizational structures, preserving many of the cottage industry features of the previous period. They were usually run by a single publisher, often with the aid of brothers, sons, or, more rarely, wives. They were lodged in unprepossessing buildings and operated by a rudimentary staff of hired hands, who took care of the various routine tasks with no organizational structure of well-defined roles and functions.

As the market for books in America expanded, in the latter part of the nineteenth century and after, to become a true mass market, the publishing of books became a large-scale industry. The editorial office was still largely run by criteria that had already characterized the earlier cottage stage of the industry. But there now developed differentiated departments, each assigned specific tasks in the making of books: production, marketing, distribution, advertisement, publicity, subsidiary rights, and still other less important functions. Even after a book was acquired by an editor, and line edited and copy edited, a whole hierarchy of departments became successively involved in its production and distribution. This is why a modern book takes usually some nine months to be produced, since it must slowly wind its way through the various departments and stages of production and distribution. The whole process can thus profitably be conceived as involving a chain of decisions peculiar to each department and made by each in turn as the book comes its way. Editors in chief and editors, to be sure, make the crucial decision to acquire a manuscript, but the ultimate sales of the book will be considerably influenced by decisions on, for example, type of jacket, print run, advertising, pre-publication publicity, and marketing strategy. Each of these decisions, though there may be suggestions from editors and editors in chief, is largely the responsibility of key personnel in non-editorial departments. If it makes sense to see editors as gatekeepers of ideas, it is also useful to conceive of the various key persons in different departments as auxiliary gatekeepers.

Four major structural conditions help determine the present character of the publishing industry in the United States: (1) The industry sells its products—like any commodity—in a market, but a market that, in contrast to that for many other products, is fickle and often uncertain. (2) The industry is decentralized among a number of sectors whose operations bear little resemblance to each other. (3) These operations are characterized by a mixture of modern mass-production methods and craftlike procedures. (4) The industry remains perilously poised between the requirements and restraints of commerce and the responsibilities and obligations that it must bear as a prime guardian of the symbolic culture of the nation. Although the tensions between the claims of commerce and culture seem to us always to have been with book publishing, they have become more acute and salient in the last twenty years.

Even though the government or private foundations or corporations may subsidize a book, the bulk of the output of publishing houses is sold on the free market as a commodity. While many products enjoy relatively stable markets, and their producers have developed sophisticated market-research techniques to predict the demands for their products, most sectors of the publishing industry are subject to sudden unpredictable shifts in consumer preferences. As a result, roughly 50 percent of mass-market paperbacks are routinely destroyed because they have failed to attract buyers. The figure for hardcover trade books is not as high. However, bookstore chains return to the original publishers between 35 percent and 55 percent of the books they, the chains, have ordered; these publishers may then remainder, destroy, or warehouse these returns. As a result of recent tax decisions, some publishers have had to refrain from storing books for any length of time and to remainder or shred many books they would earlier have kept on their backlists.

Given the built-in uncertainties of the market for many types of books, the book trade, like the fashion business or the movie industry, often operates on the shotgun principle. As one Hollywood mogul is said to have told an inquisitive reporter, "One of the films on this list of ten will be a big success"; but when the reporter queried, "Which one?" the producer answered, "I have no idea." Publishers attempt to reduce such uncertainty, as shall be seen, through concentrating on "sure-fire" blockbusters, through large-scale promotion campaigns, or through control over distribution, as in the marketing of paperbacks. In the end, however, publishers rely on sales estimates that may be as unreliable as weather forecasts in Maine.

Although in the last twenty years or so, publishing has become bureaucratized to an unprecedented degree, it still retains some features of a craft. Even low-level personnel have a measure of professional status and are seldom associated with any one firm over extended periods of time. Given the fickleness of the market for books and the diversity of "products," bureaucratic criteria are only partially applicable. The close supervision found in many other industries is not feasible; thus, low-level personnel must be delegated responsibilities, although always within budgetary limits set by executives.[4]

It can be misleading to speak of *the* publishing industry, for it has various sectors, each with its own distinct modes of operation. The production and marketing of a text in introductory economics bears little resemblance to the launching of a first novel. Most outsiders think of publishing in terms of popular trade books; yet these are only the industry's most visible line of "products" and are overshadowed in terms of sales both by college textbooks and by professional monographs. We shall discuss these three sectors of the industry, while largely bypassing more specialized types of publishing, such as art books, juvenile books, reference works, and elementary and high school texts.

Some fifteen or twenty years ago, publishing was still largely a cottage industry. In the past two decades, however, it has been growing out of that stage at a rapid pace. Many formerly independent houses have been taken over by large corporations, and other houses have "gone public" and are traded on the stock market. As a result, publishing executives now worry a great deal about how Wall Street evaluates their operations. Most major houses have rationalized their procedures by installing contemporary management practices borrowed from other industries—including electronic inventory controls, computerized marketing departments, sharply defined lines of authority and assignments of specialized tasks, and, above all, close attention to the "bottom line."

Yet even in a period when corporate takeovers, the quest for blockbusters, and the movement of corporate managers and management consultants into the front offices of publishers have pre-empted publishing news, some non-commercial aspects of the industry, together with remnants of the cottage industry mentality, are still very much alive.

The trends, tensions, and problems adumbrated in the preceding pages are discussed in more detail and probed more deeply in this book. Many other factors that impinge on the publishing process are taken up in what follows. Chapter 1 sketches the history of book publishing in

8

America. We show that what at first blush would seem peculiarly contemporary phenomena have in fact characterized the industry throughout its history. This chapter also paints in broad strokes the major changes that the industry has recently undergone.

As we discuss in chapter 2, one of the industry's key features, its remarkable heterogeneity, makes it hard to generalize about the state of book publishing. There are significant differences among the various branches of the industry. Each sector operates within a distinctive environment, with its own standards and criteria for success. The amounts of money, the size of print runs, and the chances for new authors to be discovered all differ by industry sector. Finally, the impact of mergers varies by type of publishing: some branches of publishing are highly concentrated, while others exhibit a remarkable degree of decentralization and diversity. We examine a wide range of relationships and practices within the book trade and, where possible, point out the effects of the broad changes discussed in chapter 1.

In chapter 3 we analyze a large set of sociometric data that help one to understand the role of social circles and informal networks in book publishing. We find there are distinct social circles for the different branches of the industry. In trade publishing, editors are isolated both from other trade editors and from writers. In contrast, in the scholarly and textbook sectors, editors are in frequent touch with authors and with editors in other houses. Invisible colleges as well as institutional mechanisms, such as academic conventions, serve important "linkage" functions.

In chapter 4 we analyze the career patterns of editors and show how the routes they have followed to the top are largely sex-typed. We describe, in chapter 5, the decision-making process and the various tasks that editors perform. The rise of women to positions of prominence and influence within the industry is reported in chapter 6. Here the results of a detailed survey of the occupational experiences of men and women in publishing are analyzed and the career impediments of women are described. The manner in which publishing houses are organized is the subject of chapter 7, where we discuss how formalized the work process is within firms, some of the causes of interdepartmental conflict, and some of the problems involved in managing publishing houses. Some houses are informally and loosely organized, while others are more bureaucratic and hierarchical. The growth of multi-media conglomerates and their impact on book pu' - lishing is reviewed. We report the opinions that editors have formed about being owned by media conglomerates. Our interviews suggest that up to now, few of the expected competitive advantages of mergers between film companies and publishing houses have been realized.

Introduction

Creating successful books or books that give the appearance of success is the topic of chapter 8, in which we focus on the promotional and marketing efforts of publishers. In this area, the blockbuster phenomenon has had a pronounced impact. We suggest that some promotional efforts in trade and college text publishing have the effect of overkill; saturation advertising reaches a point where the promotion becomes the event itself, and the senses are dulled to whatever merits a book may have.

In chapter 9 we report the results of a large survey of authors which examined their satisfactions and their complaints with publishers. We point out that at crucial points in the publishing process, authors are likely to be displeased with their publishers. We are reminded of the sociologist Everett Hughes's wise observation of many years ago: that what are emergencies for some are routine events for others.[5] When the parents of a sick or injured child take their loved one to a hospital emergency room, they encounter a doctor to whom the child is but the thirty-fifth patient in a long day. Authors often find themselves in a similar situation when they encounter large publishing houses. Some publishers might dream of publishing books without having to deal with authors. In fact, a number of publishers have turned this dream into reality. In chapter 10 we describe three types of "non-books," as we choose to call them; they include book "packages," novelizations, and managed textbooks.

The next section of the book moves outside of the publishing house to assess the impact of several key external forces. Chapter 11 reviews the role played by literary agents and their effect on author-publisher relations in trade publishing. Filling comparable positions in scholarly publishing are powerful brokers and patrons who "sponsor" new authors. We argue in chapter 12 that the book-review process has little influence on the success, or lack thereof, of blockbuster books but is a critical evaluation stage for books of intellectual or literary merit. The complicated, costly, and somewhat inefficient channels of book distribution are analyzed in chapter 13. Here we describe the varied ways in which books reach the shelves of bookstores. An important recent development, the rise of chain bookstores, is scrutinized carefully, as it is conceivable that these stores may become the tail that wags the publishing dog. The book concludes with a summing up of our study and with our views on some of the directions in which the industry is headed, and attempts to strike a balance between the rosy optimism of the main spokesmen for the industry and the doomsday vision of some of their jaundiced critics.

PART I

The History and Structure of the Industry

Chapter 1

Commerce and Culture: A Historical Survey of Book Publishing in America

LIKE so much else in human affairs, the history of book publishing can be viewed in both evolutionary and cyclical terms. Certain aspects of the book trade have changed considerably over the last century and a half: this transformation is best captured by a linear or evolutionary model of change. In contrast, there are cyclical movements that give the appearance of radical change but are, in slightly different form, a repetition of earlier developments. Both the evolutionary and the cyclical model accurately represent some features of the industry's history.

While we believe the cyclical metaphor is the more accurate, publishing today is in many ways very different from the trade in the nineteenth century. In the first place, instead of the simple two- or three-story buildings in which early nineteenth-century firms operated, some of the major publishing houses in New York City now have huge skyscrapers. Where there were once a few rooms in which a very few people went about their business, we now find elaborate offices on many floors with subdivisions, partitions, and spaces reserved for a great many specialized staff members. Where people used to communicate with each other by going back and forth among a few offices, they are now, at least in major firms, linked by elaborate electronic devices.

Physical appearances are but reflections of major changes in both organizational structure and style. Where most nineteenth-century houses were dominated by the publisher and a few trusted assistants, major publishing houses today have elaborate organizational charts mapping the complex hierarchical relations among top management, editors in chief, senior, associate, and assistant editors, as well as the heads of sales, marketing, subsidiary rights, production, and manufacturing divisions, along with their many staff members and assistants. Where lines of authority were once simple and clear-cut, they are now complex, variegated, and intricate.

Few nineteenth-century publishers would grasp the current importance of subsidiary rights income, which is all the income earned above and beyond the direct sale of a firm's books. In the nineteenth century, a hardcover trade book's profit was determined by the number of copies sold to individual readers. Today, it is usually determined by the sale of subsidiary rights to movie companies, book clubs, foreign publishers, or paperback reprint houses. The possibility that publishing houses would be owned by large corporate entities engaged in a wide variety of unrelated businesses would have struck nineteenth-century publishers as the fantasy of a diseased mind. In those days, publishers and their families, sometimes in conjunction with a few business associates, owned their firms and personally ran them. "Going public" and selling stock in them, as in the steel or the oil industry, did not occur to the most ambitious publisher.

While such differences between then and now are obvious, has publishing radically changed? Many observers think so. Critics of the recent rash of takeovers and mergers argue that publishers once balanced the demands of commerce with their responsibilities to culture by letting commercially successful books pay for books of high quality but limited appeal. As E. L. Doctorow, speaking for himself and the American Center of P.E.N. (Poets, Playwrights, Editors, Essayists, and Novelists), recently put it, they could "make money and be proud of their contribution to literature and ideas at the same time."[1] In the view of many critics, the hardheaded businessmen running today's publishing corporations care only for books likely to sell to a mass audience, and as a result, argues Bernard Malamud, endanger "the integrity of the trade."[2]

Yet heads of different publishing firms may conceive of their missions in different ways, depending on where they consider their responsibilities lie. Some publishers think almost exclusively in terms of producing maximum profits for owners or stockholders; others may see themselves as responsible to the educated public, or to the general public, or to the cultural traditions of America. Such differing views are more than abstract: they have tangible consequences for publishing strategies and choices. And, as we shall argue repeatedly, publishing is a highly diverse industry; and changes in one of its segments do not necessarily affect the others.

On one level, the publishing business does not differ form any other business, in that all firms, from minuscule ones to multinational enterprises, are constrained by the forces of the market to look at the "bottom line." The world of business, as Karl Marx forcefully showed over a century ago, provides little room for altruists. The pressures of the marketplace will soon eliminate anyone who remains oblivious to them. Yet the fact that the quest for profit provides the lowest common denominator for each firm in the highly diversified publishing industry is not sufficient to explain the strategies of individual publishers.

When one inquires about responsibilities other than the quest for profit, one begins to see what distinguishes most, though not all, publishing houses from many American businesses: immediate profitability need not be the main criterion when it comes to the publishing of any specific book. Precious little American poetry would be published today if the "bottom line" reigned supreme in all houses. Few first novels would appear on bookstore shelves, and scholarly books would be produced in very small print runs and only by academic presses. It is still the case that, as in the past, publishers as a group or individuals within particular houses are often torn between the requirements of commerce and their sense of cultural responsibility. As a leading editor in chief put it in an interview with one of us:

> I don't think we ever turn something of real quality down because it is going to lose money. We know that half of our books are not going to make money. My theory is let people look at the final results. I don't want to be judged on a book-by-book basis. If we are not making enough money, or no one likes us, then I am doing a bad job. If at the end of a year enough books have made themselves felt and heard, and we have come out ahead financially, everything is fine. How I got there is my business. So far I have got away with it.

A recent report in *Publishers Weekly* (*PW*)* on how marketing affects decisions to publish a book found that many books continue to be

---

* *Publishers Weekly*, founded in January 1872, is the industry's widely read trade journal published by R. R. Bowker Company, New York.

published despite low projected sales. Olivia Blumer, reprint rights manager at Doubleday, noted: "You can take any recent *PW* announcements ad and you can go through the books that are announced for each house and say, 'This looks like a conscience book, and this looks like a conscience book,' and that's fine. I'm damn glad that people can do it."[3]

Of course there are decisions and firms where profitability is the sole consideration. The *PW* report on the influence of marketing found that sales potential is an all-important criterion when the book under discussion is nonfiction. And when the financial stakes are high on any book, early advice from the marketing department is usually sought.

> According to Rollene Saal, [formerly] of Bantam, "Given a book such as 'Princess Daisy'—which we eventually paid over $3 million for—you are dealing with something that everyone in the company, including marketing, is involved with." And according to Ken Collins of Fawcett, "Who gets involved in the acquisition depends on the book. If we're talking about certain relatively inexpensive category kinds of things, it's usually one department, very frequently just one person. If you're talking about an important lead title with a lot of money, a lot of gamble perhaps, then I suppose at that level it's fair to say that all people are considered involved. If it gets expensive enough, the corporation is involved."[4]

Certainly there is some merit in the arguments of those critics who contend that publishing is in danger of being absorbed by the entertainment industry, with all the latter's tendencies to pander to the lowest common denominator of public taste. As the noted literary critic Alfred Kazin wrote in the *New Republic*, "Like so much in American life, the book world is big, busy, and commercial, driven; not likely to be too aware of its compulsiveness, special interests, many blinders."[5] He went on to express dismay at the inordinate attention heaped on a few "big" trade books.

> I open a press release about Erich Segal's "new blockbuster," 10 years after *Love Story* [Harper & Row, 1970], *Man, Woman and Child* [Harper & Row, 1980], to learn the publication plans for this story of a loving marriage on the brink of tragedy: 200,000 copies on the first printing, $200,000 initial advertising budget. The book is already a Literary Guild alternate, a Doubleday Book Club selection, a Reader's Digest Condensed Book Club selection, a Family Circle excerpt. Foreign language rights have been sold for "record figures" to France, Germany, Italy, Denmark, Portugal, Spain. [6]

Such excesses are not unusual today; however they are largely characteristic of the most visible sector of the book industry. And they are not novel: trade publishing in this country has almost always been oriented toward the mass market.

THE COMMERCIALIZATION OF LITERATURE

The Spanish philosopher Ortega y Gasset once wrote that the best clue to the study of European history was "*Eadem sed aliter,* the same thing but in another way."[7] Despite some significant changes—particularly in terms of size, complexity, and the loosening of ties between authors and publishers—when we look at some of the major facets of the publishing industry over the last century and a half, we are struck with the pertinence of Ortega's remark. Much has changed indeed, but much has remained very much the same. Even if a model stressing "progress" and unilinear evolution describes certain aspects of the history of the industry, it fails to capture other important ones, which are better understood by a cyclical model. Economic historians have stressed that longer or shorter cycles of prosperity or depression, with different economic peaks and troughs, have much in common even though they may be far apart in time. Demographic historians have shown that periods of high fertility or mortality, even though they may be separated by centuries, have similar consequences. In the same way, the history of the publishing industry is replete with "advances" and "revolutions" that strike the naïve observer as peculiarly modern phenomena when, in fact, they are rather old, although they now appear in a new dress.

Let us take a few examples, chosen almost at random. One can hardly attend a gathering of authors or a convention of publishers today without hearing heated debates about how the independence and dignity of the publishing enterprise is threatened by the "commercialization of literature." Yet a look at the historical record shows there have been many similar crises in book publishing.

In 1843 a reviewer for the prestigious *North American Review* complained bitterly:

> Literature begins to assume the aspect and undergo the mutations of trade. The author's profession is becoming as mechanical as that of the printer and the bookseller, being created by the same causes and subject to the same laws. . . . The publisher in the name of his customers calls for a particular kind of authorship just as he would bespeak a dinner at a restaurant.[8]

In 1890, *Publishers Weekly* inveighed against creeping commercialism:

> This is an age of ambition. The countersign in commercial circles is push, energy, snap. . . . While this spirit of unsatisfied ambition has brought compen-

sation and developed an activity not to be ignored, it has nevertheless been at the expense of certain elements of character which should not be abused or uncultivated. Dignity is very often forgotten. . . . If literature and art are to be treated as common merchandise . . . it will make commonplace the manners of our people and their intelligence restricted to the counting-room.

Similar complaints were heard on the other side of the Atlantic. The literary critic Q. D. Leavis protested:

> Whereas in George Eliot's time literature had paid, that is to say, a serious novelist could make a handsome living without surrendering anything, by Conrad's it had ceased to do so. Novelists of the stamp of Gissing and Henry James cannot find publishers easily to-day, and they cannot in any case hope to make a living from their novels.[9]

In November 1905, the highly respected *Atlantic Monthly* carried an article entitled "The Commercialization of Literature" by the dean of American publishers, Henry Holt.[10] In it he told a delightful tongue-in-cheek story about the founder of the house of Appleton, who said to his heir-apparent William Appleton, "The only misgiving I have regarding your success after I am gone, arises from my having noticed in you some symptoms of literary taste." Holt argued that disregard for the canons of literary distinction and lack of esthetic consideration had not generally prevailed in the past but were now becoming prevalent. "The more authors seek publishers solely with reference to what they will pay in the day's market," Holt contended, "the more publishers bid against one another as stock brokers do, and the more they market their wares as the soulless articles of ordinary commerce are marketed, the more books become soulless things." Holt was especially perturbed about the way advertising had distorted the market. "I cannot but think," he said, "that lately American publishers were as crazy about advertising as the Dutch ever were about tulips." The future, as he saw it, was dark: "All this has made it more and more difficult to get books that are not 'sellers' fairly before the public, without an amount of advertising, drumming, discounts, and credits, that makes them unprofitable; or even, with all those risks, to sell them in profitable numbers. Literature, in fact, is crowded into the cellar." What worried Holt above all was that—with rising costs of advertising, higher royalties, and the emergence of literary agents given to driving hard bargains—the quest for highly profitable best sellers would drive out concern for books of high quality but limited appeal. "Not as many books pay for themselves, as did before," Holt believed, "but the few that do sell, sell more widely. Hence the mad quest for the golden seller, the mad payment to the man who has once produced it, and the mad advertising of doubtful books in the hopes of creating the seller." Holt sounds familiar and current. So does his general assessment: "The literature of our mother tongue has been commercialized to an extent not dreamed of in any time of which I have knowledge; and . . . within our generation our literature has fallen to a lower estate than it knew for generations before." Reading Holt, one cannot but feel that there is something to Vico's view that history repeats itself, that it exhibits the pattern of *corso* and *recorso*.

An example from a less remote period in the history of publishing appeared in the *Atlantic Monthly* shortly after the Second World War. Alfred R. McIntyre, president of Little, Brown & Company, argued with considerable passion that the cost of producing books had risen so sharply that publishers were compelled "to depend for [their] profits entirely on the special income that comes to [them] . . . from book club adoptions, royalties on the leasing of plates for cheap editions, and the revenue from the sale of subsidiary rights."[11] It would be easy to cull similar statements from yesterday's *Publishers Weekly* or *New York Times*.

Authors voiced like-minded criticisms. In 1946 the novelist James T. Farrell wrote a much-discussed and prescient essay entitled "The Fate of Writing in America."[12] Describing "the tendency toward combinations and concentration in the book industry," he said, "this concentration will increase the difficulties of operation for small and independent publishers, and it will probably have the effect of requiring a higher initial investment from any newcomers in the field." He feared that "the scale of publishing will be enlarged, and money will talk more than ever. It is already common knowledge that books which have the largest advertising budgets most frequently receive prompt and long reviews, and that those selected by a large book club are generally treated as important books by the majority of reviewers." Moreover, "the enlarged scale of publishing will require increased efforts to minimize risks. Now more than ever, publishers will be forced to be receptive to bestseller books." The ties between Hollywood and the world of books had become pronounced, Farrell suggested: "Many writers have found it most convenient to adjust their conscience, their style and their themes to the dramaturgical conceptions of Hollywood. New ties are being forged between studio offices and reprint houses. . . . The direction now being taken by the big publishers has been described as the Hollywoodization of literature." Farrell warned against the possibility of Wall Street becoming interested in publishing: should that happen, "Wall Street control will mean that Money, Pure Money, becomes the boss. In other words, there will be absentee ownership." Farrell also viewed with alarm the rise of chain stores that would, through centralization and expansion, drive small bookstores out of business and help tie the book industry more closely into the networks of America's corporate economic structure. Farrell, the author of the *Studs Lonigan* series, was not only a sensitive observer of the general social and economic scene in his day: he also had a fine nose for much of the shape of things to come in the book trade.

PAPERBACK REVOLUTIONS

In the years after the Second World War, a much-discussed phenomenon of the publishing industry was the "paperback revolution." This was in fact the third such revolution in the United States: there had been two earlier ones in the nineteenth century.

Mass-market publishing began in this country as a combination of technological innovation and piracy. The advent of the steam-powered cylinder press and the use of stereotyped plates and cheaper bindings brought about a technological revolution, which was furthered by the refusal of the United States government to recognize copyright on foreign works. During the first paperback revolution in the early 1840s, newspapers printed English and French novelists in cheap editions. Called "broadsheets" or "supplements," they were hawked by newsboys on the streets and sold through the mail.[13] As more and more were printed, their price dropped. Publishing houses, whose well-printed cloth editions sold for a dollar or more, were forced to enter the fray. A brief period of vicious competition followed. Publishers sent swift boats out to meet the ships bringing the latest novels from overseas and had books printed on board. Publication schedules were calculated to the hour, since whoever got a title out first usually captured the market. These cheap books threatened to destroy the profit structure of the young publishing industry; and so, at the urging of many book publishers, the U.S. Post Office in 1845 dealt the newspaper supplements a death blow by withdrawing their permits to mail at inexpensive newspaper rates.

The second paperback revolution in the nineteenth century had many affinities with its twentieth-century counterpart. Just as the mass printing of paperbacks was powerfully stimulated by demand from American soldiers during the Second World War, so "the outbreak of the Civil War created an acute need of reading matter for soldiers in the field and camp."[14] Between 1860 and 1865, the Beadle Brothers, pioneers in this venture, sold more than 4,000,000 copies of their written-to-order dime novels. Sales of individual titles ran from 35,000 to 80,000.

The Beadles established the modern mass-market book in a form it retains today: a paperback pocket-size book with a low price—ten cents then—and with an illustrated cover and the series insignia (or colophon)—the covers were all covered orange to begin with—and distributed through newsstands. The content of the popular novel was much the same as today's romantic or violent stories, written in accord with specific plot outlines and conventions, and to a specific length. The first book in the series published by Erastus Beadle was called *Malaeska, The Indian Wife of the White Hunter* and was 128 pages long—still an ideal length for the presses when a large printing is planned. Success was immediate; a specifically American public had been uncovered—the mass market.

After the Civil War, other paperback publishers followed the Beadles into this remunerative field. Some of these popular books continued to be written to order by "Grub Street" hacks, others were pirated cheap editions of English works unprotected by copyright; and still others were legitimate reprints of hardcover editions. This paperback revolution was powerfully stimulated after the Civil War by the development of woodpulp paper, low-cost printing, and cheaper postal rates. If the pirates for a while dominated the market, they soon began to destroy one another with their cutthroat competition. Moreover, the books they issued were of poor quality. *Publishers Weekly* complained in 1884: "In the rage for cheapness we have sacrificed everything for slop, and a dainty bit of bookmaking is like a jewel in the swine's snout."[15] Not long after, in reaction against the competition of cheap paperbacks, major houses began to issue reprints of their own backlists. In 1885 Harper & Brothers, for example, began to issue nonfiction paperbacks on a weekly basis at twenty-five cents a copy, having started a few years earlier to reprint novels from its backlist at ten cents a copy.

The paperback revolution of the nineteenth century withered away in circumstances not unfamiliar to the modern paperback industry. Paperbacks glutted the market. In 1883, the American News Company returned to only one publisher 1,200,000 books it could not sell. Another publisher disposed of no less than 3,000,000 of its unsalable reprints for $30,000 to soap companies which then included a free copy with each bar of soap.[16] By 1889 another familiar problem had made its appearance: publishable manuscripts were not being received in sufficient quantity, and the industry could not rely on hacks alone.

Not only cheap paperbacks but also their quality counterparts date from the last century. For example, the New Series of Foreign Literature, published by the firm of John W. Lovell and edited by Edmund Gosse, the distinguished British literary critic, published a number of well-known authors at fifty cents for the paperback and one dollar for the hardcover editions.

By the turn of the century, the second paperback revolution encountered its Thermidor. America's belated adoption of a copyright law in the early 1890s put an end to pirated editions. Cutthroat competition, high rates of returns of unsold copies, inadequate retail outlets, and the scarcity of suitable books for reprinting killed the second paperback revolution. Hardcover reprints were common throughout the first half of the twentieth century, but paperbacks came into their own again only after the Second World War.

MERGERS, MONOPOLY, AND CONCENTRATION

Publishing mergers, so noticeable in the 1960s and 1970s, are also not without precedent. From 1885 to 1890: Merrill, Meigs & Company merged with Bowen Stuart & Company (1885); Ticknor & Company formed in Boston to take over the bankrupt Osgood firm (1885); David McKay acquired H. C. Waters & Company (1885); Houghton Mifflin acquired Ticknor & Company (1889); and the American Book Company was formed by a merger of several textbook firms (1890).[17] The latter was a classic example of a monopoly firm. At one point, the "book trust," as it was called by its critics, controlled 93 percent of the country's entire textbook business.[18]

The American Book Company initially consisted of the textbook departments of five large publishers and eventually absorbed about thirty houses, of various sizes, under its direction. But the monopoly was short-lived. The company's ability to establish a monopoly rested on control of several state textbook committees that selected texts for adoption. The monopoly suffered from internal political fights and ultimately new companies entered the field. Companies that had sold their textbook lists to the book trust went back into textbook publishing at the end of the five-year period for which they had agreed not to publish schoolbooks.[19] The American Book Company lasted until 1967 when it was bought by Litton Industries; by then the company's market share of the textbook business had diminished to 3.6 percent. In January 1980, Litton Industries, a giant diversified electronics company, agreed to sell its publishing division to International Thomson Organization, Ltd., a huge Toronto-based publishing empire. Or, to take another example of the impermanence of publishing mergers: Bantam Books, the largest paperback house, has had five owners in less then thirty-five years. Among the parent companies have been Grosset & Dunlap, National General, American Financial, the Italian corporation IFI International, and, most recently, the German Bertelsmann Publishing Group.

The example of the American Book Company adds an important historical perspective to the current debate over concentration in the publishing industry. Though the debate has quieted with the arrival of the Reagan administration, many groups are concerned about the possible harmful effects of oligopoly on the book trade. The Authors Guild has been the most outspoken, labeling the merger wave of the 1970s a "sinister process" that is diminishing competition.

There are, we believe, two important points to consider in any discussion of concentration. First, for over one hundred years publishers have sought to market fewer books in larger quantities to achieve higher profits; and over the same period, virtually every house of any size has been involved in mergers and acquisitions. Second, in industries that depend on individually created products that appear sporadically, that do not have sizable sunk-costs (capital investments that cannot easily be changed) in plant equipment or product development, and that face highly unpredictable markets, mergers and concentration trends are neither permanent nor irrevocable. Research on the popular music industry by sociologists Richard A. Peterson and David Berger suggests that industries involved in popular culture alternate between periods of competition and oligopoly.[20]

Publishers, like any business owners, prefer control to chaos. As the vagaries of public taste are not economical, it is preferable to stabilize and consolidate them, thus increasing predictability. If an owner can do this, he will. If he cannot, he is left with two options: to continue to follow the same chaotic and less profitable tradition of his predecessors; or to sell out to someone else who will begin the process anew.

What impact does market concentration—that is, an industry in which a handful of firms dominate its products and sales—have on culture? Peterson and Berger's research showed that in the music industry, periods of high concentration were likely to be ones of creative stagnation. Organizational analysts Richard Cyert and James G. March have also shown that managers place a premium on predictability, routine, and control, both for economic and for psychological reasons.[21] Firms in concentrated industries, by virtue of their market power, feel no need to risk innovation even though consumers might be interested in new products.

Concentration of market share within industries leads to fewer but significantly larger competing firms. Economists have argued that the larger a firm is, the more reluctant it is to take chances. Frederick M. Scherer puts it this way:

> In a small firm, the decision to go ahead with an ambitious project typically involves a very few people who know one another well. In a large corporation, the decision must filter through a whole train of command—the person with the idea, his section chief, the laboratory manager, the vice president for research, and if substantial financial commitments are required, several members of top management. Each participant is risking his reputation, if not his money, in backing the project.[22]

Clearly concentration could have a deleterious effect on the quality and the diversity of published books. But is book publishing a concentrated industry? The evidence is mixed.[23] Townsend Hoopes, president of the Association of American Publishers, argues that "the most fundamental measure of the health and vigor [of book publishing] is the number of active firms in the industry."[24] The AAP and a recent Congressional Research Service Report argue that, while there have been many recent mergers, the book industry remains hospitable to the entry of new firms, which have been steadily appearing.[25] This is by no means a new view. In 1931 the National Association of Book Publishers sponsored a study of the industry's health.[26] The author of the survey, in discussing the "panacea" of mergers recommended by many in the industry, argued:

> For every house which would be "eliminated" through merger, several new ones could—and would—easily spring up, because the capital need is so small and the "publishing urge" so great. The rate of increase in the number of houses by fission seems always to be at least equal to the rate of decrease by fusion.[27]

The Association of American Publishers also points to the many titles released annually (over 40,000 for the past few years) and the quantity of books in print (478,000 in 1977) as further evidence of the industry's competitiveness. Over the years, the U.S. Census of Manufactures concentration ratios—statistics that measure the percentage of total sales controlled by a specified number of the largest companies in an industry—are lower for book publishing than for many other industries. In reviewing the 1972 Census concentration data for most American industries, ratios of 80 percent, 90 percent, and 100 percent for the top fifty firms are not uncommon, as compared with 75 percent for book publishing. Unfortunately the concentration figures for the 1977 Census are not yet available, so it is not possible to assess what changes have occurred in the period from 1972 to 1977.

Historically, book publishing has been a competitive industry primarily because of the low capital entry costs. These same low entry costs have made publishing susceptible to mergers because of the many undercapitalized small firms. Additionally, the easy availability of a host of intermediary and ancillary services that can be contracted for as needed makes it easier to establish new publishing houses compared with industries where economies of scale are more important. Thus, low capital entry costs and free-lance services, along with the availability of books of all types worthy of publication, have historically mitigated trends toward oligopoly.

Nevertheless, book publishing has changed in the past two decades. It has been affected by societal trends, including a growth in real literacy, the increased number of college graduates, the expansion of the higher educational system, a worldwide information explosion, and an enormous boom in the mass entertainment industry. The economics of mass communications during the 1960s and the 1970s pushed publishing onto a path previously followed only by the larger media. The tendency in the film industry as well as in the print and the electronic media to diversify holdings has affected sectors of the book trade. International ownership of the media has also increased; and as one of the earliest media to have cultivated an import and export trade, publishing is intimately tied to this trend.

Publishing began to shed some of the traits of a cottage industry in the 1960s, when it came to be regarded as a good investment on Wall Street.[28] After the Second World War, college enrollments skyrocketed; and in the years following the 1957 shock of Sputnik, federal and state funds for education, including library budgets and scientific research, were plentiful. The 1960s were bullish years for publishing. The industry underwent huge changes, including the widely publicized "urge to merge." During the 1960s some older, established houses, among them Houghton Mifflin in Boston and Random House in New York, became public stock companies to raise capital for expansion or to avoid being broken up by estate settlements. Some publishers amalgamated with other publishers; others, such as Harcourt Brace Jovanovich and Macmillan, embarked on expansion campaigns of their own, diversifying into other fields.

The most discussed acquisitions occurred between publishing houses and electronics and/or computer corporations. In the intended marriage of electronics and education, the electronics firms planned to provide hardware, capital, and management skills; and publishers, the raw materials, marketing skills, and legitimacy. Among the corporate entrants were International Business Machines (IBM), International Telephone and Telegraph (ITT), Litton Industries, Radio Corporation of America (RCA), Columbia Broadcasting System (CBS), Raytheon, Xerox, General Electric (GE), and General Telephone. All this activity was buoyed by the expectations of increasing school enrollments and of a more widely educated and literate population with a great deal of leisure time on its hands.

The anticipated "synergy" between education and computers did not pay off quickly enough for some. A few of the marriages were unsuccessful. Enrollments declined in the schools, and some corporate parents learned that many of publishing's arcane inefficiencies could not be easily rationalized. General Electric and Litton sold their publishing interests; Xerox sold its college division to John Wiley; and RCA sold the Random House complex—including Knopf, Pantheon, Vintage, and Ballantine—to Newhouse Newspapers.

The mergers of the 1960s did not lead to less diversity. If anything, the problem was overproduction of books. Most trade books had a relatively slim chance of making it onto the shelves of bookstores and, once there, had a short shelf life. The situation was further complicated by the shotgun marketing strategy of many houses: publish many books in the hope that a few will sell very well. The very ease with which books were published clogged the distribution system.

The standard claim of publishing industry economists is that the consolidation and mergers of the 1960s made resources available without which the industry's remarkable growth could not have been sustained. New management and financial acumen resulted for the first time in orderly budgeting, forecasting, planning, and fiscal arrangements. However, not all firms shared equally in the industry's growth. The larger firms' slices of the publishing pie were expanding much faster than were those of the smaller ones.[29]

From 1965 to 1969, at least twenty-three publishing industry mergers took place annually. The peak years were 1968 (forty-seven mergers) and 1969 (forty-four mergers). Compared with merger rates in the mining and manufacturing sector of the economy, those for publishing are considerably higher. With respect to companies of significant size, mergers occurred in publishing at 2.4 to 4.3 times the rate of the combined Census category of mining and manufacturing.

In addition to acquisition from the outside, certain conditions in publishing itself encouraged mergers. The presence of many undercapitalized firms leads to a high merger rate. Established houses with active backlists have always proved attractive to acquiring firms, especially in contrast to the risks and uncertainty of starting up a new house. An industry with numerous competing firms will have a higher merger rate than an industry with few firms. This situation helps explain the frequency of publishing mergers: there are more firms available for acquisition. Yet it is also why many critics are alarmed: they fear that one of the more open and competitive industries in our economy may lose, as a result of mergers, one of its essential features.

The next wave of merger activity took place in the middle 1970s. In 1974 alone, publishing mergers took place at ten times the rate of mergers in mining and manufacturing. From 1974 to 1978, fifteen or more mergers took place annually. Unlike the "go-go" years of the 1960s, the 1970s were a period of financial austerity, and general economic conditions were poor. Both inflation and the prime interest rate increased. Production costs rose significantly for publishers. Federal spending on education decreased; and as a result, library budgets contracted, and federal research monies became scarce. The birth rate dropped, and long-range educational projections predicted, at best, stable enrollments and, at worst, a relative decline over the next decade.

The distinguishing feature of recent mergers is that they are taking place almost solely within the media business. Most prominent have been the mergers of softcover and hardcover houses—such as those between Doubleday (general publisher) and Dell (paperbacks), Viking (trade books) and Penguin (paperbacks)—or of media conglomerates with substantial publishing interests and previously independent publishing firms—such as the purchase by CBS (which already owned both a paperback line and the hardcover house of Holt, Rinehart & Winston) of Saunders (a major medical publisher), Praeger (professional books), and Fawcett (paperbacks). Successful publishing houses, such as Harper & Row, have been buying up their less successful brethren (T. Y. Crowell and J. B. Lippincott). The Hearst newspaper empire, which owns Avon Books (paperbacks), acquired Arbor House (hardcover trade books) and then purchased William Morrow, a large trade publisher, for approximately twenty-five million dollars from Scott, Foresman, an educational publisher. Time-Life, with major holdings in magazines and subscription books, bought Little, Brown and Book-of-the-Month Club. The Times Mirror Corporation, owner of several large metropolitan newspapers, also owns Abrams (art books) and New American Library (paperbacks).

Foreign publishers have opened American offices and started acquiring American firms. In addition to Penguin, this trend includes the purchase of David McKay (college texts) by Longman (a British publishing firm owned by Morgan Grampian), the purchase of majority stock in Bantam (the largest paperback house in the United States) by Bertelsmann Publishing Group (West Germany's largest magazine and book publisher), and the Canadian International Thomson's purchase of Wadsworth, a California-based text publisher for thirty-two million dollars in 1978.

The film industry has also gotten into the act. The Music Corporation of America (MCA) took over both Putnam (trade books), which had previously absorbed Berkley (paperbacks), and Coward, McCann & Geoghegan (trade books). Filmways Pictures now owns Grosset & Dunlap, and Warner Communications has founded Warner Books. Gulf & Western counts Paramount Pictures, Simon & Schuster, and the latter's paperback subsidiary Pocket Books, as part of its leisure entertainment division. Film and television studios look to book publishers as sources of new material and as outlets for novelizations of successful films.

Many of the mergers were normal, friendly business arrangements. Some takeover attempts, however, have been anything but amicable. Western Pacific backed off on its attempt to acquire Houghton Mifflin because authors and editors threatened to leave the venerable house. Western Pacific did make a tidy profit when Houghton Mifflin purchased its stock back at a higher price than the former had paid for it. McGraw-Hill, itself a diversified publishing combine, undertook a "scorched earth" policy to fend off American Express. And Harcourt Brace Jovanovich has reacted with displeasure to the acquisition of sizable amounts of its stock—first, by Marvin Josephson Associates and, later, by Warner Communications. Some merger partners never made it to the altar: Macmillan was courted by both Mattel and ABC, but vows were never exchanged. During the courtship, an outside stockholder was elected to the Macmillan board and was successful in fomenting a palace revolt, ousting chairman Ray Hagel in the process.

Corporate executives within the media business like to refer to these mergers as natural marriages that cross-fertilize the communications field. But these mergers are also business strategies in which an acquiring firm reduces its dependency in an uncertain business environment and, by horizontally and vertically integrating related interests, gains economies of scale. It is clear that large size has competitive advantages for advertising, inventory control, and distribution. Despite such benefits, the consequences of these mergers are difficult to sort out. When Harper & Row acquired two old houses, J. B. Lippincott and T. Y. Crowell, it was claimed that Harper had saved two faltering firms. However, in the process of consolidation, hundreds of employees were dismissed, the number of editorial decision makers was reduced, title output was cut back, and writers were left wondering about the status of their books.

At any given time, the character of literary output is determined not only by the prevailing methods of production, distribution, and consumption but also by the patterns of financial reward for publishers, booksellers, and authors. The mergers of the 1970s differ markedly from those of the 1960s, as do their literary and financial outcomes. The merger wave of the 1960s led to expansion, with the publication of many books that went unnoticed. Parent companies were satisfied to allow the acquired houses to operate as separate profit centers, and institutionalization of the multidivisional form and interdivisional competition within firms became common.

Mergers in the 1970s took place in a different economic climate with a new set of corporate actors and have had a different outcome. In trade publishing, an increasing emphasis on "blockbuster" books has led to multimedia tie-ins. Indeed, one of the most significant developments of the 1970s was the growth and proliferation of multimedia conglomerates, with interests in film, television, cable TV, newspapers, magazines, home video equipment, and book publishing.[30]

CHANGES IN PUBLISHING STRATEGIES

Our reading of publishing history and our understanding of the industry's socio-economic structure lead us to believe that few trends in publishing are lasting; they are likely to occur in cycles. However, current trends have had two effects that bear close attention: multimedia mergers in trade publishing have created an environment in which books, films, and even television programs are viewed as constituent parts of a media package; and a shift in the internal status order within publishing houses—a process in which the power of editors has declined, and the influence of agents, professional managers, and subsidiary rights directors has risen. In combination, these trends focus attention on "big" books and reduce the contact between editors and writers.

John Brooks, speaking for the Authors Guild, has argued:

> It is not that fewer books are being published than formerly, or even, at least not provably, that books of exceptional merit are going unpublished. It is,

29

rather, that such books are increasingly being squeezed out of sight by the conglomerate-hyped and -packaged best sellers, and not reaching the public that they deserve, and that deserve them. . . . A book on a publisher's list that does not sell to paperback or book clubs or the movies these days often becomes a sort of idiot child, to be kept out of sight.[31]

There is increasing focus on blockbusters because publishers, in both hardcover trade and mass-market paperback houses, believe that these books will generate exceptionally large profits. Even college textbook publishers have turned almost exclusively to introductory-level texts, investing heavily in the design and marketing of "snappy" books for courses with sizable enrollments. Critics, in and outside of publishing, see as irresponsible this emphasis on blockbusters and the exorbitant costs they involve. What these critics fail to recognize is that blockbusters are, in fact, a conservative approach to the problem of coping with uncertain market demand.

By carefully planning all aspects of a blockbuster, mass media industries control the risk of failure while maximizing the potential for profit. Furthermore, blockbusters have common features that allow them to be exploited as "products" by several media, with enormous financial rewards. First, heavy advertising and promotion before the book is released contributes to the appearance of a successful "product." Tie-ins between books and films are especially useful here because of the savings on joint promotions directed to different audiences. Second, for new projects, media industries increasingly depend on "products" that have proved successful in another medium. This situation enhances the importance of the subsidiary income that can be derived from the sale of "products" from one medium to another.

Signing up established "stars," or name authors, is another blockbuster strategy—but one that has escalated the blockbuster war. Although "stars" guarantee a large audience, they also shift the negotiating balance. Their bargaining power allows them to demand and win "up-front" guarantees, bypassing the wait for the royalties that may or may not be forthcoming. As a result, "stars" command huge advances. As the stakes grow higher, they sign with agents and lawyers, who win for their clients many of the subsidiary rights publishers count on to multiply their own profits. A handful of "stars"—nonfiction writers, such as Tom Wolfe and Carl Sagan, and ex-politicians or best-selling novelists, such as Judith Krantz or Taylor Caldwell—receive vast sums. One consequence, editors told us, is that there is now less money to go around for other writers.

That is not the only unfortunate outcome of the "star" system. In a *Publishers Weekly* survey (May 1980) of major trade houses, one executive, whose house depends on best sellers, voiced concern at the increased pace that blockbusters require. "It is becoming harder and harder to keep best-selling authors without paying huge amounts of money. With multiple submissions, editor and author never get together to judge the chemistry between them, and we find ourselves up against 15 other houses, having to make fast decisions."[32] An author submits the barest of outlines for review, and an editor must decide quickly. The investment in a large advance speeds up the whole writing and editorial process, and production and promotion must be coordinated and orchestrated with other media to ensure maximum exposure.

The second major trend signaled by the hot pursuit of blockbusters is a power shift within publishing itself and a significant reorientation in publishers' views of their social role. Increasingly, the key people in trade publishing houses are not editors but the buyers and sellers of subsidiary rights. Publishers, who once prided themselves on connections with writers and thinkers, are increasingly influenced by the media industries and corporate world where they, the publishers, must sell their wares. The internal shift in power and the change in outlook and operating procedures reflect the fact that, when making choices, people are likely to orient themselves to groups or individuals who are important in their lives—to their "reference group," to use Robert K. Merton's concept.[33] Publishing standards, definitions of responsibility, and conceptions of the role of publisher are likely to be powerfully influenced by the reference groups that individual publishers have chosen for themselves. Their decisions to publish or to reject specific books or categories of books will often reflect the standards of the company they keep.

The biographies or autobiographies of nineteenth- and early twentieth-century publishers show that many of them were closely associated with their authors and with other writers, as well as with literary critics and other cultivated people.[34] To be sure, such cultural interaction may have been exaggerated in these retrospective accounts; but even so, it seems to have been more frequent and intense in the past than it is now.

The decline in contact between the business of publishing and the worlds of writers, critics, and intellectuals can be accounted for partially by the greater size of many publishing firms and the consequent complexity of ownership and control. A publisher at a major house nowadays has wide and diversified tasks and spends increasing amounts of time with lawyers and corporate officers. He or she may simply no longer have the time and leisure for sustained associations with people outside the firm.

As publishing houses are integrated into complex corporate structures, they change profoundly. Communication lines grow longer, and the organizational hierarchy grows steeper. Publishers work at a distance from writers, spending more time maintaining their organization than working on manuscripts. As one publishing director, whose small house was acquired by a large publishing combine, complained to us, "After we were bought, I never had time to see authors, I spent all my time in meetings with various corporate execs and 'selling' our imprint within the parent company."

In addition, many publishing contracts are negotiated no longer with the author, but with literary agents or lawyers. Direct contact with authors has been increasingly replaced by a mediated relationship that forecloses close association between editor and author except in the special case of well-known authors. One prominent editor in chief, who recently moved from a small, high-quality house to head the trade department at a large one, told us that although he had gained considerable financial benefits from his move, he was worried that in his new position he saw "mostly lawyers and agents and [he was] in danger of losing touch with creative writers and their manuscripts." In his earlier position he could assist in the creative development of his authors; now he is in danger of becoming a well-paid retailer of ideas and entertainment.

Publishers and major editors have become so involved with businessmen, lawyers, literary agents, and key decision makers in subsidiary rights that they are in danger of losing touch with the world of the creative intellect. To the extent that they are segregated—or self-segregated—from intellectual and cultural circles, they are more likely to let their general cultural responsibilities remain on the back burner, while the front burner is occupied by immediate business considerations and calculations.

We discussed the effect of corporate ownership on publishing at length with some editors in chief, most of whom were directors of small or medium-sized quality firms that were divisions or subsidiaries of larger corporations. The parent companies were all members of *Fortune* magazine's one thousand largest corporations. We also conducted field observations at several houses in order to pursue the ownership issue in more detail. One house was a division of a large corporation; one was independently owned; and the other had recently regained its independence, having broken off from a large diversified publishing company. Each of the houses published between fifty and one hundred books a year.

We were particularly interested in the pressures and demands these firms received from their owners. No one reported any effort by a parent company to influence the content of books. Nor did we notice any discernible difference in pressures to increase profitability. There was somewhat more attention to long-range planning and budgeting in the non-independent houses; but many editors felt that, given the peculiar nature of book publishing, these were exercises in "creative writing." The independently owned firm was under the greatest financial pressure, because its creditors were constantly disturbed by its chronic cash-flow problems. This situation led us to conclude that for independent firms of this size, the marketplace, which is shaped by the nature and variety of firms competing within it, was a more insidious force than corporate managers.

One key difference we frequently observed in the corporate-owned houses was pressure to increase the number of titles published annually. This was a serious concern for the houses we were studying, which were modest in size and had a reputation for nurturing their authors. The pressures, they felt, were aimed at increasing the size of their operations and their sales volume. We cannot say if this is common in all corporate-owned houses. Perhaps in a larger house, parent company influence would be focused not on growth but on producing fewer and more promotable and profitable books. Large operations may feel pressures to increase their operational efficiency; our medium and small houses relied heavily on freelance outsiders and were most certainly not overstaffed. To our inquiries about "pressures from above," the editor in chief of a quality small house, owned by a parent conglomerate with a wide variety of interests, responded:

> The main pressures we feel are not pressures for greater profits. They don't even look at the figures on individual titles. What we feel are pressures for growth, to expand and do more books. . . . We cannot sustain growth really, they don't understand that. . . . They've bothered us partly by forcing more growth than we would normally have. They want us to do more books and we keep telling them there may not be any more books of real merit that we can do justice to.

In a 1978 *PW* interview, Charles Scribner, Jr., described some of the differences between his independent firm and other houses:

> We're putting out the "Dictionary of Scientific Biography," done in-house. It's been in the works 15 years, but it will be a perennial seller. And we're embarking on the "Encyclopedia of the Middle Ages," at least a 10-year project. Big publishers simply won't undertake such time-consuming projects. Everyone wants everything tomorrow.
>
> We enjoy being independent. The two greatest joys are these: Independence confers upon us an important business advantage, the opportunity to take the long view, to take a long time waiting. Many times the merits of an author or a work are not immediately apparent, but we can wait. Second, we enjoy the ability to follow our own judgment. When you have someone pulling up the plant to check its roots, the plant simply will not grow. We do not suffer beneath that yoke.[35]

33

Scribner pointed out some important differences between the long-term view taken by his independent house, with its consequences for publishing choices and strategies, and the short-term outlook dominant in other houses. Yet our survey of the industry revealed that changes in author-publisher relations and in the internal organization of houses are more pervasive than a simple typology of independent/non-independent houses would suggest. Crown Publishers, for instance, is the independent house that published Judith Krantz, the queen of blockbusters if there ever was one. A front-page article in the *Wall Street Journal* described the "notable departure from tradition" at the independent firm of Houghton Mifflin when the house brought in a new trade book chief, Lynn Thompson Long, who had no publishing background. A lawyer and former investment banker, Long had defended Houghton Mifflin against the Western Pacific takeover attempt in 1978. She said that her skills are "managerial, not editorial," and asserted that "publishers are now managers of ideas [for many markets], not just publishers of hardcover books." Her plans for Houghton Mifflin included raising title output by fifty to one hundred titles a year within five years. The news article went on to state:

> The old-line editors who founded and long ran publishing houses are being replaced in top managerial jobs by a new breed, the professional manager. More and more houses have been acquired by big public companies with a gimlet eye on the bottom line. Houghton, one of the best-known remaining independents, has had to bow to the new realities.[36]

In contrast, Simon & Schuster, which is owned by Gulf & Western and has a reputation for doing big, splashy, successful books, appears to be following a strategy of "growth" by becoming smaller and more diverse. Within the company, smaller lines have been set up—among them, Linden Press, Summit Books, Wyndham Books, Timescape Books, and Touchstone. Each is headed by an individual who has a record of achievement within the industry. This process of growth through the formation of small, personal imprints is an attempt to counterbalance many of the forces that are buffeting the industry. Other large, corporate-owned trade houses have also set up similar arrangements with their top editors.

The comparison of Houghton Mifflin and Simon & Schuster's different growth strategies demonstrates the difficulty of generalizing about trends within the industry. Distinguished old houses are hiring professional managers, and highly commercial houses continue to publish books of real merit. After reviewing a number of fine books published in 1980, *New York Times* book reviewer John Leonard remarked, "This year, like every year, is arbitrary, trendless, accidental, perverse."[37]

34

Commerce and Culture

Readers unfamiliar with the inner workings of publishing houses may have trouble reconciling the complex business of publishing with an author's solitary creative efforts. The myth is widespread that book publishing in the nineteenth and early twentieth centuries was a gentlemanly trade in which an editor catered to an author's every whim, whereas commercialism and hucksterism have taken over in our day. It is a useful myth, to be sure, for it permits authors to point to a golden past and allows publishers to fashion for themselves a fine pedigree going back to a time when their profession was not sullied by the crass requirements of the marketplace. There once may have been more gentlemen in publishing than there are now, but there were surely sharp operators, hucksters, and pirates galore. In publishing, as in many other spheres of social life, there is little that is new. What is different, we believe, are the changes in the work process and the status order within houses. However, book publishing in the past as in the present has operated under the pressures of the marketplace, the countinghouse, and the literary and intellectual currents of the day. The quest for profit and the demands of excellence have all too often refused to go hand in hand. One should not be surprised that these same tensions, albeit in somewhat different form, are still here today.

Chapter 2

Publishing Worlds: Sectors within the Industry

BOOK PUBLISHING is a comparatively small industry. With total sales of approximately seven billion dollars in 1980, the entire industry would rank only forty-sixth on *Fortune* magazine's list (4 May 1981) of the 500 largest U.S. industrial corporations in 1980. Most book publishers are small: in 1977, only 348 establishments (a company may own several) had more than twenty employees.[1] Geographic concentration is high. New York State accounted for 45 percent of the total industry receipts in 1977;[2] our tabulations show that 45 percent of all publishing houses in the United States in 1975 were located in the New York metropolitan area and published over 60 percent of the titles released that year.

Despite its modest size and geographic concentration, the industry is highly differentiated. It is the most specialized of all the media industries. While there is general agreement that it has many specialties and subfields, there is little consensus on how to categorize its various segments.*[3] In

----

* We decided not to use the categories that the Census Department or the American Association of Publishers employed in their record keeping, because their categories were too

order to discuss the behavior of publishers and editors and analyze the way the industry works, it was crucial to find an adequate way of sorting out different types of publishing houses. One would hardly expect the same behavior of a three-person house located in Arizona and publishing two highly profitable cookbooks a year, of a four-hundred-person house in New York producing five hundred scholarly monographs a season, and of a two-hundred-person New York house that each year has at least one blockbuster on the best-seller list, and whose staff regularly lunches with the editor of the *New York Times Book Review* to go over the season's list. These three houses all publish books; but, beyond placing words between covers, they may have little in common.

In classifying types of house, size is obviously a factor, but how to measure it? What counts the most—number of titles, number of sales, number of sales per book, gross receipts, capitalization, number of employees, number of divisions, or what? Subject matter, too, seems important; and though this may seem an easy way to slice the industry, a quick perusal of any library's classification scheme—from the Dewey decimal system to the Library of Congress method—will show that very dissimilar books can end up on the same shelf. Then there is the nature of the audience or market. Surely, selling texts to college freshmen is different from selling romances to suburban women. Finally, there are the auspices of a house. At the very least, one would expect university presses that may have a subsidy to differ from houses that are supposedly profitable. Then ownership itself may make a difference: does a publishing house owned by a few editors differ from a house owned by a television network or a movie company, and what difference does a public corporation make compared with a privately held house?

In this chapter, we will sort out some of these questions, beginning with the knotty matter of size, moving on to the relation between the size of a house and the nature of its market, then to the issue of corporate ownership, and finally to the heart of any book—its contents. Our aim has been to find a scheme that accounts for the major differences among houses, and then to demonstrate that the method we have used is closely related to editorial standards and the way editors judge the worth of

---

broad and masked what we perceived to be significant differences among houses. The AAP has a particularly awkward classification scheme for our purposes. It classifies individual books, not houses, and uses an array of categories. Some categories refer to a book's subject—such as, religions; others refer to a book's audience—that is, trade or professional; while other categories describe the mode of distribution—that is, book club, mail order, or subscription; and one category is based on the type of house—that is, university presses. Many researchers have complained about both the completeness and the usefulness of publishing industry data sources.

37

their efforts. No single classification scheme is entirely satisfactory, but we have tried to take into account as many factors as seem relevant and practical.

LARGE AND SMALL

Sociologists who study organizations have shown that size of a firm plays a determining role in influencing the behavior of individuals within the firm. One therefore might expect to find a significant difference between large and small publishing houses.[4] A large house can afford to experiment, even in one specialized area, without the assurance that all its titles will do well. Smaller houses, in contrast, must exercise greater care to avoid being saddled with too many failures. Although one might argue the converse, we speculated that larger houses may be more inclined to innovation. On the other hand, smaller houses, particularly newcomers, may have to be alert to developing trends by introducing authors or fields not yet preempted by their big competitors. Large houses can offer great potential for promotion, distribution, and sales; small houses can offer an author more individual attention. The first task in understanding the industry, then, is to classify houses according to size.

Every firm has some inputs, does something with these inputs, and produces an output, a commodity, for the market. In terms of inputs, publishing houses have traditional labor and capital; but their raw material, as it were, differs from that of many firms since it consists of manuscripts submitted by individuals who are otherwise peripheral to the industry. One could classify houses in terms of capital investment, number of employees, and number of manuscripts submitted. The number of books published, the dollar volume of the sales, and the number of copies of books sold are quantitative indicators of the size of a firm's output. In many industries, the various indicators of size are all correlated to a greater or lesser degree. For example, an automobile company that produces many cars, has many employees and a high capitalization, along with high gross sales figures. And although the differences are extreme between Rolls Royce and Ford, the generally accepted way of making money is to sell many cars of many different kinds (Rolls Royce is, in fact, no exception: its motor car division, which sells but a few expensive products, loses money). In the book business, however, these indicators of size are not necessarily correlated. A one-person firm can, as we shall see, survive very well and earn more money than one with many employees. One can make money by selling many copies of the same book or a modest number of copies of many books. These differences also affect capitalization, so that the more profitable firms are not necessarily the best capitalized.

Perhaps these facts about the complexity of industry sound obvious, but at the start of our study we had thought otherwise. Given our assumption that all the indicators of size would in any case be correlated, we thought that the easiest way to begin would be to count the number of titles each firm produced each year. The *Literary Market Place*,* an annual volume, reports the number of titles published yearly by many of the houses in its lists. It would be an easy matter, we thought, to supplement these figures by calling or writing the houses whose yearly output was not listed. To our surprise, we learned that some publishing houses do not even keep accurate records of the number of titles they publish annually. The comments of a senior executive at a large publishing conglomerate illustrate the problems involved:

> Well, the trade department did X number of titles and the juvenile division did this many. I don't know how many the college and elementary and high school texts divisions did; besides, those are textbooks and they aren't the same. Then there is the reference department—does a dictionary count the same as a single book? There is also X, which is a division of ours. I suppose we should count them, but they do their own budgeting and accounting. We also have a number of subsidiaries and foreign affiliates. So you tell me, how many books did we publish this year? I just don't know. And that doesn't even consider the books that were supposed to be published, maybe even were announced, but were delayed for one reason or another.

Nor is that the end of the complications. Not all books are comparable. Our respondents asked, "How is a textbook that took five years to produce or a reference book ten years in the making comparable with an annually published income tax guide?" The *Literary Market Place* also lists some divisions and subsidiaries separately from their parent companies. Yet we were told that the figures for one large publishing conglomerate included all the companies under its umbrella, even though several of these were listed separately. After several months, during which we learned a lot about the informal nature of record keeping in book publishing, we even-

---

* R. R. Bowker's *Literary Market Place* (*LMP*) is an annual publication that may be little known outside the book trade; but within it, it is, perhaps, the most used of books. The 1980 edition, the fortieth, runs to almost 1,000 pages and lists the names of some 25,000 individuals and companies. Available in libraries, *LMP* is a useful guide to publishers, agents, book clubs, and most facets of book publishing.

tually obtained enough data to rank almost all houses by the number of titles published.

We turned next to comparing annual sales figures. Here we saw first-hand some of the important differences among the various divisions within the industry. The trade and the college text departments of one firm published a similar number of titles. However, the former had annual sales of five million dollars, in contrast to the college text's seventy million. We conducted interviews with scientific monograph publishers that put out hundreds of titles each year; but their sales were comparatively small, as they sold only several thousand copies of each title.

We later tried to measure size by the number of employees working for various houses, and thus were led to examine how work was organized and distributed within a house. We found that almost all functions or services can be delegated to individuals or firms outside the house, and that copy editing, jacket design and artwork, and publicity are frequently contracted to such free lancers as the work is needed. Also, small or medium-sized houses rely on larger ones to distribute their books. Publishing can operate as a cottage industry in part because it is possible for a publishing house to operate with a staff of one—the editor—while handing over all other functions to free lancers or outside contractors. This is one of the reasons that book publishing is concentrated in New York City, where, as in a few other big cities, there are available within walking distance all the services one needs to publish books—from typewriter-rental firms to free-lance writers, to copy editors, not to mention all the people and organizations that can design, publicize, and distribute the final product.

Economists describe such an industry as one in which external economies prevail. And where there is heavy reliance on external economies, there are organizations with highly permeable boundaries, making it difficult to determine who is a member of the organization and who is not. The number will vary depending on when one is asking the question and on the particular project one is looking at. Several well-known, highly visible publishing houses have surprisingly few full-time employees. This was particularly true of trade houses and scholarly houses that published for a general intellectual audience. We studied several houses that had twenty-five or fewer employees yet published seventy-five or more titles a year. In contrast, we observed college text houses that had several hundred employees and produced fewer than one hundred texts a year. We also studied a scientific monograph house that had more than four hundred employees and published more than four hundred titles a year. The difference lies in the reliance of many trade and scholarly publishers on outside services, while labor-intensive text and monograph publishing requires large and specialized in-house production and promotion departments.

None of the preceding quantitative indicators of size—title output, annual sales, or size of work force—provided us with wholly satisfactory measures. Capitalization, which we discuss when we come to the ownership of houses, proved difficult to collect accurate data on; and the number of manuscripts submitted turned out to depend on many variables (see chapter 5). In the end, we used number of titles per year as part of our strategy for sampling editors simply because we judged that working conditions in firms with many titles would be different from those with fewer titles, but we are under no illusion that this single index is an adequate substitute for an over-all notion of size. In our survey of editors, we asked for a qualitative, subjective response: whether, in the editor's *opinion*, the firm he or she worked for was large, medium-sized, or small. In accounting for editorial behavior, this single subjective measure seemed to perform as well, if not better, than the objective measures.

THE DUAL MARKET

Throughout the nineteenth century the so-called mass market for books was the small reading portion of the relatively small populations of the United States and Great Britain. Today, with the population explosion and a high literacy rate, the potential size of the market for books is of an entirely different order of magnitude and has been enhanced by media tie-ins. There are now two pronounced segments of the book trade: one in which books are media properties and part of a high-risk speculative mass market characterized by a winner-take-all system of huge windfalls and disastrous failures; and the rest of the industry, in which serious publishing continues albeit quietly and without much fanfare.[5] The audience for these latter publications is not large, nor are their successes or failures grand. Persuasive arguments, theoretical and empirical, account for this two-tier development.

Sociologists and economists have for some time argued that, in modern societies, both labor and production have become segmented. In the labor market, there are a so-called primary sector with job mobility, good working conditions, and high wages, and a secondary sector characterized by unstable employment and low wages.[6] These differences in the labor market are seen by some economists as resulting from a fundamental split between industries that comprise the core or the muscle of the American economy and those that are relatively peripheral.[7] Core industries have an oligopolistic market structure. Firms within these industries have a large share of the market, are vertically integrated, and are simply big. Peripheral industries have a competitive market structure and are characterized by relatively easy entry costs, and firms within such industries tend to be small.[8]

Similar to the core-periphery distinction in the economy at large is the division within the mass media between those that are producer-oriented and those that are distributor-oriented.[9] For example, Off-Off Broadway theaters serve small audiences, have a close artist-audience relation, and reward originality and the breaking of molds and traditions. Indeed, the audience often consists of people who are themselves involved with the theater. In contrast, Broadway productions cater to large audiences not intimately involved in the theater and favor formula rather than innovation. These latter media must retail cultural developments to a large audience. The criteria for Off-Off Broadway success are often no more than the approval of one's colleagues. Indeed, some noted performers attempt to restrict access to their work. In contrast, the main criteria for the success of distributor media are quantitative rather than qualitative. Without large audiences, a Broadway play closes. Thus, prospects for delivering original and complex ideas are clouded from the outset by the economic organization of distributor media.

Though book publishing as a whole may be regarded by some people as a peripheral industry in comparison with steel or automobiles, publishing itself contains one sector more like the core industries and another more like the peripheral industries. Some publishing firms deal in large investments, big money, and fast turnover and have a hectic promotion pace. Other, smaller firms have specialized audiences, lower entry costs, and a more traditional approach to marketing. In this sense, book publishing, too, has a core of distributor-oriented firms, and a periphery of producer-oriented firms.

Whatever the terms used to describe this split into two sectors, the distinctions are certainly familiar to observers of book publishing. In a summary of the year's trends, N. R. Kleinfield noted in the Sunday *New York Times Book Review* that in 1980 "the money went even higher for the hot titles, while the money diminished for the small books, and the gulf separating the two extremes became wider."[10] The comments of Don Fine, the head of Arbor House, illustrate the two-sector argument:

The book publishing business—the one that has to do with big-name authors and big money and sexy ladies and sexy literary gentlemen—has nothing to do with the book publishing. It gets the attention of the press and the people who are dinner-party knowledgeable, but it gives a black eye to what real book publishing is about. That is something quite unspectacular but immensely satisfying to those who are part of it: finding a person who writes well, creatively and with sensibility—a Victorian phrase that nonetheless is timeless.[11]

And Judith Krantz, author of the best-selling *Scruples* (Crown, 1978) and *Princess Daisy* (Crown, 1980), pithily clinches the point:

I'm no Joan Didion—There are no intelligent, unhappy people in my books. I want to be known as a writer of good, entertaining narrative. I'm not trying to be taken seriously by the East Coast literary establishment. But I'm taken *very* seriously by the bankers.[12]

Contracts in the core sector carry high advances. For example, Carl Sagan was offered $2,000,000 by Simon & Schuster for hardcover and paperback rights to *Contact*, his first work of fiction—after the publisher had seen only a 115-page outline for the proposed book. Taylor Caldwell, the popular novelist, signed a two-book contract with G. P. Putnam's for $3,-900,000. Bantam Books paid $3,200,000 for the paperback rights to Judith Krantz's *Princess Daisy*. Bantam also bought *The Right Stuff* (Farrar, Straus, & Giroux, 1979) by Tom Wolfe for $600,000; and United Artists bought the movie rights for $500,000. The same film company also paid $2,500,000 for the film rights to *Thy Neighbor's Wife* by Gay Talese (Doubleday, 1980).

Besides giant sums of money, there is in the core sector much greater movement of authors and editors from house to house. An article in the *New York Times* stated that "loyalty [in book publishing] has a new name these days and it is spelled m-o-n-e-y."[13] Also commonplace is the signing of book projects not on the basis of the whole manuscript, but at a much earlier stage. Often an outline is sufficient indication of whether a book can be successfully mass-merchandised. The extraordinary attention paid to promotion can mean that the quality of the package, the meticulously designed jacket plus advertising and promotional materials, is often superior to the merits of the book. Publishers have come to question whether their increasingly professional promotion and marketing departments should be cranked up for books that do not have mass appeal. In a revealing response to the question, "What size advance do you usually pay?" a senior editor at a large hardcover trade house responded:

I've paid up to half a million, although I certainly have to get approval for something that big. But the amount has really gone up in recent years. I would have said $10,000 was the minimum several years ago, but now it's considerably higher. We have a highly effective publishing machine here, particularly on the promotional end, and it is not only hard to get them interested in a book that is earmarked as small, you have to wonder if it is even worth their time.

With such all-or-nothing publishing, Herbert K. Schnall, president of New American Library, calculates that "it almost doesn't pay to buy something for under $100,000."[14] Mass-market paperback publishing, college and elementary-high textbooks, and parts of hardcover trade publishing have grown into a high-stakes business. The emphasis on "big" books, which generate high-volume sales, necessarily confines a house to a predictable pattern of operation.

The French sociologist Pierre Bourdieu has described such a pattern by developing a typology of publishing houses based on whether publishing decisions are oriented toward a short or a long time span.[15] He suggests that the more "commercial" the orientation of a firm—or, in our terms, the more distributor- or core-oriented it is—the shorter its time perspective and the greater the tendency to produce books that will meet an existing demand and fulfill particular readers' interests. Such houses, in Bourdieu's view, are geared to the rapid turnover and quick obsolescence of their products, and to the minimization of unnecessary risks. Houses geared to a longer time perspective, on the other hand, tend to accept higher risks and lower immediate profitability and turnover, in hopes that once a book is part of the backlist, it will continue to find new buyers. These houses are oriented toward the future. Such firms, Bourdieu suggests, are not concerned with the immediate maximization of returns but rather tend to accumulate what he calls, in a memorable phrase, "symbolic capital." As an example of this latter strategy, he points to the Paris house, *Editions de Minuit*, that published Samuel Beckett, among other difficult authors. *Waiting for Godot*, for example, came out in 1952 and sold only ten thousand copies in the first five years; but its rate of sales increased by about 20 percent per year, so that its cumulative sales by 1968 amounted to sixty-five thousand copies.

Firms that are intent upon acquiring symbolic capital must follow different strategies from those geared to quick accumulation of financial capital. Bourdieu highlights the fact that those firms concerned with symbolic capital are by no means engaged in philanthropy. They, too, are geared to the logic of profitability, but they operate within an extended time perspective in which immediate returns and quick maximization of profit are not the primary considerations.

Since core publishing tends to preclude the publication of books that are original or experimental, and important but demanding, peripheral publishers—small trade houses as well as scholarly ones—are moving into the territory that has been vacated by the large trade houses in the quest for blockbusters. As many publishing houses have increased their expectations of the number of copies a book needs to sell in order to be deemed successful, they are less willing to take on titles with potential sales of from five thousand to twenty-five thousand copies. Many small trade publishers that have sprung up recently, particularly on the West Coast, can do very well with books in that range. A similar phenomenon occurred when television usurped radio's mass audience. Paul Hirsch and others have argued that the success of television in capturing radio's mass market led to a transformation in the latter's programming. The audience for radio was redefined: stations directed their programming at groups with discrete, specialized tastes instead of at a unitary mass audience.[16]

Scholarly publishers, both commercial ones and university presses, are increasingly aiming books of more than academic interest at a larger audience. The crush of big books has given impetus to smaller houses. The following lengthy comments of the editor in chief of a successful, commercial, scholarly firm illustrate this development:

> One of my duties is to pick several books a season from our list that I think have some trade potential and work on promoting them. We can't "make" bestsellers like trade publishers do, we don't have large advertising budgets. . . . In our business, and perhaps it is only in our branch of publishing that this is true, good books sell themselves because the book itself says something that is important. I try to help them along by bringing them to people's attention. . . . Our kind of publishing doesn't require a great deal of money. We rarely compete with other houses on the basis of money . . . our advances are quite small. We compete on the basis of services we offer authors. We like to think that we are continuing the traditions of editorial excellence.
>
> In the past it was uncommon for our hardcover books to sell more than 10,000 copies, except for the few textbooks we did. Now we are aiming for somewhat larger sales. We're advertising in places like the *New Republic* and the *New York Review* [*of Books*]. But we aren't becoming trade publishers. Our books are still budgeted to earn small profits on four-figure sales. If some of them do better, that's great. . . . It's a totally different business from trade publishing where books have to recoup their investments in six months. . . . We do it on a two year basis . . . and if a book doesn't sell big, somebody loses his shirt. Trade publishers live off their front list sales. I couldn't sleep at night if faced with that. . . . The majority of our sales are from our backlist, good books that sell year in, year out and that make life a lot easier.

45

The History and Structure of the Industry

Because firms compete most intensely with firms of similar size, the distribution of organizational size has important implications for competition. Michael T. Hannan and John Freeman have shown:

> Competition between pairs of organizations within an activity will be a decreasing function of the distance separating them on the size gradient. For example, small local banks compete most with other small banks, to a lesser extent with medium-scale regional banks, and hardly at all with international banks. . . . [A significant alteration in the size distribution of firms in an industry will serve to select for and against certain organizations with regard to size.] When large-sized organizations emerge they pose a competitive threat to medium-sized but hardly any threat to small organizations. [Thus, the rise of large organizations may actually increase the survival prospects of small organizations.] On the other hand, organizations in the middle of the size distribution may find themselves trapped. Whatever strategy they adopt to fight off the challenge of the larger form makes them more vulnerable in competition with smaller organizations and vice-versa. [In sum,] the two ends of the size distribution ought to outcompete the middle. The number of medium-sized firms will decline upon the entry of large firms . . . and the fortunes of small firms will improve.[17]

Recent developments in book publishing illustrate very well the phenomenon that Hannan and Freeman describe. There has been simultaneous concentration among large firms and a proliferation of small, geographically dispersed independent companies. The small firms are frequently pursuing projects overlooked or cast aside by larger houses. Hundreds of very small, independent, "Mom and Pop" enterprises have sprung up outside of Manhattan. Many are located in California, clustered around Santa Barbara and the Bay area. These houses survive on low overheads and with small staffs. Some are only part-time operations. They have tended to favor the trade (large-size, quality design) paperback format. Although their output is only a fraction of the industry's total, several titles published by small houses have made the trade paperback best-seller list.

Why have these small houses been successful? One independent publisher argues:

> Because our resources are limited, we have to specialize, to make our imprint stand for things that concern people these days—career-changing, parenting, health, solar housing, and the like. Few of our books are returned unsold by bookstores, most become steady backlist sellers. We've had to let very few of our books go out of print.[18]

One way of competing with core, commercial, or distributor-oriented houses is to move toward "market segmentation" without necessarily be-

46

coming producer-oriented. Thus, many small publishers have found specialized niches and have concentrated on big-selling, "how to," fad, or regional books. There are also small publishers dedicated to social causes—religious, or conservative, or like the South End Press in Boston, which is an independent socialist publishing collective focusing on books analyzing political and economic systems. These publishers are more producer-oriented, bent on accumulating symbolic capital.

Other small peripheral houses, such as David Godine in Boston, concentrate on doing books of exceptional design and beauty. There are also small firms that reissue titles large companies have allowed to go out of print. Firms such as Second Chance Press—in Sagaponack, New York—or Academy Chicago Ltd. are operating as if they were traditional, backlist publishers. A considerable amount of contemporary poetry—including poems by the Polish Nobel Prize winner Czeslaw Milosz on Ecco Press's list—is published by small houses.

The Association of American Publishers points with considerable pleasure to the growth of small houses at the industry's bottom and even argues that their proliferation offsets recent concentration at the top.[19] There is no question that the number of small entrants to the industry has been remarkable; but to argue that they mitigate the development of large vertically integrated publishing combines is, in our opinion, wishful thinking.

A recent issue of an industry newsletter devoted a page to the more than one hundred independent publishers, "growing every day," in the Santa Barbara area.[20] The focus of the article was on Para Publishing, which has released fourteen books since 1969. But while new small houses are sprouting up, there are no replacements for medium-sized companies like Lippincott, T. Y. Crowell, or Bobbs-Merrill. (Lippincott and Crowell were absorbed by Harper & Row; Bobbs-Merrill dropped its fiction list under the policy direction of its parent conglomerate, International Telephone and Telegraph.) Herman Wouk, speaking for the Authors Guild, argued in 1978 that the many small companies publish only a few titles per year and "lack the capital to produce, advertise, promote, and distribute their books effectively in the national trade book market."[21]

In attempting to make the case for the contributions made by small presses, Winthrop Knowlton, then president of Harper & Row, stated the same year:

> For a quick, easy way of gauging the role of specialization in book publishing and the role of newer, smaller firms, go into any large bookstore and examine the cookbook section. . . . The other day in a store near me in New York, I

counted more than 900 titles. Of these, 25 percent were published by small, independent firms.[22]

This, however, is precisely the point of Wouk and the Authors Guild: small houses tend to specialize in "how to" books; they do not compete in the national market for major works of fiction or nonfiction.

While small houses are able to specialize and concentrate their energies in ways that medium and large houses cannot, the former also face unique problems. The editor in chief of one of Manhattan's leading small, independent houses commented to us:

> Our freedom has both advantages and disadvantages. The disadvantage is that we don't have the clout. Sometimes we just don't have the resources or money to pay what an author asks for. It can be hard to compete with the big guys. We're like the farm team for the New York Yankees. We create the successes for the big houses. We sign an author when he's relatively unknown and then next book time, the big guys pick him up.

The houses that are popping up on the West Coast, however, find that they need not compete with eastern houses, but are locating previously unpublished authors, doing projects other publishers have found unworkable, and being contacted by West Coast writers who like having an editor near by. These houses face other problems, particularly in terms of distribution and access to bookstores. They have had to develop marketing techniques outside of normal sales and distribution channels. Growth for small houses usually involves financing problems, but the problems of distribution to libraries and bookstores on a national basis become paramount. We again quote Knowlton of Harper & Row:

> I know from my own experience that small presses are springing up everywhere. They often come to us (and other established houses) for advice and help and sometimes for marketing services. We are happy to oblige because we cannot cover the editorial waterfront ourselves and sometimes distribution arrangements with new firms help us spread our considerable overheads.[23]

Distribution agreements between large firms and small houses may sometimes be mutually beneficial. Small presses, however, cannot afford to absorb returns at the same rate as large publishers, but depend for survival on direct sales rather than on subsidiary rights sales. Small publishers have complained to us that, under such distribution arrangements, their books are always "last to be touted [to booksellers]. . . . We even make presentations to their sales force at the end of the week . . . when they have been fully satiated with books and drink." New Republic Books encountered an unusual problem when, in 1979, Simon & Schuster chose not to distribute Steven Brill's book *The Teamsters* because the larger publisher had a book on the same subject.

Then there are small firms that are part of larger firms. This fact raises the issue of what constitutes a meaningful unit of analysis. While small houses publish only one or two different lines of books, large vertically integrated corporations like Time, Inc., or Times Mirror have a foot in many aspects of publishing. Doubleday, for instance, is a leading hardcover trade publisher involved in general publishing, special interest publishing, religious books, and paperback publishing through its division, Anchor Press. Doubleday also owns Dell Publishing which includes the second largest mass-market paperback publisher, Dell, and the latter's hardcover affiliate Delacorte with two personal imprint lines, as well as Delta Books and the Dial Press. The Literary Guild is one of twelve bookclubs owned by Doubleday. Both Macmillan and Harper & Row have trade and college text departments that rank among the top ten in sales in each of those markets. Macmillan owns the Free Press, and Harper & Row owns Basic Books: both subsidiaries are well-known scholarly publishers. The Putnam Publishing Group, owned by Music Corporation of America, is another diversified operation, counting among its various operations: G. P. Putnam's Sons; Coward, McCann, & Geoghegan; Perigee trade paperbacks; and Berkley and Jove, both mass-market publishers.

Even though some operations of the small firms owned by large firms appear to be producer-oriented and involved in the accumulation of symbolic capital, the parent firm itself possesses all the attributes of a core firm. The sizable resources available to these large firms, their extensive holdings, and their market power have squeezed middle-sized firms out or led to their acquisition and subsequent absorption under large corporate umbrellas. There are people within publishing who believe not only that medium-sized trade and text houses are in decline, but that medium-budget books are in trouble at larger houses. These books aimed at audiences of modest size are deemed risky for, without mass or specialized appeal, they have no ready market. *Publishers Weekly* asked sixteen top executives in trade publishing to comment on their current publishing practices. Their responses confirmed the decline of middle-level projects:

> We're cutting middlebrow fiction—anything that is neither commerce nor culture.
>
> We're not cutting back but we have an increasing reluctance to participate in auctions for intermediate books.

For anything below the blockbuster, the paperback reprint market is no longer the reliable source of income it once was.[24]

At a 1980 P.E.N. panel on bigness in publishing, the argument that "big" books help pay for the rest of the list was challenged by Leona Nevler, vice-president and publisher at Fawcett. The effect of blockbusters worried her; she lamented that "the middle of the list doesn't make its way anymore." Ann Freedgood of Vintage maintained, "Many middle books would do better at small houses where they could be treated as lead books."[25]

These developments have been criticized by some of the publishers involved. Oscar Dystel, former president of Bantam Books, the largest paperback publisher, has been dismayed by the overattention paid to big books:

> Lack of variety and subject coverage cuts into sales just as deeply as rising cover prices do. This lack of publishing variety and innovation, this lack of broad title inventory availability, this concentration on the big book and fads, does something else too that is perhaps even more detrimental to our growth. It does not allow us to live up to our cultural and social responsibilities as fully as we should to provide the widest possible choice of books—books that are the legacy of our cultural heritage, and books that explore the fringes of the present and the frontiers of new thinking. There should be space on at least some paperback racks . . . as there was not so many years ago, for writers like Henry James and William Faulkner. There should be room for the important books published today on social, political, and economic themes.[26]

Recently, at the 1980 Bowker Memorial Lecture, Dystel observed:

> And still superhype shows no slackening. The Hollywood syndrome of dubbing everything colossal and stupendous has spread through mass market publishing like a fungus. What's more, the avalanche of imitation that follows one publisher's really innovative and successful promotional campaign has tended to debase the entire industry.[27]

HOW DO LARGE COMPANIES EXERCISE OWNERSHIP?

The diversification strategies pursued by large, core publishing firms make it difficult for researchers to decide on the relevant unit of analysis. For example, Addison-Wesley and Holt, Rinehart, & Winston both have college divisions that are among the ten leading sellers of college textbooks. They both produce books for the college market, compete for the same authors, and are roughly comparable in size. However, Holt's college department is part of a larger publishing company, Holt, Rinehart, & Winston, which— along with Praeger, W. B. Saunders, and Dryden Press—make up the CBS Publishing Division, which is but one branch of an even larger diversified company—CBS, Inc. In one respect, Addison-Wesley and Holt, Rinehart, & Winston's college departments are similar in terms of number of titles, annual sales, and number of employees. At another level, they are not at all comparable, as Addison-Wesley has neither the resources nor the clout of CBS, Inc.

Our attempts at classifying firms within the industry were further confounded when we observed that vertically integrated publishing corporations—which may include a larger trade division, possibly with several small imprints and a paperback line—have yet to engage in widespread "inside dealing." Publishers tell us that anyone who penalized an author's potential earnings by selling rights "on the cheap" to a corporate sibling would be promptly suspected and exposed by authors. As a result, publishers continue to compete voraciously, even among themselves. Richard Peterson and David Berger observed a similar process in their study of the record industry and have noted that

> diversity has been maintained because the largest firms in the industry allowed their various divisions to compete with one another. The majors [in the record industry] have a wide range of artists under contract with one or another of their various subsidiary labels, hence they can take advantage of every changing nuance of consumer taste.[28]

The following excerpt from a 1975 interview in *Publishers Weekly* with Richard Snyder, president of Simon & Schuster, who is discussing the relationship between Pocket Books (paperback subsidiary), Summit Books (a newly created trade division), and Simon & Schuster (all owned by Gulf & Western), illustrates the process of internal competition:

> PW: How do you project what Summit should be doing? . . . And can Summit compete with S & S for . . .
> Snyder: You're damned right it can. Absolutely, and indeed did as in the example of the James Wooten book about President Carter, which now looks like it's going to be a hit. Summit and Simon & Schuster were in the auction. S & S put in a certain amount and Summit did more and got it.
> PW: Does that mean that Peter Mayer as president of Pocket Books has to compete against all other paperback houses for, say, the rights to the Wooten book?

51

> Snyder: That is absolutely correct. Or if it was a Simon & Schuster book it would be the same thing. He has to go into the open marketplace just like Bantam, or NAL, and this is strictly an arms-length arrangement. . . . As to the role of S & S in an auction, whoever pays the highest amount of money and is competent to publish the book will get the book. . . . We were in an auction at S & S, the other day, for a major author, and Pocket Books did not feel the price was justified. S & S absolutely disagreed with Peter and his staff's point of view. . . . The reverse also had happened. Peter was very hot on a book and indeed acquired all rights. S & S was not interested in the hardcover rights, so he sold it to another hardcover house.[29]

While we have spoken of divisions of a publishing house as if the relation of one division to another was relatively clear, in fact there is a wide variety of relations among various divisions, parts, and subsidiaries of a house. Ownership strategies and practices vary considerably, further complicating the question of the size of a house. Many terms are used commonly to describe ownership relationships in publishing, including: "a division of," "a subsidiary of," "a member of," "distributed by," "a [name of parent] company," and "owned by." These different terms do not, however, reveal systematic differences in operational policies. Some houses that are divisions are not closely controlled by parent companies, while some subsidiaries are. If one looks at various industry publications, such as the fall and spring new title announcement issues of *Publishers Weekly* or at the *Literary Market Place*, one notices that the ads for some divisions and subsidiaries mention their parent companies, while others make no mention of them at all.

Our interviews and observations revealed that parent-company control could be exercised in a number of ways:

1. Parent company must approve all contracts issued by a subsidiary.
2. Parent company approves only contracts of an unusual nature, such as a very large advance or a long-term commitment to a project such as a major reference book.
3. A parent company's financial officer with a direct supervisory function is located within the subsidiary.
4. Subsidiary operates with relative autonomy; parent company sets annual budget and shares certain corporate services, such as warehousing, ordering supplies, and so forth.
5. Subsidiary operates with nearly complete autonomy, the parent company having no influence over its operations.

These different management policies have real consequences for the behavior of firms. We observed some parent corporations that followed a "hands off" policy with their subsidiaries, and others that became involved in daily matters such as hiring and firing. As a result, blanket statements about parent control of subsidiaries are impossible to make; corporate ownership policies are much more diverse than many critics of conglomerates in publishing would have one believe.

Further diversity has been created by the recent trend toward establishing personal imprint lines within large trade publishing houses. With such an arrangement, editors enjoy some freedom from corporate constraints, and authors enjoy the intimacy and closeness associated with smaller houses. The more than two dozen imprint arrangements allow such an editor to rely on his or her own judgment. The large firm is able to keep successful editors content and, at the same time, give them a greater financial stake in the books they bring in. Personal imprint editors are on their own as far as acquiring and nurturing authors, yet retain corporate muscle for financing, sales, distribution, and the like. Moves in this direction are likely to be more frequent in the future, as publishing complexes permit this kind of adaptation to keep editors who might be tempted to go off and start publishing houses of their own.

Other large publishers, in an effort to hold on to key personnel, have "spun off" small subsidiaries that operate more or less autonomously within the larger company. We discussed earlier the satellite imprints set up within Simon & Schuster. The advantage of such arrangements lies in "the intimacy of a small operation with no committee meetings and no bureaucracy," according to Larry Freundlich of Wyndham Books. "The allegedly virtuous editor has freedom of choice and has the financial power of the large firm."[30]

This combination of factors—large publishers buying up small firms and setting up small imprints, the practice of internal competition, and widespread variation in how corporate ownership and control is actually exercised—makes it difficult to classify systematically publishing houses as either core or periphery, or large or small. One fact is clear: as the industry strives to adapt to conditions of the 1980s, it is becoming increasingly segmented into very distinct sectors. Within each of these sectors, there are core and periphery firms, houses owned by large corporations and those that are struggling independents. But firms within sectors have more in common with each other than with firms of similar size in other sectors. We also found that large firms with numerous divisions specializing in many types of publishing are rarely homogeneous. The text and the trade departments at large houses have little contact with each other and rarely operate in similar ways. The type of publishing the various divisions are involved in—not size or ownership—is the primary determinant of the operating behavior of each.

THE DIFFERENT SECTORS OF THE INDUSTRY

In our attempt to classify houses, we have yet to look at the type of book that houses publish. In so doing, we discover the most useful of all classifications to be determined by the way editors exercise their craft: that is, whether a house is trade, or text, or scholarly or monograph or a university press. This division has several practical implications: the discount that publishers give to bookstores—about 40 percent in the case of trade books and much less in the case of the others; the kind and size of the audience to which a book appeals or whether it is technical and limited to a circumscribed audience. In each case these matters affect not only the content of the book but the actual process of its writing, acquisition, editing, production, and distribution. Sociologists call these craft-dependent matters "technologies." The term denotes the way work is done. Charles Perrow has argued that organziations should be seen primarily as systems for getting work done, for applying techniques to the problem of altering raw materials—whether the materials be people, symbols, or things.[31] The choice of technology affects how organizations are structured. The structure of an organization is the set of arrangements or relationships that permit work to be coordinated and controlled. The different branches or sectors of the publishing industry operate with markedly different technologies. Each sector seeks its own audience and utilizes different means for reaching it: the more specialized and demanding the topic, the smaller the audience and, as a rule, the higher the price of the book. Each sector operates within distinctive environments, with dissimilar amounts of attendant risk and uncertainty. Each has different standards and criteria for acceptance of manuscripts. The amounts of money, the size of print runs, and the time schedules diverge tremendously. The chances for new authors to be discovered vary according to how books are acquired and to what kind of broker is necessary in each sector. Each has its own definition of what is successful, as well as its own strategies for attaining success. There are differences in the way projects are conceived, produced, and distributed. Different sectors of the industry use different methods of distribution and offer books to retailers at different discount rates. Let us examine in some detail the organizational processes and structures that are employed in the three sectors of the industry that we studied—college textbooks, adult trade books, and scholarly publishing, including university presses.

COLLEGE TEXTS

College text publishing, epitomized by giant firms like Prentice-Hall and McGraw-Hill, operates under its own unique set of premises. Long regarded as one of the most profitable types of publishing, it is also a market that is experiencing major dislocations as college enrollments have stabilized after rapid increases during the 1960s and 1970s. "In textbook publishing in the 1960s, there was little you could do that didn't make money," says Thomas Williamson, editor in chief of the college division at Harcourt Brace Jovanovich.[32] This happy state of affairs no longer exists. As a result, large text publishers have focused their energies almost exclusively on undergraduate introductory courses. With the market for texts growing more slowly, "publishers are getting more involved in market research and more into the management of the entire textbook process," according to Donald Farnsworth, vice-president and general manager of McGraw-Hill's college division.[33]

The college market has, moreover, become more predictable. During the late 1970s, both teachers and students showed increasing interest in basic texts. As a result, these big introductory markets have become exceptionally competitive. One house may produce a number of competing texts for the same course. Textbooks sell for only a year or two, and then successful ones must be revised because students buy used books rather than new ones. College text sales topped $750,000,000 in 1978, with the largest sales in business and economics, English, mathematics, and psychology.

The production of a modern introductory textbook—with its many illustrations, its multiple color schemes, and the wide distribution of at least 5,000 to 6,000 sample copies as a come-on—requires immense outlays long before even a single copy has been sold. A detailed report on the industry noted that "the college textbook market is characterized by the dominant role which the industry leaders play."[34] The study goes on to state that "there are decided economies of scale in the college market, publishers with annual sales of over $20 million have higher gross margins, lower selling, editorial and promotion expenses and higher net income than text publishers with smaller annual sales."[35] Wall Street publishing anaylst J. K. Noble, in a study of 1976 industry statistics, found that—as a general rule—the larger the publisher, the higher the profit margin; and this relation was "clearest in college textbook publishing."[36]

The number of firms competing in the college market declined through merger in the 1970s. Rand McNally bought Markham and then sold both its text publishing division and Markham to Houghton Mifflin.

Scott, Foresman acquired Silver Burdett and General Learning from General Electric. Prentice-Hall absorbed Appleton-Century-Crofts; Wiley bought Xerox's college publishing division; Random House acquired CRM, and Harper & Row merged the college lists of Dodd-Mead, T. Y. Crowell, and Lippincott with its own college division. J. K. Noble argues that "only in the textbook industry may the number of industry participants be declining."[37]

Since the large houses have lost interest in upper-level courses with smaller enrollments, a handful of little text houses—some of them independent and some subsidiaries of industry leaders—have emerged to fill the gaps. Often located outside of New York, these small firms are identifying and supplying specialized niches that larger firms have ignored.

Textbook publishing is unique in that it is the only type of publishing where the firms are in direct competition with each other for "customers"—in this case the professor who must decide which text to adopt. While students are the main readers of college texts, they are a captive audience and must read—or at least give some evidence of having done so—whatever books their instructors assign. Consequently, professors—not students—are the market for text publishers. Thus, there are fewer "customers" than eventual buyers. The situation is even more exaggerated in elementary and high school text publishing, where adoption decisions are commonly in the hands of state boards or school district review committees. Frances FitzGerald has described the highly politicized maneuvering in which a handful of big customers, like the Detroit school board or the Texas State Schoolbook Committee, exert immense leverage over elementary and high school text publishers.[38] There is nothing comparable in college publishing, although instructors who teach exceptionally large introductory courses may find themselves being "courted" by college text salespersons.

In college text publishing, according to one editor, "it isn't what you know, it's who you know." The successful editor knows how to assemble a list of trustworthy experts who can advise him about both the scientific merits of texts and the likely reception of these texts by other professors.

Whether we are talking about the traditional introductory textbook or the new "managed" text (see chapter 10), production costs run between $100,000 to $250,000 or more before the first copy is ever adopted. Unlike trade publishing where large sums are spent externally (on advances to authors, agent's fees, promotion, and the like), the costs of publishing textbooks are largely internal. This large investment puts heavy pressure on editors to ensure the success of their books. As a result, college text editors tend to handle fewer books per year than do the editors of trade books or scholarly books and monographs, and to pay close attention to every detail of the acquisition, production, and marketing of those books. Editors can count on their own market research staffs, or on a marketing service, to poll professors for their opinions on current texts and on what new topics need to be covered. The large text houses have sizable staffs of college travelers who canvas campuses attempting to place adoption copies in the hands of every instructor of a particular course.

Text houses publish a small number of texts each year. The strategies employed in producing an introductory biology text do not differ significantly from those used to produce an anthropology text. The work is relatively routine, and we find that text publishers are organized in a more bureaucratic fashion than other types of publishing, so that each step of the production process can be closely supervised.

SCHOLARLY PUBLISHING

Within the world of scholarly publishing, we include commercial scholarly houses, major and minor university presses, and professional monograph publishers, such as Academic Press, Praeger, or Jossey-Bass (San Francisco). The major feature of scholarly publishing is that money can be made on books that sell comparatively few copies. This is the reverse of trade publishing where, because of the costs involved, money can be lost on books that sell as many as 20,000 copies. Scholarly houses can earn a profit on a book that sells as few as 1,500 copies, though most publishers much prefer to sell from 3,000 to 10,000 copies of a book. A scholarly book that sells 5,000 copies in its first year would likely be regarded as a success, while such a sale for most trade books would be disastrous. The risks in scholarly publishing are therefore minor in comparison with those in the trade market.

Scholarly publishers proceed by conservatively estimating a book's sales potential and then budgeting the book in such a way that a small profit can be made on a small number of sales. The amount of money involved in terms of advances, production costs, and advertising budgets is relatively small. It is not unusual for a small scholarly book to cost its publisher less than $10,000. Advances seldom exceed $5,000 and for many books are even less. A scholarly book is normally expected to have a comparatively small print run and to sell over a fairly long period of time; it is the exact opposite of the "current best seller" which sells in quantity over a very short time and is then forgotten. While some scholarly books are sold in bookstores, particularly in university towns, the discounts offered by most scholarly publishers are less favorable to booksellers than discounts offered by trade publishers. Scholarly books are also sold through direct mailings, professional conventions, journal ads, and library sales. A scholarly book may sell slowly but steadily, and it can be several years before it is reviewed in scholarly journals and attains any recognition. Scholarly publishers must have patience and wait for their books to be "discovered." This trait is almost totally absent in trade and text publishing.

In scholarly publishing, the editor is the pre-eminent figure. Lacking the sales forces of trade and text publishers and the promotion and subsidiary rights personnel of trade publishers, editors are jacks-of-all-trades. Their primary role is to keep informed about what is happening in intellectual circles. An editor must know his or her house's fields thoroughly in order to learn what in other businessses would be generated through market research. Scholarly houses, with their comparatively low overhead, cannot afford expensive market research. Unlike trade publishing where the importance of editors is being challenged internally by subsidiary rights personnel and externally by agents, or unlike text publishing where an editor's duties are segmented and often subservient to marketing and sales departments, in scholarly publishing the editor remains crucial.

Professional monograph houses are a specialized branch of scholarly publishing in terms of both subject matter and appeal. Monographs generally report advances in particular fields of scientific or medical research and are of interest primarily to professionals and scholars working on similar problems in those fields. Because monographs typically report research advances or new information of practical application, rapid dissemination is essential. It is not unusual for a monograph to be published in less than six months. The books are often set in cold type. Little editing is done on the manuscript, and there is minimal artwork and design. Often the books do not have jackets. It is a steady, if unspectacular, business in which cashflow problems are minimized by the small overhead costs and the short publishing schedules which allow money to return to the publisher much sooner than in other types of publishing. Cash flow, the conversion of cash into other assets and their reconversion into cash, is a crucial factor for any business. Speed is important because the faster the flow, the less borrowing is necessary, the more money is available, and the faster a business can grow. It is not uncommon for a monograph publisher to print as few as 750 copies of a book; and since the market is assumed to be both captive and inelastic, book prices are extremely high.

Monograph publishers rely almost exclusively on direct mail and library sales, as only a very few bookstores carry their publications. A monograph house must pinpoint the small audience for its publications and, thus, has extensive and particularized mailing lists. The house also has a large fulfillment department to handle mail orders that come in response to brochure and catalogue mailings.

TRADE PUBLISHING

General trade publishing—that is, adult hardcover and paperback books—is the most publicized and talked about sector of the industry. Some of these books make the best-seller lists, and their authors appear on television talk shows. Despite the visibility of trade publishing, industry data show that it is the proverbial tip of the iceberg. In 1979, adult hardcover and paperback trade books and mass-market paperbacks accounted for an estimated $1,500,000,000 in sales, or slightly less than one quarter of total industry sales of $6,300,000,000.[39]

The field of trade publishing, as we see it, consists of three components: hardcover trade books, "quality" trade paperbacks, and mass-market paperbacks. The latter two are chiefly reprints of books that originally appeared in hardcover. However, in recent years, there has been a noticeable trend toward original publication by paperback houses. Their intention is to break their dependence on hardcover houses who play a broker's role by auctioning off, often at astronomical figures, the paperback rights to their books. There are also certain genres—women's historical fiction, detective stories, and science fiction—that are seldom published in hardcover. While many people outside the industry talk of a paperback revolution in which expensive hardcover books will disappear, we view this as extremely unlikely. The library market depends on durable hardcover editions, and book reviewers rarely pay attention to books that are not issued in cloth editions. These two factors alone are likely to ensure the survival of hardcover publishing. Hardcover trade books are sold primarily in bookstores, and the booksellers are supplied the books at a discount of 40–45 percent as well as permitted to return unsold copies.

Trade books are considered "perishable": a hardcover book has a limited amount of time, less than six months as a rule, to make an impact, or else it is forgotten. Confidence on the part of the house, and attention on the part of the media and the rest of the book industry, help a book's sales immensely. Favorable reviews, serialization, selection by a major book club, movie or television deals, and author tours all help to generate enthusiasm for a book. A company's sales force then gets behind the book and pushes it with more vigor. Knowing that a publisher has invested a great deal of money in a book, booksellers order it, assuming it to be a safe item. Often publishers, through extensive pre-publication promotion, try to create the impression of success. This is where hype and puffery enter, as publishers hope the impression of a success can create a best-selling book.

59

In deciding what to publish, trade editors are pretty much on their own. As will be evident when we discuss how editors acquire books, trade editors often rely, for advice and guidance, on other people within the house; but their decisions are basically made without much outside guidance. In contrast, text, scholarly, monograph, and university press editors usually require the opinion of outside expert readers before making an official decision to publish. To be sure, these editors often influence the decision by carefully selecting their readers; but nonetheless, they are partly dependent on the opinion of outsiders who reflect the community that may eventually buy the book. Because a trade editor is so dependent on his or her own judgment, publishers have various ways of trying to ensure success. Many rely on established writers, well-known public figures, or people temporarily in the limelight to supply new books. To screen the hundreds upon hundreds of manuscripts submitted, most trade publishers depend on agents who have already extensively sifted through the ranks of potential authors. Few of the major trade publishers take chances on manuscripts from people whose names are little known. Some houses even refuse to read unsolicited manuscripts. Well-known authors or celebrities are also much more likely to receive attention from the other media and booksellers. As a result, an unsolicited manuscript from an unknown author has scant chance of being published by a major trade house. There are, however, smaller trade houses around the country who, as we have noted, function as the minor leagues for experimental works and for writers who have yet to make it big. An author can move up from this much smaller world to the larger trade houses. Another route for unknowns is to be discovered by an influential agent or to be in touch with a well-known author who is willing to act as a broker and approach a publisher on his or her behalf.

There are to be sure, trade publishers who avoid the high-powered world of mass entertainment. They are, however, much less visible, and there is some fear for their future survival. Their options are limited: they can try to compete in the mass market and face a watering down of the quality of their books; or they can aim for smaller audiences and risk alienating authors who complain that their books are neither receiving enough attention nor selling well. Some houses (like Farrar, Straus & Giroux) try to keep best-selling authors with high advances, while running the house itself on a shoestring.

The emphasis in mass-market paperback publishing is predominantly on quantity. Sold in supermarkets, drugstores, airports, and anywhere a bookrack can be squeezed in, these books have very large print runs, beginning with a minimum of fifty thousand and escalating to several million.

The appeal is usually to the lowest common denominator of reader, in order to attract the largest possible audience. Mass-market paperback houses compete furiously with each other for the rights to hardcover best-sellers. The bidding for paperback rights in recent years has exceeded one million dollars on many occasions. Since paperback publishing has primarily been reprint publishing, editors in these houses are skilled in negotiating the purchase of books that have previously appeared in hardcover. If paperback publishers are to move extensively into original publication of books other than genre categories, they will need editors who have real editorial skills and can shape manuscripts and nurture authors.

The huge sums of money required to compete in mass-market publishing has contributed to significant concentration. None of the largest paperback houses is independently owned. A small number of houses are responsible for the majority of sales, and it is almost impossible for a new paperback house to break into the market—a matter of some public concern. Hence, in June 1978, the Justice Department sought to have CBS (which already owned the paperback line of Popular Library) divest itself of Fawcett Publications. The department's suit contended that, whereas in 1972 the eight largest firms accounted for approximately 76 percent, and the four largest firms for 51 percent, of total sales, these proportions had risen in 1976 to 81 percent for the former and 53 percent for the latter.

We are currently witnessing signs of change in paperback publishing. Although the distinction between mass-market paperbacks and trade paperbacks is frequently hazy, the latter are coming into their own and attracting the attention of both hardcover trade and paperback publishers. Trade paperbacks are thought to be more serious in subject matter, are produced with materials of better quality, and are sold at higher prices predominantly in bookstores. The minimum printing for a trade paperback is usually around twenty-five thousand copies.

SETTING STANDARDS

The editorial selection process, by means of which ideas, projects, manuscripts, or even gleams in an author's eye are sifted so as to produce the forty thousand or so new titles with which we are annually blessed or cursed, is at the very heart of publishing. In this section we will test the validity of our division of the industry into trade, college text, and scholarly and monograph publishers and university presses, and demonstrate that the standards by which editors sort out books differ from one sector to another.

Although it may sometimes seem unlikely, all editors in all sectors of publishing have standards that guide them in the selection process. These standards, as we shall see, are often not articulated; but they are nonetheless there. Standards of evaluation are part of the "culture" of each house and each sector of the publishing industry. Since the nature of a culture is often apparent only to the visitor—if not from outer space, then from a somewhat different culture—we believe that as outsiders we have a special insight into publishing. We can see aspects of its culture that are invisible to its "natives" simply because they take for granted its standards and modes of operation. In Molière's famous example, the student does not know he is speaking "prose" until he is told so by the professor. With this in mind, we tried to get the "natives" of the publishing culture to talk about the whys and wherefores of choosing books, and about why some houses do a better job, in their eyes, than others do. But as it was difficult to sort out so many opinions, we also simply asked people to point to good and bad examples of publishing, leaving entirely implicit the criteria for their choices. Since editors are, after all, in the best position to know the standards by which they make their choices, we asked them to rate major publishing houses in terms of the quality of work of each.* If there are evaluative standards in the world of publishing, then a system of rating would emerge from the chaos, because the ratings would depend on the opinions that each editor had in the back of his or her mind even if the exact basis of these judgments could never be wholly explained.

We could tell that there was a system to the ratings when editors consistently rated houses in the same way: that is, if both editor X and editor Y rated the Super Press as "consistently one of the best" and Editions Tripe as one that "seldom publishes outstanding books" (the two end points of

---

* The question was, "Please tell us which houses you think are the most prestigious in the publishing of scholarly books in the social sciences and humanities (not including literature)." Editors were presented with a list of 43 houses and asked to use the following ratings:
  1. Consistently one of the best.
  2. Outstanding, but does some other work.
  3. Not especially good, but does some exceptional work.
  4. Seldom publishes outstanding books.
Many editors did not want to confine themselves to scholarly books, not knowing "what in Hell that was." We asked these editors to rate houses in terms of publishing books like the ones they themselves published. Some editors still had trouble rating houses; others were pressed for time, and the rating sheet was skipped. So what we have are the ratings supplied by 49 of the editors: 15 from college text houses, 10 from scholarly, monograph, and university press houses, and 24 from trade houses.

our rating scale), then—regardless of the reasons for their ratings—we knew that the two editors had comparable standards. When we matched up these ratings for all the editors who were willing to perform this somewhat demanding task, then we had what statisticians call a "correlation matrix." For example, if Editions Tripe and the Super Press had a high negative correlation, then most of those editors who rated the one house low also rated the other house high. We then clustered these correlations by putting together houses that had high correlations with one another.*

To the extent that all these ratings were reasonably consistent, we can conclude that there is indeed a culture of publishing, and that there are standards by which the quality of publishing is established. But if our notion of the different sectors of publishing holds true, then these standards should vary according to the sector of the industry in which the editor works. Thus, an editor in a trade house specializing in blockbusters will think a house is wonderful if it obtains big movie contracts and tremendous sales figures, while an editor in a university press may think a house worthy of a high rating if it produces beautiful, accurate, and useful concordances.

The five clusters that resulted from the ratings of editors are presented in table 2.1. The houses are listed in the order within each cluster in which they are most "typical" of that cluster. Each house appears only once in the cluster for which it received the highest rating. Beacon Press has the "most" of the attribute that characterizes the houses in cluster A; Praeger has the least. Similarly in cluster B, Viking is the most highly representative of that cluster. Houses have a rating or what statisticians call a "loading" for each one of the clusters or "factors." We do not report these loadings, but they are useful in interpreting some possible anomalies in the data. For example, even when the location of a house seems somewhat out of place, it is invariably the case that the second strongest loading does make sense. For example, John Wiley & Sons has a loading of .48 (loadings vary from 0 to 1.0) on cluster D, in which all the houses are involved in the college text market. Wiley has a large and important text division, but it is also well known for its monograph division, Wiley Interscience. Wiley also has a loading of .43 on cluster A which consists of houses that publish monographs.

Cluster A consists of houses whose lists largely consist of scholarly

---

* An oblique factor analysis—one that assumes the factors are related to one another—was performed. Five factors were rotated. The method was used more as a clustering than a scaling device. Houses were assigned to the factor on which they had the highest loading. Cases in which this produced ambiguous assignments are noted in the text. Forty-three houses were factored, but three were dropped from the clusters presented. Two no longer exist, and one was unknown to most respondents.

TABLE 2.1

CLUSTER A	CLUSTER B
Beacon Press	Viking
Free Press	Farrar, Straus & Giroux
Schocken	Knopf
Elsevier	Atheneum
Academic Press	Random House
Praeger	Pantheon
	Houghton Mifflin
	Harper & Row

CLUSTER C	CLUSTER D
William Morrow	Lippincott
Sheed & Ward	McGraw-Hill
T. Y. Crowell	Macmillan
G. P. Putnam's	Dorsey Press
Harcourt Brace Jovanovich	Jossey-Bass
Simon & Schuster	John Wiley
George Braziller	Prentice-Hall
Little, Brown	
Grove Press	

CLUSTER E

University of California Press
University of Chicago Press
MIT Press
Columbia University Press
Basic Books
Harvard University Press
Cambridge University Press
Oxford University Press
W. W. Norton
Holt, Rinehart & Winston

monographs. These houses were strongly interrelated, and each was only weakly related to houses in other clusters. This means that editors tended to rate these houses all in the same way: an editor who thought the Free Press terrific also thought well of Academic Press; someone who thought Praeger was awful also thought the same of Elsevier. How editors saw houses in this cluster, however, was not much related to the way they saw houses in other clusters, except for a general factor of personal style in rating. That is, some editors have a sunny disposition and think everything is pretty good, though some houses are better than others; while other editors think all houses are terrible, though some manage to rise a bit above the morass.

Clusters B and C are both groups of trade publishers. What is the difference between these two sets of houses? In part, as we shall soon see, trade editors rated the houses in cluster B more favorably than those in cluster C. The differences also reflect the different standards of evaluation applied by editors. However they felt about the houses, they tended to rate the houses in cluster B according to different standards than those in cluster C. Perhaps most of the houses in cluster B were better known to most editors (including those in college text publishing who might not be able to make fine distinctions in the trade world) as publishers of fine literature. Two houses in cluster C also had high loadings on cluster B. Though Simon & Schuster had a loading of .55 on cluster C, it also loaded .45 on cluster B; similarly, Little, Brown loaded .42 on cluster C but not much lower—.38—on cluster B.

In discussing the difficulty of arriving at a classification of houses, we observed earlier that several houses were simultaneously engaged in different kinds of publishing. Some houses, for example, have both a trade and a college text division. Others engage in both scholarly and college text publishing. We saw that John Wiley could readily be classified in two different ways—as a text house or as a scholarly house and, indeed, was so perceived by the editors in our sample. Random House and Harcourt Brace Jovanovich, both of which seem to have been evaluated mainly according to the quality of their trade list, also have strong college text divisions. Accordingly, both these houses have relatively strong loadings on cluster D, which includes houses that have notable college text divisions. Houses in cluster D appear to be rated by most of our editors in terms of their college text publishing. We would suggest adding W. W. Norton and Holt, Rinehart & Winston to this cluster. Although the computer program placed them in cluster E because their loadings on that cluster were just slightly higher than their loadings on cluster D, the differences are basically trivial. In our judgment, the most distinguishing factor about these houses, in terms of the way they were evaluated, is that they are strongly involved in college text publishing as well as in other kinds of work.

The last cluster is obviously composed mostly of university presses. There are also a few anomalies. We noted that Norton and Holt, Rinehart & Winston could just as well have been placed in cluster D. Basic Books is also placed in cluster E because it was held in the same high regard as were the university presses.

The clusters that have emerged as a result of editors applying their individual standards to the publishing programs of various houses correspond rather closely to our suggested division into trade, text, scholarly and monograph, and university publishing houses. There is nothing predetermined about the way the clusters emerged: they reflect the fact that editors in different types of house have different standards for evaluating a publisher's list. We interpret the make-up of the clusters as strong confirmation of the usefulness of this method of classifying houses. It captures an important aspect of publishing culture—the way editors apply standards of evaluation.

This brings us to the sensitive issue of the actual ratings that were made by the editors in our sample. We need to bear in mind that these ratings are based on the responses of slightly more than half of the editors we formally interviewed. The highest rating for a house was 1, and 4 was the lowest, with 5 indicating that the editor did not know anything about the house—not an uncommon occurrence in a differentiated industry. We assumed along with P. T. Barnum that at the very least one had to be able to get the name right. In table 2.2 we list the ratings for each cluster. The ratings are based on the average rating given each house by the editors we interviewed. Thus, we are using the editors' pooled judgments about the quality of the individual houses as representing the most likely rating of that house. For each cluster, we added the ratings so obtained to arrive at the cluster rating. The individual ratings for each house are not reported in the table, since—because of the few editors involved—the differences between individual houses are not always statistically significant. The averaged ratings are more stable, and the table shows which of these differences are significant. We will comment on some of the differences between the ratings of individual houses when there are striking findings.

Editors themselves were classified as working for a college, a trade, a scholarly or a monograph house or a university press. The most noticeable finding when editors are classified this way is that those from different types of house regard other houses in dissimilar ways. The major differences are between trade editors on the one hand and college and scholarly, monograph, or university press editors on the other. While there are different clusters corresponding to scholarly, college text, and university houses, editors in these fields must all be somewhat conversant with what editors in another field are doing. For example, in order to be able to evaluate the quality of work published by potential textbook authors, a college text editor must know something about which houses in scholarly fields are doing good work. Trade editors, on the other hand, play in a different league altogether. They tended to rate scholarly and college text houses considerably lower than did the editors who work in these houses. Part of the reason for

TABLE 2.2

TYPES OF PUBLISHING HOUSES

TYPES OF HOUSES RATED	AVERAGE RATINGS OF EDITORS IN		
	COLLEGE HOUSE	SCHOLARLY HOUSE	TRADE HOUSE
	(Pooled Average Ratings)*		
Cluster A†	3.2	3.1	3.8
Cluster B‡	2.9	2.8	2.6
Cluster C	3.5	2.2	3.5
Cluster D§	2.9	2.9	3.8
Cluster E¶	2.3	2.1	2.6
Overall Average**	2.9	2.8	3.2

* Since the table was constructed from the average judgment of each house, the house—not the editor—is the unit of analysis. Thus, the overall average has an N of 40; Cluster A, an N of 6; and so on; t-tests were used to measure significance.
†Difference between College and Trade significant at .05. Difference between Scholarly and Trade significant at .003.
‡Difference between College and Trade significant at .07.
§Difference between College and Trade significant at .013. Difference between Scholarly and Trade significant at .06.
¶Difference between College and Trade significant at .028. Difference between Scholarly and Trade significant at .001.
**Difference between College and Trade significant at .009. Difference between Scholarly and Trade significant at .001.

the lower ratings is a lack of knowledge, but part of it is a reflection of the fact that they value such publishing less highly. The only set of houses that trade editors gave consistently high ratings to is cluster B. College text editors had their "revenge" because they consistently gave trade houses in cluster B lower marks than did trade editors. Overall, as we see from the grand mean, trade editors tended to give *all* houses lower ratings than did editors in other types of publishing.

Having considered differences in perception and standards, we can comment on the absolute size of the ratings for different houses. On the average, university presses received the highest ratings. We found a general perception that university presses exist to publish books of high quality which might not otherwise be published. To be sure, trade editors ranked university presses lower than did the other editors, but even these ratings were not appreciably lower than their ratings of élite trade houses. It is worth noting that even editors at scholarly houses and university presses rank scholarly houses lower than university presses.

Some interesting discrepancies reflect the way "insiders" view a house as compared with "outsiders." Farrar, Straus & Giroux was given poor marks by college text and scholarly editors but much better ones by trade editors, though not as high as we would have expected. Simon & Schuster, for example, was given just about the same rating by trade editors as was Farrar, Straus & Giroux. One supposes that the former's continued participation in the blockbuster market weighs as heavily in the eyes of some editors as the latter's continued reputation for literary excellence. Harcourt Brace Jovanovich is grouped with the second set of trade houses but had generally better ratings than did other houses in that cluster. It was given high grades by college text and scholarly house editors who were probably responding to its successful college department.

Some famous trade houses such as Knopf were held in high esteem by scholarly and university press editors. Trade editors also gave this house a high rating; in fact, no trade house rated more highly. Anglophile as they seem to be, trade editors gave Oxford University Press the highest rating of all. Among university press and scholarly editors, Harvard, Oxford, Cambridge, Basic, and Knopf all rated tops.

The main point of these evaluations should not be obscured by the American penchant for engaging in rating games. Rather, the ratings show that there is indeed a differentiated culture of publishing. They also verify that the main strategy we adopted for classifying the industry makes some sense because editors in the different sectors of the industry, as we have grouped them, apply different standards to book publishing.

SUMMARY

As anthropologists often observe, culture never does anything. Only people do. Culture never perpetuates itself and never polices those who do not adhere to the accepted values and standards. Instead, it is the members of a culture who carry and enforce its traditions. The rest of this book will be concerned with the way people behave in response to the different structures within the publishing industry. Often, their behavior will vary because they are trade editors rather than text or scholarly editors. But sometimes size of firm, corporate ownership, capitalization, or other factors will prove to be most important. Nevertheless, were we to rely on only one classification, it would be the distinction between trade, college text, and scholarly, monograph, and university press publishing.

One reason that this distinction is so important lies in the way norms and standards are enforced and reinforced. Interaction, the company one keeps, is probably the most single important "enforcer" in the world. It became clear to us soon after we started to observe the publishing industry that its personnel commonly knew more about what was taking place in other companies engaged in the same type of publishing than in the various departments of their own company that were involved in other types of publishing. An editor's friends and acquaintances within the industry are formed on the basis of the type of publishing they are all involved in, not as a result of their working for the same company. That is, college editors will know college editors in other firms, trade editors will have contact with other trade editors; but, generally speaking, college editors and trade editors will not know each other well, if at all, even if they work for the same company. Further, publishing is known as a business within which rumor and gossip are said to travel quickly. The paths, if we were to trace them, would not be *within* companies; they would be interorganizational and would involve people in the same kind of publishing. An editor in a trade department has about as much in common with a reference book editor as a political scientist does with an astrophysicist. The analogy with universities and their departments is apt. The interests, loyalties, and friendship networks of scholars and scientists are often more directed to persons with similar interests in other universities than to local academics. Networks formed across organizational boundaries have important consequences: they act to create, preserve, and enforce values and standards in publishing. How these networks are formed and how they work, and what functions they serve are the subject of the next chapter.

Chapter 3

Networks, Connections, and Circles

O NE OF the editors we interviewed explained to us the importance of connections in publishing:

> Everyone knows each other and there is a very heavy gossip thing. We've all sold our soul to the company store. Your performance is assessed on the basis of desk politics, how you greet higher-ups, how you relate and dress.

The editor in chief of another trade house told us, "I know there are people who know no one outside of publishing." Apparently, "everybody knows" that publishing is a tight industry where everybody knows everybody else and connections are very important. This chapter explores the nature of connections in publishing, the degree to which they are important, the basis on which they are formed, and the structure that emerges from these networks of informal relations. We shall show that what "everybody knows" about networks and circles in publishing is partly wrong.

Connections are indeed important because publishing is an external economy industry, as we explained in the last chapter. Recall our suggestion that it takes but one person to be a publisher—lone and isolated, armed only with telephone and desk, finding authors and hiring free-lance editors, production personnel, distributors, and publicists. The very life of an external economy industry depends on making and maintaining connections among disparate elements. In publishing, however, relations are much looser and more difficult to maintain than most people believe. Links are formed among editors in similar parts of the industry, as we mentioned in our description of the industry as segmented into trade, scholarly, university press, and college text divisions. Some editors and some houses occupy key positions linking many other editors and houses. The most important links, however, are forged by agents, whose job it is to make connections. We shall show that editors are ambivalent about connections with authors, in part because they, the editors, are dependent upon them to produce good manuscripts and to promote their own books; and yet these crucial connections are often very tenuous. We shall show that these ambivalent feelings are structured by the nature of book publishing, and that the relationships and networks that an editor forms are, in turn, very much conditioned by the type of publishing in which he or she works. In our discussion we shall be concerned mainly with relationships with people outside houses rather than with internal office politics. We shall show what holds or links the industry together, and what divides it; what circles and networks can accomplish for editors, and what they cost. We shall describe the types of exchange that circulate through these relationships, which are ostensibly friendships or, as one editor put it, "extended families." We shall also show that publishing has looser circles or networks than does the American intellectual élite one of us studied a few years ago.[1]

CIRCLES AND NETWORKS

The word *network* has entered popular parlance to such an extent it has even become a verb. When one wishes to make or keep connections, one "networks." We have heard of "old boy" and "new girl" networks which serve to pass along news of jobs and help network "members" meet their various needs. The word *member* is in quotation marks above because the networks we are describing are completely informal. There is no official way of joining such a network—which is exactly the problem women and minorities have when they look for a job.[2] The image of a network is one of an endless skein of connections, where almost everyone in the world is linked to everyone else. Actually, most of us do not expect to be so well connected, and comment with amazement about what a "small world" it is when we discover that someone we have just met knows half a dozen of our friends.[3] If we give the "small world" phenomenon further thought, however, we come upon a paradox. Even the more socially impoverished of us tends to know at least five hundred people by name. Most professionals know at least two thousand people.[4] The United States population is about two hundred million. A little combinatorial arithmetic will show that if every person in the country knows about one thousand persons, then the number of links between one person and every other person in the United States is somewhere between two and three! Suppose that you had to deliver a message through a chain of people to the President, how many steps would it take? Most middle-class people can reach the President in two or three steps through a chain of people who know one another. We ought, then, to be surprised—not when someone we have just met knows everyone that we know—but when this does not occur.

The facts of social life, however, do not correspond to the simple arithmetic of networks, as we all know. If middle-class people can easily reach the President, working-class people and minorities may be able to do so only through five or six links. The reason we are not all better connected is that networks in real life are clustered into social circles.[5] Most of us move in several "crowds" or circles. Some of the circles have names. There is the "fight crowd," "ski bums," the "Wall Street" crowd, "Madison Avenue," and an almost infinite variety of other circles. One can add to this list several publishing circles.

Access of people to one another within a circle is easy and conforms more closely to the "small world" arithmetic we described. Some circles are overlapping, and access from one to another is fairly easy. There may be few connections, however, between very different circles—between Texas Cowboy circles and circles of literary intellectuals, for example. While circles ease access for those on the inside, they can make connections between one social position and another somewhat problematic.

A circle is formally defined as a region or a part of a network that is dense with mutual interconnections. As such, a circle differs from the more familiar notion of a group. Unlike a circle, a group has relatively clear boundaries. Members know that they belong, and outsiders know who the group members are. Interaction in a group is face to face rather than through a chain as can happen in a social circle. Finally, a group has some sort of leadership structure. A circle may have a core and a periphery, but one can hardly say to a member of a publishing circle, "Take me to your leader."

A circle develops when individuals with similar needs begin regularly to connect with one another in various routine yet informal ways to fulfill these needs. The needs do not arise at random; rather, they arise from particular social situations and structures. In publishing, the system of manuscript acquisition, book editing and production, distribution, and publicity promotion, all create needs for making connections which the formal arrangements of publishing do not altogether satisfy.

The beginning and the end of the publishing process—manuscript acquisition at the beginning and book reviewing and promotion toward the end—are the most troublesome for editors, since these are the points of contact between publishing and the outside world. The circle of editors and their connections is draped, as it were, over the skeleton of formal interactions both within the industry and outside of it. The informal connections within publishing circles serve to fill in the gaps that are inevitable in any formal arrangement. All offices have their own informal internal structure. Newcomers learn that the way to get things done is not necessarily to go through formal channels but to ask Mary or Frank who do not formally have the power. Publishing as an industry depends, as we said, not only on connections within a firm but on connections that extend far beyond the reaches of any one company. Thus publishing, if it is to survive as an industry, must form networks and circles that go far beyond the confines of a single office.

The enormous number of manuscripts received by any editor is a case in point (see chapter 5 for an extended discussion of the problem). Were editors to rely solely on formal means of manuscript submission—through agents or through authors simply mailing in a manuscript "blind" with no prior contact with the editor—publishers would soon go out of business, for there would be no efficient, low-cost way of quickly separating the good from the bad. Prior screening by friends, by friends of friends, by agents with whom an editor feels comfortable, by professors who intercede for their protégés, and by a host of other informal "brokers" is the only flexible, trustworthy, and manageable way editors can cope with the avalanche of ideas or outlines for books (sometimes called "projects") and actual full-blown manuscripts that routinely swamp editors. In fact, if the reader who is unfamiliar with publishing takes but one message away from this book, it should be that formal channels of manuscript submission are the very last resort of would-be authors. To get a book published, recommendation through an informal circle or network is close to being an absolute necessity.

The informal route has many advantages. Formal role relations—say, between editor and production manager—involve a system of clear rules about who does what, an organized *quid pro quo*, a time schedule of what

73

is expected when, and many other clear-cut mutual obligations. These are often set down in a formal job description. Even relations within families have regular and expected patterns and schedules. In contrast, relations within circles have no set of rules that govern, say, the recommendation of a manuscript by a friend of the editor. These informal relations are bound by some norm of reciprocity but nonetheless have the flexibility of apparent happenstance. The participants in such a circle have much more room for bargaining than is afforded by a system of relatively fixed rules and obligations—what sociologists commonly call a social "role." If I recommend a manuscript to an editor through my social circle connections, I do not necessarily get a 10 percent commission. I may get merely a thank you, perhaps a dinner invitation from the publisher, a free book from the editor, the affection of the author, perhaps just a personal feeling of good will and well being. Because my reward or *quid pro quo* is not fixed, my recommendation is seen as more trustworthy than one motivated by sheer avarice. Because the editor and I are part of the same circle, the editor also knows that we share the same standards, and my "gift" is worth receiving.

A social circle is not only composed of a single relation with an editor but is part of an entire system of relatively stable but flexible informal relations. This flexibility is a great advantage in publishing, since its products are constantly changing. The lack of a readily apparent structure and of clear boundary lines is not without disadvantages. The total shape and character of a circle or, for that matter, of any network is not visible to anyone who participates in it, even to those who excel at managing relations in social circles—those who are experts at "networking." Being in a social circle is somewhat like being caught in a Manhattan "grid lock," in which no traffic can move through the tangled maze of clogged streets. Only by rising above the skein of streets in a skyscraper or helicopter can one observe the pattern and get things moving.

One's constant surprise in rediscovering the "small world" attests to the lack of visibility of the total network. Circles in publishing are paradoxical. When we started our study, we were told by many of our informants how important networks were: projects came to editors via friends of friends, jobs were obtained in that fashion, rumors and gossip were exchanged, projects were passed back and forth, and the entire world of publishing was a tight little ship. There are elements of all of this, but at the same time the very factors that make the informal channels in publishing so important also make them hard to establish. To begin with, there is not one small ship of publishing but an entire fleet. Within each "ship," editors tend to be more or less isolated from other editors, owing to the way publishing works on a day-to-day basis. In college text and in scholarly publishing, there are organized mechanisms for bringing together editors from different houses. In trade publishing, however, outside forces—such as agents and the system of reviewing—serve as weak connections among editors. The best "organized" connection is the "old boy–old girl" network of people who once worked in the same house. The crucial issue for every editor, no matter what his or her specialty, is to select the right projects or manuscripts. How an editor is plugged into various networks is the paramount factor in the flow of projects, ideas, and manuscripts to publishers. The task we have set for ourselves in this chapter is to use the general theory of networks to show how circles in publishing work. The picture that emerges will be familiar to expert "networkers" within publishing but may also contain some surprises.

GETTING THE NAMES

In the course of our interview with editors, we assiduously collected names. For example, the second question we asked was, "Have there been persons who have demonstrably helped your career?" We took down not only the circumstances of any help that was offered but also the name of the helper. When we asked about advisory editors or readers, we not only ascertained whether, and how, an editor used them, but wrote down their names. When agents were discussed, we not only collected examples of how an editor worked with them but also who they were, and so on, throughout the interview. Finally, we developed a special set of questions on circles, which we introduced as follows:

> A large part of publishing, people have told us, consists of keeping and making contacts of one kind or another. A lot of this has already come up but we'd like to talk about the matter systematically for a bit.

We then asked about contacts and connections within the house, but these questions were not included in the analysis of extramural circles on which this chapter is based. The following questions produced most of the names used in the analysis, though one should remember that *any* occasion for mentioning names throughout the interview was also exploited.

- Could you tell me whom (in addition to colleagues in your house) you had lunch with this last week? Was this typical or different in some way?

- Do you keep in touch with people you used to work with in other houses? Who?
- Do you exchange information on books with them? Who?
- Are there any people you see fairly regularly who work at other houses? Who? Do you ever send manuscripts to them and do they send any to you? Name one book, if possible, for which this has occurred.
- Are there any editors, or editors in chief, whose work you especially admire? Who?*
- Do you know any reviewers (other than the ones you may have mentioned above)? Who? When is the last time you saw them?
- What about agents? Are there any you know fairly well we haven't yet mentioned? When is the last time you saw them? How do you keep in touch with them?
- How much contact do you have with people who write the books you publish? Would you say that any of them are your good friends? About how often do you see them?
- Who are your three closest personal friends? What is their occupation? How did you get to know them? When was that? About how often do you see them? Do any of them know each other?

Obviously, it takes *chutzpah* both to ask these questions and, even more, to get good answers. But even the editors who began by finding us unreasonably intrusive, came to understand our desire to make sense of the circles and connections by means of which they conduct their working lives.

We fed all the names we had gathered into a computer, using a special program that finds social circles.[6] The program was instructed to use only those questions that implied contacts with people outside of the house (as we have said, office politics is not our concern in this chapter). Most of the questions that required specific names for answers were reserved for the end of the interview, and in some cases we ran out of time and could not ask them; furthermore, one or two editors refused to give us names. This analysis of circles in publishing is, therefore, based on the sixty-seven editors who gave us data on their connections. One special aspect of our method needs to be kept in mind: people we did not interview but who were named by two or more respondents, thus forming a connection between the two respondents, are also included in the analysis. In this way, we are able to go far beyond the boundaries of our interviews.

Despite our industriousness in collecting names, the circles of editors

---

* Strictly speaking, this is what sociologists call a "reputational" question and does not belong in an analysis of interaction. On the other hand, almost all those who mentioned an editor reported some contact at some point with that person. Since our circles were sparse, we decided to include this item.

were sparse, at least in comparison with other circles we have studied.*
Almost fifteen hundred different persons were named in one connection or
another by our respondents—an average of more than twenty-two names
per editor interviewed. (One person named eighty-nine contacts outside of
his house!) Yet fewer than 15 percent of these persons were named more
than once. If everyone were connected to everyone else, then only 2 percent of these possible connections between these persons actually exist.
The sparseness of connections and the paucity of overlap are surprising in
view of claims made by people we talked with that publishing is a tightly
connected industry. The analysis that follows will show why our finding is
a correct and reasonable representation of the industry. It is paradoxical
that in an industry that places great emphasis on making connections, there
is a relatively low degree of actual connectedness. The reasons are to be
found in the characteristics of the people named, in the kind of exchanges
between the members of circles, and in the structure of the circles with
which editors are in contact.

To understand this paradox, we began by examining the characteristics of people who were named often, and disregarded for the moment the
circles to which they belonged. The person most frequently named was an
agent who was cited by twelve different respondents. Of the thirteen persons named five or more times by different respondents, seven were agents,
and one was a reviewer. The others included the editors in chief of well-
known commercial houses and university presses. Few authors were mentioned more than once; no other category was mentioned so infrequently.

These results have several important implications about the way informal networks in publishing are constructed. First, authors of trade
books are not much connected among themselves and thus do not form
bridges among editors or a community to which editors can turn. Authors
tend to write books rather slowly; so that even if each of an author's books
was written for a different editor, and that editor in turned named that author, still relatively few authors could be named by more than one editor.

---

* Our approach here has also been used to describe several open systems—that is,
those, like publishing, without definite boundaries. In each case the system studied was a national élite system. Included were the American intellectuals,[7] the Yugoslav élite,[8] and the
United States and Australian élites.[9] An additional local élite in Detroit was also studied.[10] In
each case, the circles studied were more dense than those of the publishing industry. Admit-
tedly, the only close comparison is with the American intellectual élite studied in the late
1960s, in which the overall density was 3 percent compared with the present 2 percent. Nevertheless, the present investigation offered many more opportunities to name interaction
partners than did any of the other studies. Many persons were, in fact, named; but relatively
few overlapped enough from one respondent to another to result in close-knit circles.

Authors, then, are obviously not a good source of connections among editors. The one possible exception occurs in scientific circles or what are called "invisible colleges," about which we shall shortly have more to say. Scholarly, university, and text editors are organized, and to some extent linked, by the worlds of their authors, if not by the authors themselves. In short, while trade editors may spend a great deal of time with authors, the world of the latter does not necessarily structure the world of the former.

Second, literary agents whose official function in trade publishing is to make connections actually perform this function more than any other single role in the industry. Scholarly house editors have other ways of making connections (see chapter 11).

Third, some editors occupy formal positions of power and influence within their own houses but also extend their power outside to serve as linchpins among houses. Despite these editors' appearance of informality in jeans and sneakers, they are self-conscious about power. We shall suggest that the main source of the power of leading editors is visible "success" and "style" and "taste."

To understand why the sixty-seven editors we spoke with named few authors more than once, named many agents, and relatively frequently named a few important editors, we need to know more about both the structure of circles in publishing and the way they function.

TYPES OF CIRCLE

There are a number of possible ways publishing circles might have structured themselves: a division into trade, text, and scholarly houses, for example. Within trade houses one might imagine the emergence of a small-big, or a center-periphery, or even a quality-schlock clustering. Or perhaps regional distinctions might occur in all types of publishing. The circles that actually emerged from the analysis are reasonable; yet, as so often happens in network analysis, they are not necessarily the ones even an astute observer might have picked in advance.

By far the largest circle is composed of trade editors and some college text or scholarly editors. Most of the well-known prestigious New York trade houses are included in what we call the "Big Trade Circle," as are several of the major university presses—those with ties to the trade world because of the past experience of their editors in chief or their senior editors. Two major scholarly houses are also included in this circle, but they also have close ties to the trade world, are owned by trade houses, and occasionally publish trade books. This circle is not especially dense with interconnections. Of the total possible number of connections among its members, only 4 percent were made—double the proportion in the entire system of editors. Thirty-one members of our sample are part of this circle, which also includes eighty trade editors who were not interviewed with our formal questionnaire, two scholarly house editors (both members of houses that belong to trade houses), and two university press editors in chief who were once with commercial houses. The thirty-one editors (including eight whom we interviewed) who were mentioned two or more times were mentioned a total of 90 times, an average of 2.9 times apiece.

The reason some editors were named more than others is straightforward. Editors who manage regularly to publish books that are regarded as important and are also financially successful acquire considerable prestige within the industry. This was reflected in our study by their being frequently named by other editors as persons they deal with or admire.

Agents are obviously the key to this Big Trade Circle and are barely mentioned in non-trade circles. Seventeen agents were cited, with an average of more than 4 times each. (Agents are discussed in chapter 11.) Reviewers, too, are important to trade houses; and ten were cited by this circle, for an average of 2.7 times apiece. Major newspapers and journals are the home base of all the reviewers cited. (For an extensive discussion of reviewers see chapter 12.) Finally, there were nine authors, often ones who also reviewed books, and they received about 2.5 mentions each.

There are also other circles. There is a circle of about twenty-four editors (and one famous author), much more dense than the trade book circle, who are concerned with the publication of books in sociology and psychology—the latter a substantive focus of our study. They all know one another, know what the other is publishing, and are on friendly but competitive terms. No reviewers were included in this circle. For lack of a better title we can call this the "Scholarly Circle" for it includes editors in most of the scholarly houses we studied and some major university presses (some of whom are also in the Big Trade Circle). Editors in one scholarly house that is large in terms both of the number of books it publishes yearly and of its bureaucratic management is not included in the Scholarly Circle; we got the impression that other scholarly houses ignore it.

There is a small circle of about a dozen people engaged in one of the special fields we investigated in this study—managed texts. All of those in this circle come from one or two houses specializing in such books. This is one of the most dense circles in the study—that is, almost everyone named everyone else.

There are a few other small circles worthy of note. Two are centered on the West Coast. One circle that is heavily interconnected includes twelve editors who specialize in psychology. A few authors are also included in this circle—an unusual occurrence which may be attributed to the close-knit nature of California psychology and mental health circles. There are two small circles centering around what used to be called the "counterculture." An interest in alternate living styles, radical feminist views, avant-garde poetry, and other unconventional matters is typical of their publication programs. Lest one think they are "uncommercial," we should note that one of the houses in these circles thrives on a perennial "best seller" on how to change one's career. As befits the counterculture, one circle is on the East Coast, and one on the West. Finally, there is a small circle of people based not on ideology or type of publishing but merely on the fact that they all once worked for a single large publishing house but have moved on to other places. We suspect there may be a number of such circles in publishing, though our present sample and interviewing methods picked up but this one.

There is one more circle we must mention even though we have no quantitative evidence for it. It is the "University Press Circle." The university press editors whom we interviewed usually belonged to the Big Trade or the Scholarly circle. There are other university presses, however; and an editor who works for a medium-sized university press explained this other circle to us:

> I like to think that the 68 or so university presses in this country—ranging from those who publish five books a year to those who publish 200—are really quite a challenging group, in that they compete yet they share information about new techniques, and are quite nice about getting their own staff good jobs. One of our history editors went to X house. And there is a good bit of friendly sense of unity among them even though they are very disparate. There's a marvelous group of people who obviously aren't in it for the money—serious about their work in a non-solemn way. I'd like to stress the fact that most university presses really care a lot more about the quality of a book than the sales. We're delighted with that rare thing, a beautifully written book—which is rarer than most people think. Y Press has prided itself in the appearance of its books. I think most people in university presses are really enjoying themselves. I always get a great sense of camaraderie at those meetings [of university presses]. Because our jobs aren't dependent in such a hard fashion on sales—how many are bought up, and such—we don't have that much pressure, and that makes me much more comfortable.

Obviously, our insistence throughout this book that there are several disparate worlds of publishing is borne out by the discovery of these different circles; trade, scholarly and university press, and college text publishing are simply different fields. On the other hand, there is some overlap among these fields, with editors in houses that have both trade and text departments, and with university press editors who have worked in a particular trade house. Furthermore, there is an obvious geographic bias to most of the circles (except the college text one)—a characteristic, as we have explained, of external economy industries, which require rapid face-to-face communication. Finally, the density of circles and their mode of connecting in scholarly and college texts differ radically from trade publishing. Trade circles are diffuse, while scholarly circles are dense.* The difference lies in the different types of circles in the production of manuscripts in trade as compared with scholarly and college text publishing, in the social institutions involved, and in the way editors tap the manuscript market. To understand how editors use their connections to acquire manuscripts and then to produce them, we need to know more about the dynamics of circles—about how editors actually work within and through them.

EXCHANGES AMONG EDITORS

Horse trading of one kind or another is one of the major activities within circles. One of the best ways of understanding the dynamics of circles is to see what flows through them, what is traded or what is exchanged.[11] In this section we shall explain the dynamics that we believe account for much in the observed patterns of publishing circles. The first kind of flow or exchange is obvious and is, in fact, the first one examined by social scientists interested in sociometry, or the study of connections. We are referring to

* Density, as measured in sociomatrixes, is highly dependent on the size of the matrix. Other things being equal, in a circle or matrix of smaller size, it is easier for a person to directly relate to other people. The Big Trade Circle is the largest in this study and therefore would be, one would assume, less dense. But, given its size, it is even less dense than we would expect. Our expectations are based on comparable studies and on large circles that dominate the networks in those studies. By and large, the Big Trade Circle is less dense than even larger circles in those other studies. More important—qualitatively, in terms of the kinds and the number of people who tie this circle together—in our opinion the trade circle is much less dense than are scholarly or college text circles. To be sure, the lack of density does not mean that the trade circle is functionless. Recent work in the simulation of information passing in networks of about three hundred persons suggest that a circle of even 1 percent density passes along information almost as well as one with a very high density. Due both to the paucity of research on quantitative studies of open system social circles and to the sensitivity of density measures to the size of the matrix and the nature of the questions asked, the density figures cannot be automatically interpreted; some judgment is required to evaluate them.

sociability and affection. As a prominent editor in chief explained to us, "You make connections and friends." These friends and connections lead to all sorts of consequences, as we shall see, but often simply to love and friendship. "My closest friend in the world is an agent in England. We spend six weeks a year together. She lives with us for three weeks and we live over there for three weeks a year. [Yet] we never had a book contract, almost never did any work together." (Whether this lack of a professional relationship is really characteristic of this particular friendship is beside the point. This editor feels that the relationship is one of pure friendship.) Another editor seems to have acquired both her husband and her lover through publishing: "I got to know my husband when he was here at [X House]. My lover was the author of someone else [another editor]. At one time we'd planned to marry, so after I married my husband, we maintained our relationship." This is the sort of connection—dramatic or prurient, depending on the point of view—that captures the attention of outsiders to publishing.

The flow of information, either separately or together with affect and friendship, is much more important to publishing than is gossip. Two kinds of information are especially valuable to editors: news of jobs and knowledge of suitable book projects or manuscripts.

Most manuscripts that trade houses actually publish come through agents (see chapters 5 and 11). Though agents may well be the most important points of connection in the trade segment of publishing, even they operate through informal channels. An editor in chief explained:

> Books come in various ways, but mostly from agents. Mostly from agents I am close to. . . . When I had been at X for six months they wanted to give me an expense account, but I said I don't know anyone and they said why don't you meet this young agent. I had no one else to take out and he had no one else to take him out.

And so, a twenty-year friendship began. The agent is today one of the most important and productive agents in book publishing and has sent many a profitable book to his old friend.

Ideas, information, and manuscripts also come from other editors who work at apparently competing houses. We asked each editor we interviewed whether he or she exchanged projects or manuscripts with editors at other houses. The quantitative assessment of the answers suggests that trade editors are most likely to trade projects or manuscripts with one another, scholarly and university press editors are almost as likely to refer projects to one another, but college text editors are unlikely to do so.

What lies behind the exchange process, and how do we account for differences in the various segments of the publishing industry?

Typical of college text editors was the reply, "I have never had a book referred from someone else nor have I referred any to other houses." Another college text editor explained that he did give information to editors from other houses: "But it is nothing I do regularly. I would never give information that would give a competitive edge." More than any other book market, the market for college texts resembles that for mass consumer goods in America. The character of the market is known (see chapters 4, 8, and 13), with the result that college texts tend to be similar to one another as each house tries to meet what it conceives of as the demands of the market. Just as the automobile industry comes out each year with similar cars amid a pretense of much secrecy, so college text editors, at least for introductory courses, worry about the slightest competitive edge a rival may have and attempt to keep to themselves whatever advantages they feel are theirs. The character of their market as well as the structure of their relations to authors and to consumers in that market, as we shall shortly see, makes for tight interaction and a world where everyone knows everyone else, and probably also knows what everyone else is up to, but where there is nonetheless a strong disincentive to trade with all but scholarly editors who do not directly compete with text editors.

The scholarly and university world is just as tight, and yet editors in it swap projects with considerable frequency. A university press editor's comments were typical: "I talk about books all the time [with editors from other houses]." When asked about the exchange of projects, he replied, "Yes, all the time." Although the scholarly market is clear and well structured, it is also highly differentiated. Each house tends to be tied into a somewhat different "invisible college" or circle of scientists or scholars. Houses also tend to specialize in the size of the market with which they are best equipped to deal: for example, some houses specialize in monographs, while others tend toward larger print runs with one eye on the trade market and another on the scholarly world. Trading is especially evident in the somewhat self-contained world of West Coast publishing. For example, one house does lower-level texts in psychology; another specializes in behavioral science monographs; and so on. The editors all know one another, and each can afford to pass along projects that do not fit the publishing goals of his or her house and indeed do so in anticipation that a colleague will return the favor. Then, too, by acting as an agent for an author, especially one who is well connected in scientific or scholarly circles, an editor may acquire a number of desirable manuscripts simply through having established a reputation as an appreciator of scholarship and an "honest broker" in a segment of the industry where there are no professional agents.

While some trade book editors remain secretive and do not send books to other houses, most editors comment that all they do when they get together "is to gossip, talk books and publishing"—and at such times, manuscripts may be exchanged. The minority view is that the practice has not been successful. "Not for me has it worked—for them, probably. It's likely that if I can't sell them here [a project], they can't sell it at their own house and vice versa." On the other hand, the following view about successful books and publishers is more common:

> The tremendous bulk of the success of a book comes out of the publisher's attitude toward it. We turn down a book that somebody will make a great success of. Or the opposite. We will make a success that nobody else will have made. I would say that 90 percent of the time we know what the possibilities for a book are. But that doesn't mean that we are always right. . . . It is very rare that a book we think can only sell five thousand ends up selling thirty thousand—very rare that when we think a book has a real potential, something very good doesn't happen to it. The surprises are minor rather than major.

There is, in this view, no objective sense of the market for a trade book, since so much depends on the chemistry between editor, house, and author. Successes are in large measure self-fulfilling prophecies. If this is the case, then, it is possible to pass along a book idea or a manuscript that does not have the right "chemistry" at one house but might do well at another.

The most dramatic exchange among editors is the trading of book ideas (sometimes called "projects") or manuscripts; but this is relatively rare. More important is talking about books, the exchange of opinion— especially in trade publishing precisely because the standards for success are hard to define. What is marketable, and what is not, is determined as much by the belief of an editor, and eventually of the entire house, in a book as by any objective factor. Sales are thus partly a subjective rather than an objective result, since they are in part determined by an editor's initial appraisal of a project and by his or her ability to "sell" the book to the promotion and the sales departments. Evaluation of the quality of a manuscript, of the kind of books that will sell, and of the houses that can best produce and sell a particular book occurs through interaction with other members of an editor's house as well as through contacts with editors in other houses. In trade circles, then, the exchange of evaluations serves an even more important function than the exchange of manuscripts.

Finally, there is the trading of jobs, in the game of musical chairs that is typical of most culture-producing systems, including theater, cinema, records, and, of course, publishing. Insiders in publishing have no doubt that networks help in job finding. An editor who obtained his first job at Random House "from friends who were there" is typical. The motivation to recruit one's friends is self-evident. Further, job changes are not only important for an editor's career, but some of the best connections among houses may consist of relations between editors who were once in the same house, as we have seen. The movement of editors from one house to another is therefore an important integrative device in publishing.

Throughout our description of exchanges among editors—whether it be jobs, rumor, gossip, manuscripts, love, or even venom—there is a subtheme of balancing friendship with competition and information with advantage. One way to deal with this ambivalence is to transform the business of making connections into a social occasion and turn work into what seems like play. Hence, there is a constant round of sociability which, though apparently informal, is vital to successful publishing.

A junior editor for a famous literary house told tales about her boss, the editor in chief: "Lunches are both social and business. For a while XXX [her boss] was sick for about a month, but he always came in for lunch." In trade publishing, a ritual party often accompanies the release of a new book. Some of the guests at the party are friends of the author. Most of the other guests work in publishing and come to the party because they must. We discussed this obligatory attendance with the publicity director of a major trade publishing house, and she complained bitterly that she scarcely had time for her own social life. One of us remarked that it sounded as if publishing were founded on pseudo *gemeinschaft*—a phony sense of community: that it was supposed to look like a family but really wasn't. She burst into tears.

There is a convention in polite society that one does not "use" one's friends. One sign of ambivalence about turning pleasure into business, and the converse, is crying when confronted with the unpleasant truth. Another is to reject the very notion that one engages in a round of parties, lunches, and cocktails. The following remarks were made by a prominent and respected trade editor in chief who is believed by some people to be a social lion:

> I have been to East Hampton for 15 years, [but] only had two parties, never been out to dinner. Never been to the Frankfurt Book Fair, never been to Elaine's. . . . I don't see anyone any more 'cause I don't go out. I have lunches in my office or their office, or go for a walk in the park.

Whatever editors say, regular socializing connects the different units of the industry and cushions some of the strain of selecting and promoting manuscripts in the face of uncertainty.

Trade publishing is much more likely than the rest of the publishing industry to mix business with socializing. Though college text and scholarly house editors have been known to throw a few cocktail parties at the annual conventions of the various academic disciplines, they have nothing comparable to the lunch and party circuit of many trade editors. Unless they are on the road in search of manuscripts, scholarly and text editors tend to go home after work to their predominantly suburban dwellings and engage in a social life that is separate from publishing or writing. In contrast, trade editors, many of whom live and work in Manhattan, are active in the city's cultural life—another source of book ideas and manuscripts. Our emphasis on salon life and socializing is not accidental since the problem of trade editors is different from that of other editors. In the next section we shall show that the world from which trade editors must draw their projects and manuscripts is far more disorganized than the world from which editors in other parts of publishing draw theirs. Social behavior then not only serves to cushion anxiety which scholarly and text editors do not experience, but also to make connections that text and scholarly house editors do not need.

CIRCLES OF AUTHORS

Thus far we have been considering relations *within* publishing; but the shape and character of publishing circles is determined even more by its reliance on authors and readers than by forces within the industry itself. The ideal situation for an editor is to belong to a circle of writers who know and trust him or her. Projects would flow naturally to the editor, who—as a member of the circle—would already be aware of the quality of an author, or the latter's ability to produce and deliver a product on time (no small matter), as well as of his or her status in the world of other writers. To the extent that writers are part of a large network of definers of taste, ideas that the writers favor would also be favored by readers; hence, the problem of selling books would be solved along with that of acquiring manuscripts. This ideal world is rarely borne out by current reality, although many people believe it was approached in the United States in the 1920s, or in the England of the nineteenth century, or even in London or Paris today.

The task of tapping various circles and networks of authors and readers is much easier for editors in scholarly, university, and text houses than it is for trade editors. The former deal mainly with circles of scientists and academics who are both producers and consumers of each other's books. Scientists and scholars must read the works of other scientists and scholars in their fields to stay abreast of new developments; and their students must read, and buy, the texts that their professors have assigned. These circles of scholars and scientists have been called "invisible colleges" because they are closely linked systems, even though they are not contained within the visible walls of real physical colleges.[12]

Dependent as they are on the latest "news" in particular fields, scientific circles tend to be fairly tight. Moreover, there are well-organized social systems through which scientific communication is informally channeled: universities, conferences, journals, peer review committees which award grants and prizes, and the entourage of followers who may surround leading scientists and scholars. The task of scholarly and text editors is to identify the leading circles, especially new ones; and in this task they are helped considerably by the formal structures of science and scholarship. By identifying the leading figure, or figures, of a particular scientific circle and bringing him or her in as author or advisory editor, an editor often is able to provide a publishing house with a direct line to both producers and consumers of scientific ideas. Most important, scientific and scholarly circles define for editors what is new, good, and important.

The scholarly and scientific field, therefore, organizes the life of scholarly and text editors and so provides connections among them. Academia provides settings where editors and authors (as well as readers—for they are often both) can directly meet one another. Many college editors first met on the road when they were travelers selling texts to professors. The most important method for making connections, however, are annual meetings or various smaller conferences regularly held by all academic disciplines. All of these meetings have a place for publisher's exhibits; and because professors are both the audience for the books as well as the producers of them, most scholarly, university press, and text editors attend several of these meetings a year. Much is traded at these meetings besides examination copies of books. The informal "invisible colleges" as well as the formal structures of academic life simultaneously solve the problem for editors of finding new projects and ensuring an audience for the published product. No wonder that text and scholarly publication are regularly the most profitable of publishing ventures.

The problem of tapping intellectual circles—or the "network," according to one of our respondents—is much more difficult, as intellectuals are simply harder to find than scientists or scholars.[13] An "intellectual" is an opinion leader with respect to ideas that deal with general cultural, moral, political, or social concerns. Intellectuals do not constitute an occupational category, nor do they, as a rule, work in teams. One finds people who take on the role of intellectual not only in the academic and scholarly world but also among journalists, free-lance writers, and editors. To the extent that intellectual life in America is organized at all, it centers about intellectual journals of opinion and review such as *Commentary, Dissent, Foreign Affairs, Foreign Policy, Partisan Review,* the *Public Interest,* the *Nation,* the *New York Review of Books,* the *New Republic,* and the *New Yorker.* Circles tend to develop around these journals and also around current political issues. The circles, by and large, define who and what is "in." Most important, they serve as arenas for sorting out ideas and defining literary taste. They are the salons of the twentieth century.[14]

For a variety of reasons, since the 1960s, intellectual circles in America have become more diffuse and harder to define and the "network" has been said not to exist at all. It is possible that the current conservative atmosphere may polarize and revitalize intellectual circles,[15] but at the moment the diffuseness of American intellectual circles poses many problems for editors. One editor associated with intellectual circles bemoans their apparent demise:

> At that point [when he had his first publishing job in the early 1960s], I was still outside the network [his word, not ours]. What do I mean by network? The Jewish mafia—Epstein, Podhoretz, *Commentary* [this from a non-Jew]. Now it's disintegrated. There are bits and pieces of it all over. There are different networks in publishing anyway. Does the generation coming into publishing now have a network of its own?

Whether these intellectual circles were "Jewish" (research suggests that they were not), their absence is felt. Lacking a distinct circle of intellectuals, editors find it difficult to decide what new ideas are "good," which writers are "in," which books will be reviewed, and which—if reviewed—will be given favorable notice. Any relation editors have with intellectuals is likely to be on a one-to-one basis. Furthermore, there is no systematic way for most trade editors to tap the intellectual circles that do exist; nor, if truth be told, do most editors care to do so. Only three of the people who appeared on a list of seventy leading intellectuals that one of us developed in 1974 also appeared in the circle of trade book editors in this study, and one appeared in the circle of scholarly editors.[16] Leading trade houses still try to employ at least one "house" intellectual who, as an ambassador to New York intellectual circles, seeks new authors and ideas. Because these circles are now poorly defined, one has the impression that these emissaries are less sucessful these days. The world of authors whose books sell well is, however, fragmented and loosely organized. Thus, in the end, the only systematic pegs upon which to rest a circle of connections are literary agents and reviewers. It is not surprising that the circle of trade editors is much less dense than the circle of scholarly or text editors.

There are certain specialized circles, and the editor who "belongs" to one is guaranteed projects that are of attested quality and have a ready market. For example, the editor in chief of a well-known house is a member of a theater circle. "Any important theater [book] project would come here," he explained, "unless there was a good reason for it to go somewhere else. Because everyone in that world knows I do that." Besides tapping specialized circles, editors and publishers try to engage in what marketing experts call "market segmentation." Some trade editors are well known in gourmet circles; others, in bridge-playing circles; and still others, in sailing circles; and so on. All this activity results in a steady flow of book projects that can be sold to a known market, and that account for the bulk of profitable publishing in many houses.

EDITOR-AUTHOR RELATIONS

Among legendary editors, the epitome is Maxwell Perkins, who—at Scribner's in the 1920s and 1930s—nurtured the talents of such famous authors as Sherwood Anderson, F. Scott Fitzgerald, Ernest Hemingway, and Thomas Wolfe. In Perkins's day, circles of authors and editors were smaller and, for this and other reasons, much more tight. It can be said in hindsight that everyone who was anybody knew everyone else who was, too. The literary-intellectual salon typified by Mabel Dodge's famous "evenings" in Greenwich Village before the First World War continued in other forms and other places (including expatriate Paris) throughout this period.[17] To the extent that editors and authors were part of the same intellectual circles, editor-author relations were regulated by social norms. Then, too, as we have pointed out, merely finding good authors as well as keeping them was an easier task, because the reputation of both author and editor circulated in the intellectual world.

Today, the situation is very different. The regualtion of relations between author and editor which literary and intellectual salons used to provide to some degree, is now largely absent from America. In any case, editors are still dependent on authors to provide them with publishable manuscripts. From an editor's point of view, authors are life blood; yet they are unpredictable and uncontrollable. Editors, therefore, tend to be ambivalent about their relations with authors (for authors on editors, see chapter 9). Authors need to be cultivated; yet in trade publishing an editor generally gains nothing by cultivating a single author except that author. There are fewer ways of "banking" or building up "credit" than there are in social systems that are better connected. Often the best an editor can do is to tell an author (usually a prospective one) how much the editor has done for another author. Reputations in trade publishing are best built with agents. Scholarly editors have a somewhat better chance, however, since "invisible colleges" may pass the word along.

While a manuscript is in progress, an editor's relationship with its author may be close and intense. Most editors pride themselves on their ability to relate to authors. One trade house editor in chief, with an excellent track record of working with celebrity authors, explained the process:

> Every editor by some strange responsive mechanism in his subconscious seems to know what every writer wants. Some writers you spend a lot of time with, others less. . . . In other words, you make a relationship and atmosphere in which a writer can work. How you do it depends on the writer.

But what happens after the book is published? Here there seems to be a sharp divergence among editors as to whether the author is incorporated into their ongoing publishing circle, and even their circle of intimates, or is gently but firmly dropped (as an ex-patient by a psychoanalyst). We asked each editor, "How much contact do you have with the people who write the books you publish?" and, "Would you say that any of them are your good friends?" A West Coast editor announced, "Yeah, well, I even sleep with them." Less dramatically, another editor reported that a well-known novelist, who was one of his authors, was the best man at his wedding. A trade editor replied, "Constant contact. Most of my good friends are people I've published," and then listed about a dozen persons, all authors, whom she considered her personal circle of friends. As for how often she sees them, "All the time—with tons of authors. At least three times a week I see a friend who's written a book for me."

Many editors take a different view of relations with authors, however, though admitting the intimacy that is necessary while a book is in progress:

> It's a very close relationship—working on a book together. You get to know someone well. While working on a book you become almost alter egos. It's a

very deep relationship. But after the book is over I never see them. I try to maintain a business-like relationship. It gets too complicated if you don't.

Another editor explained:

> With few exceptions I'm friendly with all my authors and some exceptionally so. But they are all *professional* friends and not that personal. I prefer it this way—keeps the distance. In a certain way I get to know authors *very well*, but not beyond the professional level.

Editor-author relations are not so intense in college text and scholarly publishing. The latter involves minimum line editing and working with authors, since the house assumes that the author is an expert. Academics may not be the best of writers, but any problems they have may be left to copy editors who are generally free-lance. In any case, since few copies of a scholarly book are printed and sold at any one time, the editor must work with as many as thirty titles a year in order for a list to be profitable; and he or she thus has relatively little time to spend with each author. College texts, however, frequently involve a much greater investment than the usual trade book, since at least several hundred thousand dollars must be spent even before a text is produced—and production costs are much higher than for trade books. So a college text editor handles relatively few projects a year and works closely with authors either directly or, in some houses that have a separate manuscript or project editor, as general manager of the entire process.

Even if a college text editor does become close friends with an author, regular contact is limited because academics tend to be scattered throughout the United States. Trade authors are more likely to be concentrated in the New York metropolitan area.* So while a college text editor may stay over at the house of an author when making his or her regular rounds of college and university campuses, the infrequency of such visits makes authors less likely to be incorporated into the editor's circle of intimates.

All in all, differences between trade publishing on the one hand and scholarly, university, and college text publishing on the other go a long way to explain different patterns of editor-author relationships. Still, many of the factors that account for the kind of relationship an editor maintains with an author seem to be a matter not so much of social structure as of individual personality.

---

* One of us has found over half of the American intellectual élite to be located within fifty miles of the Empire State Building.[18]

CONCLUSION

Circles in publishing seem far more dependent on the characteristics of the circles of authors than anyone might have suspected. Trade circles are more sparsely connected than is suggested by the attention that trade editors give to them. We have argued that this diffuseness is caused by the lack of connection among authors which, in turn, seems attributable to the decline of intellectual circles in the United States. Among scholarly, university press, and college text editors we find more closely connected circles, though none are all-encompassing and unifying. This pattern, too, has been attributed to the way scholarly authors tend to be organized—in "invisible colleges" which are relatively well organized and closely linked but do not constitute anything like a system of unified knowledge. To be sure, some circles among editors are formed around geography and propinquity, and some around an "old boy–old girl" network, but the basic patterns are set by editors' relations with their authors.

These unexpected findings raise several questions: why do trade editors emphasize networks and connections if in fact these connections are tenuous? What is likely to be the future of trade circles given the present trends in American intellectual life? And what is the likely impact of the lack of growth in American scholarly and academic life on circles in scholarly publishing?

Much of what trade editors do is to compensate for the sparseness of ties among intellectuals, authors, and themselves.[19] Lunch, parties, pseudo *gemeinschaft*, and agents are attempts to make connections where few exist. The irony is that there is so much talk about connections and networks precisely because they are so hard to establish and maintain and yet so crucial. All the talk gives the circles a semblance of reality they scarcely possess. And matters may become worse, or at least different. As parts of trade publishing focus more on blockbusters, we can expect that publishing circles will become further disrupted because they will depend even less on connections with the world of authors and intellectuals. Rather, publishing, or at least some parts of trade publishing, may become an appendage to Hollywood circles. To be sure, this may give the circle of editors some cohesion, but of a rather different kind than they now imagine. Except for the possible unifying force of one segment of intellectual life—the neoconservative movement—we see no tightening and reorganization of American intellectual circles that could counterbalance a trend toward either Hollywood or anomie.

Since the Second World War, scholarly and college text publishing has ridden the crest of American expansion in science, scholarship, and higher education. Scholarly publishing was successful to the extent that it was able to identify new and growing trends in scholarship and science. Research budgets and mere growth of the professoriate supported the scientific and scholarly book market. Will the lack of growth in American academia also lead to a slowing down of the development of new "invisible colleges"? Will the separate but related trend of a period of consolidation of intellectual gains also reduce the growth rate of new fields? If either of these trends accelerates, then we can expect an ossification of the leading edge of scholarship and science and the possibility that editors will not be able easily to find "invisible colleges" with which they can establish contact. This will, in turn, put scholarly editors into the same network disarray that their colleagues in trade publishing suffer. We already know of one important scholarly publishing house that in recent years had such difficulty in identifying the leading edge of the field for which the house had become famous that it switched to another kind of publishing altogether. The scientific circle with which it had been identified for over twenty years simply was no longer able to organize the field.

No ironclad rule determines that editors form their connections on the basis of the world of their authors, though this is the most frequent pattern. College text editors are a case in point. As academic disciplines became more and more specialized, and as the notable professors became less and less inclined to teach introductory courses, it became more and more difficult to get good texts to organize a scholarly or scientific field. The "cure," as we explain in chapter 10, was to have college text editors themselves manufacture the manuscript by hiring hack authors to write to specifications produced by the market research department. This development has led to the creation of a circle all its own devoted to the production of so-called managed texts. Not at all oriented to authors, this circle centers around the craft of producing such books—and thus resembles Hollywood circles centered around the craft of movies and blockbuster books. The wave of the future?

PART II

The People Who
Make Books

Chapter 4

Climbing the Editorial Ladder

IN MANY RESPECTS, being an editor in a publishing house means being at the top. Certainly the position has been lionized in publishing lore. Although there are many jobs—editorial director, editor in chief, publisher, vice-president, and so forth—that have more power and pay considerably better, these positions also carry heavy managerial and administrative responsibilities. Many people in these positions complained to us that, as their attention is occupied with planning and development, they have little time to work with writers. They set financial and policy goals, control the budget, organize staff, and, in many houses, report to top management; but it is the working editors at the assistant, associate, and senior levels who are cheifly responsible for seeing that a publishing house has books to publish.

An editor's duties involve developing authors and manuscripts and working with authors, agents, advisors, reviewers, and sometimes cooperating publishers. Editors must coordinate projects with other departments—production, design, promotion. Editors, to be sure, play a role as gatekeepers. They are empowered to make decisions about which "products" deserve sponsorship and distribution. Yet this is too passive an analogy. Editors are more like the salesmen on New York's Lower East Side who, rather than waiting for customers to enter their shops, move aggressively into the street and practically drag people inside. Our interviews reveal that editing is the most highly regarded position by those who make up the world of publishing. Thus, it is no surprise that few people who are now editors started off in that position. Of the editors in our sample, 90 percent began their careers doing something else. We believe that an editor's past occupations have an important impact on his or her current behavior and point of view. We begin this chapter by exploring some typical pathways to the position of editor.[1]

We think a few words about our sample of editors would be useful at the outset. The methodology of our study is described in more detail in the appendix. We began learning about the occupation of editor by informally interviewing acquaintances and friends who were editors. These people commonly suggested others with whom we could talk. After about twenty such talks, we developed a formal interview schedule as well as various questionnaires to gather hard data on personal backgrounds, working and reading habits, and impressions of the prestige of houses. The interview schedule was tested on approximately a dozen editors and evolved through six drafts. None of these informal interviews is included in our statistical analysis.

Once we were satisfied with the interview schedule, we generated a list of names, through phone calls and the *Literary Market Place*, of editors in chief, senior editors, assistant editors, and so on in the fields of hardcover trade, mass-market and quality paperbacks, college texts, and scholarly and monograph publishing. We randomly chose names from the list and contacted people out of the blue. We were surprised to find that few people turned us down. Over a two-year period, we arranged interviews with eighty-five editors (see the appendix for details). We also used the interviewing period as a means for our research assistants to learn about the industry, so they would be well informed when they began their case studies of individual houses or departments. During these field observations, we spoke with another thirty or so editors at considerable length.

The formal interviewing did not proceed entirely as planned. The typical interview was a one-shot affair that lasted around two hours. But some interviews were as long as six hours, and many took place over several visits. The editors in our sample turned out to be idiosyncratic. Some editors talked freely about their career histories, their salaries, power struggles within their firms, the success or failure of particular projects, their relationship with agents, and related topics. Others were reticent about sensitive subjects. While we tried to be systematic, not every editor responded to every question or filled out the biographical questionnaire.

As a result, we ended up with considerable variation in the response rate to our questions. For some questions, the rate was small; for others, it was large. The chapters on editors are based on these formal responses but are supplemented by our informal interviews, our field observations, and our reading of the book trade press.

THE ACCIDENTAL PROFESSION

The Association of American Publishers (AAP) did an informal study in the mid-1970s of how people got their first jobs in book publishing.[2] Their report was titled *The Accidental Profession* to reflect their dominant finding. People initially got started in publishing through a myriad of ways, from going to a company's personnel office, to knocking on doors, to personal friends or family, to "an endless chain of tenuous connections." What seemed to link the responses was the large number of people who felt they got started in publishing by luck or accident. Few had planned a career in publishing. Nor, as you will learn, is the industry organized into clear and recognized career lines so that entering novices have a sense of how to move from one position to another. These findings did not surprise us. In fact, they seemed to reflect the fact that perennially publishing has had more job applicants than positions. Because of this, entry salaries have been low, and little effort has been expended by firms on training new employees.

Editing seems such an intangible skill that publishers are on the lookout for such things in new people as "personality, intuition, and a special curiosity rather than for specific skills." For example, Simon Michael Bessie—at the time of writing, a senior vice-president at Harper & Row—said in an interview with a journalist:

> You'd like to believe the person you hire has the qualities needed for book finding and book making, a measure of curiosity and persistence, and interests in things as diverse as politics, fiction, French literature, science, and the sailing of small boats.[3]

The bias against special or seemingly directly relevant knowledge is widespread. According to former Putnam's president Walter Minton:

> Learning American literature never did anyone a damn bit of good. My son transferred from business administration to American Lit. and I think he's

crazy as far as a publishing career goes. Every degree is good *except* literature.[4]

These remarks were made by trade publishers. As we have indicated repeatedly, publishing is remarkably differentiated; and in this book we are focusing on three of its different worlds. Nevertheless, although editorial skills vary widely from one type of publishing to another, both the accidental nature of the editorial profession and the prerequisites of curiosity and intelligence rather than specific knowledge of a particular area seem to be features common to all branches of the industry—even, as we shall see, in scholarly and university presses.

The Association of American Publishers' report that coined the term "accidental profession" was not based on any systematically drawn, representative sample. From all indications, the report drew largely on the experiences of editors in trade publishing houses. Thus we find it even more interesting that, out of our sample, college text editors were the most likely to have embarked on a publishing career largely by accident. Most of them entered publishing simply because they were looking for some sort of a job, and publishing presented itself. One college acquisitions editor, after telling a convoluted story of how he obtained a job in college publishing through a combination of friends, acquaintances, and circumstances, summed it up this way: "But it was purely accidental, no question about it, and in all honesty I can say that I intended to stay for one year to do some traveling and have some fun, but then I got hooked, that's it."

More than a few college acquisitions editors were in the middle of applying for or continuing their graduate education when, for a variety of reasons, they found themselves working for a book publisher. Nor was such a shift uncommon among editors in scholarly or university press houses, although almost half of the editors in these houses told us they had "always" intended to enter publishing. A similar pattern holds for editors we interviewed in trade houses: a majority claimed to have had an eye on a career in publishing very early, though to be sure, a good number also began their careers serendipitously. Given this early interest in publishing, it is not surprising that half the trade editors we talked with had some personal connections that helped them land their first job in publishing. A good proportion of editors in scholarly houses also had some personal contacts. In contrast, few editors in college text publishing had secured their first job through "connections."

In keeping with the notion of publishing as an "accidental career," typical entry points often have little to do directly with the job of editor, or so it may seem at first blush. There are typically three starting points for editors. An editor may begin as secretary or assistant to an editor, or as salesperson, promoter, or marketer, or in an entirely different field. Not only do these entry positions vary markedly from one type of publishing to another, they are thoroughly sex-typed. The most striking difference lies in two starting points: secretary-assistant or salesperson-marketer. Almost half the editors we interviewed who are now in college text publishing houses or divisions began their careers as salespersons, and another 25 percent held a position in sales or marketing at some point prior to becoming an editor.

Career patterns in scholarly houses and university presses are more varied than either trade or college publishing. The editors we spoke with in scholarly and monograph publishing started in a variety of positions: about one quarter, as secretaries or assistants; about 15 percent, as salespeople; and about 20 percent began as editors without working their way up. The rest had miscellaneous other jobs. Almost all of the latter had academic backgrounds; frequently they were advanced graduate students who, for one reason or another, never completed their dissertations. In keeping with a point about training we made earlier, few of these people were educated in the scholarly field in which they are now editing. However, their advanced education may have given them an advantage over other aspiring editors.

In trade publishing, another career pattern is evident. Only 15 percent of the trade editors started in sales or marketing, and fewer than 25 percent were ever in those positions. Rather, the secretary or assistant position was the main route to becoming an editor. Among all trade editors, three fourths at one time or another held secretarial or editorial assistant positions, and over one third of them began in these jobs. There is a key gender difference in these figures. In trade houses, twice as many female editors (80 percent) as male editors (40 percent) began as secretaries or assistants. In college text houses, 90 percent of the men were at one time or another in sales. Of the five female college text editors in our sample, only one was in sales or marketing before becoming an editor. To make clear the implication of these figures for the way books are published, we will have a brief aside on the roles of salesmen and secretaries in publishing.

The consequences of having once been in marketing or sales are obvious: a salesman's function is to get people to buy books. This job in college text houses is quite different from what it is in trade houses. In the college field, most starting jobs have been and continue to be that of "traveler." This salesman is typically assigned a territory of various colleges or university departments to visit regularly. Depending on the size of the house, the traveler may specialize in one or several academic fields. College travelers concentrate on those instructors who are responsible for introductory courses that routinely use textbooks and have large enrollments. Introductory courses in mathematics, psychology, and economics are the mainstays of college textbook publishing. College editors who have been travelers told us that in "the good old days" before the 1960s decisions on adoption were more centralized, so that a single professor, often a senior one, would decide which texts were to be used in introductory courses. Now, with the greater democratization of universities, text adoption decisions are decentralized and are in the hands of every faculty member and advanced graduate student who teaches a section of an introductory course.

This change in universities has narrowed the role of college traveler. In the past, a traveler could call on a single professor and make one sales pitch. Not only was this efficient, but it allowed the salesman to get to know senior professors well, to learn about their writing plans, and also to sell them books for higher-level courses. College travelers today spend little time on upper-division undergraduate or graduate courses. Because there are now more instructors to visit and the big introductory classes are where "the money is," the focus is almost exclusively on selling books for these courses.

Most companies allowed the salesman to act also as a "field editor," sounding out professors on their current work in the hope that they might have something publishable, or asking instructors with reputations as popular teachers whether they would be interested in writing a text. The travelers would file reports on instructors who might prove to be useful reviewers of texts in preparation. Since the traveler had contact with senior professors, he was in a good position to assess the state of a given field as well as to collect potential manuscripts.

The college field changed in the 1960s and 1970s. It became bigger and therefore more lucrative as a result of increased enrollments. With the increase in size came occupational specialization. Now most houses prefer that a traveler confine himself to selling and leave scouting to an editor. Travelers in some houses used to report to the editorial staff; now they almost all report to the marketing and sales director. Thus, while experience in selling books in the college field once gave one a chance to develop editorial taste and contacts as well as to learn what made texts sell, it now makes one expert in knowing what instructors want in a text but not necessarily in what new ideas they may have.

What a sales background contributes to the skills of a college text editor is open to question. After all, almost none of the few successful women who are now college text editors began as salespersons; they began, rather, as copy or manuscript editors. Nor does it seem to be the case that competence in a particular discipline is particularly important either in college text editing or in scholarly editing. One editor with whom we talked in a scholarly house had a degree in biology but was now a psychology editor. He explained that he was better off working in a field in which he was not an expert because he could be more "objective." Another acquisitions editor in a college text house claimed:

> The skills of the acquisitions editor at this publishing house, in my opinion, are interchangeable from discipline to discipline. I could just as easily walk down the hall and within two or three weeks pick up the physics editorship or electrical engineering and do almost as proficient a job as I do in psychology.

Other college acquisitions editors felt that specialized knowledge was required. They contended that it takes long, on-the-job training to become competent. They repeatedly emphasized, however, that it is not the subject matter *per se* that is crucial, but rather the network of acquaintances that takes time to build. As one editor stated, "A lot of what I know are names and connections. . . . I'd say that it takes two years to make a good acquisitions editor so that you know the field and its people well."

To most college text editors, the "field" means the market. Being an editor, said one college text editor:

> is basically a job that revolves around two things: people and markets. Once you learn who the people are you can go within the academic community for advice, and once you have learned the markets for these particular products, which are of course "adoption" markets, then the rest is just matching them all up together and coming to decisions.

Since the few women editors in college text publishing with whom we talked had been in publishing long, only one of them had benefited from the current tendency, encouraged by equal opportunity policies, to put women on the road as salespersons. (Reports from the field suggest, by the way, that women salespersons can be extremely successful with both men and women college professors.) It is unlikely that saleswomen will rise as quickly to editorial positions as their male counterparts did. Given the restricted role of the college traveler today, neither men nor women can develop many editorial skills and upward mobility along this path may well diminish.

Why has sales been seen as a career route to college editing? We suggest that, aside from acquainting a future editor with the market and the authors, a successful track record in sales is simply a way of objectifying the otherwise intangible skill of acquiring salable books. What makes a good editor may be hard to define, but sales records are money in the bank.

Indeed, at one house we observed, every editor who came up through sales boasted a superior sales record, particularly in his first year on the road.

Selling backgrounds in trade publishing are different. Our interviews show that here a sales background is not nearly as common a path to the editor's desk as it is in college text publishing. Only one third of the men and but one of the fifteen women in trade publishing had ever been sales-persons. Trade books are sold differently from college texts. Most direct selling in the trade field is done by salesmen who call on booksellers. Some-times these salesmen represent several houses; sometimes, the list of a sin-gle house. The key reason for the different career lines in trade and text houses is that the point of sale in the latter is to a professor who may also be a potential author; while the sales pitch in trade selling is to a retail merchant.

Nevertheless, some editors have argued that the experience of selling books could help would-be editors stay in touch with the public's tastes. In his autobiography* Bennett Cerf wished that more editors had a back-ground of selling directly to booksellers. Cerf and Donald Klopfer began Random House in 1925 as a two-person company, with Klopfer mainly confined to the office and Cerf working as the outside man. He tells a series of amusing anecdotes about his days on the road, including such sleights of hand as his moving Random House books from the back of the store to front display racks while the owner was engaged in other tasks. Cerf felt that that first-hand knowledge of what booksellers wanted was invaluable in sharpening his skills as an acquisitions editor.

Although salesmen in trade publishing only rarely advance to editorial positions, there is some movement from the promotion department to edi-torial work. As we shall see later, promoting and publishing a book re-quires much care and feeding of authors as well as working with editors and reviewers, and is useful training for the role of trade book editor. Since the publicity department of a trade house is often defined as a women's de-partment, publicity work is one way for them to advance to editorial work without necessarily having first served as a secretary (though many women have done that as well). Recently, subsidiary rights, also a "women's field," have become extremely important in the decision-making process in trade publishing. Women in subsidiary rights departments are therefore coming to exercise some of the prerogatives of editors; and, in fact, there has recently been some movement of women from subsidiary rights departments to editorial work. Nonetheless, because editing requires many skills—some of them ineffable—one of the best ways for a novice to

* *At Random: The Reminiscences of Bennett Cerf* (Random House, 1977).

learn is to be thrown in and let "sink or swim," as Marc Jaffe, former Bantam editorial director said in an interview. "My only advice is to let [the novice] ask questions."[5]

There is a widespread belief that a secretarial position is a good entrée to publishing. One reporter for *Publishers Weekly*, in an article on beginning a career in publishing, maintains:

> Clearly, the best place from which to ask the right questions is the secretary-assistant's chair, especially if it happens to be next to a Robert Gottlieb, a Kenneth McCormick—his former secretary, Lisa Drew, is now a Doubleday editor—or a William Targ.[6]

Increasingly, because the job of secretary is a good starting point for a career as a trade editor, men as well as women are coming to occupy this position. Among current editors there still remain sharp sex-typed differences in career lines. For women, the traditional way of starting out in publishing was—and, judging from our data, still is—to become a secretary. Only during the unprecedented expansion of publishing in the 1960s was the situation any different: then 40 percent of the women in our sample did not begin in secretarial positions.

Because a job as a secretary is considered to be the first steppingstone for a woman on the path to becoming an editor in a trade house, the background of both women editors who were once secretaries, and of secretaries in publishing in general, differs markedly from that of secretaries in other industries. To begin with, almost all the women editors whom we interviewed have a college degree, as do the men. And while more than one third of all editors we interviewed received their college degrees from Ivy League or other top-rated schools, a slightly higher proportion of women editors in trade houses had received degrees from top-rated schools. Curiously, more women without college degrees had become editors without having first served as secretaries. The prestigious college education of women editors suggests that many come from a high social class—as, by the way, do most male editors. In fact, their class background is almost identical to the men's—only one fourth of men or women come from blue-collar backgrounds. Of all the editors, 40 percent had fathers who were professionals. Among the men, the higher the occupational prestige of the father, the more likely was the son to have once served as a secretary or assistant. For women, however, background makes little difference in career pattern: almost all who become editors were once secretaries.

The one background factor that differentiates women editors who were not secretaries is religion: of the Jewish women editors we interviewed, fully 40 percent had never been secretaries; this contrasts with only 15 percent of the non-Jewish women editors who had never been secretaries. If religion is related to high status, then more of the men in our sample are from an upper-class background. Nearly half the women in our sample are Jewish, compared with only 10 percent of the men. Moreover, one fourth of the men were Episcopalian or Presbyterian; just over 10 percent of the women were. If there is anything to the so-called genteel WASP élite today among editors, then it may be found among those Episcopalian and Presbyterian backgrounds. Half the men and all the women in our sample with these backgrounds were once secretaries or assistants.

There were also background differences among our editors by type of house. Half the editors in trade houses, both male and female, had fathers who were professionals or top executives; fewer than one third of the editors in other types of house came from these backgrounds. All in all, the impression that trade editors come from a relatively high social background is sustained.

SECRETARIES AND ASSISTANTS

The clash between the advanced education and high social status of women in publishing and the many menial tasks they are required to perform in their first jobs does not lead many present-day female editors to recall those jobs with any fondness. The daily experience of many secretaries in trade houses runs the gamut from such ordinary secretarial duties as typing letters, doing a variety of errands, answering the telephone, filing, and office administration, to sharing in the work of the editor. Such editorial tasks include line editing—that is, going over a text not only for grammar, punctuation, and clarity but also for meaning. Line editing, a task few editors have time for today, may also involve some rearrangement of the author's ideas within chapters or sections. An editor who once was a secretary recalled that in handling some manuscripts, "He [the editor] took one chapter and I took the other."

At many houses the "slush" pile of "over the transom," or unsolicited, manuscripts are doled out among young editorial assistants and secretaries. If an assistant spots a manuscript that his or her superiors then agree to take on, the assistant may be given charge of its supervision. A secretary may be promoted for finding "jewels" in the slush pile. One nice success story that occurred during our interviewing period was the discovery of

Judith Guest's *Ordinary People* (1976) by Mimi Jones, a young reader of the Viking slush pile. She discovered this first novel in a stock of unsolicited manuscripts that regularly numbers in the thousands (Viking receives some fifty unsolicited manuscripts a week). This particular novel was the first over-the-transom manuscript to be accepted by Viking in more than ten years. Mimi Jones went on to become a fiction editor at *Redbook* magazine.

Readers of slush piles learn to skim manuscripts very quickly, to leaf through the pages and make a decision in a matter of minutes. Such scant attention can, of course, lead to mistakes. William Styron, author of *Sophie's Choice* (Random House, 1979), recalls that, in his brief stint as an editorial assistant for McGraw-Hill in 1947, he was "forced to plow my way daily through fiction and nonfiction of the humblest possible quality." Among the manuscripts he perused and refused was *Kon-Tiki* by Thor Heyerdahl (Rand McNally, 1950). "The idea of men adrift on a raft does have a certain appeal," his reader's report conceded. "But for the most part this is a long, solemn and tedious Pacific voyage."[7] *Sophie's Choice*, Styron's narrator recalls:

> Watching this book remain first on the bestseller list for unbelievable week after week, I was able to rationalize my blindness saying that if McGraw-Hill had payed me more than 90 cents an hour I might have been more sensitive to the nexus between good books and filthy lucre.

Secretaries may also be asked to give a first reading to a manuscript submitted by an agent with whom the editor has not been in close contact. Thus, we see some of the key differences between the role of secretaries in publishing and that in other industries. While most secretaries in publishing do often work in paternalistic situations and perform typical secretarial duties, they are also asked and expected to work with authors. In most lines of work, a secretary is rarely involved in his or her boss's profession: it is inconceivable that a legal secretary would ever be asked to give a first opinion on the merits of a case and then to review the lawyer's brief for accuracy and clarity. A secretary in another business mounts a separate career ladder and does not compete for the boss's job, and hence depends for status and reward on the success of that boss. In contrast, secretaries in publishing are expected to be upwardly mobile and aspire to professional positions.

There is another important difference in the backgrounds of secretaries in publishing and those in other industries. Compare the college-educated women and men we found in publishing to the dominant pattern found by Rosabeth Kanter in her study of Indsco—her pseudonym for a major multinational *Fortune* "500" industrial firm—where secretaries were recruited from parochial high schools: these young women were not inclined to see themselves as bosses and tended to act deferentially.[8]

Secretaries in publishing encounter several problems. First, as trade publishers become less willing to read unsolicited works of fiction, and as more attention is focused on blockbusters, there are fewer opportunities for secretaries and editorial assistants to distinguish themselves. Second, secretaries are not necessarily given proper credit for their contributions. This is especially likely to occur in relations with outsiders. "When an author came to call on the editor," a former secretary recalled, "I would greet the author at the reception area and usher him [*sic*] into the office of the editor and the door would close. There was no notice taken of the fact that most of the comments and scribblings on the manuscript were mine. During these meetings with authors, my only function was to bring coffee and smile."

A secretary in publishing may work with several "bosses"; and editors vary in their attitudes toward secretaries. Some editors regard a secretary merely as a person to handle the usual clerical activities of an office, while others regard one as a junior assistant. The former secretaries in our sample of editors can recall working for at least one of the more traditional bosses, but also for men who gave their secretaries considerable opportunity to play the role of editor. Thus, despite regular blows to one's self-esteem, working as a secretary does give one a chance to watch editors at work and to join them in many crucial tasks. Since the evaluation of manuscripts is the most important task of an acquisitions editor, experience in this aspect of editing is invaluable. Today many publishing houses have attempted to recognize the larger role secretaries play by calling them "assistants." Whatever their title, men and women in these jobs still type letters and greet authors and bring coffee—and smile.

How do secretaries advance in publishing? More often than not, through the help of others. But there are some surprises. About half of the men in trade publishing told us they had been helped in their careers by other people. In contrast, almost three quarters of the women said that other people had helped them with their careers. We will have more to say about sponsorship and the career woman in chapter 13; but for now we should note that there was an "old girl" network which helped to promote women.

There appears to be considerable ambivalence among women sponsors about the secretary who might take one's job away. In typical instances, a woman director of publicity or a woman editor or assistant editor would give a secretary a chance to write jacket copy or to take over when one of the former was on vacation or sick. The eager secretary was always on the outlook for such an opportunity and would often fill in while still attempting to carry out her usual secretarial duties. If she was talented, her work would be noticed and rewarded. Nevertheless, the very woman who did give other women a chance might have her own job threatened by an especially able secretary and was often aware of that fact. Hence, ambivalence seems to be built into the situation.

The move from secretary to editor takes time. Of the dozen women editors in trade houses who were once secretaries, only seven had only one job as a secretary. Two of the others took another job as a secretary before advancing out of that role, and several had three such jobs. Slow promotion, however, seems inherent in the occupation rather than in the female gender. Although fewer men than women in trade publishing were once secretaries or assistants, the men, if anything, were more slowly promoted than the women. Four of the seven men had had at least two secretarial jobs before moving up.

CAREER PATHS

Once the people in our sample moved out of apprenticeship positions, the most important determinant of career mobility was the type of house for which they worked. In discussing careers, we have to take into account how long people have been working. There were some differences in our sample about when people at the various types of houses began their careers. Almost two thirds of the editors in scholarly or university houses started out before the 1960s. In college publishing we have a group of both newcomers and old-timers. Half a dozen of the men in the college publishing began before the 1950s, making them the largest single group of "veterans" in our study. Among the men in trade publishing, we have ten who started out before the 1960s and a slightly smaller group who began later.

The situation of the women in our sample was different. Those in trade and college publishing were much younger than the men. Nearly all of them began their careers in the 1960s or more recently. Only in scholarly houses and university presses have women been on the scene as editors as long as the men.

We expected and found that there is little shifting from one type of publishing to another. We have previously described the industry's different sectors, each with its own character and demands. In our sample, only one person in college text publishing was at one time in monograph publishing, and one person in trade publishing was once in text publishing early in his career. University presses are the one field that draws from other sectors of the industry. Since these presses combine scholarly publishing with an occasional advanced text and some limited trade publications, editorial cross-over is not unreasonable.

Keeping these differences between industry sectors and the age difference between men and women in mind, let us look at the career progression of our sample once they become editors. Publishing is noted as a profession in which there is a great deal of shifting about from one employer to another. A recent *Publishers Weekly* article, "Publishing's Revolving Door," begins by saying, "It's traditionally been an industry where job-hopping is common."[9] Our sample of editors suggests this is only partly true. We should note, however, that the *PW* respondents who were frequent job hoppers repeatedly cited, as their reasons for moving, low salaries and lack of opportunities for internal promotion. Some other respondents noted that "as more publishing firms are purchased by multinationals, employee-employer relations become strained."[10] Since our sample consists of editors, we are dealing with more established and perhaps more satisfied individuals.

We suspect that at the higher levels, such as editor or top manager, job switching is no greater than in other media industries—for instance, broadcasting. In part, the impression of high turnover and the instability it causes is created by authors who are vulnerable to any change of jobs on the part of their editors. As we found in analyzing author-publisher relations, one of the perennial complaints of an author is that his or her editor left the house during the time a book was being edited or, even worse, promoted. Authors were most outspoken about these upheavals, and their perspective may exaggerate the impression of change. Job hopping seems to be most characteristic of trade publishing. More than half of the men in college publishing, once they became editors, stayed with their firm and have held no other editorial jobs. In contrast, of the men who started out in trade publishing before 1966, and thus have had much time and opportunity to move, fewer than one in five are still in the same editorial job. Women in trade houses are less likely than men to change jobs. It is hard to say whether this reflects a situation of less opportunity for women, or whether women tend to be more satisfied or loyal, or whether their shorter careers mean they have had less time to become dissatisfied.

We asked editors who had changed jobs why they left the last one. To be sure, we did not always get clear answers, but those that were clear again reflected important differences among types of publishing houses. Trade editors were one third more likely to have been fired than were editors in other houses. (A curious sidelight is that frequently an editor thought to be awful by his or her previous house was regarded as a star by the new firm.) Personal relationships and the climate of work were especially important to trade editors. Almost half of those who left jobs voluntarily stated that they had done so because of the poor quality of both personal relationships and the atmosphere of the previous house. These reasons were seldom given by job hoppers in other types of house.

We interviewed several trade editors who had left large, well-known houses for smaller, more prestigious ones. Their comments were virtually identical, all of them noting that at the new house "the personality of the individual editor is allowed to come through. . . . We all know it is a much happier and livelier place because it is so much more personal."

One of the unfortunate features of modern organizational life is that job movement is the quickest way to increase one's salary. Publishing is no different in this regard from any other industry. As many editors told us, when they changed jobs for whatever reason, they expected to get paid more. The *PW* survey of job turnover corroborates our findings. Several respondents commented, "For most of us, the only way to get a significant raise is to change jobs." Or, "Even with a promotion, if you stay in the same company, money is not forthcoming."[11] About one third of the editors with whom we spoke who had voluntarily changed jobs said that their primary reasons for moving were more money and a promotion.

Our data show that it is generally true that editors who have had more jobs earn more money—but our salary data are not complete. We had a 25 percent refusal rate on this question—the highest in the study (sociologists know that it is much easier to get information about sexual behavior, for example, than about financial standing). We also know that pay varies with gender, type of publishing, and longevity. However, we would need a much larger data base to reach definitive conclusions. We report only trends in our sample and do not attempt causal explanations.

Nevertheless, in our relatively small sample of editors, women earn substantially less than men. In trade publishing, only 10 percent of the men in the sample who reported their salary earned less than $20,000 a year, while 40 percent of the women earned less than $20,000. this. In our entire sample, no woman earned more than $30,000 a year, while 20 percent of the men did. (These figures are for 1977–78.) About half of the editors we interviewed in trade houses were women; but only 15 percent in college houses, and 30 percent in university or scholarly houses, were women.

How do our figures on editorial salaries compare with other sources? One source, based on an analysis of the classified section of the Sunday *New York Times*, found that in March 1977 "editorial positions started at $10,000 and climbed as high as $25,000 to $30,000 although the mainstream was $13,000 to $18,000."[12] Although the lower figure may be the salary for editorial assistants, these figures generally suggest that our male editors were compensated at above-average rates. The survey noted that middle-range salaries ($13,000 to $18,000) required three to six years of experience and that higher-paid positions ($17,000 to $20,000) required a combination of editorial supervisory and production experience. A similar survey by *PW* in March 1979 found that most editorial positions offered salaries between $15,000 and $20,000. Those in editorial positions responding to the 1980 *PW* survey of job turnover reported the following salaries: senior editor, $17,000; associate editor, $14,000.[13] Although the salaries seem lower than our survey of higher status editors, we, too, found a gap between the salaries for executives and editorial positions. Executive director and editorial director's salaries began at $31,000 and went up to $45,000, according to the *PW* survey.

These figures support our point that editing is a dead-end job. If one wants to be promoted from a senior editorial position, one has to move to an executive position, such as publisher, director, or vice-president. Once having made the move into a much higher salary bracket, one does much less of the daily work of an editor, and one's contact with authors diminishes greatly. In the area of scholarly or university press publishing, we found the greatest job stability. Whether this is by choice or reflects the absence of available high-level positions, more editors in these houses tended to remain as editors: 90 percent of editors interviewed in these houses were over thirty-five; in contrast, 60 percent of the editors in trade and college publishing were over thirty-five.

A SOCIAL PORTRAIT OF EDITORS

Few editors agreed on what qualifications are needed to become a great editor. It is not even clear that there was common agreement on who or what *was* a great editor. We interviewed two editors who had edited bestselling, Pulitzer–Prize-winning books and were, notwithstanding, fired within a year of these remarkable successes. A common theme did, however, run through our interviews: editors must possess a certain sophistication, a broad intellect, and a personal style or flair.

It is to be expected that nearly all editors are college-educated, and we have already noted that many attended top undergraduate schools. Not surprisingly, university press and scholarly editors were more frequently drawn from élite schools than were trade or text editors. While a few in our overall sample had Ph.D.s (only 10 percent), approximately one third had some graduate training. The great majority of these editors were also in scholarly houses and university presses.

Though some publishers say they prefer not to hire English majors, they may well be reacting against the norm: English was the most common undergraduate major, with 40 percent of editors having such a background. Almost all the women editors majored either in English or in another humanity. One third of the men, however, had science or social science backgrounds.

Our sample was overwhelmingly white; only one editor interviewed was black. Protestantism was the dominant religion in all three sectors of the industry. The largest percentage—one third—of Jews was found in scholarly and university press publishing. In trade and text publishing, both Catholics and Jews were small minorities of approximately equal representation.

We are interested in an editor's social background because we feel it provides some clue to the personal taste that is central to an editor's decisions. In publishing, more than in other industries, taste plays this crucial role. It is not, however, a factor that can be easily measured.

Along with social background, another clue to taste is provided by an editor's political and cultural choices. Our data show that editors, regardless of type of house, tend overwhelmingly to be liberals. Fewer than 20 percent classified themselves as moderates or conservatives. Slightly fewer than half said they were liberal, while one third checked "strong liberal" or "radical." Seventy percent of the men and 90 percent of the women editors said their political affiliation was Democrat (these declarations were made in 1977 and 1978).

One can also infer tastes from an editor's leisure time activities. About 40 percent of the editors said they went to the theater at least once a month, with text editors much less likely than others to do so. About 40 percent of the men, but fewer than 25 percent of the women, attended concerts at least once a month. The women in text houses, university presses, and scholarly houses were especially unlikely to be concert goers. Remember, too, that women were paid less. Going to the movies at least once a month was common for 75 percent of the men in trade houses and for women editors in general, but men in text and in university presses or scholarly houses were less frequent movie goers. As for sports, the men in trade houses turn out to be fans: 40 percent went to sporting events at least once a month. Men in other types of house were not likely to attend, and none of the women in any type of house did.

We inquired about editors' reading habits by asking them to check a list of magazines and journals as to whether they read particular ones regularly, occasionally, or infrequently. According to their choices, we were able to group the magazines into three general clusters and to infer, to some extent, editors' reading habits by their scores on the different clusters.

One cluster of magazines could be called "highbrow intellectual" and included the London *Times Literary Supplement*, the Paris weekly *Le Monde*, *Partisan Review*, *Commentary*, *The American Scholar*, and a handful of other less frequently cited periodicals. Another cluster could be termed "middlebrow"; it consisted of magazines such as *Atlantic*, *Harper's*, *New Yorker*, *Business Week*, and *Psychology Today*. The third cluster formed around scientific publications such as *Scientific American*, *Natural History*, *Science*, and a few others. Three publications are in a class of their own—the *New York Times Sunday Magazine*, the *Sunday Times Book Review*, and the *New York Review of Books*. These were the most commonly read publications. Sixty percent of the trade editors routinely read all three. About half the scholarly and university press editors read each of them, but only one quarter of the college text editors did.

Not surprisingly, reading habits were related to the type of house an editor worked for. Textbook editors are least likely to be highbrow readers; only 10 percent said they read three or more such publications regularly; 60 percent read none at all. Scholarly and university press editors were the highest consumers of highbrow culture; one third of these editors read three or more highbrow periodicals on a regular basis. Approximately 25 percent of the trade editors read highbrow magazines, but 40 percent did not read any. Reading habits diverged sharply in regard to middlebrow periodicals. They were widely read by trade editors and seldom read by scholarly or university press editors. Text editors fell between. The editors in scholarly houses and university presses were much more likely to read science magazines; these were infrequently read by other editors.

Finally, in our survey of editorial tastes, it is useful to know the extent to which editors take on the characteristics of writers. Presumably, nothing can tell one as much about how a person feels and thinks as the actual experience of playing the other's role. We often heard that editors are failed writers who could never get anything published, so it may come as a surprise that almost 30 percent of those in our sample have published articles and 25 percent have published books. Writing articles was equally common among editors at different types of house, but editors in trade houses or in scholarly or university presses were much more likely than text editors to have written books.

The picture that emerges of trade editors suggest that they are middlebrow in orientation. They read a great deal; but their material, for the most part, consists of the standard fare for literate Americans rather than more rarefied intellectual and political works. They go to movies often, and the male editors attend sporting events. College text editors were much less concerned with high culture and read fewer middlebrow magazines than did other editors. Scholarly and university press editors showed little interest in middlebrow culture. Their concerns were either more scientific or more highbrow.

In some respects the cultural consumption habits of editors reflect their different occupational needs. College text editors are in the business of marketing a product to a known set of consumers. What is important to them is a knowledge of their market; major trends in intellectual life are of much less concern. Scholarly and university press editors need to stay informed about general intellectual currents, but especially they need to know about works in their own area of specialization. Trade editors have to cater to the broad spectrum of readers in America. We suggest that the sporting interests of the men in trade editing is not accidental: it can be viewed as a way of asserting that they are not intellectual snobs but are capable of staying in touch with the average fan. Thus, while the class background and the college education of trade editors rank well above average, their tastes must remain in step with those of the general reading public.

As one extremely successful editor in chief at a major trade house told us: "I was the perfect person for publishing because my hobby as a kid was popular books. . . . I read them, studied them . . . even tried to follow statistics on them." He went on to note that this was excellent preparation for editing, because "all editing involves is believing in your own impulses as a reader. You read something and have a strong feelinig that this is bad, he missed something here, you dislike this." He maintained that his primary job was giving writers "his own disinterested but passionate response like a therapist. I know if I had not become an editor I would probably have been a rabbi . . . or a psychiatrist."

CONCLUSION

A major sociological bias for many years has been that social background accounts to a considerable degree for how people behave in the present; that whatever one has grown up to be, one still retains the effects of past socialization. The child of a worker and the child of the owner of a large industry have simply had different life chances, learned a different culture, and had different experiences, so that there is always a subtle difference between them, even if they end up as members of the same corporate board.

The evidence for this bias is by no means clear. For example, most studies of élites assiduously collect data on the social background of political and business leaders. The assumption has been that social background predicts current political behavior and political attitudes. For research purposes, it would be nice if this were true since members of élites are hard to interview even in this country, much less in those countries whose leaders are in principle less accessible. Recent evidence shows that the social background of élites is a poor indication of its members' future behavior. Much more important is an individual's career, and—even more—the demands of his or her current position.[14] Much the same is true for editors. When we began this study, we thought that an editor born with a silver spoon in his or her mouth would perpetuate the tradition of publishing as a gentleman's profession—and, failing to find this true, that an Ivy League background would serve to uphold old literary traditions. A number of these assumptions simply were not so.

While trade editors do tend to have slightly more élite backgrounds than editors in other sectors of publishing, the differences are not wide. Further, an editor's behavior basically is not much affected by his or her social background. Editors from both high and low classes, for example, can boast of middlebrow tastes. The needs of the market, not personal preference, seem to rule.

We have shown that there are fundamental differences among editors in different sectors of the industry, in the way their careers have advanced and in what it takes to be noticed by people in a position to reward apprentices. There were also important differences by gender. To oversimplify, men in non-trade publishing first learn to sell and only then to edit or acquire books. Men in trade publishing learn to please their bosses who are themselves editors. Women type, learn to please everyone, and become expert at line editing. The way in which individuals in publishing must advance inevitably affects the overall tone of publishing, though differences in individual social background do not predict much in the way of individual behavior. The overall climate of a house and of a particular sector of the publishing industry does affect an editor's behavior a great deal. The best way to understand how editors work is to examine their behavior as they find and choose the books they publish—a matter which we take up in the next chapter.

Chapter 5

To Sign or Not to Sign

THE TASKS of editors vary from house to house and by type of publishing. While evaluating manuscripts and signing promising authors is a primary editorial function, it is by no means all an editor does. An editor at a large trade house put it this way:

> The easy part of being an editor is buying the book. The difficult parts are making sure the author delivers what you bought and generating enthusiasm within the house. You need enthusiasm for the entire chain to work.

These comments are echoed by an editor at a scholarly house:

> An editor does all sorts of things. . . . One thing that is very important but not visible to outsiders is promoting your books within the house. You have to be a real salesperson, especially with medium books. You have to keep plugging away, you know, telling the design people, "This book is better than that jacket."

Not only are editors involved in a variety of activities, but there are also different editorial ranks, ranging from editorial assistant, manuscript editor, and copy editor to assistant, associate, and senior editors. There are also editorial positions—such as executive editor, editorial director, or personal imprint editor—that combine editing with managerial responsibilities. We also encountered executives, with the title of publisher, editorial vice-president, and even chief executive officer, who also found time to sign a few books. One publisher described his work in the following way:

> I oversee all personnel, coordinate the activities of the various departments, and manage relations with the larger company. It's my job to articulate the publishing policy of the house. . . . I see to its direction. I also acquire several books from time to time, but I don't have the time to line edit.

Finally, both the range of editorial activities and positions differs by the type of publishing in which an editor is involved. This was well illustrated by one editor we interviewed who wore two hats, as editor in chief of a quality trade paperback line and also as senior editor in the adult hardcover trade department. He emphasized that "I do different things from other editors because I acquire books for different lines." As a senior editor, his aim was "to produce a book that can be sold to a mass-market paperback house. This is the only way hardcovers make money." In contrast, as editor in chief, his primary concern was nonfiction titles that had the potential to be "strong backlist sellers for a period of five to ten years." While wearing his hardcover hat, he looks for original manuscripts. In his paperback role, his books come from a number of sources—hardcover reprints, simultaneous cloth and paper publications, reissues of out-of-print titles, and paperback originals.

At several larger houses, personnel officers provided us with formal job descriptions for various editorial positions. These lists of formal duties provide a good introduction both to the varied ways in which editors spend their time and to the differences among editorial positions in different types of publishing.

The job description for a senior editor in the adult trade department of a large diversified publishing house stated that the primary function of the position was "to acquire manuscripts for publishable salable books for the general adult reader." The description goes on to list eighteen other "general duties," among them:

- Be aware of trends, ideas, and interests of readers.
- Be aware of books published and under development in competitive houses.
- Procure manuscripts and ideas that should be published.
- React to solicited and unsolicited manuscripts and proposals.
- Guide authors and agents through ideas, initial drafts, and manuscript development.
- Work out business details and sponsor project to management.
- Act as intermediary in negotiations between authors (agents) and publishing house.

- Maintain working relations with authors, agents, media representatives, and public personalities.
- Edit manuscripts so that they reflect authors' ideas in the best style and clarity possible.
- Write catalogue, flap, sales, promotion, and in-house informational copy and memoranda for each title.
- Act as information resource for each sponsored title.
- Review and supervise specific and content aspects of copy editing, production, design, marketing, and sales approach.
- Supervise all services that are provided for each book and keep high-quality control on each title's publication process.
- Supervise assigned editorial assistants.
- Carry out all other functions assigned by management.

Editors at a large text house we studied in detail were asked by a personnel officer to come up with a list of their major responsibilities. They determined their basic purpose was "to plan, acquire, and develop profitable new projects and revisions in assigned subject areas." In order of importance, they listed the following additional duties:

- Via travel, personal meetings, academic conventions, locate and commission authors to write new books and "sell" them to our house.
- Initiate and plan revisions of successful books.
- Locate and commission professional reviewers of manuscripts at all stages of development.
- Determine when manuscripts are ready for editing.
- Work closely with manuscript editors in the preparation of manuscripts for production.
- Consult with production managers and designers concerning the costs and physical aspects of books.
- Consult with sales and promotion departments regarding advertising and distribution.
- Maintain a working knowledge of the activities of competing publishers.
- Prepare sales briefs in consultation with manuscript editors and present books at sales meetings.
- Read and evaluate unsolicited manuscripts.

Editors at this text house were called "procurement editors." Each procurement editor was assisted by a manuscript editor, whose "official" responsibilities were:

- Evaluate the contents and organization of the manuscript, edit the manuscript for a clear, concise, accurate and well organized expression of the author's ideas, carefully review the index.
- Act as liaison with authors, maintaining a good working relationship.
- Exercise supervision over the work of assigned copy editors.

- Maintain production schedules from galley proofs to bound books.
- Work with designers and art editors developing the format of the book and cover design.
- Review all illustrations for suitability.
- Assess permissions and production costs, working out the price of the book, to ensure that each title is economically feasible.
- Work with procurement editor in writing a sales brief to be presented at sales meeting.
- Review and approve promotional materials.

As you may have gathered, this large text house had a penchant for formalizing the tasks associated with various positions. Editorial secretaries had eleven official responsibilities. The editorial associates, who report to the senior procurement editors, also had diverse duties, among them:

- Assist procurement editors in assessing all incoming manuscripts or proposals, following up on potential authors, and encouraging development of promising ideas.
- Prepare rejections, suggesting alternate plans to promising authors.
- Estimate costs of permissions, appealing fees, writing credit lines, persuading copyright owners to release materials.
- Prepare monthly editorial reports, keeping in touch with house editors and copy editors.
- Prepare cost estimates on contracted books and uncontracted projects.
- May act as an editor on some project.

These official job descriptions are much more clear about what an editor does *within* the publishing house than with relations *outside* of the house. It is worth noting, by the way, that these job decriptions, detailed as they are, are weak in regard to an editor's duties on behalf of a book once it has been released—a lack that may account for many complaints on the part of authors that, once published, their books are ignored. Nor do the job descriptions provide a clear picture of what editors do from day to day or of the important process of acquiring books. To capture these, we relied on both formal interviews and direct observations as well as on editors' responses to our request to fill in a rough time budget of their daily work.

We asked the editors we interviewed to fill out a form indicating how many hours per week, on the average, they spend on the following tasks: reading proposals and manuscripts, reading other materials connected with their work, reading in general, line editing, meetings with authors, meetings with various house staff or other editors and agents, just sitting and thinking, and last (and, as it turns out, least), answering mail and talking on the telephone. A few caveats are in order. It was difficult for many editors to estimate how much time they spend on what, and the answers we obtained must be regarded as rough guesses. Further limiting our data on time budgets was a low response rate—only fifty editors completed this section.

One thing is certain: most editors do not like to write letters, and claim not to spend much time on the telephone—or at least they denied that they spend much time on such matters.

A factor analysis of the ways in which editors spend their time suggested three distinct groupings: an exploration cluster—thinking, reading work-related materials, and general reading; a working-with-authors cluster—meetings with them, reading and editing their manuscripts; and a third cluster that involved attending meetings.

Most editors laughed when they saw the item "sitting and thinking." "I wish I had more time for that," was the almost uniform response. Other exploratory activities take up much more time, though estimates of how much time is spent reading varied widely. About one fourth of the editors reported that they spend fewer than four hours per week on general reading and job-related reading other than manuscripts. In contrast, another fourth said that they spend more than a dozen hours a week on this kind of reading. This time appears to be fruitfully spent, since these editors also reported that they receive more manuscripts and projects as a result of their own searching. There are slight differences among types of house in this respect. Trade house editors were somewhat more likely to spend their time this way. The big difference in the amount of time an editor has available for general reading is explained by the size of the house he or she works for: at smaller houses editors can spend more time on exploration.

Many authors, who expect hand-holding and much attention from editors, will be disappointed to learn that a majority of editors devote very little time to these activities. One third of the editors we talked with spend less than three hours a week working directly with authors, and only one fourth spend as much as seven or more hours working with authors. College text editors—who, as we shall see, are gluttons for meetings—spend the most time meeting with authors: half of these editors said that they meet at least seven hours per week with them. Another aspect of working with authors is line editing. There were considerable differences in the amount of time editors spend with their blue pencils. About half of the editors who worked in college text houses or in scholarly or university presses spend less than two hours a week on this task; however, three quarters of the trade editors spend more than three hours per week, and 40 percent reported they put in at least twelve hours a week on line editing.

Manuscript reading occupies a great deal of an editor's time. This activity can be viewed in several ways. It is part of exploratory activity because editors read many manuscripts before they find one they consider worth publishing. Editors who report spending time on manuscript reading also report a good deal of general reading and even more time than other editors meeting with agents. Manuscript reading is even more likely, however, to be associated with the cluster of activities that involve working with authors. Editors reported spending more time with manuscripts they have accepted than with those they have rejected. The typical editor puts in about seven to fifteen hours per week on manuscript reading, though college text editors spend slightly more time than others.

When the various aspects of working with authors—meetings, manuscript reading, and line editing—are added together, there were no substantial differences among types of house. One interesting finding is that editors with supervisory duties tend to spend less time with authors than do other editors. Similarly, respondents with the title "publisher," "president," and the like are much less likely than other editors to spend time with authors. They are much more likely to spend their time in supervisory activities and meetings with their staff.

We analyzed time spent in two types of meeting—those with other editors and those with non-editorial employees. We found substantial differences among the various types of house. Trade editors apparently dislike meetings. They report spending less than two hours per week on either type of meeting. Scholarly editors tend to spend a bit more time with other editors: 80 percent spend at least four or five hours per week in these meetings, and one third spend up to twenty hours per week in meetings with house staff. On the other hand, college text editors practically live in meetings. Nearly half said they meet from six to thirty hours per week with other editors, and the same number spend between six and twenty hours per week in staff meetings. The labor necessary to produce a college text, especially an introductory one, involves much staff work and in-house production. In contrast, the actual production of scholarly or trade books is often done by free-lance copy editors and designers. College text houses have much larger manufacturing and production departments than do trade or scholarly houses, and college editors spend a good deal of time coordinating the production of their texts. We also found that the exchange of information was more likely to occur formally at meetings in text houses. At trade houses and scholarly presses, information is passed informally "in the hallways."

One might expect that at larger houses more time would be spent in meetings. But, if anything, larger trade houses seem to require *less* meeting time for their editors than do smaller trade houses. Differences in time spent in meetings is explained by the type of publishing the house is involved in—not by its size—and also by an editor's position within it. The penalty for a higher rank, such as publisher or editor in chief, is more time spent in meetings, as is well illustrated at the large trade house we observed over a period of four months. There are weekly launch meetings for newly signed books. The editor in chief and the marketing director are always in attendance; other editors attend only if their books are being discussed. There are also weekly editorial meetings, chaired by the editor in chief, to discuss problems with particular books, what ideas editors are looking for, projects worth signing, and books being developed. Once a month there is a joint editorial and marketing meeting, again chaired by the editor in chief. The marketing strategies for various books are developed and discussed, and past performance is reviewed. Editors show up when their books are being considered, and then depart.

The responses to the time budget point out one of the dilemmas of being an editor. As one editor lamented, "There is always work to do, meetings to attend, and paper to push, but what I'm paid to do is find good books. I sometimes wonder where I find the time to do this." The large amount of time editors spend on organizational duties and on their obligations to books in production seems to preclude much attention to the search and acquisitions process. However, editors were nearly unanimous in saying that the greatest pressure on them is to acquire books. Moreover, some editors told us the work they enjoy most involves discovering new ideas and new writers. The tension between routine daily work that must be attended to, and the more important and—to some editors—the more enjoyable process of manuscript review, contributes to the harried pace at which almost every editor we observed works.

Many editors reported that their days are too hectic for any serious reading. As a result, many editors do their manuscript reading at home. We routinely observed editors taking a stack of manuscripts home at night and on weekends and even on vacations.

Editors agreed that much of their attention, if not their time, is focussed on acquiring, evaluating, and deciding which manuscripts to publish. Believing this to be the most important aspect of editorial work, we therefore devoted special attention to this process and asked a great many questions about it. It turned out that editors were, by and large, unable either to systematically describe how they acquire manuscripts or fully to account for all the factors involved in the decision-making process. Although our interviews with editors were informative, we learned more about the actual process of publishing from our observations of editors at work.

QUOTAS AND EXPECTATIONS

We began our interviews by asking editors about the numbers of titles they signed. We wanted to know how many books an editor signed in the previous year, how many one was expected to sign in the current year, and whether one would like to sign more or less in a year. We also asked whether there was an understanding at the editor's house about the number of books he or she was expected to sign and to what degree that understanding was explicit or implicit.

The variance in the number of titles signed in a year was large. A few editors signed almost no books; others, over fifty. About one third of the editors we interviewed signed a dozen books or fewer; one third signed between thirteen and twenty-five books; while the last third signed more than twenty-five. The type of house for which an editor works helps explain the number of titles signed. Editors in college text houses handled the fewest books: three fifths signed a dozen or fewer, and almost none signed more than twenty-five. In contrast, scholarly editors were the most prolific. Seventy percent signed more than twenty-five books a year. Most trade book editors fell in the middle and signed between thirteen and twenty-five, but the remaining trade and paperback house editors were split between the very active—more than twenty-five—and the very discreet—a dozen or fewer. In larger college text houses, editors tend to sign up more books; and editors in small text houses tend to sign fewer books but would like to sign more. Outside of text publishing, the size of a house did not have much influence on the number of books an editor signed. Editorial rank was also not a factor in the number of books signed: high-ranking senior editors are not likely to sign up more books than were assistant editors.

The number of books an editor signs is, however, not a random affair. In each house, there are clear expectations about the number of books that should be signed. The editors who signed fewer than the average number of books last year are likely to want to sign more books next year. These understandings about editorial productivity are relatively informal, or at least so editors report. Forty percent of the editors report having a specific quota or target; while 20 percent report that there is nothing in writing and nothing formal, but there is a general expectation about the number of books to be signed. The remaining 40 percent say they have neither a formal quota nor a tacit understanding. Typical of their responses are the following comments, the first by a trade editor, the second by a scholarly editor:

> Oh no—there isn't a yearly quota. It all depends, you may do many little books or a few "biggies." Its also different for different editors. Some editors are tracked by the amount of money they bring in. And there are editors who lose money, but are always signing Pulitzer Prize winners. Editors are all evaluated by the editor-in-chief, and he's right next door.

> A quota! I wish there was one—I've been here eighteen months and the vast majority of my time has been spent dealing with books that had been signed by my predecessors or that were dumped on my desk by higher-ups. I've had no pressure, but not much encouragement either.

What kind of publishing house is most likely to have quotas or formal expectations? A house's type of publishing does not affect the degree of formality of expectations about how many books are to be signed, but its size does. Larger houses were much more formal about their expectations. Thirty percent of the editors in larger houses report there is a formal quota of books to be signed, but only 5 percent of editors in smaller houses noted such a formal understanding. This is not surprising: organizational studies have shown that the larger the organization, the more formalized its behavior.[1] The argument runs that with increasing size, there is less control by direct supervision and more by rules, procedures, detailed job descriptions, and the like—all devices that formalize behavior. The adoption of formal and impersonal means of coordination and control is one strategy for increasing predictability in large organizations where direct face-to-face control is made problematical by spatial barriers.

Where formal expectations are not operating, we felt there would be more subtle pressures on editors to produce a certain number or certain type of book. Nevertheless, some editors described their houses as relatively pressure-free. One scholarly editor noted, "When we're successful financially, we have the luxury of doing what we want." An editor at a small, prestigious trade house that is owned by a diversified conglomerate put it this way:

> A bestseller supports the list for the season. I think we're atypical in this regard, but I don't know. For instance, we've had a pretty good year so now I'm indulging in a 4 or 5 volume French history book.

In marked contrast, we came across a corporate-owned trade house where editors felt considerable pressure to produce. A senior editor described the process of "blacklighting":

> If you're not doing so well here . . . not signing enough books or not coming up with commercial books, you get "blacklighted." They put the "blacklight" on you, so you only get the routine raise and nothing extra, your books get vetoed, the other departments start picking on you. . . . It creates a bad atmosphere. . . . It's really horrible and most people get the hint quickly. They never fire anyone here, they just "blacklight" you. Sometimes people can weather it out.

In our interview data, when we controlled for size of house, we did not find any differences between independent houses and those owned by another company with respect to the actual number of books signed. However, there is an observable difference among editors, especially at trade houses, who want to sign more books. This desire to be more productive is related to type of ownership: editors in houses owned by other organizations are more likely to want to sign more books the next year than are their colleagues who work for independent houses.

Pressures to increase title output can result from a variety of demands that organizations feel they must meet. A very real pressure for a number of houses is to outdo the previous year's performance. Stockholders and corporate owners expect houses to do better each year. These pressures are commonplace in many houses. What caused considerable alarm among editors, however, were the occasional serendipitous successes. When a book that is expected to sell 10,000 copies sells more than 100,000 copies, this should be cause for celebration. However, we found editors worrying that corporate parents or major stockholders would expect such successes to be duplicated, or even improved on, the following year.

We should note that concerns of this nature are not limited to corporate-owned or publicly traded firms. At one university press where we did interviews, an editor "stumbled upon" a manuscript that turned out to be a surprise best seller. After the euphoria wore off, the editor learned that the governing board of the press was considering dropping the university's subsidy to the press and charging the press rent. One editor reported that a member of the board told her, "This is the type of book you should have been publishing all along." This type of pressure, in our opinion, is often at odds with a fundamental characteristic of book publishing: it is a highly uncertain business in which the supply of commercial manuscripts cannot be guaranteed, and consumer demand is fickle and unpredictable.

We observed other types of pressure as well. In order to realize the economies of scale that are derived from a large sales force or marketing staff, large textbook or trade houses must have a constant and steady flow of products. One college editor quipped, "We've got thirty-two salesmen out there. . . . I've got to produce so that they have something to sell." Textbook publishers also have large production departments and other in-house personnel who must be kept busy. Not only are there pressures to sign books to keep staff members busy, but some houses need to maintain a certain level of output in order to help pay the rent. Richard Snyder, president of Simon & Schuster, is forthright about this:

> Once you become a large publisher, you must have books that cover your overhead. We may have a book called "How to Clean Your House" that no one here is particularly enthusiastic about personally but which we know there is a market for. That isn't the joy of publishing, but it is professionalism. It allows us to publish books like "Sideshow"* on which we didn't expect to make money. All we're doing in effect is trading off, which seems a rather mature way to deal with life.[2]

MANUSCRIPT ACQUISITION

After discussing work load pressures, we turned to look at the actual numbers of manuscripts and proposals received through various means, and the number of books that were actually signed from these various sources. We tried to get editors to talk about their sources of manuscripts in terms of hard numbers. As you can imagine, many editors found our penchant for figures trying and preferred to generalize about "a few" or "a lot" or some other rough estimate. While this vagueness is understandable in regard to the number and sources of the various projects or manuscripts reviewed, it surprised us that some editors were equally vague about books they had actually signed. For a variety of reasons, publishers do not always know how many books they have published in a particular year. First, editors are not social scientists or accountants. The very idea of keeping meticulous records of input and output is foreign to them. Second, since the early days of American publishing, book lists are thought of in terms of seasons—for example, the fall list, stretching from August to January; or the spring list, spanning February to June. Some trade publishers have also begun late

---

* The reference is to William Shawcross's *Sideshow: Kissinger, Nixon, and the Destruction of Cambodia*, published in 1979.

spring or summer lists to cover the summer months. Viewing books as parts of seasonal lists makes it difficult for some editors easily to cite yearly figures. The one exception is textbook publishing where there are no seasonal lists. Text editors were able to give us better estimates; on the other hand, they also evaluated fewer projects than did other editors. The ability of a trade or a scholarly editor to quote actual numbers of manuscripts and books handled is a function more of personal style than of organizational characteristics, since the number of manuscripts signed, the size of the house, and the status of an editor were all unrelated to accurate reporting.

Our interviews revealed six major sources of manuscripts, ideas, outlines, projects, or what-have-you that might result in a book. These include: "over the transom" (manuscripts sent in "cold," without sponsorship of an agent or some other personal recommendation); direct referral or recommendation of a project from a person known to the editor; submission from an agent or an advisory editor; discovery of a manuscript as a result of an editor's travels; discovery of a topic or an author by reading newspapers, journals, or magazines; and finally, the commissioning of a book because an editor's evaluation of the market shows a need or a demand for a particular kind of book. An analysis of the responses to our questions about these various modes of submission showed that they cluster into three basic types: personal recommendation—by agents known to the editor, by authors whom the house had published, or other people known to the editor; active searching on the part of editors—traveling, finding projects through reading or attending meetings or conferences, or directly dreaming up a project; and the ubiquitous "over the transom."

"Over the transom" submissions probably involve more publishing lore than any other type of contact between authors and editors. To authors, simply sending a manuscript or an idea to a publisher may seem a logical way of attracting attention. Unfortunately, publishers receive so many of these submissions that they cannot give them sufficient attention. For example, one third of the editors who gave us an estimate of the number of unsolicited projects they received, claimed that between one thousand and five thousand such projects passed over their desks alone (not to mention projects received by other editors in the same house) in the course of a year. The staggering number of ideas or manuscripts received "over the transom" means that, although editors may spend considerable time dealing with unsolicited projects, the actual time they spend on any one manuscript is limited. An editor at a successful scholarly house exclaimed, "You cannot imagine the tremendous amount of time we spend on unsolicited manuscripts! . . . Our reputation seems to attract people from all over. . . . Signing a book is actually something that happens rarely." The president of Doubleday, a large general trade house, estimated that it receives an average of ten thousand unsolicited manuscripts a year, out of which three or four may be chosen for publication.[3]

We encountered a senior editor at a prestigious trade house who liked supervising the flow of unsolicited projects:

> I'm in charge of the slush pile. I do a lot of reading, but I really enjoy it. I also have two secretaries who assist me with the slush pile and I have an editorial assistant. . . . A couple of times a week I'll lock myself in a back room and go through it. We get about seventy-five a week. The first decision is whether it should be read or not. I look at, but don't read everything. If it's at all specialized I will farm it out to the appropriate editor. We get a few dissertations each week. I don't think we've ever published one but someone will at least look at them. Other things I will direct to editorial assistants and they'd pass it on to a editor if necessary. I read about five a week. Maybe two a year get published. I write "reject" or "reject kindly" on them. The rejects get a mimeo letter. The reject kindly get a hand-typed letter; these go to professors or people with important credentials. Of course, if a history professor sent in a cookbook, that doesn't count, he'd get a mimeo letter too.

We thought seventy-five unsolicited projects a week was a very small quantity. Then we learned that these seventy-five are actual manuscripts, not proposals or outlines. In addition, the editor noted, "If a project is addressed to a particular person or comes in blind through an agent, we don't call these 'over the transom.' . . . We're very careful to read things sent by agents or sent to us personally . . . even if we don't know the agent or the author."

At one large trade house where we did field observations, there was an official policy of accepting "over the transom" material only from agents. Nevertheless, the editorial assistant who supervised the slush pile estimated that the house received a two-foot stack of manuscripts each week. She reviewed each manuscript and wrote a short evaluation. Once a week she and a senior editor went over the unsolicited pile. This assistant found form letters for rejection offensive, so—when she had time—she wrote a personal note and signed it under a pen name, Matthilda Fosse. We wondered where all these manuscripts came from if there was an official policy of not accepting them. We learned there were many sources: (1) the receptionist tried not to, but always ended up, accepting hand-delivered materials from struggling writers; (2) the president gave the editorial assistant any unsolicited materials sent to him personally; (3) materials were often forwarded from other divisions of the corporation; and (4) manuscripts came from friends of company employees. At one scholarly house that publishes only nonfiction, editors estimated that they had received approximately ten novels a month for the past ten years. The manuscripts were returned unread.

Trade editors received the largest number of "over the transom" projects. Sixty percent said they received more than one thousand such submissions yearly. In contrast, only 15 percent of college text editors reported being swamped by unsolicited projects. In text houses, the common estimate was between one hundred and five hundred unsolicited manuscripts a year. Scholarly, monograph, and university press houses fell in between in terms of the number of "over the transom" projects received, averaging between five hundred and one thousand for the majority of editors.

Very few "over the transom" submissions are ever published. One third of the editors we interviewed said no "over the transom" manuscripts had been signed in the past year. A bit more than one third said that they signed two or more such books. There was little difference in the numbers signed for different types of house. There is a difference, however, in the rank of the editors who sign more of these submissions. Editors who supervise few or no other editors are more likely to sign such books, while senior supervisory editors are less likely to use "over the transom" manuscripts to fill their "informal" quota. Also, as we shall see, they are more likely to receive books from other more valued sources. Surprisingly, senior editors do not seem to receive fewer "over the transom" projects than do other editors.

Why are there so many unsolicited manuscripts, and why are so few published? Sadly, although authors may do lots of work on a manuscript, they do little research on publishing houses. Consequently many inappropriate manuscripts are received by publishers. One trade editor lamented over the slush pile, "Some of this stuff is wacky, some of it is OK, some even good—it's just not for us. . . . We don't publish poetry, natural science, or English literature dissertations." Another reason for the routine rejection of unsolicited projects is that many unknowing beginning authors start out with the largest or most prestigious houses.

Many such manuscripts are about fads and fashions that have been played out. Additionally, these manuscripts are often very impersonal. They may include a photocopied cover letter addressed, "Dear Sociology Editor" or "Dear Current Events Editor." Few unsolicited projects include any thoughtful analysis of why the book should be published— such as what the author's qualifications are, why he or she chose this particular publisher, what the market for the topic is, or what competing books already cover the area. Finally, one should not take the figures presented here as evidence that there is a vast subterranean army of unpublished writers: the numbers of unsolicited projects are swelled by the simple fact that many authors send copies to many publishers at the same time.

For most publishers, the standard reason for turning down an unsolicited manuscript is "it doesn't suit our list." This noncommittal reply is often true, but there are other reasons for publishers to be vague about the rationale for rejection. They may have no desire to criticize a stranger, or they do not want to start up correspondence. A rejected author may well respond or try to rebut any detailed criticisms an editor might make. And, since the number of proposals received is vast, there simply is not time to respond to each one personally.

The various sources of manuscripts can be viewed as queues, as lines of authors waiting for attention.[4] The length of the different queues may vary from house to house and by type of publishing. However, one common rule applies: the shorter the queue an author's manuscript is in, the better its chances for publication. A recent *New York Times Book Review* article calculates the odds against publication of unsolicited novels at approximately 29,998 to 2.[5] It is no wonder that editors make use of various screening devices, from literary agents to academic brokers. Editors were forthright in telling us they preferred a personal approach—that is, having a manuscript referred by someone they knew or respected. Manuscripts submitted this way have a better chance of being published, although even this personal channel brings many projects to an editor's attention. The estimates vary, but the majority of editors told us that they receive between one hundred and five hundred projects a year in this fashion. The message to authors should be clear: use whatever contacts you have. Given the large number of projects that cross an editor's desk, any type of serious personal recommendation that will attract someone's attention can only help.

There are a number of different avenues for a personal approach to an editor. Some are built into the structure of publishing; others appear to be accidental or informal. The structured approaches are through literary agents in trade publishing, through consulting editors, advisors, series editors, and even college travelers in scholarly and text publishing. Accidental approaches may come from current or former authors who occasionally recommend a manuscript, from well-known people in a given field, from friends in other publishing houses or in various literary or intellectual circles, and from other contacts made through an editor's normal working networks.

There is, of course, nothing accidental about the use of informal networks. Editors in different types of house, however, make very different use of their contacts. Almost all the editors we talked with who were in scholarly, monograph, and university press houses found useful the recommendations of current or former authors and of important persons in a discipline. College text editors also mentioned these sources but are less likely to use them. In contrast, these avenues were not considered as important or productive by trade house editors. Agents are by far the most important source of manuscripts for trade editors. In contrast, text editors have little, if any, contact with agents, and scholarly editors only infrequent contact. College salespersons are a source of manuscripts for college text editors. There is nothing comparable in trade or scholarly publishing. An important formal source of manuscripts used by the majority of text editors are consulting or advisory editors. These "experts" are engaged by a text house and, for their services, are paid a retainer fee and possibly a small percentage of royalties on books they recommend. About half of the scholarly or monograph editors reported using such arrangements. Advisors of this type are rare in trade publishing. As we saw earlier, some use is made by both trade editors and scholarly and university press editors of their colleagues in other houses: one third of these editors reported that editors in competing houses had referred books or projects to them for consideration. College text editors rarely reported such "generosity" on the part of their colleagues.

Although the sources of direct recommendations differ by type of publishing, this is both a common and an important manner of acquiring manuscripts. About 85 percent of scholarly and university press house editors reported they received a great many projects on direct recommendation, as did 75 percent of trade house editors. Only college text editors reported this to be a less frequent, but nevertheless important, source of manuscripts. We believe this difference is explained by the fact that there is little reward in terms of academic empire building for referring a colleague to a textbook house; in contrast, much can be gained by referring a colleague to a monograph or a scholarly house. There is a symbiotic relationship between scholarly oriented houses and their potential customers and producers that does not exit in the textbook field.

A direct personal recommendation to an editor is a much more efficient way for an author to get published and for an editor to screen books and projects. Though the ratio of projects received to projects signed is still somewhat low, the common response of "a lot" averages out to about ten books per year. This may mean as much as a one-in-ten chance that a book that was directly recommended would be actually signed by an editor. This may not sound promising, but it is a considerable improvement over the one-in-a-thousand or worse chance for unsolicited manuscripts.

Agents are another matter altogether, and they are so important to trade houses that we devote a special chapter to them. Here we look at them from an editor's point of view. Seventy percent of trade editors reported getting many manuscripts and projects from agents. Senior trade editors are more likely than junior trade editors to receive many projects from agents, but they are no more likely to sign them. Our data show that books received from agents are much more likely to be signed than is material from other sources. For example, fewer than 10 percent of the editors who say they received few projects from agents report signing many of these submissions, while more than 60 percent of those editors who received many projects from agents also said they signed a great many of these submissions.

Opinions of agents seem to correspond with the degree to which editors are in sustained contact with them. Not a single college text house editor had a kind word to say about agents, and only a few scholarly, university press or monograph house editors did. In contrast, only one trade editor was clearly negative. Approximately half of the trade editors were neutral or gave mixed messages. The general impression of agents held by editors is reflected in their opinion as to whether agents are helpful to authors. Only one college text book editor thought agents were useful or helpful, while only one trade editor thought they were not useful or helpful. Scholarly or monograph house editors fell between these two extreme views.

Various intermediaries are important sources of manuscripts and ideas for all publishing houses. However, editors at different types of house, we have seen, rely on different personal sources. Only half the editors in college text houses report heavy use of personal sources, as compared with 75 percent of scholarly, monograph, and university press editors and 80 percent of the trade editors. As a result of being involved in more networks of contacts, senior editors receive more projects through personal sources, but the proportion of these manuscripts that are actually signed is no different from the number signed by other editors.

Editors are hardly the passive creatures we have thus far depicted. They travel, they read, and sometimes they think up book projects on their own. In these situations, authors do not come to editors; rather, editors search and find authors, often using their personal contacts. When trade editors look for projects they may contact one or several agents to help with the search. Scholarly editors may call upon an established scholar whom they know well. Actively hunting for authors is most characteristic of college text editors who, at the same time, place less reliance on accidental personal contacts to bring them manuscripts. The interest of college text editors in creating their own books is, as it were, based on their regular polling of their markets (college instructors, remember, not college students!). As a result, they have some idea of whether a textbook is needed and will sell. With this knowledge in hand, they are in a much better position than other editors to search for possible writers, and are less willing to wait until the right writer with the right book comes to them. In fact, 85 percent of college text editors report actively searching for books, while only half of editors in other types of houses do this on a regular basis. This search is carried out by editors in college text houses at all levels; whereas among other editors, it is much more characteristic of editors of higher rank. However, relatively few trade editors report that many of their books resulted from personal search, whereas both scholarly and text editors report that many projects resulted from actively searching for authors. Editors of higher rank in both these fields are more likely to say that many of their books were signed as a result of an active search.

Much of what has been discussed about how books are signed up suggests that the act of finding books is not only an individual matter for editors but also an act that takes place in an organizational setting. In the next section we discuss how the decision-making process is organized in houses and which departments in a house have a voice in this process. After explaining the organizational context, we can then discuss what criteria are used to make decisions.

THE DECISION-MAKING PROCESS

Once an editor has found a manuscript he or she likes and thinks is worth publishing, an organizational decision has to be made whether to publish. A few editors have sufficient power and independence that they are able to publish what they like. Most others must convince their house management that a book should be published. This involves lobbying for support and convincing some key people that a book either has real merit or the potential to generate profits.

We asked a number of questions about this process. First, we asked editors, "Who assists you in coming to a decision about publishing a book?" If there was a formal meeting where a book was discussed and evaluated, we asked who was present at the meeting. We then asked whose approval was necessary for getting an author under contract. We also asked about the degree of control an editor had over the production of a book. Finally, we inquired about the various factors editors considered when they evaluated a manuscript.

The procedure for reviewing, evaluating, and deciding to publish a manuscript differs considerably from house to house. Sometimes the process is simple, as in cases where an editor is excited by a project, decides to publish it, and the author has a contract within a few weeks. There are other situations where proposals to publish a particular book are evaluated and discussed at editorial meetings or at meetings where top staff from a variety of departments offer their opinions. At these occasions, an editor's enthusiasm for a book can be dampened by critical questions about the market, the competition, subsidiary rights potential, the cost or size of advance involved, or how the book "fits" with the overall list. Even more formal are circumstances where a parent corporation requires an elaborate profit-and-loss statement and a five-year projection of sales. A proposal must then make its way through the house and then go "upstairs" for the final stamp of approval.

Let us first look at who assists editors in the process of evaluating a manuscript. Keep in mind that the decision-making process and the process of getting formal approval for a contract can be separate and distinct. Some editors consult with no one and decide on their own whether a book is suitable, then go through a formal process of securing a contract. Other editors may be required to get sales or marketing input into the decision to publish. However, once that approval is obtained, the granting of a contract is routine.

There were essentially four categories of response to our questions about who assists editors in the decision-making process:

1. Editors decide on their own or with the help of outside readers chosen by an editor.
2. Editors decide which projects they want to do and then informally discuss them with other members of the house.
3. Editors check with their editor in chief who reviews all proposals.
4. Editors present their proposals to a formal gathering of editors and/or key staff, such as the marketing, sales, or subsidiary rights directors.

The use of outside readers is common in college and commercial scholarly publishing and is mandatory at most university presses. Editors select the readers and, by picking readers who are likely to tell them what they want to hear, can "hedge their bets" on a project they favor. Once outside reviewers have submitted their reports, editors can then make their case for a particular project. In commercial scholarly houses all that then remains may be to obtain the editor in chief or the president's signature on a contract. In university presses, an editor will enlist the support of his or her editor in chief and then submit the proposal to the press's governing board for approval. The governing boards are composed of senior professors from a variety of academic disciplines. At most presses, if the proposed book has two favorable outside reviews, approval is readily granted. This whole process may take considerable time, and university presses may lose projects to commercial scholarly houses where decisions are often made more expeditiously.[6]

Outside readers are infrequently used by trade editors to help them reach decisions. Since the material under review does not require evaluation by an expert in the field, readers are rarely necessary. Some trade editors can make decisions largely on their own. The most typical are personal imprint editors, who have set up arrangements with publishing houses which allow them to publish books under their own imprint, with the house doing the production and distribution. The risks involved are usually shared in some form or another. Most personal imprint editors either decide on projects on their own or consult with only a high-level executive of the house, such as the editor in chief or the president. Tom Congdon, a trade editor who had such an arrangement with E. P. Dutton, has said, "I saved a lot of time by not spending weeks on my knees asking for permission."[7]

The informal discussion process is another typical way of deciding what to publish. An editor may consult with another editor and solicit his or her advice and support. Or the editor may make the rounds of various departments—such as sales, publicity, or subsidiary rights—and informally discuss the book with various people and ask their opinion. A decision is eventually made, based on experience and intuition, as well as on informal consultation with other members of the house.

We found this informal process to be most common in trade houses. People with the title of publisher or editor in chief are most likely to say they discussed projects informally with others. The size of the house does not affect whether there is an informal discussion process. If anything, the very largest houses are slightly more likely to handle things through informal means. Whether a house is independent or a subsidiary of another house or owned by another corporation very much affects the degree of formality of decision making: dependent houses are more likely to have a formal process of decision making. Nat Wartels, president of Crown, argues that one of the key differences between his independent house and more hierarchical, corporate-owned houses is that "we can make a decision on a book easily and quickly. They must go through committees which take time to deliberate and reach a consensus."[8]

Two other factors help determine the degree of formality of the decision-making process. One is the actual costs involved in publishing a book. Almost any financial commitment above the norm requires a more elaborate decision-making process. Some corporate-owned houses must check with their parent corporation and secure its approval if the advance is especially large, if the contract involves an unusually long-term commitment, or if significant subsidiary rights are involved. The other key factor is editorial experience. We found that the least experienced editors, those who began working in the industry after 1966, are less likely to make decisions entirely on their own, especially in trade houses. Younger editors in houses that lack a formal decision-making process told us that they turn to their editor in chief for support and approval. One assistant trade editor described her relationships with her editor in chief as follows:

> He oversees every book that's published. I always check with him before making a final decision. He is a well-known superstar and covers all books in certain areas. We're pretty much left on our own in other fields as long as we check with him. For certain books he reads and OKs them. For books in areas he doesn't know anything about, he usually just approves them. Occasionally he dislikes something and tries to talk you out of it. Whether you win depends on your recent track record. But we have no editorial board or formal approval process here.

The decision to publish a book may, in some houses, be reached in regular meetings at which the books under consideration are discussed. Different houses vary in regard to who attends these meetings as well as to whether a formal vote is actually taken. At some houses no one votes, but a general discussion results in consensus. The editor, depending on his or her track record and influence within the firm, may prevail in spite of skepticism on the part of others who are attending. "There is not a vote," says Dan Green, who formerly served on the six-member editorial board at Simon & Schuster:

> Generally there is a discussion, and it's a question of who is most committed to the book, and how passionately. If one person feels very strongly, that can sometimes be enough. And sometimes even unanimous enthusiasm isn't sufficient, because we decide the asking price for the book is too high.[9]

Tom Congdon has described the more formal meetings he attended when he worked at the large and relatively bureaucratic house, Doubleday:

Doubleday then had a huge meeting called the publishing board, which was like the conclave of Cardinals, and it was awfully hard to get a Pope elected. It was a very thorough market scrutiny that followed an editorial scrutiny. In these meetings, marketing was always an important factor.[10]

In Doubleday's "conclave of Cardinals" editorial and marketing staff are represented. In other houses, a different mix of staff might be present at decision-making meetings. At the large college text house we observed in detail, the editorial board includes the director of the editorial department, the managing editor, the sales department manager, the oldest and most senior editor, and the editor in chief. This group determines the fate of all textbooks that are proposed for publication.

We asked each of the twenty-five editors who reported that their proposals are evaluated at formal meetings to tell us who attends these meetings. Since many editors told us that they either decide on their own or involve others informally, the number of cases upon which we base our findings is small—only twenty-five. In decreasing order of being mentioned, the following people are represented at decision-making meetings: editor in chief (85%), publisher (75%), sales staff (63%), president (58%), managing editor (50%), marketing staff (46%), publicity and promotion staff (40%), subsidiary rights staff (40%), production staff (27%), assistant editors (24%), and, last, representatives of the parent corporation (16%).* Our figure of 46 percent for marketing is strikingly similar to the 47 percent attendance reported by Michael Wendroff in his study of marketing's influence at a group of "well-known commercial New York houses."[11]

In those houses that hold formal meetings, we were interested in the balance of power between the editorial and the sales or marketing departments. An editor in the trade department of a large, diversified publishing company told us that her editorial department is no longer "holding sway." She felt that "marketing runs things, you have to sell your books to marketing first," and lamented, "At other houses the editor in chief *tells* the sales staff to sell certain books and they do it. That's not true here." And she wondered not whether important materials would be recognized by editors, but whether they would get published. "If marketing tell us 15,000 copies is the minimum it takes for a hardcover to make it, how can we push a book that should be published but will only sell 8,000 or 9,000 copies?" The director of marketing at this house said he realized there was a danger of inhibiting editorial creativity, yet he felt it was "necessary because editors saw themselves as part of an editorial guild." A number of editors told us they would not push for books to which marketing or sales were

* These titles and departments may vary from house to house.

strongly opposed. "Why should we if they won't support it?" one trade editor queried. Roger Straus III, previously a marketing director but now an editorial director of Harper & Row (and the son of Roger Straus, Jr., head of Farrar, Straus & Giroux), has discussed the problems involved in publishing a book with minimal marketing support, and wonders whether the author is being done a disservice:

> To publish a book that a number of us are infatuated with without making any marketing commitment to it is a real problem. I think in the long run you aren't doing yourself or the author any favor. If you are going to publish a book you have to put a certain amount of money behind it or it's going to be a problem. So very often what I will say is, "Hey, we love the book, but can we envision making the kind of effort that will be necessary to secure the audience, and if we don't, are we just going to lose the author, who'll be angry that we didn't do an aggressive enough job on his or her work?"[12]

In general, marketing and sales have more influence at houses where these departments are represented at formal decision-making meetings. However, we came across a number of editors who have strong reputations for "fantastic presentations" of their books and seem always to have gained the support of marketing and sales.

We also learned that most editors are more concerned with sales now than they were five years ago. Almost three quarters of the editors in both trade and college text houses expressed this opinion. Half of the editors in scholarly and university presses were more concerned with sales now than in the past. Concern with sales seems a pervasive, nagging worry common in many houses. The size of the house, whether it is independent, who participates in publishing decisions, and the rank of the editor were all *unrelated* to whether an editor reported more concern about sales. The only characteristic of editors and houses—other than being a scholarly or university press—that seems to affect concern with sales is editorial experience. Almost 85 percent of editors who got their first jobs in the publishing industry after 1966 reported more concern with sales, compared with 60 percent of editors who started before 1966. This is not a large difference and may reflect experience—older editors have seen it all and are less worried; or selective recruitment—younger editors are more likely to have experience in sales and marketing; or simply security—newer editors are less sure of their jobs. The essential point is that most editors report increased concern with sales. As a result, they told us that fewer disagreements are occurring between sales and editorial departments. In the past, trade and college editors were more likely to go "to the mat" over a worthy book with little sales potential. In today's publishing market, both college and trade editors reported that they can no longer afford the luxury of books with limited appeal.

One way publishing houses express their increased concern about sales is to place greater emphasis on getting marketing advice about whether to publish a particular book. Roger Straus III describes the use and importance of marketing information in publishing decisions:

> Marketing traditionally has been a kind of after-the-fact process. I have very mixed feelings about this. There is a very big part of me that feels that this is how it should be, that the decision to publish should be based on the merits of the work, and it's the job of the marketing organization to try to marry the book to its potential audience as best it can, and that a book shouldn't be dismissed because marketing or sales people feel it doesn't have a sufficient audience. If the book has enough intrinsic value it becomes the responsibility of the marketing department to find a sufficient audience.
>
> On the other hand, one has to be intrigued with some of our more scientific colleagues who ascertain ahead of time whether an audience exists. For instance, a publisher who essentially sells through mail order won't go ahead with a book without being convinced that a mail program will produce certain results, which can be ascertained pretty clearly from testing. Certainly, it's a hell of a lot safer, and I'm sure the success rate is astoundingly high compared to the traditional trade system.[13]

As Straus suggests, concern with developing a marketing strategy for book publishing has an impact on the decision process itself. It is one thing to attempt to market books after the marketing and sales departments have been "stuck" with a project. It is quite another matter to base the initial decision to publish on the views of the marketing group. We found considerable differences among types of house in the degree to which the marketing or sales group is involved in publishing decisions. Forty percent of the trade editors told us that they never rely on sales or marketing—as compared with only 10 percent of the college editors and 25 percent of the scholarly editors who never use the marketing or sales group in making decisions to publish. Since fewer scholarly editors than trade or college editors reported increased concern with sales, the former's greater reliance on input from marketing or sales may seem surprising. On the other hand, scholarly editors can turn to marketing or sales departments for fairly precise data on the past performance of direct mail efforts for similar books. With this information in hand, there may be less need to worry about sales.

We learned that both large houses and houses of all sizes owned by other companies are significantly more likely to use marketing and sales departments. Both factors operate independently of one another: that is, regardless of size of house, corporate control promotes the use of marketing and sales departments in decision making; and, regardless of corporate control, size is also an important factor.

Even if a publishing house ignores the advice of marketing or sales in assessing the profitability of a book, editors must rely on some method for assessing potential sales. There are basically three approaches: the use of formal market research; the use of informal market research, such as asking the opinion of salespeople or the examination of house records for similar projects; or personal experience or "intuition." More than half of the college text editors reported that they use formal market research, 20 percent of the scholarly editors reported such use, but only about 15 percent of trade editors did so. The larger houses among the trade and scholarly groups are more likely to use formal market research. While 80 percent and 90 percent of college and scholarly house editors make use of informal market research, only half of the trade editors owned up to doing any research. Intuition, of course, is the trade editor's tool. Eighty percent of the trade editors operate on intuition or the "seat of their pants," but fewer than half of the others admitted to doing so. The use of intuition is not a personal matter—determined by experience, gender, salary, and whether one has an intellectual reference group (as indicated by a high score on our "highbrow" reading index, page 114)—but is an attribute of the kind of house where an editor works. If anything, experienced and highly paid editors are slightly *less* likely to use their intuitive powers than are less experienced and poorly paid editors.

How is the decision-making process associated with getting a book under contract? Editors who have total autonomy in deciding whether to publish a book almost always have the ability to offer a contract. Even though a number of those who do not have complete formal autonomy have *de facto* freedom to sign what they like, these editors must formally obtain approval for the contracts they offer. After all, contracts are financially binding on the house, and their terms may be complex and involve more than editorial wisdom. There is a considerable difference between an editor who can simply announce to an author, "Consider yourself signed up," and one who says, "I want to publish your book, but I have to get approval," or even, "We love your book but I have to check with my colleagues before I can formally offer you a contract."

One fourth of the editors we interviewed are able themselves to offer a contract to authors; a little fewer than 20 percent can make the offer subject to token approval; about 30 percent need some kind of formal approval; and about 30 percent cannot themselves offer a contract at all. Editorial independence in offering a contract was greatest among editors in scholarly houses, almost 60 percent of whom can offer a contract either on their own or with token approval. Trade houses are most likely to have arrangements limiting editors' freedom to offer a contract on their own. Over 40 percent of the editors in trade houses reported that they cannot offer contracts. Not surprisingly, editors with the title of publisher or editor in chief are most likely to be able to offer contracts on their own: 70 percent report having such discretion. There is a difference, then, between informal consultation—which publishers and editors in chief reported that they engage in when deciding on a book—and actually having the right to sign it up. Publishers and editors in chief consult with others but in the end can offer a contract on their own. The position title of publisher or editor in chief—not the supervisory power—is the important factor. Senior editors who supervise other editors are no more likely than others to be able to offer contracts without approval. Consistent with this is the finding that gender also makes no difference: women and men are about equal in their abilities to offer contracts.

What people in what positions have to approve contracts?

- Almost 70 percent of the editors reported that the president or the publisher has to give approval.
- Sixty percent mentioned the editor in chief.
- Half mentioned other than editorial staff (including marketing, the treasurer, and so forth).
- Almost 40 percent mentioned other editors.

College text houses, if they do not allow an editor total freedom, again tend to be more formalistic. They are more likely to require approval from the president or publisher, from the editor in chief, from the executive editor (if any), from other technical staff, and from other editors. Size has a curvilinear effect: both large and small houses are less likely to require the approval of more than one individual. Medium-sized houses are more bureaucratic, since they frequently require the approval of both the editor in chief and the technical or financial staff. Fewer editors have autonomy to offer a contract at medium-sized houses, while editors in small and very large houses are more likely to be able to offer contracts on their own or with only token approval.

FACTORS IN THE DECISION TO PUBLISH

What criteria do editors use in deciding what to publish? Every aspiring author wants to know how editors judge manuscripts. This seems so basic that one might wonder why we did not begin our discussion of decision making with an analysis of the factors editors take into account. We did not because, in our view, several features take precedence. A major factor is how an author comes to the attention of a publishing house. Equally important is the way publishing houses are organized and the history of a particular house. At houses where there are formal meetings attended by marketing or sales representatives, editors know that sales potential is crucial. The project will not be approved if the figures do not come out right. At houses where the decision-making process is informal or solely an editorial matter, other factors may be predominant. Some editors feel strongly that the decision to publish is an editorial one and should be guided by an editor's experience or intuition.

The traditions in operation at a particular house are also a significant part of the decision-making process. Some houses are willing to publish anything that is at all salable; yet others will rarely publish books that are not in tune with their established traditions. The power of tradition cuts across both ownership and size. We observed large, corporate-owned houses with strong publishing traditions and small, independent houses with none whatsoever.

In our interviews many editors mentioned several considerations they take into account in evaluating a manuscript. Some are personal issues, such as "Do I have the time and inclination to work on this?" How well written a manuscript is, the clarity of an author's argument, and the book's sales potential are typical assessments. Almost every publishing house has some sort of proposal-to-publish form that must be completed on a potential book. Among the basic topics usually covered, there are four major concerns:

- Editorial—quality of manuscript, author, competition, copy-editing problems.
- Production—costs.
- Contract—advance, royalty.
- Marketing—audience, sales, price/suggested list price, and print run.

We queried editors about the information they include on these forms. No one suggested that they expect to be held accountable for any specific remarks or calculations they make on these forms. Some editors went farther and described the process as "a game. . . . You learn how to fill these out and then it's easy." We pushed editors on why one project is better than another. Unfortunately they were not expansive on this subject. We then tried systematically to collect and classify editors' responses to several questions. Almost all of the editors we interviewed went along with our attempt to rate the various factors that go into judging a manuscript. However, it was clear that we were overrationalizing a strongly intuitive process.

We gave editors a check list of factors involved in the decision to publish a book, and asked them to rate these factors as "critical," "very important," "important," or "not very important." The general positive tone of the responses comes from the obvious fact that in one sense all of these factors are important in almost every project. The factors themselves were derived from our early informal interviews with editors and were also based on our participant observations in publishing houses. The following factors were listed:

- The prestige of the author in his/her profession.
- The reputation of an author among general readers.
- The previous track record of an author in publishing.
- The timeliness of the subject matter of the book.
- The potential prestige of the book.
- How well the manuscript reads.
- The lack of competition on the subject.
- The recommendations of others in your house.
- The recommendations of outside readers.
- The low cost of production.
- The potential sale of rights.
- The commercial prospects of the book.
- The book's potential profitability in the first year.
- The long-term profitability.
- The ease with which it can be promoted.

As there were too many factors to consider in detail, we examined them in relation to each other: for example, does the editor who thinks that the sale of rights is critical think that the commercial prospects of the book are as well?

Sales of subsidiary rights and *not* using outside readers are strongly associated. We called this cluster a "trade" factor, since it is present for almost 40 percent of trade house editors but for no editors in college text, scholarly, or university press houses. Another factor that reveals some significant differences among houses is the extent of profit expected in the first year. Almost 60 percent of college text houses found this a "very important" or "critical" factor in deciding to publish, about one third of the trade book houses said it was "very important" or "critical," but fewer than 20 percent of university press or scholarly houses checked this category. Another strong differentiating factor was whether the book received support from other members of a publishing house. We found that house support was considered "not very important" among college text house editors as well as among university press editors but was cited as "critical" or "very important" by almost half of scholarly house and trade house editors. (Throughout this section we will differentiate between university press and commercial scholarly editors because their responses differ somewhat.) A fourth cluster, which we called "prestige," includes two elements: the potential prestige of the book itself, and the prestige of the author in his or her profession. To this cluster, scholarly editors, university press editors, and trade editors all responded in the same way: about 70 percent rated at least one of these items as "critical" or "very important." Only 40 percent of college text editors, however, rated prestige as "critical" or "very important."

We grouped together four items, each of which are highly correlated, and called these the "commercial" factor. This included: the prospects for long-term profit, how well the book reads, the general commercial prospects of the book, and ease of promotion. As might be expected, university press editors are least likely to care about the commercial aspects of their books (fewer than 30 percent rated two or more items as "critical" or "very important"). About half the commercial scholarly editors rated two or more items as "critical" or "very important." Over 70 percent of college text and trade editors checked off two or more times from this list as "critical" or "very important." Thus, while there are differences in the assessment of the importance of commercial prospects, the differences among types of house are not as great as one might expect.

Several points stand out. First, editors did distinguish among various factors in judging the potential success of a book: not everything was lumped together in an unseparable mass. Second, there were, for the most part, more similarities among different types of house in the way books are evaluated than there were differences. Among the few distinguishing factors, both trade and college editors were more concerned with first-year profitability, while scholarly editors paid more attention to long-term commercial success. Subsidiary rights was also key for trade editors. Scholarly editors took into account the opinions of experts in the field. Fewer than half the university press editors or commercial scholarly editors considered commercial prospects or profitability as the most important factor. In contrast, more than 60 percent of both text and trade editors listed commercial prospects as the single most important consideration.

We conclude that the major task for editorial judgment is to try to determine which projects will pay their way. The criteria for financial success, as well as the methods through which this success is realized, differ considerably from one house to another; but the principle remains that publishing is, above all, a business. Editors have very different expectations for their books depending on the type of house, and to some extent, on the type of book. We asked editors how many copies of a book they need to sell to "break even." This is, of course, an unfair question. The amount varies according to the size of the advance an author receives, the cost of the book, and the size of the print run. But we were interested in a minimum figure editors would consider acceptable. Editors at university presses and commercial scholarly and monograph houses cited between 2,000 and 5,000 copies. Trade editors set their sights somewhat higher: the lowest figure was 6,000 copies; but 70 percent said they must sell between 10,000 and 50,000 copies to break even. For text houses, the figure depends on whether one is talking about an introductory or an advanced text: the former has to sell many more copies. Among text editors, 40 percent said an introductory text must sell between 20,000 and 50,000 copies; and a few suggested even higher minimum print runs. Thus, although commercial success is important to every editor, the definition of what is acceptable depends on the milieu within which an editor works.

Decisions about whether to sign a book depend, as we have shown in this chapter, on a variety of organizational factors. Such decisions are reached in different ways in the various sectors of the industry and are also influenced by patterns of ownership of publishing houses. Formal structures of decision making, as well as informal ones, have a strong impact on editorial strategies. But finally—lest it be thought that we underestimate purely personal factors in decision making—let us note that there are books that might never have seen the light of day had it not been for the personal predilections and idiosyncrasies of particular editors. As one scholarly editor once put it to us, when we pointed to a book on his list that seemed unlikely to sell: "Yes, you are right, but I had a few beers with him at a recent scholarly meeting and I got to like the fellow. Maybe I'll make money with his next book, even though we might not break even with this one." When all is said and done, it is still the case that the remaining craftlike aspects of the publishing industry allow a measure of personal style and judgment to enter into the decision-making process which would be inconceivable in a fully bureaucratic industrial structure.

Chapter 6

Women in Book Publishing: A Qualified Success Story

BY THIS POINT, few readers will regard book publishing as a "gentlemanly trade," but it may still come as a surprise to learn that women outnumber men almost two to one. Because an estimated one half to two thirds of the publishing industry's 72,200 employees are women,* many observers term it a "women's business." Others reserve the term to refer to the increased visibility, and influence, of a few women in important decision-making positions. Women such as Mildred Marmur, Paula Diamond, Judy Lynn-del Rey, Phyllis Gran, Esther Margolis, Joni Evans, Leona Nevler, Lynn Nesbit, and Helen Wolff are well known and respected within the hardcover trade and paperback industry. Some of the most

---

* This is a preliminary December 1980 figure.[1] In November 1980, the number of employees in book publishing was 70,800.

Accurate official statistics regarding the percentage of women employees are difficult to obtain. Estimates are derived from several sources. In a 1973 survey of publishing employees in Boston,[2] at least two thirds of the employees were women. In the field-work observations of a medium-large trade house and a medium-large college text house, over half of the employees in each were women.

publicized "deals," such as the sale of subsidiary reprint rights to mass-market paperback houses, often to the tune of a million or two dollars, are negotiated—sometimes at both ends—by women.

Both uses of the term "women's business" raise a number of interesting questions regarding the nature of book publishing and the place of women in it. What role have women played in the historical development of book publishing? How does their present-day status, and work experience, differ from that of men in publishing? And how do the career experiences and opportunities of women compare with those of men?

WOMEN'S ROLE IN A CHANGING INDUSTRY

A review of the role of women in the history of book publishing illuminates their present-day status. Historically, book publishers have always utilized the talents of women. Because their roles were either informal or invisible, their contribution often exceeded their recognition.

In the latter half of the nineteenth century, the typical publisher was a small, family-owned paternalistic firm. In keeping with the prevailing practices and culture of the day, these "gentlemanly" publishers rarely formally employed women. Publishers selected successors from among their male heirs, as it was common for publishing to remain in the family for several generations. The situation at Harper's after the Civil War was typical: because "Harper and Brothers [was] exclusively a family concern, any male wishing to join the firm was welcome."[3]

But since many publishers *were* family concerns, wives, sisters, mothers, and daughters often helped out informally. Their tasks varied from keeping the books to reading and evaluating manuscripts submitted for publication. Neltje Doubleday and Amie Doran, two of the better-known wives, often acted as informal readers and, on more than one occasion, influenced their husbands' decision to publish a particular book.[4]

In the early years of this century, many small publishers retained this same informal character and relied, to a significant extent, on the assistance of wives and daughters. Their role was the same, although they began formally appearing on the payroll as well. Thus, in 1928 when Pascal Covici and Donald Friede started their own house (Covici-Friede) with only seven employees, Covici's wife took care of the "business department," and Friede's wife functioned as the chief manuscript reader.[5]

Only infrequently did husbands and wives become true partners. The first and most famous partnership was that of Alfred and Blanche Knopf who started their own firm in 1915. With Alfred as president and Blanche as vice-president, the early years of their partnership were particularly difficult; as she noted in a 1928 interview, it was virtually unheard of for a woman to hold anything but a minor position in publishing.[6]

By the First World War, women were well established in the publishing industry. A survey of eighty-two publishing firms in 1917 revealed that of the total of 1,406 women employed, 259 were in editorial positions, 321 were in publicity and promotion, and 826 were in clerical and stenographic jobs.[7] In this, the status of women in publishing is not unlike that of women in many other businesses and professions: most women worked in house, behind the scenes as clerks, stenographers, and secretaries, as assistants to editors, or as assistants and managers in what were considered women's specialties—children's books, publicity, and advertising-promotion. As children's book editors and publicity or advertising managers, many women attained visibility and esteem within the trade; yet these positions were always ceiling occupations for women—the last rung of one of the only career ladders open to them.

Because of the rapid growth of these "female" occupations, especially clerks and secretaries, and of the availability of a labor pool of educated women, book publishing has changed since 1900 from an exclusive male profession to a business dependent on a work force composed mostly of women. The original impetus for this shift from male to female staff grew out of what Margery Davies has called the "feminization of the clerical labor force" which occurred around 1900. In most businesses, male clerks and bookkeepers, working in a general capacity while "learning the trade," were gradually replaced by women. This shift occurred partly because more women than men were graduating from high school. Since elementary and high school teaching was the only profession from which women were not excluded, there were, in Davies's words, "literally thousands of women with training that qualified them for jobs that demanded literacy, but who could not find such jobs."[8]

It is not difficult to see the particular attraction book publishing held for many of these educated women, most of whom came from privileged family backgrounds. Publishing itself was solidly cast as a "genteel" profession because few publishers saw themselves as mere businessmen; instead, they viewed their calling as requiring a "sense of dedication which rose above material gains."[9] Moreover, in publishing circles it was assumed that much of the book-buying public, particularly of novels and fiction, was female. And because women were ideologically associated with domestic matters of education and culture, their active participation in the guardianship and enjoyment of culture, both as librarians[10] and as employees of book and magazine publishing firms, was justified. In the words of Beulah Hagen, long-time assistant to Cass Canfield at Harper & Brothers, "young women, getting out of college, were so anxious to get a job in something they could be proud of that they would go into publishing and work for practically nothing."[11]

Book publishers found it easy to employ women not only because they could, and did, pay them less than men, but because women were always an available, adaptable, and able workforce, to be used when and where needed. In Marx's terms, women were the reserve army of labor in publishing.* When publishers have, at various times, expanded their lower-level editorial staff to handle the increased flow of manuscripts into their offices, they have almost always turned to the writing and editorial talents of women. An extreme example attests to the value of female readers and editors. Edward Bok, editor of the *Ladies' Home Journal*, described the short-lived "literary factories" that prospered briefly in the 1890s. A group of thirty women reviewed all the daily and weekly periodicals published nationwide and looked for ideas or stories of possible "book merit." The ideas and stories were then turned over to a group of five women who created a story line which a known writer fleshed out into book form.[12] More common was the editorial work performed by women in textbook and dictionary publishing throughout this century; here, in 1914, college-educated women numbered between 20 percent and 30 percent.[13]

Within major publishing houses, few women achieved anything other than minor positions. While a handful became editors in chief of children's books or directors of publicity, and some became editors, only a tiny minority were promoted into key executive positions. As late as November 1974, there were only six female executive heads of publishing (presidents and editors in chief).[14] The unusual woman who did become an editor or editor in chief, often succeeded less owing to her own abilities, which were usually considerable, than to the politics and policies of the man for whom she worked. Thus, from the very beginning, the William Morrow Com-

---

* Editorial free lancers are the best example of this function of women as a reserve army of labor. Publishers find it cheaper to hire free-lance copy editors, because they do not involve overhead costs nor do they have to be paid benefits, compensation, and so on. Also, copy editors can be hired only as needed in peak periods which occur regularly just before selling seasons. It is not surprising that free lancers are usually women; they outnumber men free lancers almost two to one. In the college text house in which field work was conducted, 15 of the 17 in-house copy editors were women. The 1980 *Literary Market Place* listed 66 male copy editors, 105 female, and 58 individuals or firms whose gender was impossible to determine.

pany, founded by Morrow himself in 1926, was distinguished by the number of women in fairly high positions. Frances Phillips was director of the editorial department and remained in that position until 1967. Eva Colby became treasurer in 1931. And Emily Street along with Elisabeth Hamilton eventually became members of the board of directors.[15]

Women have exerted influence on publishing in the past either as independent publishers outside the mainstream or as able assistants within major male-dominated houses. In the first instance, publishing houses founded or headed by women have almost always been small specialty houses operating on the periphery of major trade and text publishing. For example, in 1917, Elisabeth Irene Craven Davis succeeded her deceased husband to become president and director of F. A. Davis, leading publisher of nursing texts until 1960.[16] When Helen Meyer became president of Dell Publishing Company in 1957, it was a significant and unusual move for a woman; yet Dell, like all mass-market paperback publishers of the time, was considered a stepchild to the more prestigious hardcover trade houses.

As secretaries and assistants, women have always had substantial influence on book publishing—a contribution that has seldom been acknowledged. Publishing historian John Tebbel credits Ellen Knowles Eayres as being the "third, unofficial partner, never given proper due" in the early firm of Alfred Harcourt and Donald Brace (founded in 1919). A Vassar graduate, she had started as Harcourt's secretary while he was still at Henry Holt & Company (founded 1873). She later moved up to do editorial and publicity work at Holt. Before she and Harcourt married, she had allowed Harcourt to use her apartment as a temporary office, then helped move the office to a dark basement where she typed letters, kept books, and helped direct the selling. She even traveled to libraries and schools in the Midwest to sell the Harcourt, Brace list. "As a result of her influence," Tebbel writes, "Harcourt, Brace was probably the first publishing house that even attempted to give women equal rights with men."[17]

The day-to-day experience of being a woman and a secretary-assistant in publishing throughout most of this century is captured in the reminiscences of Beulah Hagen, mentioned earlier as the long-time secretary and assistant to Cass Canfield at Harper & Brothers (Harper & Row since 1961) for thirty-eight years until her retirement in 1975.[18]

As the assistant to one of the most respected and hard-working editors in the trade, her work was extremely demanding. Without rancor, she described Canfield as a "slavedriver" who "if he wanted something done or wanted it done faster than it was possible to do it, he would just ask for it or expect it. You know, there was no discussion." She added that he was hard on everybody, including himself, and "usually he's fortunate to have people around him who would do the impossible at every level." Working overtime, evenings and weekends, was not unusual. Thus, for example, when Canfield was editorial director:

> He had monthly luncheon meetings for all the department heads, at which time they reported on the books they were publishing and the titles that they had lined up for the future. And I had to not only order the sandwich lunches and serve them, but take notes, which began the minute they began eating. I was taking notes all the way through most of the afternoon. Then I would have to spend the whole weekend transcribing these notes because I didn't have time to do it in the office because of the routine office correspondence.

As the years went by, her job changed not only because "the very nature of publishing changed a good deal over the years," but also "more and more . . . he left a great many of the contacts with the authors and the production side of books to me." After Canfield decided that a manuscript should be published, and what the terms of the contract would be, Hagen was often responsible for seeing that the contracts department drew up the proper papers. She almost always handled correspondence with an author after the manuscript actually arrived. Afterward she always made sure that authors received schedules for upcoming proofs, discussed who would do the index—the author or Harper's—and conferred with authors on innumerable details. She often worked with authors on pictures and maps and also with the permissions department on requests from other publishers to reprint either entire books or excerpts of books by Harper authors with whom she had worked. In other words, "once the author was committed, then I did a great deal of the work that would normally be supervised by an editor."

In her position as Canfield's assistant, Hagen wielded influence among other house employees, with authors, and with Canfield himself: "It's not immodest to say that over the years I had a rather, perhaps, subtle but important influence sort of behind the lines, and that was not only as far as dealings with authors was concerned, but also things around the house. If I felt that something was going badly, or if someone had been badly treated or there was disagreement about something he [Canfield] wasn't aware of . . ." she did something about it. In describing an "odd situation" with a particularly ornery author of whom Canfield was fond, Hagen recalled how the author "never made trouble to Canfield. If he was making any complaints or being nasty about something, Beulah was always on the other end of that." As with other frustrated or difficult authors, Hagen felt the need to remind him that "he was being a little unfair, because in the last analysis, I didn't make the decisions." In many ways, she functioned as a non-threatening sounding board, "someone on whose shoulder they could cry without offending their dear friend Cass." Yet it is also equally true that if she agreed with an author's complaints, "I might well take it up with Cass in my own way—and indeed I did from time to time."

THE DIVISION OF LABOR BY SEX

In some respects, Beulah Hagen's recollections have a contemporary ring to them. Most women continue to dominate certain behind-the-scenes in-house staff positions and exert an important influence over particular books. As secretaries, assistants, publicists, advertising managers, and occupants of other low- and mid-level positions, they do not exercise control over the goals and policy of publishing. However, within the last few years, a noteworthy minority of women have moved into key decision-making positions in editorial acquisitions and subsidiary rights.

Both conclusions are, in part, drawn from the results of a separate survey conducted in 1978. Mail questionnaires were sent to men and women in a sample of small, medium, and large college textbook, general trade, and mass-market paperback houses. The survey inquired into the backgrounds, present position, and career experiences of all employees in the sample. Responding to the questionnaire were 117 men and 200 women—an overall response rate of 34 percent. The findings are similar to those found in the survey of editors discussed in chapters 4 and 5, and are also corroborated by interviews with successful women in publishing—literary agents, publishers, subsidiary rights directors—and by field observations of a general trade and a college textbook house.

As in the past, women are overwhelmingly concentrated in some occupations and publishing specialties but are almost totally excluded from others. Sociologists refer to this type of sexual division of labor as "occupational sex typing." Occupations are sex-typed when a large majority of the people in an occupation are of one sex, and "there is an associated normative expectation that this is as it should be."[19] In publishing, the departments or specialties of advertising-promotion-publicity, subsidiary rights in general trade publishing, and art-design are dominated by women, who perform more than three quarters of the jobs in each area. Sales and marketing is the only specialty in which there are far more men than women; here there are two men to every woman. The remaining publishing functions of editorial acquisitions, manuscript editing, and production are dominated by women two to one—the same proportion as their employment throughout the industry.

A pervasive logic underlies the sexual division of labor in publishing. The hierarchy is such that many of the occupations and specialties where women dominate are at the bottom of the pyramid. The lower strata of every department is comprised of clerical-secretarial and various assistant positions (production assistant, publicity assistant, editorial assistant) which are overwhelmingly filled by women. Almost one third of the women who responded to the survey are secretaries or assistants; fewer than 10 percent of the men are in comparable positions. In fact, one reason why women outnumber men in some publishing specialties—editorial acquisitions, subsidiary rights, advertising-publicity, to name just a few—is because these departments have a higher proportion of secretarial-assistant jobs than of top administrative or managerial ones.

For the same reason, more women are employed in the larger, relatively bureaucratic publishing firms. In the survey, nearly three quarters of all women were employed by a large publishing house in comparison with just over half of all the male respondents. Small publishers employed nearly one eighth of the men polled but only one sixteenth of all the women. And nearly 90 percent of all those employed in large mass-market paperback houses were women.

In socio-economic terms, this lower level of positions in all types of publishing possesses many characteristics of a "secondary labor market": jobs are low-paying, employees are easily and frequently replaced, there is little job security, and promotion or career ladders are either very short or nonexistent.[20] At the time of this survey in 1978, secretaries and assistants often made as little as $130 a week—less than $7,000 a year. The low pay virtually assures that most secretarial-assistant jobs will remain a female enclave. This helps explain the experience of one young man, now a sales representative, who recalled his initial attempts to enter publishing:

> In the early 1960s, when I was looking for an editorial job in New York, I had the distinct feeling, later supported by facts, that most editorial positions were being given to women or single men because they were more affordable to publishers.

Others have put the matter more bluntly. "I believe women are the slave labor force of publishing," says a female assistant in a mass-market house. "It demands real determination and the desire to be there in the first place for the pressures and lack of money to be worthwhile." Another young woman, a mass-market paperback publicist, summed up the essential features of this "secondary labor market":

> I have found that publishing is a very stimulating area and very exciting, especially in the first years after college. However, the company I work for now does not try to develop its personnel or give individual opportunities for advancement. It's very conservative. Employees are underpaid, turnover big, no promotions from within. So that one day you wake up saying "Where am I going?" I think many of the very talented people in publishing leave the industry because of this. In other words, I would say that publishing is a very good career for a young person a bit confused or just starting out, but the companies do a lousy job of attracting, training, and keeping talent—especially in the sales-marketing area.

Frustration with the hard work, long hours, and the lack of concrete career possibilities in publishing leads many secretaries and assistants to try for greener pastures in other jobs in other industries. Consequently, turnover rates are very high; according to the survey, over three fourths of the women assistants have been in their present job less than a year. One woman editorial assistant noted: "There's much discontent in many offices among the 'lower ranks' who feel too bright to be doing their jobs and they no longer feel that they want to work five years to make $15,000 and get a token promotion." This sentiment was echoed by a paperback editor, also a woman: "Publishing uses people up very quickly. They should either have a lot of stamina or very personal goals."

In spite of entry-level frustrations, many women persevere and become publicists, promotion managers, copy editors, manuscript editors, and acquisitions editors—positions other than secretary or assistant. This is true for 70 percent of the women in the survey. Most of these women work in what may be termed the "intermediary" professional level where they are employed as skilled and experienced professionals above the lowest level of secretaries and assistants and below the top layer of management. Here they exert much influence over the look, style, and content of particular books but do not wield power over publishing policy.

While this sexual division of labor is hierarchical in nature, it is also governed by another kind of logic in which the content, or task definition, of the job distinguishes the work women do in publishing from that of men. The sociologist Jessie Bernard and the noted author Caroline Bird have remarked that women tend to be in occupations and organizations where they do the "inside" behind-the-scenes work, while men take charge of "foreign relations," or the negotiations with outsiders, customers, and suppliers.[21] Nowhere is this inside-outside dichotomy more pronounced than in the editorial division of labor in college text publishing. The craft of editing has traditionally included multifaceted tasks ranging from acquiring manuscripts for publication to aiding authors in perfecting the organization, the grammar, and the readability of their manuscripts. The same editorial functions prevail in contemporary publishing but are often the jobs of separate individuals.

The more autonomous, prestigious, visible role of college text acquisitions editor has, until fairly recently, been close to an exclusive male province. These editors, like their high-level counterparts in production and sales, are responsible for developing, monitoring, and negotiating relations with important persons outside the firm. In general, acquisitions editors negotiate with authors and their literary agents; sales representatives and sales managers sell to wholesalers, retailers, and individual buyers; production managers and supervisors contract with compositors, printers, and binders. In all instances, important decisions are made regarding the flow of significant sums of money in and out of the firm.

On the lower rungs of the editorial hierarchy—the detail work—there are few men. The majority of manuscript and book editors are women. Copy editors, one step below manuscript editors, are almost exclusively women. One college acquisitions editor recalled how she quickly learned the difference between acquisitions and manuscript editors:

> On the first day I was there my supervisor told me there are two aspects of editorial work in publishing: the in-house editors, who never leave the house but work on the books themselves; and the acquisitions editors who are higher paid, the job is more interesting, and are only men. There was a wall-divider literally separating the men from the women, the acquisitions editors from the in-house editors. Women never got to go on the other side of the wall.

As intermediary-level professionals, women also deal with outsiders; but, with the recent and dramatic exceptions of female trade and mass-market paperback editors and subsidiary rights directors, this contact is not critical to the publisher's financial viability. Most women at the intermediary level are either in a supportive, nurturing role or in a customer-service, "greeting" role with people outside the firm. In the first case, women copy editors and manuscript editors communicate regularly with authors and continually negotiate the finer points of sentence, paragraph, or chapter; in contrast with the acquisitions editor, these are often collaborative efforts rather than conflict-ridden ones concerning contractual and financial terms. In the second case, the women in sales customer service and publicity-promotion departments often bear the brunt of tirades from irate retailers or frustrated authors. Orchestrating authors' tours and keeping in touch with book reviewers are essentially public relations functions; this is probably why publicists are known in some quarters as the "airline stewardesses" of the publishing industry.

If men tend to be in positions where they control relations with important figures outside the firm, women smooth and ease these relations with both outsiders and insiders. The positions held by women are ones that oversee the passage of a manuscript from editorial through production and sales. Copy editors are as closely involved in production details as they are in editorial matters. Managing editors, many of whom are women, officially oversee this process.

In trade houses, the people in publicity-advertising and subsidiary rights often unofficially provide feedback and information on the internal status and marketability of various books. Not only do women in these departments informally read and evaluate manuscripts prior to publication, but they also act as communication links among departments and people throughout the firm. According to the survey, the highest rates of daily contact with fellow employees are those in publicity-advertising, production, and subsidiary rights departments in trade publishing. As one subsidiary rights manager put it, "subsidiary rights has always been pivotal in a sense of depending to a very great extent on everything that goes on in other departments—publicity, production, advertising, sales, and so forth."

Women have made their greatest inroads in trade and mass-market paperback publishing. Here editorial acquisitions is no longer dominated by men. Actually, trade editorial was never totally inhospitable to female editors; for through the years a handful of women established excellent reputations in this area. What was a gradual rise in the number of women editors at both the junior and senior levels in the last decade has, within the last few years, become an upsurge. Nearly half of trade and mass-market paperback editors are women. Many leading trade houses now boast female executive editors and editors in chief. In the twelve New York-based mass-market paperback houses listed in the 1981 *Literary Market Place*, twenty-two men have the title of publisher, editor in chief, editorial director, or executive editor, and nineteen women have one of those titles.

The rise of women in trade and mass-market editorial is paralleled by their emergence as an important force in subsidiary rights. Subsidiary rights directors, in addition to informally reading manuscripts and passing along editorial opinions, are highly visible negotiators of reprint, book club, and other such sales subsidiary to the initial sale of book-publication rights by author to publisher. The income from such sales is essential to the survival of most hardcover houses. Subsidiary rights directors are also becoming more involved in the initial decision to publish. "Forty percent of my time is involved in publishing decisions," says one such director at a major house. Another leading director commented on the extensive nature of her decision making:

> When I was hired it was understood that I'd be involved not so much in administrative responsibilities, but in major decisions—which are in acquisitions. It isn't like deciding what color to make the jacket, it's do you *do* the book? It isn't that I have the right to say, "We must print 50,000 copies" but if I come in and say "The first reprinter who read it called up and said 'You've got $500,000 from us' " obviously they are going to say "Let's raise the first printing."

Women subsidiary rights directors working in tandem with women editors are a powerful combination in the primary editorial acquisition process—a significant departure from women's traditional peripheral status.

Even though women have made important inroads in trade and mass-market paperback publishing, principally in editorial positions and subsidiary rights, the executive ranks in college, trade, and mass-market paperback publishing remain off limits to all but a small minority of women. This is evident from the 1981 *Literary Market Place*. In the larger sample of 142 publishing houses from which the 21 firms in the survey were selected, there were a total of 666 executives (presidents, vice-presidents); 103, or 15 percent, were women. Women have been most successful in achieving top executive positions in small college, small trade, and large mass-market paperback firms. In each category, women constitute around 20 percent of the total number of executives.

While more women may have been entering the "executive suite" within the last five years, they are rarely doing so as presidents or as independent publishers. In the same sample of 142 houses, there were only 9 women presidents. Although this is a 50 percent increase over the previous year (1980), when there were only 6 women presidents, it should be emphasized that fewer than one tenth of all female executives are presidents and publishers. Small general trade publishers offer the most opportunity to women, as 7 of these 9 women are in this sector of publishing. One of the newest women in the presidential ranks left an executive position within an established house to start her own publishing company. At this writing, there are two women presidents at large adult trade or mass-market paperback houses.

These numbers are significant compared with those in other industries. Although it is estimated that women comprise only 1 percent of all top corporate managers, they fare somewhat better in service industries such as banking, retailing, and advertising.[22] Women have made significant strides of late in the heavily male-dominated communications industries of television and film. A 1980 *New York Times* article described the top women in the Hollywood movie studios, most of these women only recently assumed their positions. Although many of these women hold high-level and prestigious production positions, approximately two dozen are vice-presidents in a variety of areas.[23] The percentage of women executives in book publishing clearly exceeds the percentage of top women executives in the three major television networks. Of the one hundred listed members of the boards of directors and company officers of the three networks, only seven are women. Not one of the many network division presidents is a woman.[24]

CAREER PATHS—SEPARATE AND UNEQUAL

Although women may fare well in book publishing compared with women in other industries, the important question remains unanswered: given the many women employed in publishing, why are there not *more* at the top? Differences in social background and aspirations of the women and men in publishing are not the answer. According to the survey, women and men enter publishing with backgrounds that are close to identical. They come from white-collar and professional families; they are highly educated, many at élite private colleges; and nearly all are white. There are only slight differences in religion, place of birth, and college major; women are more often Jewish, born in the New York metropolitan area, and arts and letters majors, particularly English and English literature, in college. Men are more often Protestants, born outside the Eastern seaboard, and almost as likely to be social science as arts and letters majors in college. Even though this sample includes persons in all types of publishing, the findings bear a striking resemblance to the characteristic backgrounds of editors, as discussed in chapter 4.

Reasons for entering publishing are as similar for men and women as are their modes of entry. Only a small minority—10 percent—of the men and women in the survey always aspired to work in publishing. Such was the sentiment of one young woman who "wanted to become an editor when I graduated from college; I had no idea, really, what an editor did, but I wanted to become one." Most people enter publishing "accidentally." The following is a fairly typical account of how a successful editor in chief of a mass-market paperback house, now in her forties, fell into a career in publishing: She had been an English major at the University of Iowa, was married and raising two children in the mid-1950s with "no intention whatsoever of getting into publishing. Although I was antsy, the idea of work was alien." When her marriage dissolved, she began looking for work. A friend was a proofreader at Fawcett Books, "and since I'd had an English background, that seemed the only logical thing to get into." She started out in the editorial production department at Fawcett, became a copy editor, and eventually worked her way up within various houses to her present position.

Women and men find their first job in publishing through analogous, but not identical, means. Slightly more men were actually recruited by a publisher. Although uncommon today, in the past the larger college textbook houses sent recruiters to major campuses to hire young male graduates as college travelers. While more women obtained their first publishing job through agency or ad, more men used the direct approach of "knocking on doors." Just over one third of both women and men in the survey found their first job in publishing through a family member, a friend, or contacts made at a publishing program such as Radcliffe's Course in Publishing Procedures or the Denver Publishing Institute. Almost 90 percent of the men had male contacts or relatives who aided them, while two thirds of the women used female contacts and relatives.

Any similarity in the backgrounds and aspirations of men and women prior to their arrival in publishing disappears once they enter their first job. As Rosabeth Moss Kanter so well demonstrated, when one enters an organization, he or she is placed not only in a job, but in an "opportunity structure" that defines future job prospects.[25] Because women typically enter as secretaries and men as sales representatives, travelers, or editorial or other assistants, men and women have not had equal career opportunities. As discussed earlier, the secretary or assistant position is part of the secondary labor market in all types of publishing; career ladders upward are at best weakly defined and usually nonexistent. The absence of clearcut career opportunities and the low pay contribute to high turnover rates. Extraordinary effort and dedication, long hours and non-routine demonstrations of competence and ambition are required for one to jump out of this secretarial ghetto.

In contrast, men typically entered publishing in positions that promised, but did not necessarily guarantee, upward mobility. In college textbook publishing, career paths are the most formalized and the sex typing is most pronounced. While the dynamics of editorial mobility are discussed elsewhere, it is worth repeating that editorial career paths have, until recently, been separate and unequal. Women were automatically excluded from the ranks of acquisitions editors because they were never hired as travelers. The traveler position is the first rung on a formal career ladder leading upward not only to acquisitions editor but into sales management and administration.

Not until the late 1960s and 1970s were some women promoted to acquisitions editor. Without the prerequisite sales experience, many of these women found it difficult to muster the support and recommendations of the sales staff in their unusual move from in-house manuscript editing to acquisitions editor. At one large college text house, the women who did become acquisitions editors averaged twelve years along a four-job ladder, while the male editors averaged three years on a shorter two-job ladder. While these women started as secretaries, eventually became copy editors and manuscript or book editors before becoming acquisitions editors, the men who excelled in their first year of selling as college travelers were quickly promoted to acquisitions editor.

In contrast to the formalized and clearly sex-typed career paths in college text publishing, those leading to acquisitions editor in trade and mass-market publishing are not separate, although they are still unequal: that is, men and women travel similar routes but at different rates and with different experiences. The difficulties, as well as possibilities, of a woman choreographing a career in trade or mass-market paperback publishing are highlighted in the following career biography of a successful woman.

THE INGREDIENTS OF FEMALE CAREER SUCCESS

Almost all women in publishing start out the same—as secretaries—yet the journey and the destination of each are unique. This is not to say that women do not have certain career experiences in common. Women share specific patterns of career success that make their work experiences and career advancement qualitatively different from those of men. A detailed career history reflects this difference and illustrates the ingredients of female career success.

Like most women, this particular woman started as a secretary in the early 1960s but, unlike most, is now a vice-president, assistant publisher, and subsidiary rights director of a major New York trade house. With a degree in history from a midwestern college, she considered graduate school, married instead, and, with no relatives or contacts in publishing, applied for a job as an indexer at a large, diversified New York publishing firm. The personnel director referred her to another opening in the firm. She was hired as the personal secretary to the president.

Even though "publishing *per se* wasn't really something I'd thought about," she did find the job both interesting and challenging. The publishing house was forever undergoing management changes every two years or so, and "everybody there was working seven days a week all the time." She gave notice and, in her words,

> I was going to go to another publishing company, a smaller company, again in a kind of catch-all capacity working for the president. And when I went in to tell the man I worked for about this, he said "I won't let you do that because it's just going to be another dreary job like this one's been for you. Because you're very capable and you don't know enough to say 'no' when somebody says do something, you'll end up running the place but at a level where you'll have no impact." At that point, there was a vacancy in the subsidiary rights department. So he said, "This makes so much more sense. At least," this is the very crucial thing he said, "At least you'll be learning a very specific skill that you can use somewhere else. You're very well organized; you're management oriented; now learn something in an area that you can take somewhere else.". . . I was working very closely with him and we became good friends, and still are. But it's that kind of fluke; *it was only because it was somebody who was interested in me because I'd worked really hard for him, that he was concerned enough not to let me tear off and do something else.* And that's really where it all started. [Emphasis added]

In the period since then, her career has taken off. She acquired valuable experience as a subsidiary rights manager; and when her superior was lured to another house, she soon followed. After two more years in subsidiary rights, and due to her extensive involvement in editorial decisions, the president of the company asked her to take over the house's small specialized paperback line and transform it into a broader, more commercial subsidiary. She took on the job at considerable personal and emotional cost. As she said, "It was very exciting, and if you thrive on chaos and really get high on that—some people do, I don't—it's terrific. But I just found that it was a perpetual non-stop job where on your best day you were a little behind, and on your worst day, you thought it was last month." Following a period of extensive management reorganization, she "saw the handwriting on the wall about the direction things were going to go," and "since it was not what I wanted," she resigned. In the meantime, she had been talking with a woman about the possibility of taking her place after the latter was promoted to associate publisher. Two month before our interview in the

163

late 1970s, the subject of this account was offered and accepted her present position as vice-president, assistant publisher, and subsidiary rights director.

This success story not only demonstrates various facets of career mobility in publishing but also is testimony to the hardships and rewards of the day-to-day routine. For both women and men, a publishing career can be exciting, stimulating, and demanding. During the time that she was consumed with revamping the paperback line, she was chastised by a friend for "working between eighteen and twenty hours a day." She derived a great sense of accomplishment and vitality from her efforts; however, at the same time she often found herself "most mornings waking up at three o'clock," anxious and worried about forgetting to return a call or check out a contract clause.

One of us has written about "greedy institutions," organizations that require near total commitment of their members.[26] Publishing is a good example, as it is particularly demanding of the personal lives of women. According to the survey, nearly two thirds of the women are single, while just over half (55 percent) of the men are married. This disparity does not result from the predominance of women in the lower strata of secretarial and assistant jobs, for more men than women under the age of twenty-five are single. As the men in publishing progress in both age and career, they are increasingly likely to be married; whereas older women in publishing are only slightly more likely to be married than their younger female colleagues. Similarly, a minority of women (only 13 percent), but a majority of men (over 50 percent), have children. Single women often look with awe at the successful woman who manages to combine family and career. "Some of the best women in publishing have children," says one female editor, who is single. "And they are also the most driven."

The cost of being a woman in publishing is also financial. According to the survey, over half of the women in the three sectors of publishing (college text, general trade, and mass-market paperback) report salaries of less than $15,000 a year; just under a quarter of the men fall into this category. Thus, of the people making less than $15,000 a year in 1978, 80 percent were women. Of those making more than $27,000 annually, just over one third were women. Much, but not all, of the difference in average male and female salaries disappears according to particular level and type of job. Both male and female secretaries take home the same generally low salaries—$130 to $200 a week. At higher levels, however, some salary differences remain. In many cases, these differences result from overt sexism in the form of unequal pay for equal work. In other instances, these salary differences stem from the inequalities built into the occupational structure where, even though the actual work may differ little, women occupy the lower and lowest-paying positions within departments.

Despite these claims on one's time, energy, personal life, and pocket-book (if publishing is one's sole income), few women feel they have been the victims of outright discrimination. As one successful subsidiary rights director put it, "Discrimination in publishing rarely occurs personally—rather, it's only in terms of the way the whole industry is structured." Not only have men bypassed the lowest rung—secretary—but women have had more difficulty gaining access to and using organizational resources and people important in one's work and career. Many women editors, traditionally excluded from editors' luncheon clubs, organizations such as the Century Club, and other all-male gatherings, are at an obvious disadvantage in not being part of the "old boy" network.

The same male-dominated authority structure has created other work-related obstacles for women. Unlike many other businesses that are pervaded by an implicitly male managerial ethic, book publishers are characterized by a kind of paternalism at all levels. The successful assistant publisher just described always worked for men of strong, distinctive personality. She worked in one firm where all three of the editorial directors were women who reported directly to a domineering male president—an arrangement that prompted people to call them the "Charlie's Angels" of publishing. Yet "he was somebody who did take a certain amount of pleasure in seeing 'his girls' achieve something." In the opinion of this woman assistant publisher, such relationships, especially older men dealing with younger women, are inherently ambiguous. "They can let you get away with a lot if you are willing to let them have that feeling that ultimately they still have the power over you." Such relationships also breed suspicion among the office staff, about the motives and methods of the successful woman. At the very least, the female subordinate is accused of, or assumed to be, using ingratiating tactics with her male superior. The male colleague of a well-known subsidiary rights director once commented on her "great gift for getting along with all these maniacal personalities," and added, "Of course, having long eyelashes doesn't hurt."

The real key to this young assistant publisher's success, as she herself acknowledged, is the fact that she was fortunate to have a person—again a man who was her immediate boss—take an interest in her career and, in effect, sponsor or promote her to higher and better positions. In this case, he persuaded her not to take another secretarial job, but encouraged her to take a newly available subsidiary rights position where she could learn "specific skills" that she could use somewhere else. Daniel Levinson has written of the importance of mentors and sponsors in the seasons of one's life and in the stages of one's career. This mentoring relationship occurs most frequently in the work setting and is critical in the shaping of a career.[27] In publishing, as in other businesses and professions, it is not sufficient to be highly motivated, ambitious, committed to a career, or talented: one must be noticed and supported "by the right people."

While most people receive some form of help—advice or encouragement—in their careers, one does not obtain a sponsor or a mentor automatically. As a female associate editor in a trade house put it:

> It's important to work for *someone* who is interested in sharing information, passing responsibility, encouraging your progress, and has the *influence* to help you move upward. Lacking influence, your immediate boss can at least train you to prepare you for a move to another company in a better job.

Even though in the survey more women (almost three fourths) than men (nearly two thirds) reported receiving some form of help in their careers from certain people, it is likely that more men had sponsors who were influential.

The nature of sponsorship as an informal mechanism of recruitment into the middle and upper levels in book publishing, automatically favors the promotion of men over women. From the point of view of the mentor, sponsorship is a way of selecting suitable candidates for training, promotion, and advancement. In the absence of tangible measures of talent or ability, editorial directors, publishers, and sales managers probably favor, select, and therefore sponsor aspirants they perceive to be like themselves. This is particularly the case in the uncertain social environment of book publishing, an exceedingly personal business dependent on interpersonal ties and loyalties. In publishing, as in any profession or business, the informal sponsorship system results in the perpetuation of the social types in power—in this case, white upper–middle-class males.

It is not hard to understand the difficulties encountered by women, minorities, and others who, on the surface, do not fit "the mold." Lamenting what she calls the "homogenous, unidimensional staff" among editors, one young female assistant editor feels that "publishing as a career should be open to a wider range of people—as it is now, it is too homogenous a group." Another black male trade sales representative feels that "minorities and women are hired in various departments merely to satisfy some 'guideline,' but that their opportunities for advancement are severely impaired by the attitudes and actions of their white male superiors." He added that the "young, up-and-coming celebrities are always young, white males from the East or Midwest, never a woman, never a black or chicano."

Yet some women do acquire influential mentors, most often men, and have been sponsored into key editorial and subsidiary rights positions.* The built-in male bias of sponsorship acts as a kind of screen to facilitate the rapid advancement of outstanding and talented men to the top; it also makes possible the not-so-rapid movement of less-than-exceptional men to the middle levels. This same process virtually assures that the women who are sponsored and make it to both levels, top and middle, often surpass many of their male colleagues in drive, intellect, and experience. Says one trade editor: "To be a successful career women in what is still a man's industry . . . one has to work harder, be brighter, more articulate, and more consistently businesslike in demeanor than one's male counterparts." Consequently, the women who have been sponsored into editorial, subsidiary rights, and even a few marketing positions arrive more than qualified, having developed expertise and acquired well-grounded experience along the way.

By virture of such credentials, it has behooved the men who are publishers to promote their female talent. Being in the right place at the right time certainly helps. "If you have a man running the department," says a leading subsidiary rights manager, "the likelihood is you're going to have a woman in number two. And, if she's any good, she's going to eventually get the job." As Michael Korda, editor in chief of Simon & Schuster, wrote, "Publishers did not set out to promote women as a deliberate policy; they simply had no choice."[28]

There are no two better examples than in the careers of the women in mass-market paperback editorial and in subsidiary rights in trade publishing. Many women in mass-market paperback earned reputations as readers and editors of "women's fiction." This market for gothics and historical romances is strong and steady. "The women's reading public is so important," according to a woman paperback editor, "and few men can read well for it."[29] Similarly, Judith Rossner, author of *Looking for Mr. Goodbar* (Simon & Schuster, 1975), believed only a female editor was interested in her first novel "because she *felt* for the heroine and let herself be moved by the story."[30] These women had developed an expertise that fueled their careers when the paperback industry took off. "Boom—paperback publishing comes into its own," says an editor, "and there are many women who've been around and know their business."

* A majority of both men and women in the survey received career assistance from men. Eighty percent of the men had male "helpers," while nearly 60 percent of the women also had career "helpers" who were men. Female respondents in the survey tend to receive the same kind of assistance from their male and female "helpers"—support and encouragement and on-the-job training. In contrast, male respondents reported very different forms of assistance depending on whether their "helper" was male or female. From female "helpers," men receive support and encouragement; from male "helpers," men receive on-the-job training.

The changing structure of trade and mass-market paperback publishing in the 1960s gave rise to the unanticipated dominance of women in subsidiary rights. One director recalled the status of subsidiary rights "in the old days," when it was the "lowest job on the totem pole before there were auctions and new money; it was an accounting process and very dull." The details and handling of reprint sales and permissions was either done by an editor's assistant or by the women in a contracts and permissions department. What was "once a clerk's job" was radically transformed "when the money started coming in and women were in those jobs. And they knew all the people, who to talk to; they were there on the scene." As another subsidiary rights manager recalled:

> Until ten years ago, subsidiary rights wasn't even considered to be important.... Then when the paperback industry went "cuckoo" and when the heavy competition started for buying paperback rights, then there were all these women sitting in what had been considered not terribly important jobs—just another service department.... And all of sudden, they have an enormous amount of power.

By accident, women were in the right place—editorial assistants and contracts and permissions managers—at the right time, and publishers and editors had little choice but to promote them into higher positions.

It is for the same reasons that women are said to have more career opportunities in a smaller house. As one experienced senior trade editor said, "A smaller firm, if it is sound, gives more opportunity to generalize and more scope for individual progress." Not only are there advantages in the informality and the opportunity to learn in a smaller house, but there is more opportunity to be visible and "selected" by a sponsor simply because the pool of candidates is smaller. In a system where sponsorship is critical to career mobility, and where the nature of sponsorship tends to favor the recruitment and sponsorship of men, the smaller house offers more opportunities for a woman to become visible, to voice ambition, to demonstrate competence, and thus to acquire a sponsor who takes an active interest in furthering her career.

PRESENT TRENDS AND FUTURE POSSIBILITIES

Will book publishing become a "women's business" controlled by women and not just dominated by them in terms of sheer numbers? Much depends on the outcome of present trends. Women appear to be entering publishing at a greater rate than men. In 1978, a personnel director at a large well-known publishing house reported that between May 1976 and April 1977, two thirds of its applicants were women. Popular publishing courses, such as the Denver Publishing Institute's, report that around three quarters of their applicants and graduates are women.[31]

The sex typing of entry-level jobs, and their contingent career ladders, has ceased. Popular opinions about women's aptitudes, such as "women do not have editorial minds," are no longer publicly espoused. Yet it does not appear that women and men are equally taking advantage of this opportunity. Secretaries are still overwhelmingly female, although men are now entering at this level. Many starting sales positions are now filled by women who are thereby entering the pool from which future sales managers will be selected.

Clearly the presence of many women at the lower levels in all types of firm puts more pressure on the middle and upper levels to absorb them. Ambitious young women are increasingly reluctant to remain stuck in secretarial and other low-level positions that women in the past gladly accepted. "I was a secretary," says one woman who entered publishing in the mid-1950s. "Pre-women's lib. With a master's degree. For four years I worked, during which time I thought it was an honor to read books and write reports and put books together and write flap copy." Even with such sentiments, many women are still unwilling to trade the glamour of a job in publishing for slow career advancement.

The pressure is probably more acute in the middle and upper levels of publishing. As one female subsidiary rights director expressed it:

> Sooner or later everybody finds herself blocked at any major management level. A lot of women have very elegant titles now. But it's like the men have bought off their ambition with the titles. It's an interesting time right now. And there are a lot of fairly young women who are pushing at the bottom of the top. And what will happen in the next five years?

Whether women will break through what are now their mid-level ceiling occupations and assume top management positions remains to be seen. The relative youth of the men at the top in many houses poses an obstacle to the career advancement of ambitious women and the men just below them. This, in combination with the relative paucity of upper-middle and upper management positions and the vast pool of ambitious aspirants, suggests that the latter's wholesale promotion into the very top may be a long time in coming. Due to the dynamics of sponsorship, women will still face stiff competition from men.

It is likely that more women will move up, but only as the men at the top move up into a parent company or out of publishing altogether. As publishing houses grow larger and, simultaneously, as more publishing houses are bought by larger conglomerates, women may become directors of the "publishing subsidiaries," but they will continue reporting to male presidents or chairmen. As an executive, and perhaps as a member of a board of directors, the woman publisher will find herself, once again, operating in a predominately male environment where a great deal of club-manship exists. This was the experience of one female publisher who reported to an all-male board of directors of her parent company. She found them "not very kindly disposed to the notion of women as heads of the houses they own." As she explained, "It's still in New York, and in publishing we're all used to women achieving things and being treated with a certain amount of respect. That doesn't go on in the rest of the world."

By the same token, as trade publishing comes more and more to provide material for the larger, more powerful media/entertainment industry, women in key editorial and publisher positions will be increasingly negotiating and working with men in those largely male-dominated industries. A female vice-president in publishing points out the difficulties she encounters in these transactions:

> I've always felt it [discrimination] outside of publishing. I mean, when I was in the advertising world, or every time I've ever gone into a world that is not ours . . . or out into Hollywood which I have to do a lot. I can be traveling with my editor-in-chief and I can be saying the words and they're looking at him. That happens all the time in Hollywood.

This is not to say that women do not continue to encounter great obstacles and male prejudices within publishing. Because women executives at the top are still in the minority, interaction with male colleagues is often fraught with difficulty. A woman executive and co-publisher explained:

> It is a continuing struggle to be taken seriously. . . . One has to establish *bona fides* daily. . . . another problem is the lack of ease in staking out responsibility and in finding a voice that is listened to, but doesn't grate. The line between whispering your ideas and intimidating men is finer than you would imagine.

If more women gain entry to the top levels, the extent to which women will be doing business with women would exceed present levels, which are already significant. As it is now, the following scenario is not rare: a female author represented by a female literary agent submits a manuscript to an editor who is a woman and who, in turn, seeks publishing approval from her editor in chief, who also is a woman. The paperback subsidiary rights subsequently would be sold to a female mass-market paperback editor. In both firms, the book would be promoted, advertised, and publicized by women. Men in sales management would oversee sales and distribution, but the odds are that a woman would buy the book, especially if it were a historical or a modern romance.

According to many women, there are decided advantages in dealing and negotiating with other women. Since gender is taken for granted, sex does not interfere with the relationship. As one woman publisher put it, "Women are in publishing because for the most part they're very serious women and not just working for a lark." Such mutual respect makes for direct and forthright encounters, often devoid of "a lot of maneuvering."

While the qualitative nature of women negotiating with women may be open to debate, the fact of these continuing relationships—an emergent and increasingly important network of sorts—is not. Barbara Bannon, executive editor of *Publishers Weekly*, recently commented that "women are networking more" and helping other women advance to the top faster.[32] This women's network functions not only as a mutual support system but also to relay important job-, work-, and career-related information to women in many quarters.

The pervasiveness and strength of a women's network would not counter the forces already affecting the status and the future of the women in subsidiary rights. Since subsidiary rights *is* a profit center, will more men move in and take over? Or will subsidiary rights fall from power as quickly, and unexpectedly, as it moved to center stage?

At least for the short term, it appears that women will continue to dominate subsidiary rights. In some circles, it is widely held that men will not be drawn to subsidiary rights because of the low salaries. As one leading subsidiary rights director put it, "The middle-level executive jobs women would take for salaries that men wouldn't consider—especially in subsidiary rights." Some subsidiary rights managers in the survey reported salaries of less than $20,000 annually. One director of subsidiary rights disclosed a salary just under $30,000 a year; her male colleague in sales management received over $40,000 annually.

Although the number of men in subsidiary rights may be increasing slightly, the supply of female candidates still far exceeds that of male ones. In looking for a replacement for her former position of subsidiary rights director, a newly promoted vice-president conducted a thorough talent search. "I could find five possible people—all young women. And there was not a man to be seen. Nobody. In terms of established people, the men just didn't measure up. They didn't come close."

It is more difficult to assess how changes in the industry will affect subsidiary rights sales. It is perhaps significant that by the 1960s, just as women became a dominant force in subsidiary rights, the traditional control that hardcover publishers exercised over these rights was being eroded.[33] As literary agents become more successful in retaining subsidiary rights to their authors' books, subsidiary rights managers will be left with less to sell. Similarly, if mass-market paperback publishers acquire *all* the rights to books, including first-time publication, they will be shopping for a hardcover trade publisher, rather than the reverse. Many mass-market paperback houses have created their own hardcover trade imprints. Further inroads into the power of subsidiary rights occur when a trade house, in conjunction with its own mass-market paperback line, acquires and publishes books. Stripped of major sources of revenue, especially paperback reprint rights, subsidiary rights managers will perhaps return to "filing contracts and processing permissions," in the words of a subsidiary rights director.

Changes in the industry's structure affect changes *within* publishing firms which may reduce the status of women even as they assume top editorial positions. As publishers scramble to stay profitable, and as the financial risks and stakes become greater, financial and budgetary considerations increase the power of sales, marketing, and finance departments at the expense of editorial departments. In college textbook publishing, for example, the acquisitions editor may become less autonomous, more specialized, and more circumscribed by "management objectives"; the acquisitions editor may become subject to more strict control and tighter supervision. Many trade houses, infused with a new "managerial ethic" are introducing new criteria of editorial "financial accountability," also known as "performance standards." Such measures range from computer-based profitability formulas intended to calculate projected profit-loss figures for given books, to increased market research expenditures, to the hiring of business and financial managers to quantify editors' "track records."

With such changes, editorial acquisitions may become yet another female ghetto. Bernice Hoffman, former editor at McGraw-Hill, explained in a 1974 interview the connections between such changes in publishing and the status of women:

> Committee choices are based on budget considerations largely, which probably did not happen before. It raises the question of whether editors have as much power as they once did, whether their power is more circumscribed and

the whole question of who controls what editors want to do. The minute any jobs are open to women and minorities, you think maybe the nature of the jobs has changed.[34]

If these trends continue unabated, there may be associated changes in the traditional career ladders leading to the top. Finance and legal people, usually men, from the parent company may with more frequency be introduced into top publishing management positions. Or, upper management may be instead recruited directly through in-house sales, marketing, or finance departments, thus bypassing editorial altogether. This would simply be an outcome of a long-standing conflict between a managerial ideology dependent on financial and legal controls and a professional ideology rooted in the traditional craft-based lore infusing the publishing of books. Since women are joining the executive ranks with extensive editorial backgrounds, and men are entering as controllers, lawyers, and accountants, this conflict is also gender-based. The fact that women *are* doing business with figures, negotiating important financial deals and enjoying it, does not mitigate the extent of this conflict. The reason is that the breadth of publishing experience acquired by women en route to the top may challenge the authority of male finance and legal managers who, in contrast, enter with little direct publishing experience. In any case, trade, college text, and mass-market editorial acquisitions may well become a low-ceiling, low-power enclave much like children's book editorial or publicity-promotion-advertising departments.

CONCLUSION

Over the years, changes in the nature and structure of publishing have resulted in occupational changes, most of which have been conducive to the increased employment of women. Yet, with few exceptions, women have remained at the bottom of the occupational hierarchy, dominating secretarial and assistant positions, service and staff departments such as publicity and advertising, and less prestigious departments such as children's books. Compared with other industries, however, women have been modestly successful in achieving middle, and even some top, executive positions. Publishing may truly become a women's business in that women will be doing business with women, generating revenue, and making publishing policy. This may occur just as publishing is increasingly controlled by outside interests. These interests may not only homogenize the product—namely, books—but also bureaucratize and standardize the organization—namely, occupations. Women may be disenfranchised even as they move to the top.

The woman who desires more autonomy and power may have to follow the lead of many women who have left successful careers in publishing to become literary agents. Becoming independent publishers is another option, as yet not greatly utilized. If women continue to dominate subsidiary rights and also become publishers and literary agents, they will become an even more powerful force in publishing, leaving behind the days when women were influential in unseen and unsung ways.

Chapter 7

Craft and Corporation: The Organization of Publishing Houses

IN MOST INDUSTRIES, cottage features and modern bureaucratic and corporate features appear in historical sequence; they belong to distinctly different historical periods. But in book publishing, cottage and corporate features exist side by side, although not always in harmony. In today's publishing world we have struggling two- and three-person firms alongside huge conglomerate enterprises with many subsidiaries involved in books, newspapers, films, and cable television. Within the publishing subsidiary itself there may be college text, scholarly monograph, and hardcover trade divisions. For example, McGraw-Hill has both trade and text divisions as well as scholarly and reference book divisions. McGraw-Hill is also a diversified, transnational "information" corporation involved in many activities—such as *Business Week* magazine, Standard and Poor's credit ratings, and economic forecasting—that are remote from book publishing. Random House has a trade division, both school and college text divisions, and a juvenile book division. Under the Random House um-

brella, there are a number of other publishing imprints and houses, including Vintage Books, the Modern Library, Ballantine Books, Pantheon
Books, and Alfred A. Knopf, Inc. Random House, Inc., is itself a subsidiary of Newhouse Newspapers which purchased Random House from
RCA, Inc., for $65,000,000 to $70,000,000 in 1980. Random House also distributes the publications of a number of very small publishing firms.

The continued survival of both cottage and corporate features makes it
impossible to point to a particular period in the industry's history and de-
finitively state that then publishing underwent a profound transformation.
Some houses have changed significantly and look more like other modern
corporations than like nineteenth-century publishers. Yet the economics of
book publishing being what it is, small houses continue to survive, and
even proliferate. However, we can trace some changes, in the structure of
publishing organizations and in the philosophy of publishing practices,
that illustrate the transition from craft to modern corporation that many of
today's firms have undergone.

A review of the industry published in 1913 noted that the tendency of
general trade publishers to diversify into textbook and subscription publishing was becoming more pronounced. The author, George P. Brett,
president of Macmillan, stated:

> Among the larger publishers of the country, that is, those who carry on the
> business of book-publishing in its original meaning, and as it is still under-
> stood by the general public, there now remain only a few who confine their
> publications to books in general literature.[1]

Brett was describing the origins of the multi-divisional publishing firm that
is now typical of almost all houses of any size. As houses moved from general publishing to several divisions, the number of customers and the range
of "products" increased. People at the top of a publishing house found
themselves less concerned with day-to-day activities and more involved in
developing long-range plans, coordinating and reconciling the activities of
various departments. Since close supervision of routine work is no longer
possible in multi-divisional houses, publishers began evaluating their departments on the basis of performance criteria. The shift from a simply organized house that published for one market to a more complex firm that
published for several markets and encountered a variety of environmental
demands can be viewed as a key stage in the transformation of publishing
from a cottage business or occupation to a corporate enterprise.

However, this change primarily affected people in top management
positions. The impact on editors was probably not immediate, and change

in their role occurred gradually. In the 1948 Bowker Memorial Lecture,* Ken McCormick, then editor in chief of Doubleday's trade department, described the emerging new responsibilities of editors:

> Maxwell Perkins took the position that an editor had no interest in anything but the book itself; that his responsibility lay solely with the author and that once he had discharged that responsibility his part of the work ceased. For the generation to which he belonged he was right; but the fact remains that publishing is not that simple today. Editors must have some business sense, which should be directed to the benefit of the author and publisher alike. . . . The publisher now concerns himself more than ever before with business management. . . . The most important change in an editor's job today is that he has slowly acquired the publisher's responsibility.[2]

William Miller in his excellent survey of the book industry, published in 1949, reported that, "As more American houses become big and bureaucratized . . . financial terms tend to be the only ones different departments are likely to retain in common."[3] He went on to say that finance "becomes the basic language of the firm." This is because only in financial terms can a publisher measure the performance of a department selling textbooks against that of a department selling children's books, and thus estimate the contributions each makes to the overall enterprise. Miller stated that "in big companies, company-wide policy can only be made in [financial] language, and values that cannot adequately be discussed in it tend to atrophy and their influence to diminish."[4]

This change in perspective means that the performance of an editor, "as well as the performance of his authors, come increasingly to be judged by their financial showing." Miller argued that, especially in periods of narrow profit margins, an editor's doubt about the financial merits of a book or an author may prompt him to abandon both. Simultaneously, "an editor is less likely to compromise his firm and his job in the opposite way: by passing over reasonably sure financial coups." This situation leads editors to be particularly tempted by manuscripts offered by a "friendly movie company or magazine, or a neighborly book club or reprinter, or a newfangled market expert."[5]

Another significant step in the transformation of book publishing occurred when various firms became public stock companies. Some firms chose this route to raise capital for expansion. The owners of other houses saw this move as a means of protecting their interests. In the late 1950s,

* The Richard Rogers Bowker Memorial Lectures, in remembrance of the former owner and editor of *Publishers Weekly*, have been given annually since 1938 at the New York Public Library by leading publishers, editors, and authors, and are published by the library.

Donald Klopfer and Bennett Cerf, the founders of Random House, were fretting about problems of inheritance taxes in the event one of them died. They were also concerned that if the government set the value of their business too high, the survivor could not afford to buy the other half. These worries led Klopfer and Cerf to consider a public stock issue to establish the market value of their house. On 2 October 1959, 30 percent of Random House stock was sold to the public. In his autobiography, Cerf recalled, "this marked a big change":

> . . . the minute you go public, outsiders own some of your stock and you've got to make periodic reports to them. You owe your investors dividends and profits. Instead of working for yourself and doing what you damn please, willing to risk a loss on something you want to do, if you're any kind of honest man, you feel a real responsibility to your stockholders.[6]

Random House went public at the outset of a period of wild speculation in publishing stocks. The prices of these "unseasoned stocks" escalated "without rhyme or reason." Cerf stated that from the time of the stock offer on, "we were publishing with one eye and watching our stock with the other."[7]

After going public, Cerf and Klopfer discovered that, although they felt they had deliberately passed up real wealth by going into the publishing business, suddenly they were rich in spite of themselves. During the 1960s, Cerf's attention focused much more closely on expansion and profits. He merged Random House with Alfred Knopf and acquired Pantheon Books, assuring both firms that they would remain entirely independent in their editorial decisions. Cerf, in his autobiography, expressed admiration for Knopf's excellent music books and distinguished South American authors but noted that "very few of them ever showed a profit." He then quipped that "the books that Alfred is most ashamed of are the ones that have made him the most money."[8]

The next step in Random House's evolution was another key phase. In the 1960s many publishing companies merged with other publishing houses, a common practice in publishing history. However, the entry of outside interests into publishing, which was widely prevalent in the 1960s, did not have historical precedent. In 1957, Cerf discussed a merger with another publishing house that, to his delight, placed a value of $2,000,000 on Random House. Cerf later discussed a merger with Holt, Rinehart and with Time-Life, before settling with RCA, Inc., in late 1965 for $40,000,-000. It is doubtful that the real value of Random House increased twentyfold in just seven years; however, Cerf's expectations certainly did. Cerf had RCA agree in writing not to interfere with what Random House published.

The transformation of many publishing houses from a craft occupation to a corporate enterprise involves several major changes. Initially, a publishing house may expand and operate several distinct divisions. The next phase involves establishing financial accountability and performance goals for the firm's editors. Then a firm may go public in order to raise capital; at this point the interests of outsiders become a significant consideration. Finally, a firm may acquire several other publishing houses, or it may itself be bought by a larger firm. Not every publishing house has gone through each of these phases; nor have those that have necessarily followed this exact sequence. It is important, however, to recognize these various steps as distinct. Both popular attention and criticism of book publishing has focused almost exclusively on the merger phase. This is, by all means, an important step, at least symbolically. However, fundamental changes in organizational policies and practices may be more affected by the three other phases. Here again Random House is a good example: Cerf went to great lengths to ensure that it maintained editorial independence after its merger with RCA. Of course, not all merged firms retain this freedom, and some that have independence promised find that agreements can be reneged.

In our interviews and field work, we initially paid a great deal of attention to the question of what type of influence a parent company exerted over the activities of the publishing houses it owned. We found that the effects of outside ownership are often subtle and not overt. Editors have opinions about the merits of being owned or being independent, but these opinions are not necessarily objective analyses. In fact, employees of dependent houses may be biased. We spoke with personnel at a variety of levels who expressed satisfaction with the improved financial benefits that accompanied corporate ownership. For decades, publishing had been a quiet and neglected business. Now, as a result of mergers, trade publishing is a "glamour" industry, an integral part of the entertainment business. Salaries have increased in an industry that has long been known as one where people were underpaid and labored for "psychic" income. Conglomerate ownership has effected not only higher salaries but better health and retirement benefits as well. We will see that financial strength is one very positive factor associated with conglomerate ownership. Moreover, being part of a media conglomerate has greatly raised the possibility of corporate mobility and expanded job opportunities for many employees.

Despite the fact that editors are not likely to be objective judges, any allegations about the effect of ownership of publishing houses cannot be evaluated without taking into account editors' opinions. In our interviews with editors, fifty-eight of them were willing to discuss in detail the consequences of ownership. A slightly higher percentage of college text editors worked for independent houses than did trade editors. University press editors, whom we group with scholarly and monograph editors, are in a special situation. In one sense they are a part of another organization—the university. The university often provides space, helps pay for overhead costs, and may set salary and budgetary limits. There are also university review committees that approve books for publication. Yet many editors told us they regarded university presses as highly independent. The issue seems to be which exerts stronger control: a parent organization or the marketplace? Since university presses are not under great pressure to make money, many editors view them as being autonomous. In the discussion that follows, we exclude university press editors and concentrate on editors whom we can more readily assign to an independent or a dependent status. However, the reader should keep in mind the distinction between control by the demands of the impersonal market in which a house competes, and control stemming from the demands of a parent organization.

There were thirty-three editors who worked for houses that were part of other organizations or corporations. When we asked them about the advantages of being one part of a larger unit, we received three general answers. The availability of capital was far and away the most often mentioned advantage accounting for about half of both their first and their second responses. Every editor mentioned capital at least once. The services available from a large corporation and the technical expertise that various units of the corporation could offer were the second most frequently mentioned asset associated with corporate ownership. Financial and accounting expertise were commonly mentioned as the type of technical support that larger corporations could readily offer. The third most frequent response was financial security and personal benefits, both of which were said to be better than those offered by independent publishing houses.

The most surprising response to our query about the disadvantages of dependent status was "None" or "Nothing." Eleven of the thirty-three editors specifically said that there are no disadvantages to being "dependent." As to the disadvantages actually cited, thirteen editors said that they felt that their corporate overseers do not understand book publishing. A second, and perhaps related, concern cited by nine editors as a disadvantage was that the parent corporation is too concerned with the "bottom line."

We probed in detail to determine whether editors encounter corporate censorship. Not a single editor could recall an example of parent-company censorship. Several editors cited books they had published that were in fact critical of the parent company. The parent company, they felt, was concerned not about what a book said, but about how much money it could make. Ultimately, then, if there is any censorship, it concerns profitability. Books that are not profitable, no matter what their subject, are not viewed favorably.

It may make more sense to speak about the disadvantages of independence, since twenty of the twenty-five editors in independent houses mentioned either lack of money or financial security as negative aspects of "going it alone." Other editors noted that their independent firms lacked technical expertise commonly associated with corporate ownership. One editor in chief of a formerly independent monograph house remarked, "Our parent company provides us with an unlimited line of grade A credit, excellent accounting services, and cheaper warehousing. So far they haven't interfered—what more could we ask?" The general pattern of responses from editors in independent houses suggests that, in comparison with dependent houses, they perceive themselves to be at a competitive disadvantage in regard to both financial security and management services. Not surprisingly, the main advantage of independence, cited by eighteen editors, was having few constraints. Fifteen of the twenty-five editors said being independent enabled them to follow their own tastes. Less red tape and less pressure were also frequently mentioned as advantages.

In our interviews and field work, we found that when pressure from a parent company was exerted, it was felt most directly by editors in chief and publishers. At a scholarly house we studied, the editor in chief acted "as a screen to shield his editors from the influence of X [the parent corporation]." He did not want his editors affected by corporate policies; he felt they were his concern. He was very successful at this, as most of the editorial staff reported they felt no pressures from top corporate management. There are other cases, however, where executives or editors in chief are less successful at protecting their editors from pressures to increase sales. A parent company may gradually replace or add top executives until a point is reached where the editor in chief no longer feels comfortable working at the company. In June 1981 the editor in chief at Bantam Books, Rollene Saal, found herself in such a situation. The post of publisher at Bantam was given to the marketing director. A few years earlier, when Oscar Dystel stepped down as chairman, his position as chief operating officer was filled by Alberto Vitale who had previously been with Fiat, which through ownership by the Agnelli family, was the previous owner of Bantam. The new executive group at Bantam had become heavily sales-

and marketing-oriented. Saal decided to leave Bantam because it had become a company "run by people with a different kind of background," and she felt that she was going to "lose some of her prerogatives"—ones that she regarded as "essential to an editor in chief."[9] At almost the same time, John J. Geoghegan resigned as chairman of Coward, McCann & Geoghegan after twenty-one years with the firm. He charged that the parent company, MCA, and their subsidiary the Putnam Publishing Group had allowed "finance and administration guys [to tell] editors what kind of marketing will be done."[10]

The majority of editors in non-executive positions who belong to the corporate world reported that they were not strongly affected by it. Many of the editors who stated that ownership has an impact on their work felt that it was a positive influence. For example, parent corporations provided publishing subsidiaries with financial security that enabled the latter to make long-term strategic plans. However, the corporate proclivity for planning was not always satisfied by publishing subsidiaries. There are aspects of book publishing that are not easily amenable to strategic planning. Not only is it hard to predict in advance which will be successful books by authors who are not well known; it is difficult to plan exactly when a successful author will deliver his or her next manuscript. The vagaries of public taste are not always ascertainable in advance, and the productivity of creative individuals can be equally unpredictable.

One area about which critics have expressed concern with corporate ownership is the matter of inside trading. When a film company and a hardcover publisher are owned by the same parent corporation, does the film company get an advance look at a promising manuscript? None of our editors mentioned this happening; however, a *Publishers Weekly* article on Hollywood and book publishing suggests that the day may not be far off when "sneak preview arrangements are built into merger agreements."[11] Questions have also been raised about whether hardcover publishers favor their paperback or book club corporate siblings in subsidiary rights deals. Do they sell to them "on the cheap" as it were, and deny the author a competitive market price? Our data show that best-selling hardcover books *are* auctioned off to the highest-bidding book clubs and paperback publishers with no deference to conglomerate brethren. A former president of Harper & Row—a firm that does not own a mass-market paperback line or a book club—maintains that such "sweetheart" deals would be far too obvious, and that everyone in the industry would complain. The power of agents and attorneys is another strong deterrent to selling "on the cheap."

Nevertheless, conglomerates possess the option of engaging in tactics such as inside dealing—or "reciprocity agreements," as they are known in economics—and cross-subsidization. These tactics are not open to non-conglomerate firms. Several editors at independent hardcover trade houses suggested to us that there may be subtle forms of reciprocity or favoritism. "Of course, best sellers go to the highest bidder. We have no problem there," said one editor, "but take a look at the smaller books, the respectable works that don't have mass market potential written all over them. I have a hell of a time selling the rights to them, but my competitors who have affiliated paperback lines and book clubs seem to be doing just fine." Cross-subsidization is another option open to conglomerates. By operating in a number of markets, the conglomerate can use profits in some markets to subsidize losses in other markets. If the subsidized markets are small in comparison with the overall operations of the company, the impact on profitability can be minimal. Subsidization can pay for price cuts or for a large advertising campaign that can establish a subsidiary's position in a particular market. The advantages of conglomerate ownership in this case are summarized by the economist Corwin Edwards: a conglomerate "can absorb losses that would consume the entire capital of a smaller rival. . . . The big company can outbid, outspend, or outlose the small one."[12]

Even though many editors tended to underplay the consequences of outside ownership, because being owned has had little direct effect on their work, there are subtle but nevertheless real ways in which outside ownership effects editorial behavior. First, we must recognize that few top managers bark out orders all the time.[13] Instead, they define the limits of appropriate and acceptable behavior. They set priorities that unobtrusively shape behavior. Many organizational theorists have pointed out that "the vast proportion of the activity in organizations goes on without personal directives and supervision—and even without written rules."[14] In complex organizations, superiors have the power and the tools to control the premises on which decisions are made. The control of the premises of decision making sets up expectations about what should and should not be done. When premises are effectively controlled, subordinates voluntarily restrict their activities to those projects on which they are encouraged to work.

Any complex organization faces the problem of control. Organizations where work is routine can rely on hierarchy, standardization, and technology. In the case of the assembly line, the technology itself controls the work process. In most organizations, a bureaucratic division of labor works well as a common control device. However, when work is non-routine—as in publishing, with its many, unique products—direct controls are not as feasible. Work cannot be standardized or governed by rules; therefore, unobtrusive controls become much more important. This

is true both in independently owned companies and in corporate subsidiaries. However, what may distinguish independent from dependent
houses is the nature of the premises that guide editorial decision making.
For example, parent-company pressure to increase growth, to go after big-
volume best sellers, and to maintain a steady flow of commercially successful products does affect the types of books that get published. No one
has to tell editors which books to select; but when the premise is well established that sales volume and subsidiary rights sales are the overriding
concerns, editors are encouraged to pursue authors with successful track
records whose work can be "exploited" in a variety of media formats.

Certainly not every corporate-owned publishing house follows the
same policies. Some parent companies operate with a "hands off" policy
and assess a subsidiary's performance by evaluating, on an annual basis,
sales, profits, or return on investment. Other parent companies may go so
far as to get involved in such minor issues as job promotions or the advertising campaign for a particular book. Based on the limited sample of
houses in which we did field work, we noticed more daily interference
when the parent company was a book publisher rather than an unrelated
business. The common element in all outside ownership of book publishing is money and the greater access that subsidiaries have to it. As we suggested in chapter 2, the entry of outside firms into publishing has exacerbated the industry's two-tier structure. Greater sums of money now go to
employees, to best-selling authors, and to advertising campaigns. Conglomerate capital allows some hardcover houses to pay huge sums for
books by popular authors; and, in turn, conglomerate money enables paperback houses to pay millions for the paperback rights to these same
books.

The entrance of outside interests into book publishing has drastically
raised the stakes and the costs of doing business. Thus, one merger can
beget other mergers, as independent houses respond defensively to competition with conglomerate-owned houses that can avail themselves of their
parent company's "deep pockets." Mergers can thus become contagious, as
less powerful firms feel they must merge with outsiders, lest they be
"snowed under" by the superior resources of their conglomerate rivals.[15]

In general we found that outside ownership has strong indirect effects
on the operation of publishing subsidiaries. Direct, daily interference or
supervision is infrequent. The setting of premises for what is permissible
and what is not is a powerful, but not necessarily overt, influence. In addition, the entry of outside interests can have an impact on competing independent houses which must compete with rival houses with greater access
to money and resources. This is perhaps the most profound effect of merg-

ers and outside ownership; competition for "big" books heats up, and the ante required to play the game is raised. Thus, even editors in independent houses may feel pressures similar to those of editors in non-independent houses.

THE INTERNAL ORGANIZATION OF HOUSES

For the most part, what directly affects an editor's daily routine is not corporate ownership or being one division of a large multi-divisional publishing house. Instead, on a day-to-day basis, editorial behavior is most strongly influenced by the editorial policies of the house and the relationship among departments and personnel *within* the publishing house or division. These relationships are frequent sources of conflict: a considerable amount of "office politics" stems from the power struggles among departments.

The design of an organization is one of management's key decisions. An organization's structure is its skeleton, its basic building block. The structure of an organization coordinates individuals and departments for the maximum control and efficiency to fulfill the needs of a particular house and to allow it to adapt over time to changing circumstances. The key structural decisions are how to allocate tasks and how to group activities. There are a number of different bases for grouping the activities of individuals. One can group work activities by the means used to produce products and services. For example, departments can be set up on the basis of business function—production, marketing, finance, sales, and so on. This is a common divison of labor. Other means are the knowledge or skills required to do a particular task. Another way to organize work is by the ends involved—the characteristics of the markets served by an organization. For example, work can be divided up on the basis of product lines, geographic location, or clients served.

Any organized human activity gives rise to two basic and opposing demands: the division of work into a number of distinct tasks that must be performed; and the coordination of these diverse tasks to accomplish the overall mission. There are significant benefits to be realized from a formal division of labor: common supervision is established under a manager who is in charge; the linking of managers creates a formal system of authority; a department shares common resources and tries to achieve common stan-

185

dards of performance; decision rules and organizational routines are established, and work proceeds in an orderly fashion. Each department or unit can thus give particular attention to its special problems.

At the same time, however, that a division of labor into departments encourages coordination *within* a department and creates a chain of command, it can create problems of coordination *among* departments. Members of a department may band together and treat others as outsiders. Departments can become isolated from each other; they develop their own goals, style, language, and time perspectives. A production department may want to produce beautiful, well-made books, while other departments may be concerned with cutting costs or getting books out quickly.

Publishing houses can be organized in a variety of ways and to different degrees of formality. Typically, at the very least, there is a department of which editors are the members, usually called the editorial department, and a production department. The latter is in charge of seeing that manuscripts are turned into printed and bound books. All of the actual production work is almost always contracted out to printers and binders. Preparing the manuscript for the printer is usually done by copy editors, who may be free-lance outsiders or members of the production or the editorial departments. Artwork, layout, typography, and other aspects of a book's contents or appearance are also often handled by the production department. A house may also have a promotion department concerned with advertising books and getting reviewers and the public to notice them. This department is different from the sales department which is devoted to selling and distributing books. There may be a financial department in charge of accounting and financial control. Depending on the formal chain of authority, all the departments are overseen either by the editor in chief, the president, or the publisher. In larger houses, there may be several very large general divisions—an editorial group, a sales group, and a financial group. An editor in chief is in charge of the editorial group, while other executives are in charge of the other major divisions. All of these executives report to the publisher. Sometimes publisher and editor in chief are one and the same person holding different titles, but the functions are separate. A large multi-divisional publishing company may have a college division, a grade school division, an adult trade division, and so on, each with its own internal departmental arrangements.

Many steps in the publishing process may be delegated to persons or firms outside of the house. A few examples from our interviews illustrate the degree to which publishing houses rely on outsiders. Of the editors we interviewed, 85 percent said that the copy and line editing is at least sometimes sent out to free lancers: that is, the actual manuscript is entrusted to outsiders to be put into final shape for the printer, sometimes even to be revised. And 80 percent of the editors reported that artwork is also sent out. College editors were most likely to report using outside artists. Jacket design is done outside of the house 40 percent of the time, according to our editors—a practice most typical of trade houses.

In chapter 5 we described a textbook house that had attempted to develop a formal list of tasks and responsibilities associated with each job. We also mentioned houses where responsibilities were not clearly defined, where everything seemed "up for grabs." A more detailed look at the formal structure of the textbook house and a brief picture of the informal format of both a trade and a scholarly house illustrate the continuum along which publishing houses may be organized.

The college textbook division that we studied is one of several major units within one of the eight groups in the parent corporation. The organization of the textbook division is standard; the various stages of the publishing process, from acquisition to sales, are each set up as separate departments. The management of each department is the responsibility of the department head. Thus the editor in chief supervises all acquisitions editors whose duties are divided by subject area; the managing editor coordinates the work of manuscript and copy editors; the director of production oversees the production and design staff and keeps tabs on the art manager who is responsible for the art editing staff; the director of promotion and publicity supervises copywriters and publicists; and the sales force reports to four regional sales managers, who in turn report to the general sales manager. In addition, there are a business and a personnel manager. There is also a separate West Coast office.

The division employs approximately two hundred people. Each department has several levels of hierarchy. At the top of the departmental totem pole are the department heads. The next level is the senior staff, which includes senior editors, production managers, and regional sales managers. They are followed by the junior staff—assistant editors, sales force, designers, and so on. Then come the assistants in each department, and on the bottom are the secretaries. The department heads report to the deputy director who answers to the director of the department. The latter is an officer of the corporation.

In sum, it is a tight ship with clear-cut lines of authority and responsibility. As the managing editor commented, "I've never worked at a place that was so well organized. In fact, at times the place gets downright boring." Each department's activities are thoroughly routine. Superiors and managers keep a close eye on their subordinates through frequent contact and weekly activity reports. This carefully organized division is not devoid of conflict or idiosyncratic arrangements, both of which we will discuss in more detail. For now, we should also note that exceptions to the chain of command and formal task assignments are not uncommon.

Editors sometimes poach on other editors' subject matter, particularly if they happen to like working with authors from a particular university. One senior editor said, "I refuse to be pigeon-holed. If I think of it first, I'm going to develop it." Occasionally a copy editor is permitted to sign up a book. Sometimes acquisitions editors copy edit. One editor demanded to be allowed to write copy for advertising and the catalogue for her books, even though that is clearly the job of the publicity and promotion department. There were other examples of work that accidentally "fell into someone's lap" even though it was not formally assigned to that person.

However, in contrast to other houses we studied, the textbook house is a model of order and well-established routines. At a small prestigious scholarly house, responsibilities are never clearly defined, and new employees have a hard time learning what they should and should not be doing. This firm is a subsidiary of a parent company. It relies on the parent company's sales force. On a daily basis it is largely autonomous, but the parent company keeps close tabs on the subsidiary's financial performance. The house has between thirty and forty employees and is loosely organized into two departments, editorial and production; other key functions, such as sales, design, and subsidiary rights, are handled by single individuals, each of whom is assisted by several young employees.

There are few, if any, formal assignments or specifications of duties. Who does what varies enormously from book to book. If an editor is particularly enthusiastic about a book, he or she may do the copy editing, work with a free-lance artist on the jacket design, write catalogue and jacket copy, send out page proofs to reviewers and people thought to be influential, discuss subsidiary sales with paperback houses and magazines, and ride herd over the commission salesmen and the parent company's sales force to make sure they get behind the book. In other cases, the editor will sign a book, do minimal copy editing, and pass the manuscript on to another staff member. The sales manager, for example, might then take up the book's cause, oversee it as it moves through the house, and promote it to the world at large. Responsibilities are not fixed but are constantly changing; and somehow work gets done, and respectable books are published.

We observed similar informal arrangements at a small well-known trade house. Here, too, responsibility shifts on a book-by-book basis. But there is an added element of chaos—or creativity, if you will. Some employees do not work out of the New York office. One editor lives in a cabin in Vermont; another peripatetic editor is based in London and Paris. Sometimes copy editing and design are done in house; on other occasions they are farmed out to free lancers. Some employees work at their homes and come in only occasionally to check their mail. There is no division of responsibilities by subject matter among editors: they simply work on books they want to be involved with, whether they deal with sailing or politics, experimental fiction or Victorian romance. Rampant informality notwithstanding, everything manages to get done more or less on time; although the editorial director always seems to work seven days a week.

The choice of formal or informal organization clearly involves trade-offs. Decisions may appear to be inconsistent and arbitrary when formal rules are absent. A "loosely run" organization may have a lack of clarity about what is expected of people and how their performance is assessed. However, rigid formal arrangements may mean that decision makers are too segmented into separate units, and that coordination cannot be achieved. There may be conflicting goals, as the organization lacks a single set of objectives. Personnel may find themselves at cross-purposes.

What makes for these differences in organization style among houses? Independent or conglomerate ownership is not a factor. Size, however, is an obvious influence. Recall that in chapter 5 we found that large houses were most likely to have a formal quota of books to be signed. Similarly, large houses were more likely to be divided into separate and distinct departments than were small houses. This is hardly surprising; however, size is not the only, or the most important, factor. The effects of the size of the house can be mediated by the age of a firm. An old, tradition-bound but small house can be formally organized, while a medium-sized house that is relatively new can be in flux. We conducted a number of interviews at a medium-sized trade house, with some 125 employees, that publishes approximately 250 books a year. Despite the house's size, it is overwhelmingly staffed by newcomers. As a result of having many new employees, the firm's organizational design is not firmly set. There are vague boundaries among departments, and few employees have a clear picture of the overall operation. Even the managing director, who is the chief financial officer, had trouble drawing an organizational chart for our interviewer.

A good example of this house's lack of a clear chain of authority was the constant movement of a new position, the media development director. This new job was designed to help develop books into movies and coordinate the release of media tie-ins. Initially the media development director reported to the subsidiary rights director. The tasks of these two positions are obviously related, and the media director's background was in subsidiary rights. Because media tie-ins generated large revenues, the new position was transferred, with the director reporting to the managing director who was in charge of finances. After several months, media development was moved again; this time the position fell under the editor in chief's wings. The hope was that this move would permit media development to be involved from the outset in the acquisition of hardcover titles. After we finished interviewing at this house, we learned that the media development director had been moved once again, to the paperback subsidiary of the hardcover house. This young trade house was constantly experimenting with its organizational design.

While both the size and the age of a publishing house affect how formally it is organized, the key variable, once again, is type of publishing. It is almost axiomatic that text houses are more bureaucratically organized than trade or scholarly houses. They have clearer departmental boundaries; members spend more time in formal meetings as opposed to encounters in the halls, have larger in-house production staffs and rely less on outside free lancers, have the most formal decision-making processes, and are least likely to ignore the advice of marketing or sales when it comes to deciding what to publish. As we have shown, the production of textbooks is a routine process that involves publishing a limited number of costly products that do not vary a great deal in format from one discipline to another; nor does a text on a particular subject change markedly over the years. All these factors augment a formal, bureaucratic organization.

In contrast, each year scholarly and trade houses produce a range of diverse titles that may have little in common. These houses lack reliable predictive powers. They have no cause-and-effect models to ensure success. Since their work is non-routine, flexibility is important. Most interesting to us were the patterns of variation within trade and scholarly houses. In trade publishing, paperback houses were more likely to be formally organized than were hardcover houses. Since so much of the initial work on paperbacks has already been performed by the hardcover publisher, a more formal structure is possible. So far most of the original publishing done by paperback houses is of the genre or category format, such as westerns, mysteries, or romances. These, too, can be processed routinely. However, if paperback houses continue the present trend toward becoming full-fledged publishers and not just reprinters, they may have to decentralize their operations and adopt a less formal structure.

Among scholarly publishers, the most formally organized are the houses that publish monographs, such as annual reviews, proceedings of symposia, or yearly summaries of a field. Obviously the production of such titles is so routine that it fits comfortably with a bureaucratic structure of administration.

THE EDITORIAL DEPARTMENT

Regardless of the size of house or the type of publishing, most editorial departments have a flat hierarchy. There are certainly differences in rank and status among editors; but, with the exception of editors in chief and editorial directors, few editors directly supervise the work of other editors. Typically, an editor supervises a secretary or an assistant. To be sure, editors have a say in the work of other departments and sometimes can exercise a veto over their work; but editors are hardly at a pinnacle of authority. About half of the editors we interviewed have either no one or but one person report to them. Fewer than 20 percent of the editors have administrative authority over other employees who are not in decision-making positions; typically, these employees are copy editors. About one third of the editors noted that at least one person in an editorial position reports to them; thus, these editors have control over others who make editorial decisions. About the same proportion of these supervisory editors were interviewed in each of the three kinds of house we studied—college text houses; scholarly, monograph, and university press houses; and trade houses.

What are the differences between the editor who does not supervise other editors and the one who does? To begin with, editors in supervisory positions make more money than other editors—or at least do not make as little. Almost 40 percent of the editors we interviewed who have no supervisory responsibility make less than twenty thousand dollars per year, as compared with only 5 percent of those with management duties who make this little. But at the higher end of the scale, the picture is more complicated. If editing retains some of its cottage industry features, then all an acquisitions editor needs to be successful, and hence to be financially well rewarded, is to select salable manuscripts and productive authors and to turn out good books. To do this, an editor does need a secretary (but, in our definition of supervision, we are not counting that kind of assistance) and has to be able to assure a steady supply of manuscripts which will be produced, promoted, and distributed effectively. In trade houses, access to reviewers is also important. The successful trade editor also has to be concerned about subsidiary rights. Not a single one of these aspects of an editor's job, however, are necessarily under his or her direct control or supervision but either lie outside the publishing house altogether or are services rendered by other departments. An editor can negotiate with these departments but does not have administrative or executive control over them.

Not surprisingly, then, we find a bit more than 20 percent of editors who do not supervise other editors earn more than thirty thousand dollars a year. This compares with an even slightly lower proportion, 16 percent, of editors with supervisory duties who earn that amount. Only in scholarly and university press houses do we find that supervision is closely associated with high salary. In other types of house, the editors in the middle-income range are most likely to oversee other editors.

What explains this curious state of affairs where editors in middle-range salary brackets are likely to have management responsibilities? The mystery of what accounts for supervisory authority among editors is resolved when we see, first, that in both text and trade houses not a single editor who was with the firm before 1969 (these interviews were conducted between 1976 and 1978) is in a supervisory position. On the contrary, editors who have arrived more recently are likely to be supervisory editors. Second, only among women is there a strong linear relation between salary and authority. Women with higher salaries are much more likely than other women to be supervising editors, and the progression is even: none of the women earning under twenty thousand a year is a supervisor, but four of the five women earning twenty-five thousand or more are supervisors, as are half of the six in the middle range. The picture that emerges suggests that management responsibilities in publishing are not necessarily strongly coveted or desired by editors. Newcomers to a house with some experience can be lured, perhaps, with the promise of running a department. Old-timers can remain where they are and earn a decent salary without having to supervise anyone. One way for women to advance is through management. It appears to be harder for them to be lone editorial stars. That position is much more a male province. Finally, if one considers the career path of editors who become supervisors in both college text and trade houses, they are likely to have started out in sales, marketing, or promotion. Presumably, persons with such experience are either more willing or more qualified to take on administrative responsibility—a responsibility that we see does not carry with it the same status among editors as it carries in more hierarchically organized industries.

One of the most common conflicts in editorial departments occurs between an individual editor's aspirations and the overall house editorial policy. For example, a young trade editor, who wanted to make his mark in the industry, put all his energy into searching for a smash best seller; however, he had to change his ways as the publishing strategy of the firm was geared to a balanced list. Or, there was the neophyte trade editor we interviewed who dreamed of Maxwell Perkins but worked for a house that published many "how to" books. At a scholarly house we studied in detail, a new senior editor with a successful track record at other houses was hired. Despite his experience and extensive contacts, he never established himself at the new house. His experience in the field had taught him to sign books for which ready markets existed. The policy of his new house, however, demanded more: prospective manuscripts had to pass intellectual muster with the editor in chief. Such conflicts stem from a lack of fit between an editor's self-image and ambition and the constraints imposed by the policies of management. These conflicts are usually resolved by the departure of editors who "do not fit," although occasionally a house will be flexible enough to make adjustments to individual interests and requests. Our interviews suggest that the discrepancy between personal interests and house policy is a major cause of the frequent shifting of editors from house to house.

At almost every house we studied, members of other departments were envious of the editorial department. One reason for the envy was summed up by the marketing director at a trade house, who saw himself as more radical politically than other members of the house and was jealous of editors because "I am unable to express my personal values in and through my work the way they are." Other employees envied editors for being accorded special treatment. One sales director likened his publishing house "to a hospital where there are doctors on top and then comes everyone else. . . . We also have a two-class system, editors and then the rest of us."

Jealousy was heightened when editors had unique arrangements by which management gave them considerable autonomy, unusual responsibilities, and freedom from organizational routines. The marketing manager of a large text house complained about the special status of a senior editor:

> X is two years beyond retirement age but no one is sure what his arrangement with the boss is. He had a lot of power. . . . After all, he's been here over 20 years. As for now, it's all very vague but everyone acts as if he is still very powerful. I'd just like to know what his status is. He continues to sign some good books, but many of his books are bombs. But no matter if someone dislikes his ideas for books, he always gets them through.

Editors, for the most part, did not care to respond to such charges. Most of them acknowledged their special status but pointed out that they were responsible for finding authors and "that is our life blood."

INTERDEPARTMENTAL CONFLICT

As we have shown, decision making in publishing firms is often decentralized and dispersed. Even low-level personnel, such as editorial assistants, are given a measure of responsibility. However, the tasks and sense of craft vary from one department to another. Few common criteria guide all participants in the publishing process. The absence of common standards can lead to poor interdepartmental coordination, which, in turn, leads to interdepartmental conflict. Members of one department frequently have unrealistic expectations about the services provided by other departments. Unfulfilled expectations can create dissatisfactions that may result in excessive interference in the operations of other departments. Not surprisingly, members of one department are likely to resent any interference on the part of another department. Such resentment is exacerbated because each department has its own task and sense of craft.

Despite pronounced craftlike aspects, publishing firms also operate like bureaucracies, parceling out and dividing up labor among people and departments. One consequence of this division of labor is that it is rare that any one person oversees or controls the entire publishing process from manuscript selection to sales. Moreover, not only are the tasks of different departments varied; but in addition, each department affects a specific book at different points in the process between manuscript and bound copies, so that coordination among departments can be difficult. Editors, for example, may be preoccupied with selecting manuscripts for a list that will appear two or three years from now, while the production department is feverishly trying to get last-minute material out of an author for a book that is expected to be in the bookstores within a few weeks. The overall task facing every publishing house is not easy: it involves achieving efficient cooperation and coordination among departments so as to fulfill the organizational necessity of turning out a specific number of titles on a regular basis. The process is one where conflict among departments can easily occur.

At the college text house where we did field work we encountered considerable conflict between editorial and sales departments. Although at times the disagreements were harsh, we found them to be typical of textbook publishing. The basic issue was the problem of attributing responsibility for the success or the failure of individual titles and of the list as a whole. Each department usually blamed the other for failures and patted itself on the back for successes. A few examples will illustrate. Editors felt that the sales department should be "doing more market research as well as doing its primary job of selling better!" One editor alleged that sales was "neither thorough nor systematic." Several editors complained that the sales department resisted editorial suggestions and failed to push the big books on the list. One editor pointed to a large introductory accounting book that flopped, and said, "We put an awful lot of time and money into it, and sales refused to get behind it." One angry editor griped, "When a book does well, sales is congratulated; when it fails, editorial is to blame."

It was clear to us that the sales department was biased in favor of selling English, history, humanities, and psychology textbooks, and with apparent reason: these are the texts that sell well. The sales department's criticisms of editorial were also extensive and vocal. At an important meeting where the fall season's list was being reviewed, the editorial director touted a new mathematics text as the year's "ace in the hole." A regional sales manager whispered loudly to members of the sales staff, "Then we got *no* ace in the hole!"

Members of the sales force criticized many of the books signed by editors as lacking sales potential. They also charged that unorthodox books were signed, that editors "don't look at what the competition is." Salespeople felt editors believe each book is their biggest book, and reserved their praise for a few editors they considered to be "credible and able to deliver their books on time." Both the sales and editorial departments were quick to blame other departments for another common problem—the failure to get books published on schedule with all their necessary support materials. Editors and salespersons faulted the publicity department for not meeting deadlines and for delivering unimaginative promotional materials. It was hard for us to judge the accuracy of these charges, but a good case can be made that the publicity department serves a scapegoating function and allows sales and editorial to agree on something.

As we have said, we found similar quarrels in other textbook houses. In general, editors estimate sales figures high and are enthusiastic about a book and its author. This enthusiasm is necessary if one is to work with an author. On the other hand, the sales department routinely estimates a text's sales prospects conservatively. These limited expectations can become self-fulfilling prophecies. Conflict is also created by scheduling problems. Editors often have to write a summary or brief for a text, which the sales department can use before it sees the final manuscript. If the text fails to live up to its advance billing, sales blames editorial for unrealistic expectations.

The publicity department was also a bone of contention at the medium-sized trade house where we did field work. Members of the house, particularly editors, either were unclear about the tasks of the publicity department or felt publicity was "not doing enough." The publicity director and her staff reported to the marketing department head. Tension finally rose to the point where the marketing head called a special conference in order for the publicity director to explain to the rest of the house what her department's duties were. She proceeded to tick off a lengthy list: send review copies to book reviewers and keep after the reviewers if a book is overlooked; schedule author tours and arrange radio and television appearances; provide necessary travel service for authors; collect biographical information and photographs for each author which is used to write publicity releases for each book; send out catalogues; submit books for literary awards and prizes and mount appropriate campaigns; see that each book is listed in or by *Books in Print*, the R. R. Bowker catalogues, and the Library of Congress;* schedule press conferences and manage press relations; schedule and arrange promotional lunches and publication parties; and clip book reviews of all house books. Our observer at this conference was impressed by the work load handled by the publicity director and her staff of four assistants. However, other members of the house were considerably less impressed; as soon as the publicity director finished talking, she was bombarded with questions about why this or that was not done or why was the department not doing more creative things. Once again, in the debate over who was responsible when a book did not sell, the publicity department became everyone's whipping boy.

One of the main sources of confusion and conflict at the university press we studied in detail was the classification of some titles as trade books. The decision to classify a book as trade, and offer it at a 40 percent discount, rests largely with the sales manager, although on occasion an editor may campaign for the trade designation for one of his books (see chapter 2). The sales manager has a vested interest in classifying as trade at least a few of each season's books. First, while the sale of academic titles by direct mail is the advertising manager's responsibility, the sale of trade books is the sales manager's exclusive domain. Second, to sell its trade

* *Books in Print* (published by R. R. Bowker & Company in New York) is an annual catalogue of all books, hardcover and paperback, currently in print; they are indexed by author, title, and subject; details—such as publisher, dates of various editions, and Library of Congress catalogue number—are provided for the use of booksellers and anyone interested in ordering a particular book from its publisher. *Books in Print* is available at bookstores.

R. R. Bowker also publishes such specialized catalogues as *Paperbound Books in Print, American Library Directory, Biographical Directory of the American Psychiatric Association,* and *The Publishers' Trade List Annual* (listing books as they appear in each publisher's catalogue). These catalogues are available at bookstores and/or libraries.

Two copies of every book published in the United States are sent, upon publication, by the publisher to the Library of Congress in Washington, D.C., for copyright purposes and so that one may be kept in the Library itself.

books to booksellers, the university has recourse to the small sales force it shares with other university presses. The acquisitions editors at the university press are happy when even one of their books is classified as trade by the sales manager, because a trade book will reach a larger audience than will the typical academic title. It is also true that having books sold in bookstores is something of a novelty at the press. Outside of the editorial department, however, the consensus is that the sales manager is overly liberal in his selection of trade books. Even within the lower ranks of the editorial department (for example, copy editors), this opinion is widely held.

The sales manager's liberal classification of trade titles creates the most trouble for the advertising and the publicity departments, which are responsible for advertising and promoting trade books in a different manner from academic titles. While these departments virtually have nothing to do with the decision to designate a book as a trade title, they frequently disagree with such classification. These departments are obligated to do as much as they can to get the media exposure needed to sell trade books. Since their funds are extremely limited, the advertising and the publicity departments have adopted the practice of selecting one of the designated trade books as the title with the most general trade appeal. They spend most of their time and energy and their available funds on this book and more or less ignore the other books designated as trade, treating them as typical academic titles. These subversive practices greatly disturb the acquisitions editors, who frequently make eloquent appeals to the advertising and the publicity departments for more media exposure for their "trade" books.

Tension between the editorial department, on the one hand, and the advertising and the publicity departments, on the other, also exists even with typical academic books. As is true at almost any publishing house, the editors, as well as their authors, are rarely satisfied with the advertising and promotion efforts planned and carried out for their books. Editors and authors alike view their books as their "babies" and suspect that others will shortchange them. Such intense feelings of ownership lead press editors—however much they lack expertise in these areas—to meddle in the affairs of the advertising and the promotion departments.

IMPLICATIONS

Conflict is endemic in the publishing process, and the preceding examples should be regarded as typical and not unusual. One trade editor in chief summed up the problem at his house in the following manner:

> Given that it is not all that clear what sells books under what circumstances, we follow a strategy of encouraging excellence in each department. . . . This way we cover all the bases. . . . Of course, by building strong departments we can set the stage for competition and departmental in fighting.

Other publishing executives also see conflict as inevitable and, in some cases, as healthy. "Disagreements between departments," according to the director of a scholarly house, "are a part of a natural learning process, one side gives a little, a bargain is struck." My job, he stated, "is to make sure things don't get out of hand." This particular house has a practice common to many houses: each new book is the subject of a launch meeting. At such a meeting, representatives of various departments attend and discuss the publication plans for a specific book. The sponsoring editor may formally turn the manuscript over to the production department. These meetings are largely successful efforts to build camaraderie and to create confidence that the house, as a collectivity, is embarking on a worthwhile project that everyone should support.

A certain amount of both the conflict and the informal organization of the book industry stems from its craftlike character. An "accidental profession" has both costs and benefits. The lack of a formal system of education for a career in publishing, and the absence of orderly career paths and compensation and reward policies, contribute to problems of coordination. When the training required to perform work is learned in advance, work is easily coordinated. An anesthesiologist and a surgeon can meet in an operating room and have little need for communication and little cause for conflict: as a result of their training, they will know what to expect of each other.[16] Instead, publishing relies on a master/apprentice or protégé system of training which can easily lead to charges of favoritism and create conflict. However, it should be recognized that one of the industry's key flaws is also a virtue. If various individuals and departments within a house agreed all the time, it is likely that fewer books would be published. If publishers knew that by doing x, y, and z, they could guarantee that n copies would be sold, conflict within a house would undoubtedly be reduced, but the diversity of titles would likely be as well.

In place of the personal and idiosyncratic management style found in houses run by a single individual, publishing houses, particularly in the textbook market, are adopting professional management principles and techniques that allow a house to grow in complexity, while at the same time they are attempting to maintain coordination and control. When properly instituted, the principles work well. But they are not a panacea: we often observed large, formally organized houses where one department rarely knew what another department was doing. The loser in this situation is usually the poor author. As we shall see in chapter 9, the author often feels caught in a shooting gallery as his or her book is processed by the publisher. Although we both regret this situation and sympathize with authors, our analysis of the industry suggests that a reduction in conflict and an increase in coordination and control on the part of houses could well lead to fewer books being published.

Chapter 8

The Manufacture of Appeal

GETTING BOOKS into the hands of readers has been the most vexing aspect of the publishing industry at least since the invention of movable type. Books are inherently a medium that provides information in a highly selected way to a selected audience of persons interested in particular information. This selectivity occurs naturally because books are "random access devices": that is, a reader can find any particular matter of interest merely by finding the right book and opening it to the right page. Though this may appear to be a trivial point, consider a scroll, the form in which most works appeared before the development of the printing press. In order to read a particular passage in a scroll, one must roll it up to that point—whether beginning, middle, or end—rather than simply opening a book to the right page. The same is true of books on a shelf. One can simply go to the right place on the shelf and pick up the book one wants. Readers who have used microfilm on which more than one document has been stored are familiar with both the scroll and the shelf problem. In other words, books are a medium whose message and audience are highly "targeted." The goal in distributing books is to get the message to the right people. Until a book is opened, however, no one can tell what its message is; thus, the main problem in promoting books is to get people to want the message they have not yet received—no small task.

Recent entrants into the ranks of promoters and sellers of books have included at least one former executive for a soap company. Fawcett used thirty-cents-off coupons to help promote a romance series. "Coupons are the surest way to promote sampling short of hanging samples on someone's doorknob," James Young, formerly of Procter & Gamble, told the *Wall Street Journal* recently.[1] Getting people to try the product through the use of mass-market tactics for consumer goods is a worthy goal, except for one problem: in most cases, each book is a new product with a new message. When mass-market experts plan the introduction of a new product, hundreds of thousands of dollars, sometimes millions, are expended on market research and product development. To expend this kind of budget and effort on even ten books a year would strain the capabilities of almost any publishing house as it now exists, much less to try to accomplish this for every book on the list. Further, not every book is directed to a mass audience; the advantage of books as a medium is that they do not have to have mass appeal; and as we have seen, the book industry is highly segmented so that *most* publishing is not for the mass market.

One obvious solution to the problem is to market "staples"—books that are unchanging, or relatively so. This is the appeal of reference books, Bibles, handbooks, and the like. The *Encyclopaedia Britannica*, for example, in 1977 spent more than five million dollars on advertising, mainly in newspapers and magazines—more than any other publisher. Though the entire industry in the previous year spent about $45,000,000 for newspaper and magazine advertising, and about $7,000,000 to $8,000,000 on other media, no single book publisher appears on the *Advertising Age* list of the one hundred top advertisers.[2] An investment in advertising generally pays off only if the product is relatively familiar or can be made so by advertising. Although the industry average expenditure on advertising trade books is only a "frightfully small" 2 percent to 4 percent of total sales, book clubs—which market as a product each club's taste in books, rather than the individual book itself—average a high advertising figure, about 8 percent of total sales.[3]

The book club thrives by selling an unchanging single concept, rather than a set of constantly changing new books. Similarly, if one can get across to the public that the messages contained in books are all basically the same, then modern marketing strategies can be used. Harlequin Books, a house that, like Fawcett, produces "romantic" novels, understands this strategy very well. Using the language of supermarket national brand marketing, it claims, "Our readers perceive us as a brand of books with special flavor and image."[4] Publishing thirteen new titles each month, the company strives to have happy endings, exotic settings, but no premarital sex. A third solution is to concentrate on blockbusters, with projected sales in the millions of copies.

Despite the evidence that the book industry is increasing its promotional efforts, selling expenses as a percentage of total amount derived from sales are not large in the industry. The problems of investing money in promotional efforts in an industry where *most* books are for specific audiences rather than for the mass market—that is, in which books are targeted—are best seen in the relative costs of promotion in the different sectors of the industry. Advertising, publicity, and promotion expenses are less than 10 percent of sales in trade, but only 3 percent or so in mass-market paperbacks with their larger audience. In contrast, the costs for scholarly and monograph books, the most highly targeted segment of the industry, run about 20 percent, most of which is invested in direct mail.[5] This targeted market is at the heart of what publishing is all about, and we now turn to the problems of promoting and distributing these less than blockbuster books. After we explain the "bread and butter" of publishing, we shall advance to the more exotic world of big deals and Hollywood tie-ins.

BOOKS AND THE DIFFUSION OF INNOVATION

Even publishers molded in the image of P. T. Barnum, banging the circus drum, agree that word of mouth is still the most effective way of promoting books. The reasons for the importance and effectiveness of word of mouth lie in the character of new ideas, new products, and other innovations. One of the more important discoveries of modern social science is that the mass media generally do not directly change most people's minds. They are changed, rather, by the intervention of other people, called "opinion leaders."[6] Opinion leaders are those persons who are so attuned to messages from the media as to be in general better informed than others in their social network, and who are thus consulted, or whose opinions are especially valued, by them. Opinion leaders are not otherwise socially exalted above other members of their social circle. On the contrary, they tend to share the same social milieu, and that is one of the sources of their influence. In this view of the flow of ideas and innovation, messages are transmitted through a continuous chain of people—the "word of mouth" that book people talk so much about. Under some conditions, opinion leaders get the "word" initially from the mass media; in other situations, from salespeople; in still others, from specialized sources such as their own research. Under some conditions, opinion leaders are the innovators in a particular field. For example, one study showed that physicians in a community who first adopted a new drug were opinion leaders who influenced other physicians who eventually adopted the drug.[7] It can happen, however, that the so-called innovators are so marginal as to have little influence over others. In traditional villages peasants who adopt new fertilizing methods may have little influence and are looked at askance by other villagers. Then, too, the innovator may simply be a fool. In a study of early users of heavily advertised convenience foods, it was shown that the "innovators" were ill informed about food and nutrition.[8]

The typical publisher is not necessarily an expert on theories of innovation and opinion making but does know that it is imperative to reach the right kind of opinion makers in order to activate the word-of-mouth system, and that timing is of the essence. Campaigns that attempt simultaneously to reach opinion leaders and the general public may be less effective than promotion that first reaches opinion leaders and only then goes to the public. Different forms of influence have different effects depending on timing and the particular media involved. In selling to physicians, for example, salespersons for drug houses are often more effective if the physician has first seen an advertisement for the product which "legitimates" the efforts of the salesperson.

Publishers have been so impressed by their one-of-a-kind type of product—each book presumably different from the next—that they market books mainly on the basis of inspiration, intuition, and experience. Organized, systematic, empirically based strategies for marketing have been rare. Only recently have some publishers seen the connection between the diffusion of innovation and the marketing of books.

Publishers have tended to feel that, dependent as it is on word of mouth, the book market is utterly inexplicable. As a result, most editors do not know, for example, what kind of jacket really sells what kind of book, though most editors have strong opinions on the matter. Similarly, except in one or two cases of actual experimentation, publishers have no firmly based knowledge about whether advertising sells books, much less whether advertising in one medium is better than advertising in another. Again, there are firm opinions on the matter. Some editors say television sells books; others deny it. Some acclaim the *New York Review of Books* for certain types of book; others find it worthless. We even found that editors and managers in some houses did not check sales figures against their pro-

jections for different books, nor did they systematically compare sales figures for books for which their promotional activities were different. A
rampant belief in the fickleness and unpredictability of the public is
matched only by the widespread belief that promotional activities are a
kind of magic, which, if properly invoked, will sell books but which, if
tainted by lack of faith or lack of enthusiasm, will utterly fail.[9]

The Trobriand Islanders (Pacific Island natives described by anthro-
pologist Bronislaw Malinowski) are not the only ones who employ magic
when faced with uncertainty, but rely heavily on empirically based
methods when matters appear to be under control.[10] Whatever systematic
research publishers have done seems to be concentrated in those segments
of the industry that, in our terms, produce "staples," or where the market
is large but easily located, as is that for college texts.

A good example of "staples" research was Roger Straus III's efforts on
behalf of Harper & Row's new edition of Roget's *Thesaurus. Publishers
Weekly's* report by Nancy Evans, herself an authority on promoting
books, is worth quoting verbatim because it illustrates several important
principles:

> Straus was planning a 100,000 print run. He was also planning to jazz up the
> old standby's image with a colorful new jacket and a TV campaign. That was
> before Harper & Row's advertising agency suggested that they hire Yankelo-
> vich, Skelly and White, Inc., the polling firm, to survey reference book
> buyers. For $5,000, three focus groups of 12 consumers each were convened
> in the New York City area.
>
> Findings indicated that, unlike a dictionary, a thesaurus is a one-time pur-
> chase; dog-eared copies are just as good as spanking new ones. And as for that
> homely old cover, people liked it, and counted on it to distinguish Roget's
> from other thesauruses on the market. The upshot? Scratch the fancy cover
> and stick with the brand-name look. And since the book is a one-time purchase,
> scratch the TV campaign. Harper & Row decided to concentrate on reaching
> the first-and-last-time buyers through print media in three different ways: by
> placing ads directed to young people in high school and college papers; by
> contacting English teachers and urging them to recommend purchase to their
> students; and by approaching parents at graduation and Christmas time about
> giving the thesaurus as a gift. According to Straus, the research paid off. Sales
> of Roget's Thesaurus are up 40%.[11]

Observe that it was the advertising agency—a firm with considerable
experience in marketing consumer goods—that recommended the research
firm, which, by the way, had done all of the *New York Times* market research for a number of years. The firm's findings and the strategy invoked
follow the principal of finding the right kind of opinion leaders and mar-

keting the book to them. A strategy directed indiscriminately to a mass audience would have completely failed.

Research of this kind is no panacea, however. Only success stories find their way to *PW*. A major publishing house recently brought out a new one-volume encyclopedia. The advertising agency for the publisher also suggested doing focus groups.* The encyclopedia was expensive to produce, and the nationally advertised promotion campaign that followed was also expensive. The highly touted venture turned out to be a losing one. Does this result demonstrate that research is a failure, and that magical practices are still the best guarantee of success? Not necessarily. If the aim is to reach a mass market, then focus groups are only a first step. A focus group produces interesting ideas that must be subsequently tested in a carefully designed statistical sample if one wishes to know the true distribution of types observed in the group. In the case of the encyclopedia, the ideas produced by the focus groups were not representative.

This example of failed research only demonstrates how inexperienced publishers are in the use of research, and how difficult it is for them to engage in it. Several focus groups of eight persons are cheap; scientific sample surveys of five hundred to twenty-five hundred individuals are expensive, and their costs may not be justified. It depends on the market. Research in publishing can be successful only if one understands that most books are directed to particular networks and circles (see chapter 3). The goal of most book market research should be to understand and identify the chain of opinion leaders involved in the subject matter of the book. This is true even for many mass-market books. People in publishing by tradition and culture sense this truth but, when confronted by statistics and "research," seem to forget it.

HOW MARKETING AND PROMOTION ARE ORGANIZED IN PUBLISHING HOUSES

Making sure that the message about a book gets to the right people, and that the book is bought by them, involves a set of operations that have traditionally been carried on by several different departments within a pub-

---

* A focus group consists of six to twelve people recruited to discuss a single topic in a special kind of group interview.

lishing house. Each house organizes these functions differently; and with the few exceptions of houses that have instituted a marketing manager, the operations tend to be difficult to coordinate. Though we discussed the organization of publishing houses in the previous chapter, we have reserved an analysis of marketing coordination for this chapter because the way marketing efforts are structured often determines their effectiveness.

All trade houses and some text and scholarly houses have a public relations department, more often than not staffed by women. This department is supposed to get the book noticed by the right opinion leaders, including reviewers. Advertising—paying for space in other media so the publisher can say something favorable about the book—is considered by all houses to be a separate function from publicity, and is usually handled by another department. Many houses have almost all of their advertising handled by outside firms; but other houses have their own department, write their own copy, and place their own ads. Some houses call the advertising department the "promotion" department, others reserve the word for what the marketing experts in business schools call "point of sale merchandising"—that is, the design of displays and other vending devices. Then there is the sales department, usually separate from either publicity or advertising. Some houses have their own sales force, while others do not—one of the primary distinctions, as we have seen, between larger and smaller houses. Nevertheless, someone has to look after the sales figures and make sure that books get to the ultimate consumer. Distribution is often handled by still another group.

Variability and overlap of responsibility between the marketing group—as we would prefer to call all these departments—and the editorial department can be considerable. It is often difficult to coordinate functions within the marketing group as well. Take, for example, copy for the flap of a book's dust jacket. In some houses this is a job for the publicity department; in others it is a responsibility of the editor. Though the advertising department prepares and writes copy for the advertising, it generally does not write copy for the dust jacket. The catalogue which lists a house's books—an important document in every publishing house—is sometimes written by the editor or editors themselves, sometimes by the publicity department, and sometimes by the advertising group. Marketing information or research, if the latter exists formally, is generally handled by the sales department. The care and feeding of mailing lists, a key function in scholarly and monograph houses, can be housed in a separate group or may be attached to sales or advertising. The actual handling and shipping of books may take place in a faraway warehouse. There is at least one publisher of scholarly books, however, who insists on going through the daily orders received from individual scholars so that he can get a feel for the market.

Publishers try to stay on top of promotion, advertising, distribution, and sales; but the small house solution of having one person do the job is not possible in larger houses. Nor can publisher, president, or editor in chief examine the daily new orders. Meetings are the only answer; but, as we have seen, trade editors dislike meetings, so many promotion and advertising decisions are made without an editor's presence—to the consternation of some authors. College text house staffs are saturated with meetings, not necessarily on promotional matters. Publicity and promotion are carried on somewhat differently in scholarly houses, since their mode of distributing books is drastically different from that of trade and text houses. As with all other aspects of publishing, the manufacture of appeal differs drastically from one type of publishing to another. To get a feel for how this works, let us start with university presses, for they must decide whether to treat each title as a trade book, a scholarly book, or a text.

Money is at stake. The main difference between trade and other kinds of books is that the former carry a "long" discount, which means usually at least 40 percent off to the bookstores, which are then motivated to stock it (see chapters 2 and 13). The university press where we did field work estimated that it had to sell three times as many trade as scholarly or professional books in order to make the equivalent amount of money. Promotion, publicity, and advertising all cost money, of course. The requirement that a trade book sell three times as many copies as the same book put out as a professional or scholarly work, on top of the costs of a trade book promotion, makes for a natural conflict of interest between author, editor, and publicity or marketing manager. The author wants to sell as many copies as possible. Promotion and advertising costs are the publisher's, not the author's, problem. Besides, the author's ego is at stake. Although television appearances are rare for all but a few very tradelike university press books, it is generally true that the more such appearances, and the more ads visible to the author and the author's colleagues and friends, the happier he or she feels. The editor, as we have often noted, is the classic person in the middle. On the one hand, an editor is happy if the author is happy. An editor has an ego, too, and would like books he or she has worked on to be noted in the media and to sell many copies. Most editors refer to books they have worked on as "my" book. On the other hand, editors are profit centers, if only informally. If an editor's books lose money consistently, the publisher is not happy. One way to lose money is to spend it promoting books that do not sell.

THE SCHOLARLY BOOK MARKET

In University Press X, where we spent some time as participant observers, public relations and advertising personnel felt that the editorial
department always wanted more publicity and advertising. The marketing
group felt they could not abide by the editors' "whims," some of which
might eat up the group's entire yearly budget. The conflict is most apparent over which books should be given a trade discount and which put
on the scholarly market at a lower discount. For a trade book, the expectation is that a news release will be written, that major media advertising will
be written and placed by an outside firm, that some effort will be made to
get the author on television talk shows, and that other forms of free publicity will be explored. Scholarly books, in contrast, are treated in a much
lower key. There is no press release, no attempt for free publicity or television talk shows, and no major media advertising. Professional journal ads, if
any, are written by the house advertising staff, rather than by an outside
firm. The major promotional effort goes into preparing brochures for the
mailing lists. Direct mail occupies at least three fourths of the time of the
advertising manager. Given this expenditure of time and money, most
scholarly and university press houses tend to send out mailings with two or
three or more related books in a single brochure or in a single packet. The
need to save money on mailings influences editorial policy, since editors
like to sign books in areas where the list is already strong, and thus combine several books in a single mailing. The decision whether a book is trade
or scholarly therefore influences a host of subsequent marketing actions.

Scholarly book marketing depends very much on utilizing the network and the "invisible college" (see page 83) of the author, a fact that
most authors do not fully appreciate. Publishers give each author a questionnaire asking him, in effect, to describe the key nodes of his network,
and the key access point to the "invisible college" or colleges to which he
may belong, as well as the professional journals that he thinks relevant.
The author by definition knows much more about these circles than does
the publisher. More frequently than not, however, the author naively
thinks that book promotion is solely the publisher's function. The publisher may know the *principles* of promotion, but the author knows who
the *targets* are.

Scholarly book publishers typically use their proven mailing lists for a
book on a particular topic, unless the author has access to a special list. Of
all the marketing methods in publishing, the mailing list gives the clearest
indications of success or failure. Were it entirely legal, publishers would—
"to test the waters"—advertise for a book that was not yet written. If the

return on mailings were sufficient, the publisher would then commission a work on the advertised topic. At least one publisher has been enjoined from doing this on the grounds that the consumer was being sold something that did not exist. Even so—in order to test price and promotional copy— publishers sometimes advertise books that are still in production.

Just as important as the mailing list is getting a good pre-publication blurb from a noted person in an author's "invisible college." Though all types of book publishers depend on such blurbs, they should have the most impact on the scholarly market, since the circle of potential readers and their opinion leaders are so clearly delineated. It is our impression, however, that scholarly publishers make even less use of this strategy than do trade publishers, perhaps because scholars feel that overtly soliciting praise from their senior colleagues is unseemly.

Then there are advertisements in professional journals. Marketing experts in scholarly houses are split in their evaluation of these ads. Most believe that they at least have "institutional" value, in that they promote the publisher as one that cares about its authors—at least well enough to advertise their books. Since in the scholarly field, readers are also potential authors, advertising current books may secure a future supply of publishable manuscripts. Whether the ads also sell the books is a matter of dispute.

Authors themselves have access to various circles or publics, not the least of which are captive audiences of students or others at public lectures. Most academics, however, are reluctant to push their books in such settings, though this is exactly what many successful trade book authors do as a matter of course.

Displays at scholarly and professional conventions complete the list of what publishers do to promote and advertise a scholarly or professional book. Since all this takes considerably less money and time and effort on the part of the staff than does a trade book promotion, it is no wonder that whether a book should be considered trade or professional can be the subject of considerable argument in houses.

SELLING TEXTBOOKS

Texts are another matter altogether. Their market is a curious blend of both trade and scholarly publishing. The market for texts may be very large, as is the case for trade houses. Big bucks ride on reaching the text market, which—unlike the trade market and much like the scholarly market—is highly segmented. Like trade houses and unlike scholarly houses, text houses employ a sales force. College texts are sold in bookstores—but highly specialized college bookstores which are much dependent on both professors and publishers (see chapter 13). As a result, some aspects of college text marketing departments are like trade marketing departments; but other aspects are more akin to scholarly book houses.

Similar to scholarly houses, text publishers do not have a publicity department which arranges television appearances, writes news releases, or cajoles reviewers. A typical large college text house has one department that handles all promotion, publicity, and advertising. Called the "college promotion department," the official description of the duties of the department manager includes:

1. Hire, train, and supervise both the regular and free-lance employees of the promotion department, assigning projects and setting priorities.
2. Plan the advertising and promotion programs for the academic year, consulting with editorial and sales departments as required.
3. Prepare the promotion department's budget.
4. Edit all copy; coordinate and supervise copy and design activities.
5. Supervise production of college catalogue and all copy for college books listed in catalogue.
6. Work with printers on paper order, press run, and general scheduling problems.
7. Instruct data processing on list to be used in each mailing, checking counts; and work with sales and data processing on list maintenance.
8. Act as liaison with data processing and direct mail in dovetailing labels, deliveries from printers, and processing mail.

The manager of the promotion department described her group as a "small in-house agency." This text house, part of a larger publishing operation, is the only division of that firm that does not utilize an outside agency for advertising. Copywriters and designers are therefore also part of the group.

The reason text houses do not use outside agencies is that their needs are highly specialized and are likely not to be understood by advertising agencies that deal with the general public. As we explained earlier in reviewing career patterns of college editors, texts are "sold" to college professors, not to students, much in the same way that prescription drugs are "sold" to physicians rather to the ultimate user, the patient. The analogy continues. As we have explained (chapter 4), both text and drug companies employ a small army of salespersons (called "travelers" in the college field and "detail men" [sic] in the drug industry) who call upon their customers—physicians or college professors. These salespersons are crucial in reinforcing the message carried by the advertising. Similarly, samples are critical. College text editors repeatedly told us that the single most important factor in selling a text is getting the text into the professor's hands at the right time.

The Manufacture of Appeal

College text houses usually have a separate sales department that coordinates the activities of the travelers. As we pointed out, sales departments once had a close relation to the editorial department, and a few travelers are still seen by text houses as potential editors. Nonetheless, as the stakes in the market for introductory texts get higher, and as the market itself shrinks, conflict between sales, advertising, and editorial departments has increased. Houses now have the concept of a coordinated approach: the content of the text itself, the character of the advertising, and the approach of the traveler are supposed to be orchestrated. Yet coordination has not been easy; and when there are failures, departments tend to blame each other. Failures these days can cost at least $250,000 to $400,000.

One of the differences between college text houses and pharmaceutical houses in the way they market their products has been in the use of research for both marketing and product development. Drug companies have been using research for both purposes for years; college text houses have just begun. The market—that is, the professionals to whom the products must be sold—is known, limited in size, and described by computerized lists. The needs of physicians for new kinds of drugs, and why physicians adopt particular drugs, have been carefully studied. Equivalent research for college texts is still in its infancy, is underbudgeted, and is often amateurish. Even so, research has shown what college instructors want and how to sell books to them. The content of the texts has been subjected to more careful study than have methods of selling, perhaps because sales departments feel they already know how to sell. To take advantage of their newly acquired knowledge, some text houses have begun to coordinate the entire process of text production, from selecting the topics to be included to actual writing of the text. These efforts have resulted in the controversial "managed text," described in chapter 10, "Books without Authors."

Despite considerable differences, similarities between text and trade houses are worth noting. Both sell, when successful, hundreds of thousands of hardcover books. Both have a sales department to help. Both have produced books without authors. In segmenting their market and in engaging in market research, text houses are more sophisticated in their marketing practices than are trade houses, most of which are unaware of how college text departments—even when in their own house—operate, much less of what has been happening to the college market.

TRADITIONAL TRADE

Until the recent past, the promotion of trade books concentrated on tapping the "right" literary circles or connecting with the "right" set of opinion leaders. Publicity for a forthcoming volume consisted largely of writing sober press releases, placing some advertising in the *New York Times* and a few other newspapers, soliciting some blurbs from authors, reviewers, or other authorities or opinion makers, perhaps throwing a small party where the author would meet with some of his or her peers as well as with a variety of book people, reviewers, and editors. Occasional get-togethers among publicity people and key journal and magazine editors, alerting the latter to forthcoming publications, were also part of this pattern. It is still the predominant type of promotion and publicity in those sectors of the industry that deal with quality products.

In that section of book publishing that caters to the blockbuster and the best seller, a true revolution has been taking place in the last twenty years or so. At present the trade publishing industry operates in two different sectors when it comes to promotion and publicity, and these sectors which we called "periphery" and "core" in chapter 2, have distinctive characteristics.

The traditional trade book market (which we now note has become "peripheral") expects to sell between 7,500 to 40,000 hardcover copies, with a modest sale of first and second serial rights, translations, and paperback editions. A book club sale might help by increasing the print run of the number of sure-fire sales. In contrast, the "blockbuster market" may involve sales in the hundreds of thousands even in hardcover; and the simultaneous orchestration of hardcover sales, eventual mass-market paperback sales, and, for fiction, a possible Hollywood movie version. Trade book publicity, advertising, and sales departments are basically organized to handle the traditional market, and are quietly being torn apart by the different mode of operation required for the new market; though, in truth, many houses have not yet fully grasped the contradictions involved. Further, trade authors themselves are confused. Many now expect the blockbuster treatment; but, in fact, almost all will end up with the relatively perfunctory traditional promotion, and wonder why.

The differences are most easily understood by noting who is involved in the promotion and sale of books in the two types of market. In the past, and in much of present-day quality trade publishing, the promotion of a book involved only a relatively few concerned actors: editors, publicity people, people in subsidiary rights, booksellers and, infrequently, a set of other people believed to be in key positions to spread the merit of the book by word of mouth. What has been happening in recent years in the mass market is that the number of significant, and often decisive, people who must interact in order to promote a book has been significantly enlarged. The fate of a book in the blockbuster age might hinge not on the previous set of role partners of author and editors in the book industry and the connected circle of interested readers, but rather on people who are not part of the book business at all but are in key positions to make or break a book. Hollywood movie producers, the hosts of major talk shows, television executives, and congeries of lawyers and other intermediaries now link the book publishing business to the world of mass entertainment, so that there is emerging a Hollywood-TV-Publishing Complex that may well affect the cultural life of America. We shall argue when we discuss the creation of "non-books" (chapter 10) that the mere possibility of selling a book to the movies or to television affects its style and content because, when writing, an author willy-nilly keeps in mind the needs of the visual media. Finally, the successful author of blockbusters has assumed, in the promotion of his or her "product," a central and active role that bears little resemblance to the largely passive role of the author in the promotional aspects of all publishing in the past and of quality publishing in the present.

The blockbuster promotion has received much attention recently; but the traditional market still predominates, at least in number of books published, and is little understood outside of publishing circles. Although trade editors and publicists do not understand the business school jargon of "market segmentation," the goal of effective traditional public relations has been to locate that part of the book market which will be most receptive to the message of a book and to inform that segment about the merits of the book and how it will serve its needs. The author's circle is just as important to trade promotion as it is to scholarly selling; though, again, traditional authors may not be fully aware of this.

If the book is a literary work, then the public relations department attempts to get literary opinion leaders and makers to endorse the book. Getting reviewed in the right places is part of this process but, as we shall see in chapter 12, is not all that easy. Dealing with reviewers and opinion makers occupies a good deal of a public relations department's attention. For both reviews and blurbs, the amount of effort the public relations department spends is determined by its own enthusiasm about the book. In turn, this enthusiasm is fed by the general atmosphere within the house.

A good public relations person in a trade house can almost guarantee good quotes from the right people and a review in the right places for a few books a year—but only a few books. A house, an editor, or a public relations person with credibility can assure key reviewers they know personally that the book is important. It takes but a few failures in judgment to lose this leverage. Similarly, public relations people have been known to send hundreds of hand-written notes to important literary people, along with galleys or pre-publication copies of a book, assuring the recipient that the book is really worth their reading and commenting on. Again, the publicity department can seldom afford to do this.

To assuage the average author, and to hope against hope, public relations departments have routine releases sent to potential opinion leaders and reviewers; but whether these efforts catch on seems a matter of pure chance. The same holds true for television appearances, which are simply not in the offing for most authors. Television shows are indeed sent announcements of the book, mainly to show authors that the house has been active on their behalf; but television producers and public relations people generally know which approaches really count and which are mere window dressing.

Most trade books, like scholarly books, are in fact specialized and appeal to a known, locatable market. It is for these books that traditional public relations efforts often fail, unless the book catches the imagination of the publicity group, or the editor puts something special behind it. Public relations departments are caught up in the routine of providing for many more books than they can adequately handle.

BANGING THE CIRCUS DRUM

One of the best ways to understand the new mass marketing of books—marketing that attempts not to penetrate a particular circle but aims at a relatively undifferentiated set of readers—is to begin with the role of the author. Traditional trade book authors can do much to help the sale of their books. If they do not, however, the book may still be a success if it strikes the right chord. But authors of mass-market books can almost never afford to take a backseat when it comes to the promotion of their "products." They must be out in front. They must be salesmen or saleswomen of their own wares. When Procter & Gamble engages in a sales campaign for a new product, the company may utilize glamorous models or stars in promoting it—but the commodity cannot speak for itself. In contrast, authors sell books by selling themselves.

A well-prepared promotion campaign for a new blockbuster carefully pre-programs the author's appearance on a variety of talk shows on the major networks, but in addition whisks him or her all across the country to appear in innumerable local television and radio shows. Even a five-minute slot on the "Phil Donahue" or the "Today" show may sell fifty thousand copies.[12] Local appearances, especially if the bookstores are informed beforehand and can stock the author's book in a prominent place, may sell hundreds, perhaps thousands of copies. It is well known in publishing, however, that a common complaint of authors is that they indeed went on tour, appeared on the local radio or television show, but that the local bookstores did not have the book in stock (see chapter 9). We know one author who routinely bribes men at the publisher's warehouse and drives a van to the back door to load up books to place in local bookstores. Coordination, once again, is a major problem for publishing houses.

In fairness to them, we can repeat the sad tale of an author who went on tour, was interviewed on a local radio talk show in Columbus, Ohio, and then sat for hours amid a sea of yellow dust-jackets in a local department store waiting to autograph his book. No one came. Finally, a woman came with her obviously disturbed child and managed to get a short free consultation with the psychologist author. She left without buying the book and was the only result of that particular talk-show appearance. The department store shipped the books back to the publisher. One author we know systematically guards against this possibility by slipping into stores and autographing his book without the bookseller's knowledge (thus marked a book cannot be returned).

The economics of an author's appearance on national or local shows partakes of a curious alchemy in which both the networks and the publishers come out ahead. The network fills a slot with an "entertainer" for whom it does not have to pay. The publishing house does not pay the author either, except to reimburse travel and hotel expenses. The author puts in time and nervous energy and may even put his health at risk, but he is made to feel that all this is justified by the sales boost at the end of the tunnel. Popular authors such as Gay Talese or Carl Sagan have spent literally weeks on the radio and television circuits. Sagan even became a highly paid entertainer in his own right. Judith Krantz said in an interview:

> I never realized before how much hustling was involved. Touring for a book—it's the literary equivalent of war.... When you leave the hotel early in the morning ... the publisher has a limo to get you out to the studio, and

your suitcase is going to be in that limo all day while you make your sixteen stops.

She recalled that she was so exhausted at one point that she decided to stop; but one of her bookseller friends told her, "You get back on that road. Irving Wallace does it. Sidney Sheldon does it. You do it. If you want your book to sell, you finish up that tour." And finish it up she did. Ambition, so it would seem, is a most powerful stimulant.[13]

Most of the hosts and interviewers on talk shows—whatever their personal interest (or lack of it) in the person they interview—rarely, if ever, have time to read the book they are ostensibly discussing. Rather, assistants provide capsule summaries. This is not necessarily a drawback for the author about to be interviewed. He or she has already received elaborate instructions from the publisher's office on what to highlight, on how to direct the conversation in the most advantageous direction, and on how to turn the whole affair into a publicity success. Inexperienced authors are frequently accompanied by a member of the publicity department who hovers backstage to make sure all goes well. Real pros, such as Judith Krantz, learn to beat the system. She interviews herself and prepares typical questions and answers for shows on which she is to appear. These are taped and go out to every show ahead of time.[14]

Not every author and every book is suitable for a television or radio appearance. Far from it. Only a few are chosen. What differentiates the author who appears from the one who does not? To begin with, television commentators, hosts, and reviewers are themselves part of "show business" and share the standards of that world. "Celebrity" status, topical relevance, and slick self-presentation are critical in ensuring that the phone call from the publisher's public relations department will be heeded by the people responsible for scheduling authors for the mass media. Since authors are thought to be poor judges of their qualifications as celebrities or entertainers, media scheduling personnel almost never respond to a direct attempt on the part of an author to arrange an appearance.[15] Because the media are interested in celebrities, there are countless television interviews with celebrity "authors" of so-called autobiographies which have actually been written by ghost writers. The content of a book also has some bearing on the probability of its author's being interviewed: the sexier the topic and the more sensational the book, the better the chances that the author will appear on television. Aware of this need for "sex appeal," editors often push academic authors to be more outspoken than they might naturally be. Thus, the mere existence of television has an indirect effect on the content of books. Nevertheless, every conceivable topic may have its day. The author of a modest scholarly book with a print run of only five thousand copies may suddenly be in demand for a television show if for some reason (for example, if the country on which he or she has just published a book is invaded) the topic of the book becomes "news."

Celebrities are almost by definition expert in self-presentation. For other authors, interviewers and producers may exercise discretion when inviting authors for interviews. Pre-interviews are conducted to find out whether an author has stage presence. You may have written a splendid book, and produced an appealing set of ideas, but if you stumble in your delivery, if you have an unprepossessing appearance, if you are too timid and lack forcefulness, you are not likely to get many interviews. Conversely, the more of a "character" you are, even if the book itself is not so interesting, the better the chances of a television appearance.

All these factors account for the difficulty of getting literature reviewed on television. A novel, unless its author is already notorious, has no inherent news or show business value. First novels, therefore, are entirely out of the question as television topics. While television has every right to devote itself to the picturesque, in so doing it drives one more nail into the coffin of good literature: television appearances by authors do sell books, and authors of fiction are unlikely to appear on television.

Despite its neglect of fiction and serious nonfiction, the interview business thrives as never before. In 1977 the "Today" show, for example, aired over 250 author interviews, generally in five- to seven-minute segments.[16] The "Phil Donahue" and the "Merv Griffin" shows seem to air about the same number of interviews each year, and other national programs are not far behind. If one adds the innumerable local shows, such as "AM Tulsa," on both radio and television, the audience mounts well into the millions. Although no one seems to be able to estimate with any accuracy the specific effect such programs have on sales figures, most book people believe the impact to be significant. The enormous advances hardcover, and especially softcover, publishers pay nowadays for what they believe to be blockbusters depend in part on their anticipation that the power of the mass media will be available to help promote books via pre-packaged interviews.

The tie between the promotion of blockbusters and the media via pre-packaged interviews is, however, by no means the only—perhaps not even the most consequential—link between them. The recent ties between Hollywood producers and publishers of blockbusters are at least as significant, as will be seen in chapter 10. Books slated for Hollywood are given circus-like promotions, and the line between book publishing and show business becomes further blurred.

The People Who Make Books

People within the book industry, on all levels, are well aware of the changes brought about by close links with the movie industry and related developments. As a subsidiary rights director told one of our interviewers:

> When I arrived here, the first serial rights and the movie rights were done sort of in a half-assed fashion by the general editors. It was a madhouse.... [Later] there were always the same sets of rights, but stakes changed. Properties changed. The money started changing. And the whole industry started turning around.

The new name of the game is "tie-in." Instead of the traditional pattern in which hardcover houses sold movie rights to Hollywood, new patterns have emerged in which both hardcover and softcover publishers publish a book in conjunction with the release of a movie bearing the same title. Tie-ins may take several forms. A book in either hardcover or softcover is issued six months or even more before a film of the same title is to be released, but the book's jacket will state that a motion picture is imminent. When the film is actually released, a newly packaged book appears on the racks as a mass-market paperback. The tie-in cover, often with stills from the movie, draws attention to the film. The book first helps to promote the film; then the film helps to promote the book and gives it, so to speak, a second life. Of the movies produced each year, roughly one third are based on published books.[17] There is the further symbiotic relation when the script of a movie not originally based on a book is "novelized"—a process that will be described in detail in chapter 10.

Nowadays, tie-ins may be arranged directly between studios and publishers, or they may be put together by packagers on the West Coast and by a variety of agents. They have become a central link between the publishing and the entertainment industries, and they are a key component in the activity of the promotion departments of both. Of late, publishers such as Bantam have even established their own movie-production companies.[18]

Not only the movies but also television has helped boost the book-promotion business. Of late, bids from television producers have become competitive with those offered by movies. For example, the most successful tie-in between television and publishing has been Alex Haley's *Roots* (Doubleday, 1976). Shown as a mini-series on television, the program attracted an audience of over 100,000,000. Following the showing of the series, the hardcover book sales rose, within two years, from about 600,000 to over 1,000,000. Early in 1979, hardcover and softcover sales reached nearly 6,000,000. In the same year, Gerald Green, the author of the NBC mini-series "Holocaust," wrote a novelization under the same title which sold 1,-700,000 copies in paperback.[19]

Hype lies at the core of the tie-in trend. Without such tie-ins, neither *Roots* nor Erich Segal's *Love Story* (Harper & Row, 1970) would have sold as many millions of copies as they did, and Judith Krantz's *Princess Daisy* (Crown, 1980) would never have earned her $5,000,000 three months before its date of publication.

Contemporary marketing demands concentration on every detail but especially on what a book will look like on a bookstore shelf. We know of houses where the acceptance of a book for publication will involve only one or two editors; but where editors in chief and other editors, together with many others lower on the totem pole, will spend untold hours on the selection of a cover—or jacket, as it is commonly called for a hardcover book. It is the cover, more than the contents, that counts in the paperback world. Says Oscar Dystel, until recently president of Bantam Books, "The cover is our first job in launching a book in the mass paperback market. We feel it's one of the most important single elements of the book's eventual sale." Says Dale Phillips, when a director at Fawcett Books, "You've got to be drawn to it immediately. It's an impulse buy. I look at it as a little box of Tide up there on the shelf for choosing, alongside of all the other soap flakes."[20] The comparison to mass-market methods in selling other consumer goods is apt. One historical romance or science fiction thriller is as much like another as are different brands of soap. What David Riesman, years ago, called "marginal differentiation" becomes critical. A distinctive cover may seem at least as important, perhaps more important, than a distinctive message or story line.

Covers must be eye-catching, provoking, memorable. They need not necessarily be sexy, although they often are. In an age where palates have become jaded when it comes to nudity, sexy books are often wrapped in plain white covers with subdued type and a cameo picture of a woman's face. The very search for impact leads to the curse of mass-marketing promotion—sameness and conventionality. Books all tend to be promoted in the same way, and this promotion includes covers whose very purpose, it would seem, is to make the book look different from other books. "Let's face it," said Phillips, "everything is a gimmick in this business." Hence, covers follow fad and fashion just as do the contents of books and the style of promotion. One year blue is out, and the next year it is all the rage. One year it is gold stamping for titles or fold-out covers. The next, Day-Glo and die-cuts are the thing to do.[21] Even college texts have borrowed from the mass-market mentality. One year a successful text had an Impressionist painting on the cover for no reason we could discover. Next year every publisher's new introductory sociology text had an Impressionist painting on its cover.

Whatever the fad of the moment seems to dictate, an appealing come-on is of the essence if a mass-market book is to survive the fierce competition for shelf space. A book buyer may know precious little about the contents of the book he or she is about to buy, but will respond to the cover—or so book people firmly believe.

Promotion campaigns for both hardcover and softcover books have always ranged from the sophisticated to the vulgar, but the latter seems to be winning out in the marketing of blockbusters. Here are just a few examples of both the ingenious and the vulgar:

When Julia Knickerbocker, director of publicity at William Morrow, mapped her strategy for selling Silvia Tennenbaum's *Rachel, the Rabbi's Wife* (1978), she decided to send advance copies not to rabbi's wives but to rabbis. Since the book portrays its rabbi protagonist in unflattering terms, the rabbis were incensed and preached against it to their congregations. Naturally, many congregants immediately ran to the nearest bookstore to buy the book.[22] This was surely an ingenious and sophisticated approach; but now consider the following instance of vulgarity.

A New York company that goes by the name of Oh, Dawn, has been printing on toilet paper some of the most popular books of recent years. The books so reprinted include *The Book of Lists* (William Morrow, 1977) and *The People's Almanac* (Doubleday, 1978) and sell between $3.00 and $3.50 a roll. The houses that sell the rights to such reprints plainly hope that people, after having used up the toilet paper, will run to the bookstores to buy the paperback for more leisurely reading.[23]

Book reviewers are not only deluged with advance galleys and attached news releases that carry blurbs from "famous people" and boast of big printings, major sales to book clubs, and Hollywood tie-ins; they may also receive a variety of other come-ons. A review copy of Guy Lombardo's autobiography was accompanied by a $1.50 box of Lanzi's Cashew Nut and Rice Crunch candy. Other such give-aways include T-shirts, long-playing records "not available to the general public," and special limited editions.[24]

Finally, nothing indicates better the increasing importance of mass-distribution methods and mass-product-selling attitudes in the publishing industry than the trends in book advertising. Though, as we said, book publishing spends much less on advertising than do other consumer industries, advertising expenditures are on the rise: newspaper advertising billings are up from $16,000,000 in 1975 to over $24,000,000 in 1980; magazine advertising (excluding trade and professional magazines) is up from nearly $41,000,000 in 1975 to $63,000,000 in 1980. But the real bellwether of mass merchandising—radio and television advertising—has shown by far the greatest increase. Radio is up tenfold from $220,000 to $2,395,000; network television increased from $843,000 to over $5,000,000; spot television went from nearly $9,000,000 to nearly $27,000,000 in this period, and has thus now surpassed all newspaper advertising, which was once the standby of book advertising. Further, while total media spending has not quite doubled between 1975 and 1980, spot television ads have tripled.[25]

Best sellers are not born, they are made. And they are made largely through promotion. Once a book is accepted, its editor must promote it successfully within the house, so as to create enthusiasm on the part of the editor in chief as well as among other editors and people in sales, promotion, and subsidiary rights. When the in-house people have been sold on a book, there begins a long pitch to convince outsiders, from book clubs to reprint houses and the movies, that the book is indeed a valuable property. Most of this activity typically takes place long before the book is published. Only the last stage involves the promotion of the book to booksellers and, ultimately, to its prospective readers. If blockbusters have created one fundamental change in publishing, it lies in changing the source of profits. Until recently sales of books to the public counted the most. But now that a large part of the profits comes from other sources, promotion involves much more than selling to the customer in the bookstore but, rather, movies, television programs, and T-shirts. In fact, the tail wags the dog, for successful promotion through movies, television, and various tie-ins, in turn, guarantees the sale of books to the public.

In sum, the promotion of blockbusters is an entirely different ballgame from promotion of quality work. While major favorable reviews largely determine the success of a book in the quality market, they play a minor role in the mass market for blockbusters. The major promotion for the latter has already occurred before any reviews have appeared. Press releases and advance notices to writers running book trade columns in the dailies,[26] or to booksellers and librarians, continue to quote endorsements from famous names, but they show, above all, that the house believes in the book as a future best seller. Hence, high publicity and advertisement budgets, national tours of authors, sales to book clubs, high initial print runs, Hollywood or television tie-ins are amply publicized. They are the name of the game. Some years ago, the historian Daniel Boorstin, now the Librarian of Congress, published a book, *The Image* (Atheneum, 1962), in which he dealt with the cult of celebrities in contemporary culture and provided a memorable definition of a celebrity: "The celebrity is a person who is known for his well-knownness."[27] To borrow from Boorstin, it would seem to us that best sellers are mostly books that are known for their "known-ness" long before a single copy has become available to the public. This is not to say that all well-known persons or books are shallow, without merit; but that merit is hardly the sole, or even main, criterion for success.

It is possible for the so-called mid-list book (neither a foregone lost cause nor an obvious blockbuster) to be successful, but such success requires a measure of care and devotion that most houses cannot regularly afford. When previously unknown Mary Gordon brought her first novel, *Final Payments* (1978), to Random House, it generated considerable enthusiasm there. A subsidiary rights director of another large major trade house described the process to us:

> The publicist who worked on the book, a young woman named Lynn Goldberg, sent out something like 400 handwritten notes to people who might logically give quotes, saying, "I think you'll like this book." She got back an incredible number of quotes from these people. Basically, if you have ten, you are ahead of the game. The subsidiary rights department alerted the movie people and did everything it could to launch it and it worked. It was wonderful. But that's a lucky situation. You don't always luck out. You can have a marvelous first novel with an absolutely terrific review, and nothing much happens.

This combination of hard work on the part of the public relations department, a work of genuine literary merit, enthusiasm within the house, and—perhaps most important—sheer good luck is alas all too rare.

CONCLUSION

Not only is publishing itself a highly differentiated industry, but the product it sells is, for the most part, highly specialized and its audience highly targeted. Publishing shines when it is able to bring the mysteries of automobile repair to mechanics and do-it-yourselfers, the latest in revisionist criticism of Yeats to experts on Irish poetry, and the best new work on cognitive psychology to workers in that field. Always in search of the new, the book industry strives to let people know about its "products" and what they contain. Paradoxically, it is only with the advent of mass marketing that the concepts of "opinion leader" and "market segmentation" have been developed. While book publicists have known all along that their problem was to find the right keys to the public, they have also felt that their task was suffused with mystery and magic. Some campaigns worked, others did not. Since most editors and publicists have a background in the humanities (see chapter 4), the possibility that some systematic help from the social sciences might be on the way is by and large not appreciated.

The lore of book promotion and book marketing differs in each sector of the industry. The mailing list is the tool of scholarly houses, travelers are the key to text marketing, while the cajoling of reviewers and the soliciting of celebrities are the methods of quality trade promotion. Inherent in all these techniques is the attempt first to find, then to understand, and finally to convince specialized networks and circles to adopt a new book.

The Sages of the Talmud well described the predicament of book promotion, though it was but one Book that they had in mind: "The day is short, the work is plentiful, the laborers are sluggish, and the reward is abundant, and the master of the house presses."[28] Careful attention to the process of interjecting a book into the appropriate circles is simply not possible, given the number of books a house handles, and the number of laborers. To be sure, the author's typical view is simply that the workers are sluggish. Given the size of the rewards, masters of the publishing houses are usually content to let tradition be the guide. It is basically unknown whether larger budgets and innovative methods would sell enough targeted books to justify giving increased attention to all books, rather than only to those inspired by God.

Although promotion in college and scholarly markets is not always effective, the fact that the circles there are fairly easily identified means that promotion is rarely a total disaster. Not so in trade book publishing, where locating the circles at which to target a particular book requires more effort. The tendency in trade lately has been to eschew the role of books as a specialized medium and to market them as a consumer product for a very wide market—an approach that leads to many of the absurdities we have described.

Chapter 9

Authors:
A Worm's-Eye View

PUBLISHERS and editors usually refer to authors as their partners. Except in rare cases, no book can appear without the services of a publisher, and little can be published unless someone writes a manuscript. This formal partnership is, however, a source of considerable conflict, because the power positions of authors and publishers are asymmetric. What cooperation there is is likely to be what American sociologist William Graham Sumner long ago called "antagonistic cooperation."

The relations of authors to publishers can run the gamut from close friendship and mutual esteem to deep-seated antagonism and even hatred. Sometimes relations have been so good that an author has been ready to make financial restitution to a highly esteemed publisher who has lost money on one of his books. Thus, the nineteenth-century British prime minister and author, Benjamin Disraeli, had received the unprecedented sum of ten thousand pounds from the house of Longman for his last work of fiction, *Endymion* (1880); when it did not sell as well as expected, he told an associate, "My conscience will force me to disgorge," and offered Longman a new contract that virtually amounted to returning three thousand pounds to the firm. Longman at once replied that it "could not think of availing [itself] of Beaconsfield's [Disraeli's] liberal and considerate suggestion."[1] But such instances of "*Après vous, Gaston*" are rare indeed.

At the other extreme of the continuum of feelings between authors and publishers, one finds a letter from the nineteenth-century writer of books on Japan, Lafcadio Hearn, to his New York publisher, Harper's, (which had resented something Hearn had done): "Please understand that your resentment has for me less than the value of a bottled fart, and your bank account less consequence than a wooden shithouse struck by lightning."[2] In the same vein, it is worth recalling that Rudyard Kipling once sent to one of his American publishers an angry missive that he had had privately printed on toilet paper.[3]

Then in recent times there was the author of a well-selling trade book who wrote us four single-spaced pages explaining the ins and outs (mostly outs) of his long relationship with a particular publisher. "Would I publish with X again? Will Rosemary have another baby? Then again, I said that about Y [a big paperback house] and I am quite pleased with what they are doing this time around, as well as with their plans to reprint my first book. Try to figure it out." And that we are about to do here.

"Put two authors in a room together and invariably they will begin telling tales of horror about how their publishers handle their books." In fact it's the abundance of such stories that has led the *New Yorker's* Calvin Trillin to threaten repeatedly (and only partly in jest) to compile "An Anthology of Authors' Atrocity Stories about Publishers," or so begins an article for *Publishers Weekly* on such stories.[4] In this chapter we, too, will refer to a rich mine of anecdotal material but will also rely on responses to a scientific sample of authors at several different types of publishing house. More important, we will show the sources of the tenuous and multifaceted relations between authors and publishers.

Beneath the apparent reciprocity between author and publisher, there lie structural differences in power. The bases from which one can exercise power are, of course, varied and many; but in a capitalist society, privileged position in the marketplace for goods and labor is certainly among the most potent resources that power holders may employ in order to impose their will. It is useful to recall Marx's well-known argument about the power differential between workers and factory owners in negotiating the conditions of labor contracts. If workers are able to gain their livelihood only by selling their labor power to those owning the means of production, then— even though the labor contract appears as a transaction between equal partners—it in effect amounts to instituting the unilateral dependence of one class upon the other. Ownership of the means of production assures the power of owners over laborers and hence produces the asymmetry of relations between them. This is not to imply that capitalists do not complain bitterly about workers, and certainly not that editors and publishers do not have an equal number of atrocity stories to tell about authors; but the difference in power is still considerable and has been so since the beginning of the publishing industry.

There have been two key aspects to the commercialization of writing and literature since the eighteenth century.[5] The first, which forms one of the continuing themes of this book, is the creation of two inherently contradictory stances. Editors and publishers must serve as interpreters of market trends and public demands, even as they also wish to be seen as arbiters of aesthetic or scientific quality. Second, there has been a drastic change in the relation of authors to their public and to the publishers who mediate between them and their readers. With the rising demands for books that marked the eighteenth and, even more, the nineteenth centuries, authors were able to emancipate themselves from the dependence on patrons that had shaped their careers for many centuries. The publishers and booksellers, who exploited the rising market for books, helped writers in significant ways in their struggle to attain independence. Yet the relations between writers and those engaged in the publishing and distribution of books remained tense and ambiguous throughout the eighteenth and nineteenth centuries and after.

Writers of the period understandably differed in their assessments of the new situation in which they found themselves. What is more, a writer might, at times, be lyrical about the services rendered him by a publisher and, at other times, curse the book industry. Thus, in the eighteenth century, Oliver Goldsmith, author of the *Vicar of Wakefield* (1766) and of an enormous variety of compilations, essays, translations, and reviews, could write upon occasion about the virtues of the new marketing system that allowed men of letters to attain financial independence. "The ridicule," he said, "of living in a garret, might have been wit in the last age, but continues such no longer, because no longer true. A writer of real merit now may easily be rich." "I look to the booksellers," he also wrote, "for support, they are my best friends." But the same Goldsmith could also write, "The author, when unpatronized by the Great, has naturally recourse to the booksellers. There cannot perhaps be imagined a combination more prejudicial to taste than this. It is in the interest of the one to allow as little for writing, and of the other to write as much as possible."[6] Goldsmith's ambivalent attitude echoes even more insistently throughout the nineteenth century and up to our own day.

Writers and publishers were, to be sure, natural allies when it came to mobilizing the resources of the market for particular books. Yet writers found again and again that even though they owed to publishers and booksellers some of their freedom from the servitude of patronage, they were also bound to both by a new set of ties that were nearly as restrictive as those of the patronage system. Authors were often appalled at the ways in which publishers advertised and peddled their literary wares in order to increase sales. Moreover, many authors bridled at publishers' attempts to make them lower their literary standards so that their work would be more palatable to the shopkeepers, apprentices, housewives, or clerks who formed a large part of the newly literate audience of the nineteenth century. The very democratization of the reading audience endangered quality. Many authors felt that publishers, in catering to new audiences, exercised pressures on them, the authors, to relax standards and to disregard the canons of established literary taste.

But, over and above the threats to the author's vocation and craft that came from the rise of the mass market for literature, there arose the specifically modern tension caused by the fact that the book had now become a commodity like any other, over whose price authors and publishers had to haggle, just as farmers and merchants haggled over the price of eggs or wheat. In addition, whereas the price of most commodities could easily be ascertained at any given time from the publicly available quotations on commodity markets, the real market value of a book was largely a matter of an educated guess when the contract between publisher and author was written, and would become fully ascertainable only after the book was published. Prices for wheat or eggs will change, within a given range, over time; but the market value of a book upon publication may be next to zero or hundreds of thousands of dollars. Given this situation, publishers naturally tried to get away with treating their authors—especially those among them who had not yet established a secure reputation—with extreme niggardliness.

Well-established and popular authors managed to make a good deal of money in the new mass market for books, especially if they were, like Walter Scott, willing to make concessions to popular taste. Thackeray and, above all, Dickens, while making some concessions, made sizable fortunes from their various books. George Eliot, on the other hand, heroically resisted any effort of her publishers to make her novels more "marketable": she attained commercial success but never compromised her artistic standards. Some of the great writers achieved financial independence or even a measure of opulence in nineteenth-century Britain, but many others—and not only the untalented hacks that then as now crowd publishers' anterooms—fared much less well. Wordsworth and Coleridge earned £30 from their *Lyrical Ballads* (1798), while George Eliot's literary income over the years amounted to some £45,000.

What was true for nineteenth-century Britain applied *a fortiori* to nineteenth-century America. In this country—where up to the end of the century no international copyright law was recognized, and where, as a consequence, cheap reprints of Britain's writers flooded the market—native American authors had a hard time selling their products and receiving adequate rewards for their literary labors. Melville gave up writing in despair after the miserable reception, both critical and in sales, of *Moby Dick* (1851), and Hawthorne's angry complaints about "a damned mob of scribbling women" who inundated the marketplace with cheap novels to the detriment of serious writing are well-known.[7] Hence, a high proportion of American authors in the last century worked in customs houses, on consular missions, in various civil service jobs, or as journalists and reviewers. Just as Coleridge and Hazlitt in England worked as debate reporters, and Lamb wrote jokes for newspapers (at sixpence apiece),[8] so their American counterparts resorted to a variety of labors to eke out a living. To be sure, *Uncle Tom's Cabin* (1851–52), which sold some five million copies in a few years after publication, made a fortune for Harriet Beecher Stowe; and Louisa May Alcott, the author of *Little Women* (1868–69), received, all told, some two hundred thousand dollars in royalties for her books, exclusive of fees from magazines. But these were exceptional success stories.[9] Most of the great American writers of the nineteenth-century—Whitman, Melville, and Hawthorne, for example—sold so little that they could never have made a living from writing alone. Even after the turn of the century Henry Holt could still argue with conviction that

> few men have ever [depended upon their pen for daily bread]. Few men have ever done it happily.... Most good authors, from Shakespeare down, have had other resources. There are some pursuits in which it is almost as dangerous to make money the main end, as, in the general conduct of life, it is to make personal happiness the main end.[10]

This being the case, one can hardly be surprised that, despite instances of exceptionally good relations between authors and their publishers—instances that are usually lovingly recorded in the company histories of publishing houses—cases also abound in which authors protested contract terms slanted in favor of publishers and low royalties, argued over what they perceived to be mass market-oriented biases, and complained about being cheated through a variety of bookkeeping devices. In the nineteenth century, as in the twentieth, authors were largely a discontented lot, even though a few managed to establish warm relations with their editors and publishers. Contemporary authors, however, face a much more complex set of relationships than did their nineteenth-century counterparts. Publishing itself is more differentiated; the organizational structure of houses is more bureaucratic; and agents, packagers, and authors' unions have entered the scene and interposed themselves between author and publisher. The best place to begin to understand author-publisher relations is the formal legal contract between them.

ASYMMETRY IN POWER

The asymmetrical relations between authors and publishers are symbolized by the publishing contract. Publishers still account to authors in their own way and frequently at their own pace. As in Islamic law, where men can divorce their wives at will but no such right is accorded women, a publisher has the right to refuse to publish a book even after a publishing contract has been signed. In contrast, an author cannot "divorce" his or her publisher. Every standard contract contains a clause specifying that the publisher will accept for publication a manuscript only when the publisher finds it satisfactory. No contract ever specifies that an author can terminate a publishing contract if he or she finds the publishing house's services to be unsatisfactory. Sloppy editing, insufficient provisions for advertisements, and so on, are not considered a breach of contract in law, and so provide no way out for an author who has become dissatisfied with a publisher; although, under some circumstances and with the permission of the publisher, the author can buy out his or her contract. Nevertheless, a publisher remains free to contend that the final manuscript does not live up to initial expectations, and so is not required to publish it. Moreover, the publisher who finds a manuscript "unsatisfactory," can sue the author to return the advance. The author can discover that he or she has spent several years working for no pay. We will have more to say about the so-called satisfactory manuscript clause; but suffice it to say here that the Authors Guild, the nearest equivalent to a generally recognized union for professional writers, has mounted a heavy attack on this aspect of the standard publishers' contract.

The clause has more than practical significance. Just as divorce procedures in Islamic law are emblematic of the inferior status of women in Muslim societies, so the clause specifying that a manuscript will be published only if judged satisfactory by the publisher is emblematic of the inferior status of authors in their relations to publishers. It is one of the main indicators of the skewed power relations between them.

It might be objected that an author who has been refused publication by one publisher may always submit to another. There is some merit to this argument, but it is nevertheless far from convincing. The author is likely to have received an advance from the first publisher which, economic conditions of writers being what they are, he or she is likely to have spent long ago and is in no position to return. This means that the author approaches another publisher with a heavy handicap: the necessity of informing a second publisher of the earlier rejection, with the result that the latter, in taking on this work, will have to repay to the first publisher the advance paid to the author. The latter's position is, therefore, a bit like that of a pregnant woman in desperate search of a husband to legitimize her offspring: a situation hardly conducive to great bargaining power.

Moreover, for many a book, there may even be few desirable alternative houses to approach. With increasing differentiation and specialization in publishing, a book may fit the publishing programs of only a few houses. If a scholarly book in, say, economics, does not appeal to the major university presses, it may interest only two or three commercial houses of the first order; if these happen not to be interested, the author is forced to submit the manuscript to less prestigious houses whose services might be second-rate at best. Thus, an author is likely to think twice before refusing a publishing house's request to revise a manuscript so as to make it "satisfactory."

The contract is just the beginning of the relationship between author and publisher. There are more opportunities for sorrows (and joys) during the process of editing, production, promotion, and distribution. Authors are, of course, neither helpless nor necessarily hapless in this entire process. Let us review the results of a systematic survey of authors at the various publishing houses we studied.* We will look at some of their characteristics, and ask if these affect the way publishers handle their books. We will then inquire how authors become connected with a particular house, and what authors like and dislike about publishers; we will study some individual cases of content and discontent; and, at the end, we will return, with systematic evidence, to an analysis of the author-publisher relationship.

As background for our inquiry into the characteristics and attitudes of authors, let us keep in mind several facts about author-publisher relations. First, all houses are organizations that operate in a market economy. Ex-

* This survey was designed and analyzed by Laurie Michael Roth.

cept for some university presses, all strive to show a profit better than that which could be obtained by investing money in the savings bank. Even university presses must earn money on some books to offset losses on others and to counterbalance the limited subsidies on which some university presses operate. Second, the asymmetrical nature of author-publisher relations is basically set forth and expressed in the contract, as we described it. Third, while money is important to all publishers and surely not irrelevant to authors, each party earns a profit in ways that can lead to a clash of interest between publishers and authors.

The publishing houses we studied each publish between sixty and four hundred books a year. Each author, however, may write only several books in a lifetime. The publisher earns money even if only some of the books do well; the author who may have invested several or more years in a book must earn money on each book or find some other means of support. Some publishers are fond of pointing to the figures on successful individual books and showing that, after federal corporate taxes, authors make more money than publishers do.[11] If this is true, then publishers are indeed in sad shape, for a recent survey of Authors Guild members shows their median 1979 income from writing to be under $5,000 per year.[12] Moreover, publishers' computations rarely take into account subsidiary rights sales or corporate tax writeoffs. These arguments notwithstanding, they mask the simple fact that what is routine to a publisher is exceptional to an author who nurses but one baby at a time. The book is a loved one to the author, as well as a potential means of support; and an author's ego is intimately tied up with its fate. In contrast, the publisher is more like the old lady in the shoe with so many children she can hardly keep track of them all.

WHO WRITES BOOKS?

Our questionnaires come from thirty-four authors who recently wrote for a large university press; forty-five who wrote for a large publishing house specializing in professional and scholarly books; thirty-one who published with a major college textbook house; and sixty-three who wrote for several trade houses—a large one and two smaller ones. In addition, we sampled forty-six authors of psychology books. By and large, the psychology authors exhibit patterns similar to those shown by the authors from the trade houses in our study.*

Let us begin with the way authors in our sample earn their living, since this indicates much about what they expect from publishers. Many authors are academic. Almost all the authors for the university press, the scholarly house, and the college text house were professors, the majority of them having Ph.D.'s. Even among nonfiction trade authors, 40 percent were professors (we did not include fiction in this survey). Our figures are almost exactly the same as those reported for Authors Guild members who wrote part-time—38 percent of whom were university professors. Guild members are almost exclusively trade book authors.[14] Thus while books are important to academics professionally—as expressed in that much-mis-used admonition "Publish or perish"—few of the authors count on books as a basic means of livelihood; even though, for textbook and trade authors, royalties may be an important income supplement.

Despite the low economic return publishing brings to most academics, book publication is an increasingly important component of a successful career. The constriction of the academic job market in recent years has placed great pressure on young academics to publish. While in the past, one book may have been enough to qualify a young professor for tenure, today we find that a book may be a prerequisite for an entry-level job at one of the better universities. And in tenure decisions, some universities no longer count an author's published dissertation, on the assumption that turning a dissertation into a book is both commonplace and expected these days. Consequently, the increased pressure to publish has lessened the credential value of any one single book but has magnified the overall importance of a strong and lengthy list of publications.

We found many editors in scholarly and professional houses, as well as in university presses, who complained that the pressures on academics to publish have become too severe. Editors have claimed that academics are now trying to stretch articles into books and are submitting manuscripts at a very early stage of preparation for evaluation. The editors with whom we talked were all too conscious of their possible role in tenure decisions and frequently resented being thrust into such awkward situations.

Most non-academic authors are also not dependent on books for their basic income. Among the non-academic writers in our study, about half were professionals of one kind or another, and the rest were employed as

* Response rates vary from about 55 percent to 80 percent for the different samples of authors to whom questionnaires were sent. These rates are higher than those obtained in the *Columbia University Economic Survey of Authors*, which averaged 46 percent. Among Authors Guild members, 58 percent responded, but the response was only 21 percent for those invited to be members but who had declined.[13]

editors and journalists. There were few free-lance writers, those who are dependent on the sales of their work to various publishing sources. Our sample suggests that most contemporary writers of nonfiction do not depend on book publishing as their main source of income. The survey of Authors Guild members finds that 35 percent have no other job but writing and, by their own count, spend at least twenty-five hours per week writing. Even so, the median year's income from writing of these "committed full-time" writers is only $11,000 per year—about one third of their total family income.[15]

If book writing is a part-time occupation for most writers, then we might expect that a significant proportion of books would be written by women, given their systematic exclusion from equal access to labor markets and the fact that many women, until recently, worked in the home. Nonetheless, records show that in the 1880s only about 15 percent of the nonfiction published by Macmillan, a leading trade and intellectual house in England at the time, was written by women.[16] Considering the fact that almost all books today are written by people with at least a college degree, and that the number of women graduating from college has dramatically increased since the nineteenth century, we would expect a sizable proportion of nonfiction writers today to be women. And this should be particularly evident in trade houses that publish fewer academics, in whose profession women have experienced significant obstacles. But only 20 percent of our respondents were women—a figure just 5 percent higher than that of Macmillan in the nineteenth century. There was *no* difference by type of publisher: that is, trade houses had no more women authors, at least in our sample, than did scholarly and college text publishers.

In both England and the United States in the early nineteenth century, novel writing exemplified the "empty-field phenomenon"—that is, a field with neither tradition nor entrenched practitioners. As a new form of literature intended for a broader audience, the novel did not quickly win the admiration of the guardians of literary taste and morality. The early novel's characteristics, coupled with the prominence of women as authors, subjects, and readers, assured it a low intellectual and social position. But as Gaye Tuchman and Nina Fortin show in their study of novelists in nineteenth-century England, as novel-writing became a more high-status profession in the latter part of the nineteenth century, men entered the field in much greater numbers.[17] At several of the larger English houses for which data are available, as the percentage of men submitting novels passed the 50 percent mark, the acceptance rate for men went up and declined for women. The length of book reviews for novels greatly increased, with almost all of the increase to be found in longer reviews of novels by men.

In the United States, the nineteenth century saw a clear separation of the novel into high culture and popular culture. Ann Douglas has convincingly argued that the high-culture novel became an almost exclusively male preserve; the popular novel became associated with women and the clergy, both of whom were "dis-established" by the waning of Puritanism and the rise of industrialism.[18]

To complete the picture of the book writer today as a member of the "establishment"—male and well educated—we found only 2 percent of our respondents to be black. And youth was hardly served: almost two thirds of the authors in our sample were over forty. Only the scholarly house had younger authors—about 60 percent were under forty. Its relatively youthful set of authors is a consequence of the nature of its publishing program, which stresses research on the frontier of science in some of the newest sub-disciplines which naturally attract younger scholars.

Since such a sizable proportion of the writers we surveyed were academics, we should say something about the universities with which they are now affiliated and from which they received their advanced degrees. We know from studies of the academic profession that the most prolific scholars are located at élite universities, so it was no surprise that our survey confirmed this finding. Among the university-affiliated authors who wrote for the scholarly house, the college text house, and the university press, fully 60 percent came from the top-rated categories of university,* as did almost half the academics who wrote for trade houses. We were somewhat surprised at such a large percentage given the current academic marketplace, where it is certainly no longer true that the most talented persons teach exclusively at élite universities. When we look at our sample of writers, academic or not, who earned at least a master's degree, we find that 80 percent of them received their degree from the two top-rated categories of university—a percentage that includes trade book authors. Only the college text house and psychology authors deviated slightly from this standard; about 65 percent of these authors graduated from the top two categories of university.

* Barron's rating of the competitiveness of universities on the basis of the entering class's Scholastic Aptitude Test scores was used as a general rating of the universities, rather than the American Council of Education's rating of specific fields.[19]

THE INFLUENCE OF ACADEMIC STATUS

What effect does the letterhead of a prestigious university have on an author's chances of getting published? Sociologists of science have demonstrated that having obtained one's Ph.D. at a major institution is a substantial advantage to a scientist.[20] The dean of American sociologists of science, Robert Merton, has suggested that scientific recognition exemplifies the "Matthew Effect"—to him who hath shall be given.[21] Merton argues that there is a continuing interplay between the status system, based on honor and esteem, and the class system, based on differential life chances; this interplay locates scientists in differing positions within the opportunity structure of science. Without deliberate intent, the Matthew Effect operates to penalize the young and unknown and, in the process, reinforces the already unequal distribution of awards.

In deciding which books to publish, are editors influenced by academic status, and do they consequently make decisions that perpetuate the scientific status system? And is there anything wrong with this? Some scholars have argued that the most talented scientists are to be found in élite schools, and that science is a highly universalistic system which admirably rewards merit.[22] Obviously, scholars employed at élite colleges and universities have better facilities, more research support, lighter teaching loads, and more release time that they can use. Such a system of accumulated advantages would result in the "rich getting richer at a rate that makes the poor become comparatively poorer."[23]

Nevertheless, the question of the influence of status is a complicated matter. To publish the work of a well-known academic seems eminently sensible, but it is another matter to accept the work of an unpublished graduate student or junior faculty member solely on the basis of institutional affiliation. Even though most eminent scholars come from élite universities, there are plenty of non-eminent scholars who also received degrees from the top universities, and whose manuscripts may not be especially good.

The comments of several editors emphasized the importance of academic status. A psychology editor at a leading scholarly house stated:

> Sure, if I get a project that has a Harvard letterhead on it, I'll handle it with dispatch. . . . I might even take it home to read that night. There's no question someone from Harvard has an inherent advantage over others. Why shouldn't they?

The editor in chief at a scholarly house quipped, "People at good schools write good books and people at poor schools write bad books or no books at all. It's that simple. You can't go wrong publishing the books of people at the élite schools."

However, the majority of editors whom we asked about academic status responded that few decisions are made solely on the basis of where an author is employed. These editors noted that academic credentials are increasingly difficult to evaluate. Also, recent trends in the job market for academics have forced some editors to adjust their thinking. The comments of the editor in chief of a major university press are illustrative:

> As a matter of fact our director was asking me about that just yesterday, whether I paid attention to what college the letter came from. It used to be that that was a fairly good criterion of what you could expect. . . . It isn't that they may not be good colleges, but many of these colleges are teaching institutions almost exclusively; and they may be fine teaching institutions, but they don't allow much time for, or do anything to encourage research and writing, and so they don't support this kind of thing. But the way things are now, people are getting jobs where they can find them, so I am reading a lot more carefully something that comes from some college that I never heard of.

Moreover, in our field observations we observed editors receiving projects almost daily from people at élite universities, and of these they accepted only a few for publication. As one of us has shown elsewhere, editors at two leading scholarly houses were very selective even when they reviewed the manuscripts of faculty at élite schools.[24]

Yet status remains influential because graduates and occupants of positions in high-quality schools have a much greater access to effective socialization: that is, they are more confident, they will probably write better letters of introduction, they will have better contacts—all because they have learned the ropes from people who already know "what matters." Sociologist David Caplovitz has made use of the concept of "effective scope" in illustrating that more well-to-do individuals make far greater use of facilities and cultural resources than do others.[25] It is well known that class position influences the degree of knowledge and the use people make of labor- and money-saving opportunities. It is thus no accident that scholars in élite schools have a more "effective scope" than their counterparts located elsewhere. They more often have contacts or are involved in a network of relationships that enable them to contact an editor directly. It seems likely that academics in élite schools who, lacking contacts or connections, send in their materials unsolicited are treated the same as others who use this route. Such an explanation would account for our observations of manuscripts by people in élite schools being rejected. We asked editors at scholarly houses how they would react to receiving unsolicited material from faculty at Harvard or Chicago. Most responded that the letterhead alone would not sway them. Two senior editors at two scholarly houses remarked, "Something must be wrong with the guy, doesn't he have any colleagues who think highly enough of his work to recommend it to me?" and, "I know plenty of people there and if no one mentioned him or her to me, I'd have to wonder."

How much of the difference in an author's relationship with a particular house *after* a contract has been signed, is accounted for by the author's basic attributes? Actually, very little. There are important differences, to be sure, between older and younger authors; but these are almost entirely explained by the differences between greater and less experienced authors. Gender seems to make no difference at all. In none of the matters into which we inquired were women writers appreciably different from men. One would think that the academic prestige of an author might make a great deal of difference—that editors would pay more attention to books by writers from Harvard than from Podunk U. Perhaps, but our sample is one of *published* authors and cannot tell us how, and on what grounds, editors winnow out authors from less prestigious universities. We did find a slight tendency for authors now teaching at less prestigious universities, and who were eventually published, to send their manuscripts in "over the transom" and not to have previously been in touch with or to have worked with a publisher; but the differences are not as strong as some of the folklore of editing would suggest. Once the houses that offer no advances were ruled out, writers teaching at eminent universities were somewhat more likely to be offered larger advances.

There are a few other advantages—particularly in the case of multiple submissions—that accrue to authors at these universities. An author teaching at one who sends his manuscript around to at least one other publisher besides the one with whom he is now publishing, is more likely to be offered a contract than is an author teaching at a lesser university. More than half of the authors from the top universities were offered more than one contract for the same book, compared with one third of those from the lesser universities. But we are talking about a small minority of the authors who sent their manuscript to more than one publisher. Finally, it is true that writers now affiliated with prestigious universities are more likely to review manuscripts for publishers than are authors from less prestigious universities. Since trade houses rarely ask for pre-publication review by outsiders, this finding does not apply to trade publishing.

Our sample of published authors—as well as the Authors Guild sample—leads us to conclude that academic status and the background of an author do not account for many significant differences in treatment by book publishers. Far more important are an author's previous contacts with a publisher. We should not be surprised that authors in prestigious schools have more and better contacts; but once we control for prior experience with a publisher, many of the differences between élite and lesser universities disappear.

NEW AUTHORS AND OLD HANDS

Recipe for a book. First find a publisher. The first question we asked authors in our questionnaire was how they initially decided upon a publisher for their manuscripts. The process differs for authors who have previously published with a house and for those who are newcomers. The way an author approaches his editor, the way the house responds, the terms that are offered, and almost anything else one can think of depend on whether the relationship between author and house is new or old.

From the house's point of view, the issue is author loyalty; from the author's point of view—and that is our point of view for this chapter—the issue is satisfaction. An author who is satisfied with a house will be more likely to return to it than will one who is not. Putting matters this way, however, oversimplifies a complex relationship.

If our sample of authors is a good indication, then most authors are new to a house; in fact, two thirds of the authors were with houses that had never before published them. Does this mean that most authors are dissatisfied? Not necessarily, because 40 percent of the authors in our sample who were new to a house had not previously published a book, while another 15 had published only one previous book. In sharp contrast, more than half of the 33 percent who were not newcomers to their current house were veteran writers with more than four previous books.

The policies of a house have a great deal to do with whether authors stay with it for other books, though satisfaction is not always related to the same house. For example, the scholarly monograph house in this sample has few repeaters (fewer than 20%); but this house also has the highest proportion of satisfied authors. This anomaly is explained by the house's strategy of being constantly on the lookout for frontiers in science. It does not necessarily like the esoteric; but, rather, judges that, for its type of publishing, books in new areas of science sell best—areas that are most likely to be populated by new and less experienced scientists. It is also the case that, having once published a book with modest circulation, an author may aim for a house that offers distribution to a wider audience. Authors apparently leave the scholarly house not because their expectations on their first book are not met, but because they have different expectations for their next one.

Except for the scholarly monograph house, the more frequently authors are satisfied, the higher a house's proportion of returning authors. The repeat rate for other houses in our sample runs from about 20 percent to 60 percent; and to order houses by proportion of highly satisfield authors is also to order them by rate of repeating authors. Yet there are important differences among the trade houses, the university house, and the college text house. Trade houses in our study have repetition rates for authors ranging from 20 percent to 30 percent; the university press's rate of returning authors is 33 percent; and the college text house has the highest rate, at 60 percent. These rates are not necessarily related to the size of advances offered former authors compared with new authors. For example, the college text house offers smaller advances to former authors than to new authors. This seemingly counterproductive practice is partly explained by the fact that repeating authors frequently get a chance to publish a higher-level text, which contains more of their original ideas but has a smaller market potential. New authors at this house are usually authors of beginning texts, which have a potentially large market. On the other hand, most other types of house that do give advances offer larger amounts to repeat authors. Differences in rates of return of authors to publishing houses are probably as much a reflection of type of publishing as they are of the manner in which a particular house treats an individual author. Trade publishing is inherently more uncertain and trendy than other types of publishing. Hence trade authors are more likely to switch publishers (so are trade editors, as seen in chapter 4). University press publishing is similar to scholarly and professional publishing in that successful authors are likely to move on to other publishers who offer wider distribution. On the other hand, one significant feature of university presses is that they have a built-in tie to authors at their own institutions who may feel more comfortable returning to their home press.

CONTACTING A PUBLISHER

Bearing in mind the differences between authors who have previously published with a house and those who are new to it, we shall see how authors go about contacting publishing houses. As we said earlier, most editors think that sending manuscripts "over the transom"—that is, sending a publisher an unsolicited manuscript—is a total waste of time and energy. Fewer than 1 percent of all manuscripts received in this fashion are ever published. While this perception may make sense to an editor, it is irrelevant to authors who have actually overcome the barriers and been published. The proportion of repeaters who simply send their manuscript in to their old publishing house without any prior notice or ceremony is extremely small; in fact, one wonders whether the few repeat authors who checked this alternative on our questionnaire actually understood our question.

But there is a substantial number of authors who are new to a publishing house and whose manuscripts have arrived "over the transom." The proportion depends on both the subject matter of the book and the nature of the house. Over 40 percent of new authors in the field of psychology originally sent in unsolicited manuscripts, as compared with only 5 percent of new authors of books of all types published by trade houses. Since some of the authors of psychology books did publish with trade houses, there must be something special about the field of psychology: either editors are especially on the lookout for books in it and/or are sensitive to them, or psychology authors are both naïve and lucky. Scholarly and university press houses are much more receptive to unsolicited manuscripts than are trade houses. About 25 percent of the scholarly houses' new authors sent in their manuscripts in this way, and about one third of the university press authors did so. The college text house was much like the trade houses in that a *very* small proportion of new authors sent in their manuscripts "over the transom." As noted in our discussion of textbook publishing, it is a business with significant sums of money involved, and editors are not likely to risk these sums on persons unknown to them. For the university press, and especially for the scholarly-professional house, a variety of complicated and non-standard ways of getting a new author in touch with a publishing house were also important. Being part of a series edited by a senior professor with whom the author worked, getting published as a result of an academic award, being part of a special project, and the like formed the basis for initial contacts of a not insignificant number of authors. Sources of this type were far less important for other kinds of house.

Editors told us that they spent a good deal of their time hunting down prospects. How productive was this work from the authors' point of view? In most houses we sampled, from one fifth to one third of all new authors came to the house as a result of an editor's initiative. The proportion of repeat authors who were approached by an editor (usually their former editor) to do another book is also about one fifth to one third, depending on the house. (We must caution that who initiated the contact with a house, and who merely reacted, is usually not easy to disentangle in the case of repeat authors.) Editorial initiative was most important in the case of college text publishing. Most able academics would rather write scholarly books or professional monographs; they need to be persuaded to write a textbook. Not surprisingly, then, two thirds of the new authors of the college text house came to it as a result of its initiative rather than as a result of their own search for a publisher.

The subject of brokerage and patronage has been the substance of many myths. We devote more attention to it in chapter 11 on agents and brokers. In our sample of authors, between 15 percent and 25 percent of new authors came to a house as a result of an introduction by a friend or a colleague who already knew someone at the house. But the success of this informal route leads us to question another myth—namely, that it is agents who *initiate* the contact with a publishing house. Agents are not important sources for university presses, scholarly-professional houses, or college text houses, but they are the reputed kings and queens of contact with trade houses. Our data, however, show that only 25 percent of new authors at the trade houses in our sample were sent to the house by their agents. The other authors may also have had an agent, but the initial contact with the house for 75 percent of them was made in some other way.

Finding a house is not the same thing as deciding to publish with it, for almost half of the authors had sent their manuscript to at least one other house beside the one where they ultimately published. We asked authors in some detail what influenced them to sign.* There were four basic reasons. The first was the nature of the relation between publisher and author. Examples included: "I had done previous books with this publisher and liked them," or "I had a previous professional or personal relationship with the publisher or an editor at the house," or "A colleague recommended the

---

* Each author responded to a list of eleven "factors" that might have been important in the decision to sign with the particular house that brought the author into our study. Authors told us how important a given reason was to them. These reasons were then clustered empirically, using McQuitty typal analysis of the correlations between the reasons. Here we report only the reasons given as the *most* important reasons for signing.

house," and, "This publisher was the first to offer me a contract." This first factor reflects a lack of search and in effect says, "I signed because it was the most convenient thing to do." Over 60 percent of the repeat authors noted that prior relationship with a house was their main reason for signing with it again. The mere fact that the relationship continues must signify that it is at least satisfactory. Not surprisingly, then, more than half the repeat authors who signed as a matter of convenience also indicated that they liked the house. A new author is, of course, less likely to have a prior relation with a house or to know one of the editors; and so these reasons are seldom involved in new authors signing. Even among new authors, 15 percent indicated that they signed with a house because of some prior relationship with it or with a staff member.

The mere fact that a contractual relationship was offered was the major reason for signing given by one third of the new authors; they signed up because the house was the first to offer them a contract.

The qualities of editors constituted a second reason for signing and was cited by about 10 percent of the repeat authors and by 20 percent of the new ones. We were surprised by these low percentages. Clearly relatively few authors flock to a house because of a new Maxwell Perkins. This fact is important to bear in mind when we discuss authors' complaints, which frequently center on turnover in editorial staff. Although we know that most authors tended to approve of their editors (more about this shortly), the presence or the absence of a particular editor is apparently not a very frequent reason for signing with a house. Other factors count more.

Attributes of the house itself were a third reason for signing and were given as the most important factor by one fourth of the repeat authors and by almost two fifths of the new authors. These attributes clustered into two groups: (1) the books a house had published in the past—that is, the reputations created by the books and the traditions associated with the house; and (2) the services a particular publisher could provide for a particular author—such as good financial terms, quick publication, effective advertising and promotion, or wide distribution. In view of the fact that money, timing, advertising, and promotion eventually cause considerable grief to both authors and publishers, it is interesting that these factors are apparently not as important reasons for signing as is a house's reputation. Only 10 percent of repeat authors, and 20 percent of new ones, checked services as their main consideration.

Money will be discussed again when we analyze relationships with agents and other representatives; but some comments about money and choosing publishers are relevant here. Money can be divided into three components: royalty rates, size of advance, and share of subsidiary rights sales. Until recently, royalties tended to be fairly standard (about 10% to 15%) and the item least subject to negotiation, as we infer from the fact that having an agent does not increase an author's royalty rate. Thus, it is fairly easy to understand why royalites were not an important factor in the decision to sign, even among authors for trade houses.

Advances are another matter. There is a wide difference in the size of advances that authors receive, and here agents do seem to make a big difference. The few advances that university presses pay are as a rule only for manuscript typing, and for that as seldom as possible. College text houses have been known to pay large sums for introductory texts that appeal to large markets. Yet in the house in our sample, advances were not large. Only 20 percent of the authors received advances between $5,000 and $20,000, and only a handful received more. It is for trade authors that advances may be a critical factor in the decision to sign with a publisher. In a recent Authors Guild survey of contracts received by authors in 1977 and 1978, only 5 percent of those replying did not receive an advance.[26] This compares with 7 percent of the authors for trade houses in our sample—about the same. But the Authors Guild respondents received more money than did the respondents in our sample. One fifth of the Guild survey of nonfiction authors, but only one tenth of ours, commanded advances of $20,000 or more; one third of ours and a bit more than one third of the Authors Guild's received $5,000 to $20,000. Finally, half of ours but only a third or so of theirs received less than $5,000. We did not ask about the size of the split with the publisher on the sale of paperback rights to another house, but over 80 percent of the authors in the Guild survey received the standard 50 percent, so there was not much variance. Money can therefore be an important matter in signing but seems to be a sizable issue only for a relatively few authors who can demand large advances. Further, when it comes to the big sums, in most cases agents or attorneys—not the author—handle the bargaining. Since authors are less involved, it may be natural for them to find financial terms less important in deciding about a house than some other factors, such as the nature of the editor or the list—matters that are closer to an author's professional concerns. Then, too, it is important to remember that although authors certainly like financial remuneration as much as the next person, the typical nonfiction author does not initially write a book for the purpose of making a lot of money (though dreams of gold may occur later in the process). As we said earlier, most writers are employed in some way and do not depend on book writing for their main source of income, a fact that publishers themselves remember extremely well.

In sum: some authors do respond to the image of a house; far fewer care about the editor; and some consider what a publisher can do for them; but the most important reason for an author's signing with a house is either sheer inertia or gratitude, if you will. Merely having been there and not doing too badly the last time around influences an author to return to a house; for a new author it is important simply that a house be the first to offer a contract.

AUTHOR SATISFACTION

Most of the "disaster" stories one hears from both authors and publishers occur after the honeymoon that accompanies the signing of a contract. Upon signing, both parties to the contract are full of hope: the book is important, will sell well, and will enhance the reputation of both author and publishing house. As we said, there are many forces in the publishing process that work to separate author from publisher and eventually tend to produce a conflict of interest. Consequently, it is by no means a certainty that an author who is intially happy with a house will remain so after his or her book has been published. We therefore asked authors to tell us not only what induced them to sign with a publisher but to indicate on a check list what they liked and disliked about the publisher after their books had been published.

Two basic factors stood out: technical and editorial services.* Technical services include mostly things that authors are unable to do for themselves, such as the actual production of a book, advertising, and distribution. Those who like or dislike a publisher's advertising and promotion are especially likely to also like (or dislike) a publisher's marketing and distribution. Though publishers distinguish between marketing and distribution, authors are apparently less likely to make this distinction. Also included among technical services are book design, production schedule, and financial terms. Editorial services include advice about the basic concept of a book and copy editing. Respect for the scholarly value of the author's ideas falls between the two clusters and is closely linked to pleasure or displeasure with advertising or promotion, for it is here that many authors express opinions about the way a book was treated. Promotion and adver-

---

* The result of a cluster analysis of an eleven-item check list about what authors liked and disliked about publishers.

tising, though much desired by authors, may also be carried out in such a way as to denigrate, in an author's view, the basic quality of a work.

In general, most authors we sampled responded favorably to their editor's ideas. Almost 90 percent of authors at trade houses thought well of their editor, although only half of the authors at the scholarly house did. Copy editing was another matter that pleased most authors. The university press and the college text book house authors were particularly likely to be satisfied; authors at the scholarly house and trade houses were somewhat less likely to be satisfied, though we are still talking about at least a 60-percent-satisfaction rate. Among technical services, book design and even production time seem to satisfy most authors; but on the latter point there were more complaints by trade authors, one fourth of whom complained that their books were produced too slowly.

Advertising and promotion as well as marketing and distribution turn out to be an author's nemesis, particularly at trade houses. Over three fifths of the authors at trade houses complained about advertising and promotion—mainly the lack of either; while half were dissatisfied with marketing and distribution. Fewer than 25 percent of the trade authors were satisfied with advertising and promotion; about one third were happy with marketing and distribution. Almost every other service received better rating. What is especially interesting about authors' complaints were the different responses we obtained from the authors of the monograph house, which does little advertising, except by direct mail. Seven of ten authors were satisfied with these aspects of the house, and only one in ten had complaints. These authors were obviously aware of the limited appeal of their highly technical research monographs and were pleased to have them brought to the attention of the few scholars working in the same or related fields. Authors for the text house were also content. But the authors for the very same company's trade division were as dissatisfied as the authors at other trade houses. Authors for the university press fell in between the trade authors and the monograph authors in their evaluation of their publishers' attempts to market and advertise their books.

The satisfaction or dissatisfaction of authors with marketing, promotion, advertising, and distribution is related more to expectations authors have about different types of publishers rather than to the characteristics of either individual authors or publishers. The authors of scientific monographs have no expectations of appearances on the "Today" show, full-page ads in the *New York Times*, or a copy in every bookstore into which they might wander. They expect direct mail distribution and advertising of their books and, in many cases, know by name half of the two thousand or so potential customers of their books. Though text books are distributed by college travelers, and are given some advertising in academic journals as well as through direct mail, the marketing of texts is also fairly standardized, and the text authors found that their expectations were routinely met. This was definitely not the experience of authors of books for trade houses. The structure of that segment of the industry almost guarantees that many authors will be dissatisfied with marketing and advertising.

The signing of a book—an act determined from the publisher's side by the acquiring editor's enthusiasm—is an occasion for great expectations, at least on the author's side. The author has usually lived with the book for at least a year or two, and hopes it will repay him or her for the time put into it in terms not only of money but also of fame. At a time when one reads in the newspapers, often on the front page, about authors of trade books earning millions and becoming overnight sensations as a result of a single book, every author of a trade book has high hopes for his or her own book. The editor, the "good guy" in the plot, probably has more realistic expectations for a book, and yet it is the editor's role to convey as much enthusiasm as possible. Enthusiasm is important because most books are signed when they are incomplete—often only on the basis of an outline and a chapter or two. The editor schedules the book, works with the author, and is responsible for turning out a publishable product. Skepticism and moderation are hardly the ways to encourage an author to meet his or her obligations. And, indeed, our data show that editors and even copy editors are well appreciated by authors.

Yet in dealing with a publishing house, especially a large one, authors are in a somewhat Chaplinesque situation. An author is typically a lonely individual who must deal with a huge machinery consisting of a variety of specialized employees whom he usually does not know, and who wish to exercise some control over his work, which by now has been removed from much of his control. Many accounts of authors stress the frustrations they experience when faced with a setup of specialized personnel who often reveal a trained incapacity to think in any way other than their ritually prescribed routines. An author is likely to feel that a cherished brainchild has been treated routinely by many of those who were supposed to give it tender loving care. This situation is by no means due to happenstance but is rooted in the structure of publishing.

One major structural cause of potential conflict derives from the temporal flow of activities in a publishing house. In chapter 7 we saw how this flow affects coordination of work within a house. Here we examine the consequences for authors. As we said, the work flow is typically organized in terms of the requirements of two, or sometimes three, annual lists of publications. An editor, for example, might aim at publishing a particular book nine months from the time he or she has worked on it with an author, so that it can be placed on the fall list. This means that three months later, when the manuscript may have moved to the copy editor or the manufacturing department, the acquiring editor will already be at work on a different set of books for, say, the spring list of the subsequent year. As a result, when an author complaining about copy editing or production approaches the acquisitions editor—who, by the way, is usually the *only* person who can be approached, since other personnel concerned with the book are not known to the author—he or she will likely have neither time nor energy to spend on a book that, even though it is not yet published, is already "ancient history." Editors are taught to think prospectively rather than retrospectively.

Editors are people in the middle who stand on uneasy ground, trying to mediate between authors and the demands of the marketplace. They are torn between contradictory expectations: those of the firm's top executives and those of the authors over whom they exercise a measure of power. Editors know that publishing houses, particularly trade ones, release many books, but that not all are successful. No one likes to fault one's own work, and it is much easier for an author to cite lack of appropriate advertising or poor marketing and distribution as the reason his or her book failed to meet expectations. And failure is inevitable for a large number of the trade books published annually. The author sees that X book is receiving much publicity and therefore thinks that it will sell well. A book may show evidence of sales potential or receive a strong review and as a result be given strong promotion. Yet it is also true that a book in which a publisher initially invests a big advance also gets more advertising and promotion (see chapters 8 and 13). For the moment, let us stick with the authors' view that their expectations for their precious offspring have not been met.

Let us contrast, in different types of house, the relationship between an author's expectations, as reported to us, and his or her satisfaction with the publishing house. We should expect some relationship between current views of the house and initial expectations for a book if only because the two were reported to us at the same time. Nevertheless, there are important differences between different types of house in the way authors' expectations of various aspects of publishing were or were not met.

Positive expectations about the editorial process were by and large met in most houses. Every one of the authors who was delighted with an editor in the text house at the time of signing still, when we sampled them, had a favorable reaction to that editor. And for those for whom the editor was not an important factor in signing, 60 percent became pleased with him or her. About the same holds true for editors of the university press, though not quite so many authors were converted to a favorable view. Trade houses were not as successful in preserving authors' good opinions of editors, although three quarters of those authors positive upon signing retained positive feelings. However, among those who did not hold a fine opinion of editors at signing time, only half changed to a more favorable view.

During the process of editing, an author develops a sense of whether the house has a high opinion of what he or she is trying to say—that is, the scholarly or literary value of the book—or tends to denigrate its content. If a university press, text, or scholarly house author felt at the outset that the house valued the content of his book, he continued to do so after the editorial process was over. Further, an author who did not list the house's high opinion of the scholarly value of the book as a major reason for signing in the first place, felt—by the time he filled out our questionnaire—that the house did indeed care about the book's content.

None of this is true for authors of trade books. Almost all of them mentioned the high regard of their respective houses for the content of their books as an important reason for signing. On the other hand, by the time we asked them about their current views, half of those who had initially thought well of their houses were now reconsidering.

Advertising and promotion show a different pattern; although again, trade houses stand out as creating author dissatisfaction. There is relatively little change in authors' views in the scholarly and text houses. In the scholarly house which essentially does no promotion and little in the way of advertising, except through direct mail, only one—among those authors who were initially pleased about the prospects of whatever advertising and promotion the press was going to do for them—became disaffected. And of those who did not expect much, some were later pleased. Very few authors at the university press expected much in the way of advertising and promotion, but almost half of those for whom this was not a factor in signing with the press later reported satisfaction. Among authors of trade books, two thirds of those who were happy about advertising and promotion prospects at the time of signing, were dissatisfied with them currently, though half who expected little got more.

In sum, authors at trade houses basically like their editors but blame the houses for not sufficiently respecting the content of their books and for not having met their expectations about advertising and promotion. Authors in other types of house have, to begin with, lower expectations about advertising and promotion and tend to be happy about whatever a house has done for them.

The main predictor of discontent or satisfaction with publishers that we have been able to deduce through our quantitative analysis has been the type of house with which an author publishes. Generally, scholarly houses and university presses seem to produce the greatest author satisfaction, college text houses are close behind, but trade houses seem to engender as much discontent as satisfaction. We attribute these differences to the varying expectations authors bring with them to the different types of publishing, and to the different organizational setups found in each.

AUTHOR-EDITOR RELATIONS

Despite the fact that publishing houses, especially trade houses, create a great deal of disappointment among authors, editors seem to be relatively immune from criticism. Indeed, we find in certain circumstances a good relation with an editor increases author satisfaction with a house. An author of previous books with a house who came to it mainly because of his prior relationship with an editor was twice as likely as other authors to be highly satisfied with that house after the publication of his current book; moreover, not a single author checked any dissatisfactions. The picture that emerges from our sample is logically contradictory: authors dislike publishing houses but like editors, who are the houses' employees.

Let us look in more detail at the relations between authors, editors, and publishing houses. We will begin with scholarly publishing and then turn our attention to several cases in trade publishing. Though we have seen that scholarly and university houses generally tend to meet author expectations and engender the least difficulties (for example, "The entire enterprise was a great joy. The editors were helpful, encouraging and intelligent"), several examples will illustrate some of the problems scholarly houses can get into. The role of the editor appears crucial to the author in each case. These examples, which have had their subject matter modified to conceal identities, will provide some understanding of how authors and editors interact.

A young female author with good academic credentials and considerable, though recent, reputation, submitted a book on the history of music to a high-level publisher of scholarly books. She was previously acquainted with the woman music editor of the house, and the two soon established an excellent working relationship. The editor was glad to accept the manuscript and to sign a contract. She spent time on the manuscript; in fact, she went over it line by line, a practice that, by the way, has become increasingly rare. The author was most grateful for what she considered a decided improvement. Editorial work being completed, the manuscript was sent to the production department, and the author naively assumed that it would now be processed routinely. The production department in this particular house, which produces a relatively large number of books, consisted of only a handful of production or project editors. A production editor usually works on six or eight projects at a time, farming out much of the copy editing to free-lance copy editors who work at home on a fee-for-service basis. This means that an in-house production editor coordinates the activities of free-lance editors and has only a surface acquaintance with any particular manuscript.

In this case, the manuscript was given for editing to a free-lancer who was supposed to be knowledgeable because he had previously worked for the musical page of a national magazine. Thus, a person who had no official position in the house but claimed expertise, found himself in a position of power over a recognized expert who happened to be relatively young and a woman. The copy editor liberally dotted the pages of the manuscript with corrections and made many revisions, critical comments, and nasty remarks.

When the disfigured manuscript reached the author, she—understandably and predictably—exploded. Not knowing who had disfigured her brainchild, she went to see her friend, the editor, hoping that the latter would do battle in her behalf. But by now her friend and confidante was preoccupied with an entirely different set of books. Though personally sympathetic to the author's trials and tribulations, she could not really attend to them; having long before passed the book on to the production department, she had checked it off her list, and renewed concern with it would upset her tightly organized schedule. She nevertheless promised to look into the matter with the production editor. The latter, however, as it turned out, backed his free-lance copy editor and felt that any interference from the editorial department in the production process constituted an infringement of his prerogatives. (Conflicts between editorial and production departments are by no means exceptional.) At this point the young author was near a breakdown. She made brave attempts to revise the manuscript but realized soon that she was simply unable to follow the instructions of the copy editor.

This particular case finally had a happy ending. It was at last brought all the way up to the head of the company, who ruled in the author's favor and assigned a new copy editor to the manuscript who made only minimal demands on the author. But be it noted that, in the last analysis, the favorable resolution of the case depended on the benevolence of the head of the house rather than on regular procedures. Much as in an oriental autocracy, justice was done not because of the application of legal norms to the case at hand, but through personal favor of the autocrat.

Needless to say, this is not the only case of officious editing that we encountered. On the other hand, editors can be constructive and creative. To take but one example among many that we have accumulated, the editor in chief of a scholarly house that occasionally published trade books contacted a well-known author and psychotherapist and asked if he could do something with a number of European papers on existentialism and psychotherapy that the editor had accumulated. The author agreed and now believes in retrospect that, despite the many trials of translation from the German, battles with a co-editor, and the usual production problems, the book cemented his own interest in the field. He was "very moved" by the papers and wrote a preface and two essays himself, and the book was successful and "made quite an impression on the psychiatric world." Though he now publishes with trade houses, he remains on good terms with the editor in chief who proposed the project and who has now moved on to another house.

These two examples come from similar publishing houses. The differences are in the relative statuses of author and editor. In one case, we have an inexperienced author who was delighted that her book was going to be published. She assumed that publishing houses know what they are doing, and that everything would be all right, and, if not, that they knew best—or at least she at first thought so. Her editor, though sympathetic, was not powerful and was located in a middle-level position. In the other case, we have a famous author approached by the editor in chief himself. Despite many trials (mainly bickering with the translator), the intellectual integrity and control over the marketing of the book were maintained by the editor in chief who would not allow the star author to be alienated. Moreover, the editor in chief, having himself created the idea of the book, had a strong intellectual investment in it. Finally, he was the president of the house as well—it was his baby, a rare situation these days.

Given the position of the editor as man or woman in the middle, and the author's need to have someone in the house to believe in, yet the frequent ability of the rest of the house, and even of the editor, to anger the author, it is no wonder that authors have kind words to say about their editors while being angry with their houses. An author frequently attributes all of his or her woes to the fact that "my" editor left the house either in the middle of the production process or soon after the book came out. Had "my" editor only remained, everything would have been all right.

The following narrative, written as a six-page addendum to our author questionnaire by one respondent, may seem bizarre but it is not unusual. A newspaperman published a nonfiction book with one of the more commercially successful New York City trade houses, which we will call house B. Between paperback and hardcover advances, he got about ten thousand dollars. He then wrote another book—this one a novel*—showed it to the editor of his first book, who told him to "quit my newspaper job to become a big-time author." The editor also asked the author to revise the manuscript to read like a final draft, the better to impress the editorial board. Two months later, the author still had no contract, but the editor told him he was moving to another house, M, to be editor in chief. Though the new house had indeed agreed to buy up many of this editor's books that he had signed up with his former house, it had already used up its available cash (or so our author reports; the truth may well be that the editor no longer believed in the book). Nevertheless, "he pressed the book on his former friends at House S," and an editor was found who one year later brought it near to press. But now the editor in chief and the publisher read it and "neither understood it nor liked me." Our author withdrew his book.

Three years have passed since the beginning of this narrative. The author and his agent found his original editor who, for some reason, had just quit his job as editor in chief and joined a new small house, P. "I revised the book twice that spring. In the summer the editor retired from publishing because of ill health and his replacement at house P did not want the book." Our hero and his agent once more found a new house, R, a subsidiary of C. The new editor and our author worked on the book for another year and a half, "with several time-outs for exhaustion and frustration. We both nearly quit/killed each other several times." But now the editor moved to become editor in chief at a very large house, X. "A brief tussle between R [the old house] and X [the new house] ensued in which both sides were careful not further to reward the author." The new house, X, however, made specific projections for the size of the first print run, the price, and so on. The old house, R, promised nothing "but pointed to its own enthusiasm." Our author went to the new house, along with his editor. More rewriting, more battles, this time over a jacket. The Book-of-the-

---

* Our policy in this chapter has been to exclude fiction. In this case the author writes both fiction and nonfiction, and his story about his fiction book is not atypical of nonfiction work.

Month Club took the book as a main monthly selection and sold more than one hundred thousand copies. Y paperback house, a subsidiary of a publishing conglomerate, bought the rights for nearly half a million dollars. (A further sidelight: this same paperback house, when owned by another firm, was sued by the author for not keeping his nonfiction book in print.)

Yet this is not the end. "In June ... with my book a Book-of-the-Month Club selection, a sizable profit for X House, and the book already a critical success, my editor was fired. He was not replaced until several months later. ... Meanwhile, X House violated my contract by running monstrous ads that ate the $65,000 ad budget and infuriated my agent, me, and Y paperback house. I begged them to kill the last $10,000 worth and simply give the money to Y for their paperback campaign. They did. I did a twenty-four-city promotion tour, hating my publisher all the while." Our author concluded, "I wish you luck in trying to rationalize the author-publisher relationship. I'm afraid it is a bit more complicated than most people imagine. We haven't even gotten to questions of editorial quality, etc."

The author in this case was not naive and eventually became very successful. Yet his success seemed to hang by a thread tied to one editor or another. Or did it? We have a collection of many stories of poor editing, unfaithful production, inadequate distribution, unconscionable delay, inept promotion, and sheer venality with only one editor and one house; though, to be sure, authors more often blame a change in editors for their predicament than they do the structure of publishing.

Some authors are less persistent than our hero. In 1981, the Pulitzer Prize for fiction was posthumously awarded to John Kennedy Toole, who had committed suicide in 1969 at the age of thirty-two. Robert Gottlieb, at the time with Simon & Schuster and known even then as one of the best editors in publishing, had rejected the very work that, when published in 1980 by Louisiana State University Press, received critical acclaim. Besides showing that editors can indeed differ in taste as well as in the ability to gauge the market (the book, *The Confederacy of Dunces*, has already, in 1981, sold forty-five thousand copies in hardcover and has been bought for the movies), this sad story also suggests that an author needs much patience and a thick skin. According to the late author's mother, he had an extensive correspondence with Gottlieb over a two-year period during which Gottlieb asked for a number of revisions. "You can't stand the heartache of the correspondence," the mother told a reporter from the *New York Times*.[27] Though Gottlieb remembers neither his correspondence with Toole nor the manuscript, the author got—according to his mother—an unusual hearing, with Gottlieb apparently investing far more effort than is usual for such unsolicited projects. But this young author, not hardened by years of dealing with agents, editors, and publishers, simply gave up in despair.

Editors received their turn in a previous chapter. Authors themselves are hardly blameless for problems in the production and distribution of books. From an editor's point of view, the greatest problem is the unpredictability of author performance—in terms of both meeting deadlines and producing a quality product. For example, we have a story in our files of an edited handbook that has been in the works for over seven years. The academics who were putting the volumes together reported the familiar story of broken promises, vagueness, switches in editors, and delay on the part of the publishers. With much moral indignation, they finally took their project to another house. What the authors did not realize is that their obsessive editing created so much delay that the original publisher lost faith in the project, and his interest understandably waned. Having lost interest, but nonetheless having a contract, it appears that he created such a smoke-screen that the authors gave up and went elsewhere. This is perhaps not the most straightforward way of doing business but, on the other hand, was not entirely without justification.

What kind of author has successful relations with publishing houses? Authors who do not publish with trade houses, as we saw, tend to be more satisfied. Are there individual characteristics that count? Our data suggest that individual attributes may not account for much variation. Nevertheless, our anecdotal material offers a number of clues. To begin with, authors must recognize the asymmetries of the author-publisher relationship. Competition, if any, among publishers (this varies according to the field and the nature of the manuscript) operates only at the time of contract signing. The Authors Guild, agents, and some authors have been nibbling away at contracts, trying to redress the imbalance between publishers and authors not only with respect to financial terms but including such matters as the nature of accounting for royalties, liability (who is responsible for suits against author and publisher), the return of advances should the author—though working in good faith—fail to deliver a satisfactory work, and the related right of publishers to refuse a manuscript that has been contracted for, as well as the perennial issues of control over book production, distribution, and promotion.

According to an Authors Guild survey of royalty forms of twenty-four publishers, some straightforward information on how authors get paid seems missing from most publishers' accounting to their authors. Books are often discounted at various rates, thus affecting the amount and the rate of the royalties. Most publishers do not report how many books are sold and returned in each royalty rate category, or the amount of money earned in each category. The same information reported for trade sales is often not reported for wholesale, mail order, special, Canadian, export, and remainder sales. Statements often do not give sufficient detail on subsidiary rights transactions. An issue that almost all authors are concerned with is never reported by publishers: How many copies of a book have been printed? How many have been sold or distributed for review or other purposes? And how many remain undistributed? While there does not appear to be much that individual authors can do about these matters, awareness of these issues can at least avoid later surprises. Trade books are distributed in more complex ways than are texts or scholarly books and are thus more subject to royalty variations. Trade authors are probably more dependent for their livelihood on royalties than are other authors. Hence, trade book authors tend to be more dissatisfied in this area. Our data suggest that accurate expectations on the part of authors reduce dissatisfaction. Authors who are more aware of the ins-and-outs of royalty statements are less likely to be shocked by the outcome, though their lack of surprise does not necessarily change the fact that the statement may not be altogether fair.

Novice authors who have met with great success are the most vulnerable to publisher-author imbalances, for their expectations for their book diverge the most from the actual outcome. (As Durkheim pointed out, anomie is occasioned by sudden unexpected success as much or even more than by predictable failure.) Shere Hite's problem with her report of a survey on female sexuality, called *The Hite Report* (Macmillan, 1976), is not atypical.[28] As a young inexperienced social science author with a "hot" topic, she placed her faith (and continues to do so) in her editor, Regina Ryan. A contract with Macmillan provided for an advance of $20,000 and no more than $25,000 per year in royalties, the latter limitation allegedly for tax purposes. (For a similar situation, see the account given by an agent on page 291.) According to Ryan, the limitation clause remained in the contract despite her advice to Hite that it be removed. In three years the book had actually earned the author over $875,000, of which, including the advance, she has realized only $95,000. According to *Publishers Weekly*:

> Hite says that she signed the contract containing the limitation clause without benefit of a lawyer or agent and with no knowledge of authors' entitlements in such contracts. She acknowledges that when the agreement was drawn neither she nor Macmillan anticipated the large profits the book would generate. Her contract with Knopf [for a subsequent book] contained no limitation [of yearly income] clause."[29]

Meanwhile, according to Hite, Macmillan has not paid her nor has it placed the money in escrow, nor paid any interest on it, and uses it for its own purposes. Hite was angry with Macmillan, her publisher, but not with her editor who presumably supervised the contractual agreements. Hite is now suing Macmillan. Obviously, she would have benefited from an agent or a lawyer to begin with, but did not believe her book was worth the trouble or that such expertise would have made a difference. In line with what we have said about author-editor relations, Hite's book on male sexuality has recently (1981) been published by Knopf, where her editor was the same Regina Ryan, who is now an independent book producer.

Financial issues, though crucial to some authors, are, as we saw, less important reasons for signing for many others. What does rankle all authors, however, is the publisher's reaction to their manuscript. Most trade house books are signed before there is much more in hand than an idea or an outline. Scholarly manuscripts are often signed on the basis of a prospectus and several sample chapters. In either case, publishers demand, and get, the unilateral right to reject a manuscript as not satisfactory even though the author labored in good faith trying to produce it. If there had been an advance, publishers are legally within their rights, in almost all contracts as they are now constituted (as we have noted), to demand that the advance be returned. Authors claim that they risk a year or more in wages, and that publishers should be required to share some of this risk. A 1977 court case, which established no precedent because it was eventually settled out of court, seemed to support the author's side. A. E. Hotchner, a veteran author originally recruited for Random House by Bennett Cerf, found that his last book for them was rejected after it had been handed in well within the deadline. Again, we find an author's loyalty to the editor: "Bennett died shortly after ... the contract was signed: it was a loss I felt keenly. Even though I had the same editor as I had had [on the last two books] I was nonetheless apprehensive about the Random House changes that Bennett's death would provoke."[30]

Random House demanded back the $11,250 already paid as an advance. Though Hotchner's book, *King of the Hill,* was immediately published by Harper & Row to "widespread favorable reviews," Random House went to trial; and the author, a law school graduate who had practiced for all of a year, acted as his own attorney. Hotchner apparently established in court that the book was satisfactory, and that Random House did not know what the standard clause, "satisfactory in form and content," actually meant. The judge noted in chambers that courts have held that if a salesman is given an advance, has worked hard to sell the product, and fails to do so, the advance is not necessarily recoverable, and that writers might benefit from such decisions. Random House had invested far more in the case than the amount of the actual advance to the author, presumably because of the precedent it might set in cases when large advances are involved. For this same reason, perhaps, after seeing how the case was going, it agreed to withdraw its lawsuit and pay all costs, if the author would agree to withdraw his counterclaim. Hotchner agreed, claiming that Random House would in any case appeal a lost verdict, and that he could not afford the costs of an appeal. So there is still no legal precedent on the matter, though the legal power of a publishing house to recover an advance in a case where an author appears to have performed satisfactorily is now open to question. But the outcome of cases in which the author, though hard working, admits that he or she has failed, still seems to favor the publisher: the author takes the risk, not the publisher.

As we noted earlier, the Authors Guild has been much concerned about the implications of the "satisfactory to the publisher" clause and has been mounting pressure on publishers to alter it, suggesting that "professionally competent and fit for publication" might be less arbitrary. A veteran observer of the book scene, Herbert Mitgang, has wryly noted the following, which we think sums up the situation:

> If a satisfactory clause could be worked out about the meaning of "unsatisfactory," one of the tensions between authors and publishers could be removed—and everybody could go back to writing and publishing enthusiastically. "You must not suppose," said George Bernard Shaw, "because I am a man of letters that I never tried to earn an honest living."[31]

A similar issue, more directly related to the author's probity, is the indemnity clause which "obliges the author to pay all or part of the publisher's expenses and attorney's fees incurred in claim or suits for libel and invasion of privacy—and to pay judgments awarded against publisher."[32] Even when a book is judged not libelous and not an invasion of privacy, an author is still required to pay the publisher's legal expenses and fees. Many publishers, who benefit from the present state of affairs, tend to find the issues "quite complex," which means they do not wish to change anything. Nevertheless, others are concerned because of the recent increase in suits against authors which publishers must, in any case, be party to, and for which they must always enter a defense. The Authors Guild believes that indemnification clauses violate the First Amendment, public policy, and state insurance laws. At this point, indemnity clauses favor publishers and subject authors to considerable risk.

Again, authors have been active on this issue. In 1980, author Gwen Davis was successfully sued for libel by a man who claimed that her novel *Touching* in fact gave an unflattering portrait of himself that was too close to life to be called fiction. The author's publisher, Doubleday, then sued Davis for the damages it was required by the court decision to pay. A number of authors protested and later Davis and Doubleday reached an out-of-court settlement.[33] The matter of who should bear responsibility for libel has hardly been settled, however.

This far we have dealt with issues that revolve essentially around acts of commission by publishers—acts that some authors find onerous, and most of which concern various contractual matters or the editing and production process. But as we saw, these errors of commission are not the major complaint of authors. What also makes authors angry are the things publishers do *not* do—not distribute, not publicize, not reprint, and the like. The stories in our files are numerous—jackets misprinted, TV appearances arranged before a book has been placed in stores, failure to have the book available at conventions, placing a book in the wrong discount category, forgetting to put it on the list for salesmen, failure to send out review copies, failure to follow up on successful reviews, and so on. Most of these acts of omission occur after publication at a point when the author is in a weak bargaining position.

Yet this is part of the problem. Most authors believe their job has been completed when they finish writing a book. In theory this is true; but, as our examples have illustrated, in practice it is not. Judith Appelbaum and Nancy Evans, authors of *How to Get Happily Published*, have suggested a number of ways authors can counter the forces that will work to keep their book just one more title on the rest of the list.[34] They suggest that authors need to know how to berate their editors, how to get their books stocked in bookstores, how to keep after everyone from the copy editor to the sales director, how to suggest promotion lists, how to organize their own author parties, and, in short, how to be a one-person brass band. Though many authors may find tooting one's horn unpleasant and not consistent with their notions of an author's proper role, such an activist stance has its rewards. The suggestions of Applebaum and Evans are intended for trade authors. We believe their remarks to be even better suited to scholarly publishing, although scholarly authors tend to be more retiring than trade authors. In many scientific and scholarly fields, the author knows by name exactly who should read his or her book, and how to reach them; for if the author has something new and worthwhile to say, chances are that he or she belongs to an "invisible college" of other scientists or academics. Though authors use this network for preprints,* they rarely do so for books, assuming the publisher will take care of distribution.

---

* Since scholarly articles accepted for journal publication may not appear in print for many months, their authors circulate copies, or *preprints*, of them to other specialists in the field in order to keep them abreast of current developments.

With all these horror stories, one may wonder whether publishing houses are so rife with incompetence that their future is doomed. If authors must in any case promote their books themselves, perhaps they should by-pass publishers altogether and publish their own books? If the past is any guide to the future, self-publication is likely to continue to be rare. The problems that writers have with publishers date back at least to the eighteenth century, and are built into the very nature of writing and book publishing, and will therefore continue. Writing is a solitary act, and authors are not necessarily entrepreneurs or outgoing salespersons able to market their own work. As solitary workers, authors also may not possess the kind of organizational wisdom to enable them to understand and work with the complex business organization that the modern publishing house has become. On their side, publishers are in the business of organizing and producing the works of many idiosyncratic, even recalcitrant individuals. It is inevitable that the mesh between author and publisher will be less than perfect, and that many authors will get lost in the shuffle. The ultimate inequality between authors and publishers is that the latter face all these problems as part of their daily routine and are therefore fully aware of them; publisher-author relations are, however, but a small part of an author's life. While agents, publicists, brokers, and the Authors Guild can to some extent mediate author-publisher relations, authors themselves must develop a greater awareness about publishing and the way it works if they are to have any hope of improving the balance of power between themselves and publishers.

Chapter 10

Books without Authors

NON-BOOKS are to real books what frozen TV dinners are to home-cooked meals. They are not the creations of individual authors; they are much more like products manufactured on an assembly line. Non-books have assumed such an importance in the publishing industry that to ignore them would seriously distort a picture of its workings.

What mainly distinguishes non-books from books is not the quality of their contents. After all, few books are really outstanding. That most non-books are mediocre or worse is no surprise. What is most characteristic of non-books is that their authors, instead of being autonomous creators of ideas and symbols, are wholly subject to the demands and constraints of others.

When Marx wished to characterize the condition of wage workers in a capitalist society and contrast them with medieval craftsmen, he argued that workers, as distinct from artisans, were "separated" from the means of production. These means of production were owned by others, and workers hence lost their autonomy and lived in an alienated condition. Max Weber averred that what Marx had said of wage workers was merely a special case of a more universal trend in modern society. The modern soldier, Weber argued, is equally separated from the means of violence; the scientist, from the means of inquiry; and the civil servant, from the means of administration.[1] We can now add that the writer of non-books is separated from the means of exercising his craft and is subject to the dictates of others, just as assembly-line workers are subject to the dictates of the machine and their supervisors.

There is a great variety of non-books. We will discuss some of the more prevalent contemporary examples, including mail-order books manufactured and custom-tailored for mass audiences; paperback fiction, churned out by independent "book factories" or by in-house series editors; novelizations of movies and television scripts; packaged multi-media products; and "managed" college textbooks.

MAIL-ORDER PUBLISHING

Mail-order publishing has been around for many years. It is an effective way to reach book buyers who live in areas not well serviced by bookstores or to supply consumers with books that have been selected for them by "experts." In this manner, book clubs have functioned for half a century. Many scholarly and professional books are largely sold to their specialized audiences through mailings sent to members of various academic or professional groups. Both of these means of direct mail distribution involve books that are published in a typical fashion: they are written by individual authors who sell their manuscripts to publishers who then produce and distribute the books.

In another type of mail-order publishing, books are specifically created for direct distribution by mail to consumers. Most of these non-books are part of a continuous series of books with a common overall theme, though individual titles may also be marketed in this way. For such books, the publishing process is reversed. The publisher first ascertains whether a market for the "product" exists. Once satisfactory market projections of sales are attained, the publisher will hire a writer to produce these books according to strict specifications. Writers are paid a flat fee, not a royalty.

The advantages of this process should be obvious. Publishers are able to "rationalize" the publishing process and reduce the uncertainty associated with temperamental authors, with ideas that are difficult to evaluate, and with unpredictable markets. This type of publishing can be most lucrative. At Time-Life Books, for example, the market projects have been so accurate that the titles in *every* series offered to date have been profitable.[2]

Time-Life has sold way over two hundred million books in this fashion since 1961. Meredith, American Heritage, and Reader's Digest are other major producers in this field. The all-time champion series is the Life Nature Library, which has published over forty million copies of its twenty-six volumes.

The history of a line of mail-order books begins with a brainstorm in the head of an editor. He thinks that a series on, say, mushrooms or airplanes might appeal to a wide public. He reasons that many people who would never enter a bookstore might buy such books if properly motivated to do so. Next, market researchers—either within the firm or, more often, from outside—assess the probable response to such a series. If the response is encouraging, editors will be assigned to find writers who can provide the needed materials. Some months later, promotional materials are sent out to a large mailing list, and different formulas for circulars and pricing approaches are tested. Once a satisfactory response has been received, final editorial plans are made, and a massive mailing goes out. In the case of Time-Life, a series might be launched with a mailing of over ten million flyers. All these preliminary steps are, of course, very costly. By the time the first book is out, the publisher may already have invested several million dollars. However, consider that a return of even 2 percent or 3 percent on such a gigantic mailing may bring several hundred thousand orders, and that initial buyers of one book are likely to buy subsequent volumes. Further sales are generated through television ads or aggressive telephone solicitations. Giant print runs reduce unit costs. By the time the buyer acquires a third or a fourth book in the series, the publisher has covered the marketing, promotion, and production costs, and future sales of the series now make a hefty contribution to profits.[3]

This form of book production brings mass merchandising to the publishing industry. The "products" are not spontaneously created by individual authors but are manufactured, according to formulas, by stables of underpaid writers, who are most often female and are taught that individual touches spoil the outcome. The process is deadening to the spirit of the writers involved. Just like Grub Street in its day, subscription book publishers rely on a large reserve army of underpaid, and yet eager recruits, who sell their talents for minimum wages. Nonfiction books of this type are highly profitable for the industry and boost the number of people who buy books. Yet, unless the books convey specific technical knowledge on subjects such as photography or gardening, they are not likely to contribute much to individual readers or to the general cultural atmosphere in this country. Fortunately, the books that can be sold in this fashion are limited—only those that appeal to extremely large audiences. Were this not the case, the publishing of books might soon come to be indistinguishable from the making and distribution of soap flakes.

FICTION FACTORIES

While mass-produced mail-order books aim at reaching a wide undifferentiated market for nonfiction, fiction "factories" follow a different strategy. They produce books specifically targeted for a particular readership—for example, action stories for men or romances for women. The most successful of these factories is Book Creations, Inc., operated by Lyle Kenyon Engel with the help of his wife, son, and a dozen editors and typists in Canaan, New York. Over the past fifteen years, this factory has turned out an astonishing five thousand paperback titles. Some eighty professional writers "authored" these books, by filling out story outlines provided by the Engel enterprise. Most authors prefer to use pen names. When these books are sold to paperback publishers—and most of the leading mass-market houses are among Engel's customers—he gets 50 percent of the royalties. Why should authors be willing to part with half of their royalties when the normal literary agent's fee is only 10 percent? Most of these authors had earlier attempted, without success, to sell their wares in the conventional way. Engel's formula, on the other hand, can work wonders. One of his authors, John Jakes, has—despite the 50-percent cut—become a multimillionaire from the thirty-million-copy sales of his seven-volume *Kent Family Chronicle*. Most of Lyle Engel's stable are much less successful, but they can earn a living.

Engel usually dreams up ideas for an overall series and for individual books in the series. He currently has seventeen series under way and is busy preparing another thirteen. When an idea has jelled, he contacts a paperback publisher and hawks the idea. No writer's name is mentioned. Only after the book has been sold will Engel approach a suitable writer from his large stable. Once the book is written, Engel's seven editors see that the formula has been successfully followed. Engel spends a considerable part of his advances on publicity—a hefty publicity budget, since his advances run between $15,000 and $150,000 per book. He usually controls the subsidiary rights to his books and thus supplements his large income from book sales by selling television rights to his properties. He must run a successful shop as he profits despite $1,000,000 a year in overhead costs.

One of his authors, using Dana Fuller Ross as a pen name, has this to say of Engel's enterprise:

> I have, God help me, turned out some 200 books in my career, and I have never run into a character like him. Some of the books I have done for him I wouldn't be ashamed to have my name on. Others have been pure schlock. But they sell. His taste seems to mirror the mass public's taste. He seems to be everybody rolled into one.[4]

That seems an apt description: Engel, like a steamroller, homogenizes the products of diverse writers so that they turn out identical products to be packaged and sold in huge numbers.

Engel and similar owners of fiction factories pre-cook their wares and then sell them to paperback houses. But some paperback publishers have succeeded in excluding such middlemen, and do their pre-cooking of a series in-house. The Canadian publisher Harlequin once dominated the steamy romance market for female readers, but now other major publishers have developed their own brand-name lines of Gothic, Regency, or contemporary romance. These books are created by hack writers along guidelines provided by the series' editor, usually after some market research. *Publishers Weekly* recently printed excerpts from the guidelines for Jove's "Second Chance at Love" series. We wish we had space to quote the whole outline, but will have to limit ourselves just to one point.

> Sex: The hero and heroine make love even when unmarried, and with plenty of sensuous detail. But the explicit details will be used only in foreplay, and the fadeout will occur before actual intercourse. The setting and circumstances of the lovemaking are also crucial and should contribute to a slow build-up of sexual tension. The hero and heroine should not make love too early in the plot. In the Regency novels the sex can stop before intercourse, since the lack of birth control devices creates an element of worry that isn't present in the contemporary romances.[5]

Jove will release three titles a month, in one-time 150,000-copy print runs for each title. This series was created by a free-lance editorial consultant who felt that romance readers were "tired of trembling 18-year-old virgins and ready for more experienced and worldly women."[6] Jove is taking an enormously successful formula, the romance, and bringing it into the twentieth century. Spurning market research, the publisher has found that word of this line has spread quickly among writers: "The writers of these books are, to a certain extent, the market for them."[7] One imagines that Grub Street writers received similar instructions in the eighteenth century, but things have been streamlined in our day. The art of manipulating readers has been refined, and the degradation of public taste, it would seem, is now pursued without the least shred of bad conscience. But, be that as it may, such non-books sell, and sell, and sell. And that is, of course, the whole point.

BOOK PACKAGING

Book packaging as a means of creating non-books has been a part of the American publishing scene for a long time. The Beadle Brothers we alluded to in our first chapter were book packagers, even though their activities did not go by that name. But packaging has become a major activity only in the last two decades. There now exist well over one hundred book packagers, and some twenty of them have recently founded their own trade association, the American Book Producers Association. Most packagers are small firms, usually operating out of Manhattan offices. They commission writers to put together a book that they, the packagers, think can be successfully marketed, and deliver it, ready for publication, to a publisher who will distribute it. The emphasis is mainly on "how to" and reference books, where many experts are brought together under the auspices of a packager. The new *Oxford American Dictionary*, for example, was put together by a packager, the Hudson Group. Other packagers concentrate on books involving complicated graphic layouts that a publisher would find difficult to oversee.

Yet these book packagers, and the fiction factories discussed earlier, are much less visible than the large-scale wheelers and dealers who have accompanied the entry of media conglomerates into book publishing. These new packagers combine books with films and television. They commute between Hollywood and Manhattan, and the name of their game is the novelization of movies and the packaging of multi-media deals (see chapter 11).

The packaging of products across a variety of media has become a very big business. Hollywood film producers, independent agents, and trade publishers may take part in the joint development of a project and then commission a writer to develop a script as well as a subsequent or simultaneous novel. Thomas Whiteside has aptly termed this process the "spontaneous generation of literary property."[8] This generation does not have to take place in the mind of a writer; it can occur around a conference table in the office of a producer or an agent, who may then add additional elements, including the writer, who is "acquired" during the packaging process. Here is the story of one such deal as told by Mr. Whiteside:[9]

David Obst, the president of Simon & Schuster Productions, wishing to strengthen the ties between trade publishing and the movie industry, recently moved from New York to Los Angeles. While sitting in an apartment overlooking Los Angeles with the movie producer Peter Guber, the latter speculated what would happen if the city below burned down. Obst picked up the idea and found a writer to write the outline of a story, and both men provided the major story line. After some revision, the hired hand produced *The Great Los Angeles Fire* (1980), and Simon & Schuster agreed to publish it in hardcover. Columbia Pictures bought a share of the book rights as well as the movie rights for more than ten times what Guber and Obst had paid the author. Then the paperback house Fawcett paid them a six-figure advance for the paperback rights. Before the book was even published, the subsidiary rights to the book were close to four hundred thousand dollars. The author had been paid a thirty-thousand-dollar advance to write the book, Guber had only invested ten thousand dollars as his part of the author's fee, and both Simon & Schuster and Guber's Hollywood studio is likely to turn a tidy profit even if the movie and the book is not spectacularly successful. Obst concluded, "This is an example of almost-no-risk publishing."

NOVELIZATIONS

Another popular non-book of the 1970s was the novelization. This product begins when an original screenplay is turned into a novel, either by an individual writer who can do this with great facility, or by a committee. The book appears in paperback shortly after the movie's release, usually coordinated with covers and stills from the film. This movie-to-book process was a rarity before the past decade. Previously, reprint rights to screenplays were regarded as unprofitable by Hollywood and were even given free to publishers to serve to promote the film. The movie company would hire a few free-lancers to produce a book in return for a percentage of the royalties from the sale. The Hollywood producers, when they charged anything at all for publishing the book adaptation of a movie, rarely asked for more than two thousand, five hundred dollars.

Things began to change drastically when David Seltzer published a mass-market paperback, *The Omen* (New American Library, 1976), adapted from the screenplay of a movie by the same title, also written by him. Twentieth Century-Fox, which had produced the movie, thought of the novelization in the traditional way, as a promotional device. But when the softcover edition acquired a life of its own and sold three and a half million copies, Hollywood pricked up its ears, and novelization became the name of a very big game.

In the past, novelizing was a trade for hacks. The pay was usually a flat fee of between one thousand, five hundred dollars and two thousand, five hundred dollars, and the novel was often written within a few weeks so as to coincide with the release of the film. This is no longer so. After Erich Segal transformed a screenplay outline into the immensely successful book *Love Story* (Harper & Row, 1970), reprinters began to pay larger sums for novelizations, and literary hacks have been joined by highly paid professional writers.[10]

Even though by no means all novelizations and other package deals succeed—there have been some spectacular failures recently—these practices are surely here to stay, since they enhance the profitability of movie making as much as that of manufactured non-books. Furthermore, what until recently were largely individual deals between consenting firms brought about by skilled packager-agents are now moving to formal ties between book publishing houses and Hollywood studios. Film people look to trade publishers for "fresh materials" or "first looks," and publishers have their people in Hollywood doing the same thing. The relationship is not only between publishers and film companies; it also extends to television.

The media conglomerate, Music Corporation of America (MCA), entered book publishing in the mid-1970s when it acquired G. P. Putnam's Sons and its associated companies Berkley, Coward, McCann, & Geoghegan, and Richard Marek. During the first few years, MCA apparently ran its publishing operations separately. But in 1978, MCA's vice-president Stanley Newman, whom the publishing world considers "the father of novelization," announced the formation of the MCA Publishing Group, which he now heads.[11] MCA bought the Jove paperback line from Harcourt Brace Jovanovich and now uses Jove as its outlet for media tie-ins. The new MCA Publishing Group institutionally links MCA book-publishing activities and Universal Studios film properties. Newman is thought to be ideal for this, as he previously headed Universal.

In the fall of 1977, MCA's Universal Studios released a television series called "Battlestar Galactica," which received a high rating. Thereupon Berkley Books released a novelization of the series that soon made the paperback best-seller list. When the book continued to be the rage, an editor of Grosset & Dunlap, a publishing sibling of Filmways, one of MCA's rivals, saw opportunities that MCA had apparently missed. He sent a junior editor to Hollywood to develop two tie-ins with Universal Studios. As a result, Grosset & Dunlap came out with two "Galactica" titles in the bookstores in time for the 1978 Christmas season.[12] Such mishaps will presumably no longer happen now that MCA has integrated its book and film operations.

Let us give one more example of an integrated media tie-in, this time from Warner Communications, which owns Hollywood studios as well as Warner Books. For some years, Warner Communications—through its DC Comics Division—owned all rights to "Superman," which over the last forty years has appealed to youthful readers through comic strips, books, and radio and television shows. At the end of 1978, Warner released its *Superman* film, in which it had invested thirty-five million dollars, in seven hundred theaters across the country. Warner had already licensed the use of Superman motifs to more than one hundred manufacturers of thermos bottles, hosiery, beanbags, bedspreads, T-shirts, and pinball machines. Warner Records was producing Superman records. Warner Books, the conglomerate's paperback arm, got into the act by releasing *nine* books dealing with the Superman theme—including two novels, a story of the movie's production, an official Superman quiz book, a reproduction of the movie's sets and props, a telephone and address book, and so on *ad nauseum*.[13] Such "creative," as they say, tie-ins are not always successful; but even though they may often not work out for the run-of-the-mill movie, they will surely continue to be profitable for the blockbuster film and the sexy movie promising more between covers than could be seen on the screen.

The liaison between Hollywood and the publishing industry started as a fleeting and impermanent affair; it then blossomed out into a permanent relationship and has now led to a marriage that only repeated failures will break up. This, as one of us has argued, is the "Blockbuster Decade"[14]; and the captains of the blockbuster industry from East Coast publishing to West Coast movie making are now closely intertwined. The hired hands who produce the "stuff" of publishing-movie tie-ins may make a good deal of money. But even those who write in the sun next to their Hollywood swimming pools have to admit to themselves that they are completely removed from any writer's craft they may once have possessed.

Television and the movie industry may have an invidious effect on the quality of books that are being written today, at least on those written for larger audiences. Talking to a staff writer of the *Los Angeles Times,* an agent, Lee Rosenberg, had this to say:

> The indirect impact of TV [and we would add Hollywood] is much greater than the direct impact. It's subtle and subjective, but I think it's there. It seems to me that material for books is being developed more and more along the lines of visual images, action structure and externalized exchanges, rather than with internal character development. I think that TV has shaped readers'—and publishers'—appetite for books like that.[15]

Even if a book is not initially packaged by a committee and is, instead, written by a single author, such an author—by way of what sociologists call "anticipatory socialization"—will already, wittingly or unwittingly, tailor it in such a manner that it can easily be turned into a movie or a television show. Under such conditions, the writer's craft becomes subverted by virtue of the fact that one is no longer concentrating on appealing to readers of books, but is adapting to the non-literary standards governing the entertainment media.

MANAGED TEXTS

"Did you know that the King James Version was a managed text?" asked an editor at a leading textbook publishing house. "King James wasn't the author of the translation of the Bible, was he?" she continued. "And when you buy a Sara Lee cake, do you think there is a lady named Sara Lee who does the baking?" The Bible, frozen cakes, and modern college textbooks all have something in common. Those names credited as authors have an uncertain relation to the product the consumer sees.

A "managed" text is one that has been written and designed by a team of authors and researchers under the general direction and control of a publishing house. Often, but not always, an individual academic or set of academics are credited with having actually written the book—though, in fact, they have merely participated in its design. The term "managed text" has also been used by the publishing industry to cover a variety of ways of writing textbooks that differ in some way from the traditional model of a book written by a single professor or by several. Textbooks ghost-written or openly co-authored by a professional writer hired by the publisher, texts with research assistance supplied by the publisher, and many other combinations of writing, research, design, and table of contents supplied by or coordinated by the publisher according to a strict timetable—all have been called managed texts.

Since its appearance on the college market in 1969, the managed text has been the source of much controversy, at least one lawsuit, considerable profits for some houses, and large losses for others. Yet so far there have been few attempts to deal with the questions examined here: how such books got started, what needs they have met, and the serious consequences they have for college text publishing.

Credit for having produced the first managed text at the college level generally goes to CRM Books, an offshoot of *Psychology Today* magazine. Nicholas Charney, a psychologist who founded the magazine that popularizes the latest findings in the field, together with David Dushkin, then head of CRM Books and formerly editorial director of the college department at Random House, decided to borrow from the format of that successful magazine and produce a textbook by the same name. Since the readers of the magazine were by and large recent college graduates, Charney and Dushkin reasoned that college students would respond to the same format: excellent graphics, elaborate production, and a set of chapters written by experts in each area—and rewritten by the CRM staff to produce a snappy, readable text. Tight editorial control and deadline pressure would be exerted, magazine-style, and the book would be finished within a year, rather than the five years that most textbooks take.[16]

Though it cost much more than expected, the text took only thirteen months to produce. Priced two dollars above its competitors, it sold 186,000 copies in its first year, 1970—compared with the 50,000 or so sales typical of most very successful texts. College text publishing would never be the same again.

CRM subsequently produced several other books in various social science fields using the same format—different chapters drafted by experts who received a flat fee rather than a royalty, and rewritten by CRM. *Anthropology Today* (1971), *Society Today* (1971), and *Developmental Psychology Today* (1971) sold well for a few years; but then their sales plummeted. CRM was later sold to a larger text house.

Irving Louis Horowitz, editor of *Society* and one of the so-called contributing consultants to *Society Today*, wrote a scathing review of the text in his own journal in an article entitled "Packaging a Sociological Monsterpiece."[17] Calling the text a "bureaucratic book," he complained of poor organization, of lack of integration owing to multiple authors, of the lack of any clear indication of who did the actual writing, and of the attempt to appeal to a wide market by reducing complex controversial issues to a simple formula based on market research. Horowitz felt that no bureaucratic book could match the standards of a book written by one or even several scholars. CRM and other publishing houses agreed with many of Horowitz's criticisms of the text but felt that the fault was in the way these first books were produced, rather than in the general concept of a book assembled by a commercial organization.

In order to understand the unique properties of the managed text, we should remind ourselves how the traditional textbook is written. Typically, an acquisitions editor reviews current market figures, consults with college travelers, draws on personal experience, and comes to the conclusion that the firm can successfully market a new introductory book in, say, psychology. The editor already has a potential author in mind, a professor at a midwestern school with large introductory classes, someone who writes well, is known to be a good teacher, and who, for a variety of reasons, needs some money. But that professor, it often turns out, does not want to write the book and recommends someone else instead. Finally, after a year's search, the editor signs a contract with a professor who more or less matches the description of the original candidate. The academic gets an advance of perhaps twenty thousand dollars, half paid immediately, half on delivery of the manuscript. That manuscript, however, is slow in coming. Although the professor has hired a secretary and a graduate assistant or two, various other academic obligations delay completion of the book, which is delivered to the publisher only after five years. The original editor has meanwhile moved on to another company, the new editor wants a somewhat different slant, and the academic reviewers to whom the manuscript is sent put in their criticisms, all adding up to more delay. Eventually the book is published, but by this time the market for psychology texts may have changed dramatically. The process is slow, tortuous, and uncertain.

By contrast, in theory at least, the managed text is geared to a known need of a carefully defined market. There are only so many instructors of introductory psychology at universities and colleges. If one knows what these instructors want and can find a way of producing it, then one has gone a long way toward reducing the chaos of the marketplace—the goal of every product manager.

In fact, CRM did not invent managed textbooks. They had already been around for some time at the elementary- and secondary-school level. What drew college textbook publishers to the field were changing conditions on college campuses in the 1970s, both in the size of the market and in the needs of students.

In the 1960s, college textbook sales held strong. Dollar volume grew 91 percent in the five-year period between 1958 and 1963. This growth reflected the increasing numbers of students going to college—40 percent in the college-age population from 1964 to 1974. Around 1970, however, increases began tapering off. And the National Center for Education Statistics predicted a drop in college-age population in the decade after 1975, a prediction that has proven correct. In 1973, dollar volume in college textbooks grew a paltry 4.5 percent.

Not only has the sheer size of the market remained stationary or declined, but the nature of the students has altered. The 1960s students, inquisitive and unconventional, were rejecting standard textbooks in favor of monographs, articles, and source readings. Many text houses published a variety of books in addition to texts. But a study of faculty members conducted for the Association of American Publishers by Daniel Yankelovich, Inc., suggested that there were "strikingly abrupt changes" in campus attitudes between the late 1960s and the early 1970s.[18] Two-year colleges now were relying on textbooks rather than on a set of readings. Perhaps most indicative, 80 percent of the faculty agreed that "most students just do not seem able to learn the necessary material unless a course is structured for them with a text, assignments, tests, and grades."

Students today apparently need not only structure but material they can read. College Entrance Examination Board scores in reading comprehension have been declining steadily for a number of years. This decline, together with the expanding percentage of the college-eligible population attending at least a two-year college, has meant that the reading levels of textbooks present a serious problem to instructors. Many of the editors we spoke with were not the least bit shamefaced about producing texts at the so-called tenth-grade reading level for one of the various standardized tests.

A set of instructions for writers of a managed college text in geology makes this clear:

> The reading level appropriate to the student in this market is grade nine or ten. This means short sentences and short words. The style should be similarly terse. Students will not follow long explanations, nor will they participate in exercises in reasoning. They simply want to be told the information as clearly and quickly as possible. . . . You cannot expect them to be interested in the material itself. . . . It will not occur to the readers to question the validity of the initial assertion, much less to ask how it was arrived at. They just want to know the "rule" and how to apply it.

The sudden return of the textbook as a key teaching aid, together with stable or declining enrollments, led to heavy competition among houses for textbook sales. Textbook editors we interviewed unanimously felt that the major change in text publishing in the last five years has been an increase in competition. Rather than continue the traditional "shotgun" approach of putting out many books and hoping that at least some would sell well—many text publishers decided to make sizable investments in a few carefully chosen "products." Large investments require corporate strength, so we can expect to find a concentrated industry. In 1975, the ten largest college publishers accounted for 75 percent of college textbook sales, and the top twenty had over 90 percent of the market. The four largest (which are Prentice-Hall, McGraw-Hill, the CBS Publishing Group, and Scott, Foresman) garnered 40 percent of all college text book sales.[19]

While managed-text publishing originated with smaller firms, larger houses soon took over, as they have done in other aspects of college publishing. Part of the reason for this interest by the bigger houses may be the large capital outlay required to produce managed texts—capital more readily available to the large companies. Then, too, the orderly bureaucratic way of producing managed books may be more congenial to conglomerate corporate life—though, as we have seen, the idea was invented by smaller firms. Among the companies now involved in one form or another of managed books are McGraw-Hill, Harper & Row, Little, Brown, and Company, Holt, Rinehart, & Winston, and Worth.[20]

There are almost as many ways of producing a managed text as there are publishers. To cite but a few variations, textbooks can be wholly ghost-written or openly co-authored by professional writers hired by the publisher, with research assistance supplied by the publisher; or texts can be produced "in-house" or farmed out to one of the specialized firms that produce managed texts on a free-lance basis. But whatever the chosen path, the techniques have much in common.

Let us suppose that a publisher has decided to do an introductory text pitched for a particular market—whether it be the community colleges or the large state-college system. The publisher may first embark on some elaborate research undertaken by a market research department or (rarely) by an outside research firm. One house sent out a sixteen-page questionnaire with forty-seven questions, which took about an hour or more to complete. The publisher, who had quality trade books to offer as an inducement to respondents, got back close to 40 percent of the questionnaires. Most returns are much lower, however, and average in the 10-percent to 20-percent range. On the strength of the questionnaires, a market research report as long as 150 or 200 pages is prepared.

Editors frequently have ambivalent attitudes about the value of marketing research, but it can apparently be a useful safety device in at least one area. According to one editor in chief, a major purpose is to avoid law-suits, or at least to be prepared for them when and if they come. There has been at least one major suit charging plagiarism in the managed text area, and a solid market research report can show that the reason textbook A is similar to textbook B is that, in fact, both books are responding to the needs of the market. This copying of success extends even to book bindings. A curious similarity in new sociology texts is the use of impressionist paint-ings on the covers (see pages 219–220).

Next an academic consultant must be found. This is the person whose name will generally appear in some capacity—usually as author—on the cover of the book. Finding the right academic is not an easy task, and dif-ferent editors look for different qualifications. One described her perfect author:

> Ideally, he's someone *not* from NYU, Columbia, or the City University of New York [this, from a New York–based editor]. He's from the University of Delaware, the University of Maryland, maybe one of the Big Ten. Those schools represent something that's not too difficult, a more acceptable level for the audience they're trying to reach. He's someone who knows his material, has taught the course for a while, has good ideas to contribute, but who doesn't write himself. If he could write it himself, he would. He should be a rigorous reviewer who's competent, reliable, and a good teacher.

"You need as good if not better authors for a managed text as you do for a regular text," argued the managing editor at another house. "Most important, he must be a team player. The house wants control of the con-tent, and many academicians aren't interested in what we have to say."

How much does an aggressive editor really need an academic author? Hardly at all, some textbook houses say. Graduate students can supply writers with materials, and editors in any case solicit outside reviewers to go over the chapters as they are written. One editor, who had done a book with an author from a university, said bluntly, "He might as well have sailed off to sea for all the good he did." One graduate student interviewed said that the "author" gave very little help on the chapter he was research-ing on social class. The author suggested reading Max Weber and the Ben-dix-Lipset reader on social class and checking the recent issues of the *American Sociological Review*. To a sociologist who knows anything at all, this constitutes no help.

So much for the "authors." Their names are useful, but the book can be done without them. On the other hand, writers and especially editors can make or break the book. Editors are the real managers of managed texts. In a publishing house that produces its own books, there are two kinds of editor: the acquisitions editor, who is responsible for finding the rest of the team and coordinating the entire job; and the project editor, who works on a daily basis with one book at a time until it is finished, reads all the manuscripts, and regularly works with the writers. An editor may work with as many as thirty people on a book, though more often with ten or fifteen.

Most editors feel that writing up the blueprint for the book—an outline of anywhere from ten to well over two hundred typed pages—is the most creative stage in production. It is here that editor and author will decide on the book's tone, style, content, and approach, as well as on such matters as schedules, budgets, and organization. Researchers and writers are expected to adhere closely to the blueprint.

When managed texts were just getting started, academics usually wrote the chapters, which were then severely edited. Sometimes academics still do, for a flat fee of $1,000 to $1,500. But most editors today use professional writers, on the grounds that few academics write well, and professional writers can make academic prose more accessible. The writers work from research generally supplied by graduate students who, according to one expert, "know the latest stuff in the field, know the new literature, the new hot trends." They are also paid much less than professors; but, as one editor pointed out, "This is not unlike the process on books which are authored by one professor. His trusty graduate students do the research and a good deal of the work too."

Once the detailed research has been completed, a professional writer is usually called in. Some professional writers seem to wander into managed-text publishing accidentally, but others are recruited through ads in the *Village Voice,* the *Free Lance Newsletter,* or *Writers Digest.* One very successful writer of managed texts began as a free-lance editor; but an editor in chief felt that she was a better writer than an editor, and converted her. An undergraduate from Berkeley with a Phi Beta Kappa, she had a strong behavioral science undergraduate background and was an ABD ("all but dissertation") in comparative literature from Rutgers. She discovered that there was no market for a Ph.D. in comparative literature in the New York area, and did not want to move elsewhere. She thus took up managed-text writing. Another house discovered a network of "Westchester Mafia"—older women whose children are grown and out of the house, and who are intelligent, educated, and looking for something to do. One woman recommends another, and they seem to be working out well. The writer's job is to make the material clear, interesting, anecdotal, and as "jazzy" as possible, and to get it done fast. Writers are not supposed to invest much ego in the material itself.

Extensive reviewing is crucial to the production of any college text, but especially to managed texts, which exist only to sell to a specific market. The first draft is reviewed by the author, by the editors, and by five, six, or sometimes more academics who teach the subject. Reviewers function in three different ways: as academic experts on a particular topic, checking the author for errors of omission or commission; as pedagogues checking for teaching methods; and as a test audience of users. Careful attention is also paid to artwork, photo research, and design. Managed texts are noted for their use of color and arresting artwork. An instructor's manual, films, film strips, transparencies, and other aids are also coordinated with the book. Recently, the competitive market has forced publishers to offer ever more free aids as an inducement to adoption.

The topic of managed texts stirs up much controversy, among both publishers and academics, and we would be remiss as observers if we did not present our own reactions to the issues raised by proponents and denigrators of the form. What is good about a managed text? First, and perhaps foremost in the view of advocates, is speed. In a competitive industry with shifting intellectual fashions, it is very important to be out front in the market with the newest, if not necessarily the best. One editor in chief explained that he was brought in to revitalize the college department of a famous and respected trade publisher with a weak college list and lagging sales. If he had to rely on the usual way of producing new textbooks, he explained, it could be at least five years from the time he set out looking for authors until he had a text selling in the field—and that was an optimistic estimate.

A second important aspect of managed texts is close editorial supervision. Academics tend to write what they want to write and what they know about. But what one academic likes is not necessarily what other academics like or want in their textbooks. To sell the most copies, a book must cater to what the majority of professors teaching a particular course want, or think they want. The managed-text blueprint takes care of this, and the concept of team authorship ensures that some expert or would-be expert can cover every topic the market demands. Language and reading level are also important in text sales and are similarly closely controlled.

One element of editorial supervision is so important that it deserves special mention, and that is teaching technique. Most professors pride themselves on never having taken a course in education. The typical graduate student is well versed in research and in the content of a discipline but rarely has thought much about how to present the material to students: even if one acquires great teaching skill in the classroom, one may have

276

some difficulty in transferring those techniques to paper. Along with their uncertainty about teaching skills, academics tend to write in a shorthand suitable to academic journals but not to the mass market. Writing well for the millions is a special skill, seldom found among professors. A successful managed-text editor spends considerable effort finding a workable educational formula and then, through the vital blueprint, enforces that formula on professional text writers. If the editors do not get the kind of writing they want, they fire the writer. This control is possible only when style is divorced from content, writer from scholar; and it is basic to managed text production.

Fourth, and a matter closely related to editorial control, is the integration of graphics and text. While publishers nominally control design even in a traditional text, with the managed text design becomes part of the enforced blueprint, and the entire conception of the book is related to the way it will look.

Finally, cost control is a vital factor. This is an advantage in principle, which some publishers have found to their sorrow that they have not met in practice. A well-run managed-text operation that pays authors a low royalty and holds down manuscript acquisition costs can be much more profitable for publishers than the usual way of financing and writing texts. Not only does the publisher reduce his risks by producing a product more acceptable to the marketplace, but he reduces the size of the ante.

Very often, however, these ideal financial conditions are not realized. Developing a managed text can be very expensive. Several books published by CRM and the Dushkin Publishing Group had costs of about $100,000 for manuscript acquisition alone. One book cost over $450,000 and sold only 23,000 copies in two years. Its pre-tax loss was almost $300,000. The cost to produce textbooks in the usual way is also high, since traditional textbook authors get higher royalties—as much as 18 percent of list compared with the managed text's low percentage. Royalties, however, are paid out a year after the publisher has sold the book; managed-text costs are incurred mainly before the book is sold. In an era of high interest rates, the timing of costs is crucial.

Thus, cost control is only an advantage if carefully monitored. It seems that manuscript-acquisition costs and general overhead and management are much higher for houses that produce their own managed texts than for firms that specialize in producing managed texts for other publishing houses to distribute and to get credit for. We have been quoted figures of $90,000 to $100,000 for manuscript acquisition for in-house managed-text production. A specialized firm quoted a price of about $15,000 to

$25,000 in 1979 for manuscript preparation, or about 40 percent to 45 percent of total cost (exclusive of manufacturing and distributing and sales). Publishing houses may not yet know as well as specialized firms how best to squeeze dollars in the production of managed books.

Perhaps the best counter to the claims of control of speed, content, language level, writing style, and expense is simply to concede that managed texts have some advantages in these areas and then to ask: At what cost?

There is much to say about moral and intellectual objections to managed texts. Yet if they fail, their demise may have more to do with poor profitability than moral inadequacy. The very control exercised over managed texts tends to make them bland and uniform, if not outright uninteresting. As a result, some have sold very poorly. If one adds to poor sales mistaken methods of estimating profits that do not take proper account of manuscript acquisition costs, then we can understand why some houses are beginning to abandon the managed-text concept.

While most managed-text contracts specify that the academic whose name appears as the author of the book has full "rights of refusal," as it were, over the contents of the book he or she purportedly has written, in practice it is difficult for the average academic to keep track of all the things that are said in his or her name. We referred earlier to a now well-known case of plagiarism. In 1975, Prentice-Hall bought Appleton-Century-Crofts, one of the first producers of managed texts at the college level, from Meredith Corporation, and inherited some of the staff and the know-how of Appleton. It also inherited *Child Psychology* (1974), a managed text designed by a well-known developmental psychologist and released under his name without full acknowledgment of how the book was produced, though this was apparently not his intention. It seems that considerable portions of *Child Development and Personality* (3rd edition, 1969), written by Paul H. Mussen, John J. Conger, and Jerome Kagan and published by Harper & Row, appeared in the same sequence in Appleton's book, without acknowledgment or permission. According to trial testimony, Appleton knew that the Harper & Row book was the leading text in the field and had decided that Mussen, Conger, and Kagan should serve as the model for its new text; but the nominal author has claimed that he did not know of this decision. What then followed is not clear, but it seems that a harried writer hired by Appleton took instructions too literally and simply copied portions of Mussen, Conger, and Kagan. Since, after all, there are just so many points of view with supporting research in developmental psychology, and since the Appleton group was inexperienced in directing the production of a managed text, it is not clear that Appleton was aware of the extent to which it was infringing on the Harper & Row text. One editor and the author himself, however, did point out in a memo that a chapter was "almost a direct paraphrase." The author then went on:

> This writer has to go. I have not felt the others were like this but did a good job assimilating a diverse mass of material. But this particular effort has illegal overtones and I will have nothing to do with it. . . . I felt the need for a lawyer. This is not what the enterprise was meant to do. . . . What's the good of losing the whole effort because of this sort of behavior?

The author was assured that the matter would be taken care of, but it never was. The Appleton book was an instant success, and some fifty thousand copies were sold before Harper & Row sued for plagiarism, first obtaining a temporary injunction then an opinion that an infringement existed, and finally a settlement for $487,000.

Though it was not the first suit for plagiarism in the text field, the case had many serious repercussions. The author, his faculty, and his president became embroiled in the rights and wrongs of the case. Prentice-Hall, the largest college text publisher in the country in terms of sales, and one of the largest producers of managed texts, has become extremely circumspect about the way it produces its books and has abolished its managed text department. And other publishers, as noted, are taking particular pains to get long and serious reviews of managed texts, in case they have to explain why one of their textbooks looks like another that is the leading seller in the field. Finally, publishers are now very careful in using models for managed texts. For example, one firm preparing a managed text gave its writers the following instructions: "T&L as a reference. This is the leading competitor in the market segment at which we are aiming. *Use only to check level and tone*" (italics ours).

Other consequences arise when a book is supposedly written by an academic but is in fact written by others. The ghost writers begin to regard themselves as more knowledgeable than the academics in whose names they are writing, and this may well be the case. If intelligent people do nothing else but write introductory sociology and psychology books for several years, they probably learn more about these subjects than anyone else, and possibly more than professors whose main interest is some special corner of the behavioral sciences. Consequently, the writers begin to fight bitterly with the academics whom they represent; often they begin to demand to have their names on the books. In the case of at least one well-known introductory sociology book, the writers managed to insert their initials in small letters after the acknowledgments.

Academics, for their part, begin to feel that writers have become high-handed, show no respect for academic wisdom, and are generally un-cooperative. Some academics come to believe that they have actually written the book to which their name is attached; they refer to a managed text as "my" book. At least one academic "author" submitted a text bearing his name to a tenure-review committee as evidence of his competence.

This delusion of academics may even affect publishers' profits. In principle, revisions for second and subsequent editions ought to be easier with managed texts. But some academic authors of managed books, convinced that they are essential to the project, have demanded more royalties for revisions than were originally contracted for. They have even held up work on revisions by insisting on one or another of the prerogatives of real authors.

Which brings us to the peculiar matter of the way credit is assigned. We have reviewed a number of prefaces in managed textbooks. These generally cannot be distinguished from the preface of a book written entirely by an author. The spouse, the children, the secretary, and assorted colleagues and graduate students are profusely thanked for having helped in the difficult process of giving birth to the book in question. All this seems to indicate that the person (or persons) whose name appears as the author of the book has actually written it, when in fact she or he has not. Some publishers use code words to indicate that a book is a managed text. One publisher includes in prefaces the key words, "assisted by a team."

We talked with several editors who said that they wished to acknowledge fully in print how a book was produced, but that they were vetoed by the editor in chief or senior executives or, more likely than not, by the marketing department or people ultimately responsible for the "bottom line," since names sell. Because publishers have been burned by bad publicity and one court case, and because some editors feel proud of their creations, some managed texts are becoming more clearly identified. Some publishers now give credit to the writers, and some describe elliptically the market-research process. By and large, however, little indication is given as to how the book was really written.

In an attempt to remedy this situation, the American Psychological Association has refused to carry advertising for managed texts in its journal unless the authorship or lack of it is clearly identified. Enforcement of this edict will probably prove difficult, because it is not easy to distinguish a managed text on the basis of its appearance.

Misleading the potential buyer into thinking that a book was written by the famous person whose name is on the cover is perhaps unethical; but, in the long run, we believe that the anti-intellectualism implicit in the entire process will be even more damaging. Granted that managed textbooks are necessarily a synthetic product, is there any room in them for true brilliance or original thought? Most textbook editors sadly acknowledge that there is not. Personally, editors would rather have Samuelson's classic *Economics* (10th edition, McGraw-Hill, 1979) than any number of good but not great team products. On the other hand, great texts are obviously few and far between. Should we then settle for a machine-produced intellectual product?

The purpose of a text is to instruct; and at the college level (and probably at other levels as well), instruction in science and the humanities consists not so much of informing students about the achievements of science, literature, and art as of taking them along on the journey—however difficult or downright tedious it may occasionally be—that led to those achievements. The problem with managed texts is that they tend to acquire a blandness and a sameness, and fail to transmit the excitement of discovery that can be conveyed by even a flawed and incomplete presentation by an individual scholar or a small group of scholars. In fact, as we have pointed out, this very blandness may be responsible for the failure of some well-conceived managed books to sell well.

If one believes that the process of thinking, rather than some end product of intellectual work, is crucial to learning, then one must be concerned about the anti-intellectual process by which managed texts are produced. There is no question about the contempt felt and shown by producers of managed texts for academics and intellectuals. Most editors are simply looking for "who's big in the field" in order to "buy him" for his name. Once an academic has been secured, they give him perfunctory instructions, and he naturally turns in, more often than not, perfunctory material. Many able and intelligent writers have commented on the appalling quality of the outlines submitted to them by academics. When academics actually do some writing, more than half of their manuscripts are totally ignored. Thus, we have the self-fulfilling prophecy: the academic is seen as ineffectual, ill informed, and incapable of systematic thought or writing or of following through on a job—and produces accordingly. It seems that an enterprise so thoroughly permeated with contempt for intellectual life cannot help but subtly transmit this contempt to students.

Despite the protestations of those associated with managed texts, several facts are clear. First, no managed text can be said to have an author in the conventional sense of the term. It may have advisors, consultants, contributors, editors, writers, a team of researchers, or what have you, but not an author or two. Second, the editor who compared managed texts to Sara Lee products was correct: a name, especially if well known or one that has been made well known through advertising, is very important in selling a product. This is particularly true for a book, which the consumer automatically links with a name. Hence, the publisher lists on the title page the name of a well-known academic and so implies that he or she is the real author of the book. No one but the publisher understands the qualifications about authorship, if any, that are in the acknowledgments or the preface. Furthermore, the introduction reinforces, for the average academic or student, the impression that the author listed on the title page actually wrote the book. But it is all a lie.

The real sin is not so much the immorality of the lie about authorship but that the lie is one more indication of contempt for intellectual life, art, and science. The pride of discovery, of having one's name attached to one's work, is a major motivation for creativity in science and art, unlike the anonymity of industrial production where the reward is cash rather than glory. How can one motivate students toward artistic and intellectual careers if one begins with lies about authorship?

We have frequently been told by editors that academics—failing to write good texts and buying managed texts in quantity—get what they deserve. Publishers, after all, give consumers what they want. The ultimate irony is that at least some managed texts have sold so poorly that some publishers have begun to question their own wisdom. Have these texts sold poorly because they were not adequately marketed, or because—like so many synthetic products—they proved bland and boring? Perhaps, in the long run, academics will demonstrate to publishers that they are neither undeserving nor foolish.

PART III

Key Outsiders in
the Book Trade

Chapter 11

Middlemen in Publishing

M IDDLEMEN have come to be as indispensable in the publishing industry as custom agents in the import business. As publishing has become a large-scale enterprise, shedding many of its early cottage industry features, the relations between authors and publishers have become less personal than in earlier periods; and middlemen have emerged to bridge the gap between the two. Literary agents perform this function in trade publishing, and academic brokers and patrons do it in the publishing of scholarly and professional books.

LITERARY AGENTS—AN OVERVIEW

Literary agents are men and women who, either alone or as members of firms, sell the manuscripts of their clients to publishing houses. These agents receive a commission—customarily 10 percent, but occasionally up to 15 percent—of all receipts, and they negotiate the terms of the publishing contract on behalf of their clients. They know, or claim to know, the ins and outs of the literary marketplace so that they can direct the manuscripts of their clients to the houses most likely to be interested. At the same time, they know, or claim to know, the value of a manuscript so that they can market it at more advantageous terms than can the author alone.

Literary agents first appeared on the British publishing scene in the 1880s and were soon followed by American counterparts. Both the early British and American agents argued that, in an age of mass production of books, and given the new complexities of the book industry, the old personal relationships between publisher and author no longer afforded the latter the necessary protection. The new complicated copyright laws, the growing importance of first and second serial rights, the syndication of fiction to newspapers, and the dramatization of books, they argued, were too complicated for authors to handle unaided. Matters would be appreciably improved if two business people, agent and publisher, would negotiate the terms of the contract between themselves.[1]

Understandably, publishers resisted the advent of literary agents as a threat to the pattern of unilateral control that the former had exercised over their writers. The American publisher Henry Holt came to spearhead the opposition around the turn of the century. Written contracts, he believed, detracted from the warmth of author-publisher relations, and he refused to sign any. "Royalties exceeding ten percent are immoral," he said.[2] Publishers generally attempted to characterize agents as predatory middlemen who would disturb the cozy intimacy between author and publisher. Their arguments had much of the flavor of anti-union propaganda in industry, with unions being cast as villains disturbing the paternalistic intimacy of factory owners and workers. In both cases, the propaganda failed. Literary agents and unions stayed on and prospered, if for no other reason than that around the turn of the century, the vaunted intimacy of author and publisher, or owner and worker, had become an inadequate smokescreen for their divergent interests. While the hostility of publishers toward literary agents as unwanted middlemen has been muted in recent times, it has by no means disappeared.

Hostility has become less pronounced due to the gradual discovery on the part of publishers that, even though agents serve authors, they can serve publishers as well. As the business of publishing expanded, and as more and more books were produced, the number of aspiring authors increased even more. As publishing came to be seen as a new frontier where anyone could stake a claim and climb the ladder of success, the flood of manuscripts submitted became a rising tide which publishers seemed unable to control. It gradually dawned on them that agents might well serve as flood controllers. An agent's primary function came to be conceived by the editor-publisher as that of unpaid controller, sifting manuscripts before they ever reached an editor's desk. In the words of a well-known agent, Max Gartenberg:

> From the publisher's point of view, the agent's primary function is that of a screen. Winnowing good books from bad, the agent saves the publisher money he would have to spend on [hired] readers going through a lot of gibberish. Apparently this is worth the better terms an agented work gets compared to an unagented one. And some publishers now are simply not looking at so-called unsolicited manuscripts.[3]

WHAT A LITERARY AGENT DOES

There are over 240 independent literary agents and agencies in the United States, according to the 1980 *Literary Market Place.* Among these, executive positions are about equally split between men and women; but overall, women predominate in the profession. Of the 240 agents and agencies, we interviewed 15 people, which we cannot claim to be a representative sample. Yet, since on certain points our respondents replied almost unanimously, we believe that additional interviews would not have produced major differences. Of the 15 agents we interviewed, there were 10 women and 5 men; while 7 were independent agents, and the other 8 were employees of literary agencies.

One of the agents we interviewed defined the tasks of an agent: "We have three functions—*editorial:* we help writers define their own ideas for books, we find writers ideas for books, and we revise the manuscript after submission; *placing:* we find the best publishers and subsidiary rights outlets; and *selling:* we get the best possible terms." Though agents may vary in emphasis on these three activities—some agents, for example, doing relatively little editorial work—these are indeed the three major tasks that an agent performs for his or her clients.

Agents must be knowledgeable about both the tastes and the idiosyncracies of publishing houses and their editors as well as about the intricacies of the rights and duties defined in a contract. Agents also need editorial skill—and, perhaps above all, editorial flair. In addition to these key tasks, however, agents may have to play a broader role. As a knowledgeable observer who is married to an agent remarked:

> Agents can be all things to all writers. They are the authors' surrogate family, if need be, and can fulfill any function from best pal to governess or scoutmaster . . . or if none of these roles are wanted, the agent can also act as business manager, scold, tax consultant, editor, teacher, or drinking companion.[4]

Thus, agents may do all sorts of things—but, first and foremost, they read. They read in the office and at home; they read while eating and while taking a bath; they are living reading machines. As one of them put it in the interview:

> I am [in my office] from approximately quarter to ten until about six-thirty every day. And I read at home every night, and I read all weekend. . . . But then, I like to read: I read in the bathroom; I read before I go to bed. I cannot envision not reading, so I suspect that if I weren't doing this, I'd be reading magazines or the backs of cereal boxes. . . . If I am up against the wall on something, then everything else goes, and I have to finish *that* manuscript. But that does not happen that often.

When agents are not reading, they are likely to be talking on the telephone:

> We do most of our business on the phone. I sell almost everything by phone. I am on the phone all the time—to the point where at night, sometimes, I just don't want to use the phone. Sometimes I have to make business calls at night, but for me to call a friend at night . . . it's almost impossible for me, so I send a note.

When they are not reading or using the phone, agents are at business luncheons. Some agents say that they try to restrict such luncheons to three days in a week; others seem to go to such luncheons every working day. Literary parties also consume a good deal of an agent's time. Major agents may lunch or negotiate with seventy-five to one hundred different editors and publishers in a year. Even if they have their pet publishers with whom they do the bulk of their business, they can still not afford to neglect others who may be willing to buy manuscripts that their preferred publishers reject. Since it is not uncommon for a book to be finally placed only after ten or fifteen rejections, a large circle of contacts and aquaintances in the industry is an absolute requirement.

No wonder that under these conditions most agents have to curtail various leisure-time activities to which they were once attached. The world of literary agents, just like that of many editors, makes great demands on one's time; it is a "greedy institution"[5] in that it tends to "devour" the entire person and is not satisfied with partial and limited commitment. Said one of our respondents:

> We used to play the piano together. Lovely evenings. Talking, music, friends sharing the piano. [Now] I'm working an incredible number of hours, and I find I don't have much time for my friends. I barely have time to *play* the piano much less have a friend over for a little musical evening.

Said another:

No, I would love to spend more time playing the guitar, doing photography . . . learning Italian, traveling . . . cooking. There are any number of things that I love to do that I don't do now.

This mother of four children added defensively, "But it's not because I'm in publishing . . . it's because I'm doing *something.*"

AGENTS AS MIDDLEMEN

Modern literary agents are typical middlemen. Like middlemen from time immemorial—Jewish traders in medieval Europe or the Chinese in southeast Asia—they build bridges between buyers and sellers and serve as buffers between otherwise antagonistic groups. Middlemen can absorb strains that would make it difficult for members of such groups to deal directly with the other side.[6] The fact that middlemen belong to neither of the groups between which they mediate allows them objectivity and distance that makes them particularly useful for people who need to deal with functionally necessary partners whom they may or may not like.[7] Middlemen are able to plug status gaps and to lubricate social relations.[8] Yet while they thus serve as crucial bridges, they are viewed with suspicion and a measure of hostility by both sides to the transactions they mediate. Often the middleman becomes the ideal scapegoat on whom is heaped all the scorn and contempt that partners may feel is too dangerous and disruptive to vent against each other. Even when not serving as scapegoats, middlemen are bound to evoke mixed feelings in those with whom they deal. And so it seems that precisely the more indispensable literary agents have become, the more they are viewed with ambivalence.[9]

Our interviews with literary agents indicate that at least some of them are well aware of this ambivalence:

One has to be very tough because the agent is caught in the middle. The agent is always wrong. The publisher says we push for too much money. The writers say we do not get them good enough deals . . . so you have to be very thick-skinned. . . . We have to work very hard and be very tough . . . insensitive.

This agent also remarked perceptively that editors nowadays prefer to negotiate with agents rather than with authors. "If negotiations with the author didn't go well," she said, "there can be very hard feelings." If editors negotiate with agents, on the other hand, "at least the author is free—there are no bad feelings."

Agents all mention some editors with whom they enjoy excellent, often close relationships, and others whom they hold in high regard. Yet almost all agents, when asked to compare their position with that of editors, stressed some distaste for the world of publishing. "Editors do not take chances," said one agent, "because they have to answer to their marketing people." Said another in regard to a book she admired but publishers have refused:

> It's a novel that I absolutely love, and my experience has been that editors love it. But they cannot get their publishers to agree to take the book. It's a risk. . . . It's not a book that is going to make a great deal of money. . . . I've sent it to everybody I know, and it will break my heart if I don't sell it because I love it.

Said still another, "I would never want to be an editor. Editors have to steal writers from other publishers and spend their time in in-house political battles instead of devoting themselves to editing." The interviewer noted that "throughout the interview ran a theme of bitterness and disappointment with the change in publishing from a trade or profession to an industry where the business ethic prevails."

Whatever generalized hostility, or at least ambivalence, that agents may feel about publishing is reinforced by specific experiences. Several of our respondents cited concrete examples of ways in which their clients have, in their view, been mistreated and short-changed by editors and publishers.

One respondent remarked upon his latest fight with the college department of the Z Company:

> Several people worked on a book for three years. Then, when the market changed, the publisher lost interest and tried to back out, charging plagiarism by the authors. Now they want the advance back. It is a violation of trust not to publish a book just because the market conditions have changed, but this goes on all the time.

An energetic agent who feels that in the end she usually gets her way with publishers, nevertheless noted in a 1977 interview:

> The business types are rewriting contracts that used to be standard. We fight a lot over the small print. . . . At X, for instance, the traditional clause saying that an advance for an unaccepted manuscript would have to be paid back when and if the book found a new house, they wanted to change, requiring immediate payment *with interest.* They wanted to turn publishers into usurers! In addition, the conglomerates are insisting on the rights to technologies that have not been invented. We do not give them movie rights, but they try to get past us by asking for rights to pay-TV, which has not [in 1977] come into being yet.

Another agent expressed more openly bitter feelings against some publishers, perhaps because he is not as sure as the former respondent that in the end he always gets what he wants. This particular agent, who also runs a real estate business, averred that "You would be surprised; there are a lot more nice people in real estate than in publishing." Here are some of the incidents he cited to sustain his judgment that, "in publishing there is a lot of pseudo-friendship, but they really all hate each other," and that they can be much more ruthless than people in real estate:

> This writer was really getting screwed by Y. For his first book, he got $5,000 advance, which was OK since it was a first novel. But the book brought in $400,000 in paperback rights. For his second book the author received $200,-000 advance, but under a clause that was ostensibly meant to protect the author from income tax, but which was no longer valid at the time, Y was obligated only to pay the author no more than $10,000 a year. Later it was upped to $20,000. This was really unfair for the author, since the publisher was sitting on more than half a million. The second book brought in $1,500,000, so they were sitting on $2,000,000 over many years without being required to pay any interest on it at all.

He reported an incident concerning an author whom he represented and who should, he felt, command an advance of at least $300,000, even though her last advance was only $75,000:

> The editor at Y tells her that this is unreasonable and puts the most incredible pressure on her, claiming my man [another agent in his agency] is dishonest, no good, having other writers call her and tell her the same. Well, she withstood the pressure. . . . This type of thing goes on all the time in publishing, but not in real estate.

Such strong feelings were by no means the rule in our interviews; most respondents were much more muted when expressing their dislikes—and much more positive when talking about editors they liked.

Some agents are hostile to the publishing world because, as former editors or sub-editors, they left publishing owing to their distaste for what they perceive as its highly competitive atmosphere and the prevailing backbiting and politicking. While they are aware that their income and success depend on selling books to willing buyers, and thus they must cultivate editors, relations between the two are usually distant and "business-like." As a knowledgeable observer put it:

> Relations between editors and agents . . . are much less symbiotic [than relations between agents and their clients]. There is the bond and the distance— of professionalism. Agents and editors are business associates and competi-

291

tors. They wheel and deal, sometimes together, sometimes against one another. And when they negotiate, they must use the common shorthand of their business.[10]

While sentiment is, hence, usually excluded or effectively minimized between agent and editor, it plays a significant part in the relations between editor and client. Whereas the relation between agent and editor tends to be functionally specific, the relation between agent and client is usually diffuse.

Agents, to be sure, are salespeople; and bargaining is an integral part of their business. But their relations with their clients are built on trust and personal knowledge. Agents not only market manuscripts; they may serve their clients as financial advisors, marriage counselors, real estate agents, and tax consultants. The theme of "mothering" authors occurred frequently in our interviews with agents, especially women:

> I enjoy a much closer relationship with an author than an editor does. . . . I love watching someone just starting out, grow.

> I run interference for a writer.

> I provide personal contact in an increasingly impersonal and large industry.

> A lot of time is spent mothering.

Still another agent put it neatly:

> I hold hands all day, pat hands, make nice. Agents are date bureaus, travel bureaus, mothers, psychologists. We are a writer's closest friend, sometimes his only contact with the outside world. . . . You have to get him started again if he stops . . . , you have to go through his divorce with him, find him dates.

Common sense readily suggests, however, that clients, while feeling helped, protected, even coddled by agents, may also frequently be dissatisfied with them. If one charges another party with the care of one's intellectual creation and interests, one may well have reason to be angry if the transaction does not turn out as desired. It has been said that agents are midwives to their authors and deliver their brainchildren. The metaphor makes sense, however, only when one realizes that most of these brainchildren are stillborn and will be bought by very few readers. When this is finally realized by an author, he may well be motivated to turn against his agent, rather than against his editor or himself. Said an observer:

Since the agent-publisher dealing is so much beyond most writers' ken, many regard their agents with distrust and suspicion—especially after the agent has told the author that his latest magnum opus is barely worth $1,500, not the $15,000 the often desperate writer has mentally set as the rock-bottom figure. Nor does it help when the agent is proved right.[11]

One of our women respondents found that the biggest complaint against agents on the part of authors is that "you do not care about me," and that she is forced to spend much time giving moral encouragement to insecure authors. To be sure, the symbiotic relation between author and agent, the play of friendship and intimacy, is likely to be more enduring than the relation between author and publisher. It seems to be true that authors change agents less frequently than they change publishers. Even so, as one observer put it, "Some authors change agents as easily and as frequently as they change lovers."[12]

As we stated at the beginning of this chapter, agents are middlemen and, like all middlemen, frequently become scapegoats for the anger of both parties between whom they are dealing. But even though agents are aware of this drawback, the attractions of the profession seem to outweigh it.

Most agents interviewed stated that a high proportion of their clients have become personal friends over the years; but only a few, that they have personal friends among editors. One agent, when asked whether she has friends among editors, burst out, "Oh, nonsense. You see, I only work with people I like. . . . It's often very friendly, very cordial, but that doesn't mean that I am going to see them outside of work hours." In contrast, most agents interviewed would seem to agree with one who said, "Most of my clients are my good friends."

This respondent went on to explain that such friendships are time consuming: "I used to have friends who were not clients, but after a while, after I had to break dates because of business engagements, they just drifted away." The demands on an agent's time are stringent indeed. He or she is likely to take work home after office hours; lunches are usually spent on business deals; literary parties have to be attended; the telephone is an all-intrusive presence at the office or home. Hence, the social circle of an agent and his or her friends gradually becomes restricted, as the preceding quote indicates, to the world of publishing. Yet few editors become friends, and many clients do. One agent put it precisely, "Sixty percent of my friends are clients; fifty percent of my clients are my friends. Twenty percent of my friends are editors." Another agent stated that fifteen of her clients are good friends and then added, "It works when clients become friends, but not when friends become clients."

Though interaction often leads to increased liking, under some conditions the correlation may not hold or may even be reversed. In this case, our interviews show that frequent interaction between agent and editor does not seem to be conducive to personal attraction; while possibly less interaction between agent and client often leads to personal friendship.

HOW EDITORS AND PUBLISHERS VIEW AGENTS

The overall hostility that publishers expressed in regard to agents around the turn of the century, when the latter first appeared on the scene, has almost vanished—mainly, it appears, because publishers and editors now generally recognize an agent's value in screening manuscripts and thus perceptibly lightening a publisher's workload. Said Roger Straus, Jr., president of Farrar, Straus & Giroux:

> Some agents understand publishers' problems, and to the more hard-nosed agents, that makes them Uncle Toms. As far as I am concerned, though, agents are a friend at court. Some are good at coping with authors' problems and aren't simply interested in getting the last buck.[13]

Robert Gottlieb, now president of Knopf, sounds even more positive about agents:

> You know that a manuscript from a professional, knowledgeable agent is worth your attention. They have done a good professional reading for you for free. You get garbage from agents too, but they are usually the ones who send out anything to anyone, and you simply don't consider them professionals.[14]

"Good agents won't let bad manuscripts reach editors' desks," says Thomas Weyr, a good observer of the scene.[15] That would be fine, if only agents and editors could agree on what a "good" manuscript is. But such judgments vary widely, so that one house may enthusiastically buy a manuscript that previously was rejected by fifteen others. Hence, tensions between agents and editors are built into their relationship. For example, an agent may believe that a property is worth $100,000, while a publisher may think it worth barely $10,000. Indeed, the market value of books is not as standardized as is real estate, so that sources of conflict are effectively maximized. The relationship is further stressed in that agents have the understandable tendency to overvalue their clients' work, while publishers evidently are subject to the opposite tendency—at least before signing up an author.

Since editors are wont to utter only pious platitudes or positive statements when they talk about "good" agents, the best way to find out what tensions exist is to inquire what editors think of "bad" agents. By far the most venomous description of the bad agent comes from the pen of a leading editor in chief, now retired, William Targ, in his memoirs entitled *Indecent Pleasures*. Targ—who, incidentally, is married to a literary agent whom he evidently considers a good agent—has this to say about the bad variety:

> It is the bookkeeper mentality of an agent that gives the profession a bad name. An author wants a competent and trustworthy agent, not an accountant. . . . Another example of the "bad" agent is one who fidgets over commas and semantics and forgets the basic deal . . . constipated, paranoid, uptight, these agents waste time trying to chip away at the publisher's profits, wrangling over language and small type. They fail to realize that legitimate publishers use standard language that is accepted by most agents and authors and their lawyers. The amateur challenges every word and is a pain in the ass. He negotiates with belligerence, as though the publisher were an enemy. . . . Agents sometimes drive an editor up the wall with telephonic raillery and repeated questions about sales, reviews, and ads.[16]

Though Targ claims that all this applies only to a minority of bad agents, it seems fairly obvious from his highly emotional tone that he got something off his chest in his memoirs that must frequently have bothered him. He seems to let the cat out of the bag when he concludes his tirade against bad agents by remarking, "He is the man who only renders dissension and confusion . . . for his is the soul of a mean prosecutor or accountant. . . . He tries to preempt certain prerogatives of the publisher, and aids and abets the author's paranoia."[17]

Targ feels that bad agents aid and abet the paranoia of their authors; yet it would seem obvious that what is perceived as paranoia by one side may well be perceived as legitimate defense of its interests by the other. The old ditty

I am firm,
Thou are obstinate,
He is pigheaded,

has its sociological counterpart, as Robert K. Merton has shown in his brilliant essay on the ways by which in-group virtues are subtly transformed into out-group vices.[18] Both parties have come to realize that they depend on each other; yet both also feel, often strongly, that the other side, by "unduly" advancing its interests, departs from the rules of the game. When editors and publishers try to distinguish between good and bad agents, they try, one suspects, to make a verbal distinction that is far from corresponding to empirical reality. Just as there are no real girls or boys who are all good or all bad, so real agents, one feels, are likely to be a bit of each. The publisher's or the editor's categorization of the moral characteristics of an agent is a kind of word magic disguising a reality that is much more muddled and full of ambiguities than either wishes to recognize. As one of us has argued, the closer and more sustained the relationships between partners, the higher are the chances that hostility and conflict between them will emerge alongside respect and even admiration.[19]

Hostility and conflict are likely to emerge when there is intense interaction between people who occupy different positions and have different power resources, yet who are engaged in what each perceives to be similar tasks about which each claims equal competence. As Rose L. Coser has shown in her study of the interaction between nurses and physicians in a hospital, the fact that different degrees of power are held by both while engaged in caring for patients, makes for a high potential for friction.[20] In similiar ways, the power differences between editors and agents lead to conflict, as both are engaged in serving authors. Editors have the power to accept or to reject a manuscript, but agents can retaliate by insisting on strict definitions of terms. What is more, just as physicians complain about the "rule-bound" and "compulsive" behavior of nurses, complaints about the "bookkeeper mentality" of agents and their "fidgeting over commas and semantics" can be explained by resentment on the part of the powerful toward people whom they perceive to be of inferior status, yet who exercise control over their own activities.

JOB SATISFACTION

The literary agents whom we interviewed all reported great satisfaction with their work—regardless of age, regardless of stage in career, regardless of sex, and, perhaps most surprisingly, regardless of income. Whether they make fifteen thousand dollars or fifty thousand, whether they are vice-presidents of an agency or work on their own out of a bedroom, whether they belong to the generation of the 1960s or to an earlier one—all love their jobs. The agent who said, "Being an agent has been my whole life," spoke for many agents. All seemed to feel that "this job is it"; and none expressed any interest in moving into other types of work. Needless to say, such enthusiasm is not likely to be found among many types of worker in the American labor force, who are often alienated from their jobs. Two factors seem to account for much of this response: the high degree of autonomy and freedom agents enjoy in their professional lives, and the satisfactions that come from intimate association with their authors.

It is much more rewarding [to be a literary agent] than an editor because then you are structured by the publishing house. I can take on anything I want. I can represent anyone I want.

I would go crazy dealing with in-house politics [as an editor].

The things that confine me as an editor would bug me too much.

As an agent and on my own, I can do whatever I want to do.

Stress on the rewards that come from making autonomous choices, as opposed to the restricted scope for such decision making in publishing houses, ran through almost all our interviews. No matter whether our respondents identified themselves as liberal, radical, or conservative, they all seemed to feel that their work allows them to live up to the traditional American ideal of the rugged individualist cutting a path through the jungle of competition. Unhampered by bureaucratic routines and the departmentalized and hierarchically parceled out responsibilities that they see as prevailing in the publishing industry and in the corporate world generally, they can freely do their work and enhance their careers. Distaste for positions in publishing or in other corporate organizations is perhaps especially pronounced among those literary agents who worked previously in such settings; but this feeling seems to be held generally and is part of the professional culture of literary agents.

Autonomy of decision making is, however, only one of the factors that make agents so surprisingly unalienated. Many of them stress the rewards that come from close contact with their authors:

Writers are the most interesting people, and meeting them is a terrific bonus of the job.

You do not make very much money, but you do meet a lot of interesting people, and that is something important and special.

We have already seen that many clients of agents become, in due course, personal friends. But whether such friendships develop, it is apparent that most of our respondents enjoy the company of their clients partly because, to put it in sociological language, they enjoy the reflected status that comes from associating with creative and glamorous people. The pleasures of such association seem to be increased by the fact that, in contrast with other cases of reflected status (for example, a secretary who basks in her boss's glory), agents feel that clients are dependent on them at least as much as, or more than, they themselves are dependent on their clients. We have come across only a few dissenting voices regarding the pleasures of close association and friendship with writers. One agent argued: "You cannot be yourself with your clients. You cannot talk about other writers or money . . . because they get jealous. Essentially, you enjoy a business relationship with your clients, no matter how warm." This is decidedly a minority view.

Another major factor that seems conducive to the remarkable lack of alienation among literary agents is the sense they all have that they do not have to sell books they dislike. Some agents volunteered that they would never have touched a book by Richard Nixon or the Watergate crowd. They are aware, of course, that not all they sell lives up to high literary standards, but they feel that in order to be successful, they must believe in their wares:

> Ninety percent of the selling of books is believing in them.

> I like to be enthusiastic about my books, and I am about all of them.

> I have to care about my books. When I believe in the book, I can sit through fourteen rejections.

When the interviewer probed further, asking, "Can you be enthusiastic about something that you don't think is that good?" this third respondent replied:

> Look, there's schlock and there's literature. And I know the difference between them. If it's a good piece of schlock—you know, a wonderful gothic romance—and if I am going to tell someone that this is Proust, then I am really out of business. But I never do that. But if I called somebody and said, "This is such a great read, and she's so sensual, and it's wonderful," then I know what I mean by that . . . and I would not send that to Bob Gottlieb [of Knopf].

Still another respondent made a nice distinction:

> Yes, I have to like it, but I can like it on a lot of different levels. I can like something because I think it is going to sell and we are all going to make a lot of money, and that makes me like something very much. But I can also like something because I think it's got literary value. Or I can like something because I think that there is a message there that should be heard.

In sum, almost all our respondents agreed with one of them who put tersely, "One has to believe in a book on some level to sell a book. It is impossible to sell something that is a piece of shit, unless you are a very good liar." We shall see later that at least some editors think that such "very good liars" are not as rare as one might suppose from our interviews with agents; but our respondents were unanimous in stating that selling a product means believing in its quality.

Still another factor that would seem to contribute to agents' satisfaction with their work is that, as compared with the world of editors, the rewards are immediate. One respondent specifically referred to this advantage:

> The thing that really decided me for this job [instead of a job in publishing] was that [in the latter] the moment of return is much farther off. I get a manuscript here that I like . . . and it's not very long before I have it set in the right house and sold. Whereas, for an editor, from the time you sign up something . . . you are probably not going to have that thing to hold, or feel it's done, for at least two years. That's a very long time to wait for your rewards.

RECRUITMENT AND SALARIES

It has been said that publishing is an "accidental profession" in that most people in it have reached their positions by a series of accidents, chance encounters, or personal connections. People also often similarly drift into being literary agents. Yet many agents have previously been employed in a publishing house. Some may have been only editorial trainees or secretaries; others, however, had fairly responsible editorial positions when they decided to switch professions. While an agent may, at a later stage, become an editor, this change is less common than that from editorial work to employment in a literary agency. To some extent, then, publishing houses serve as the breeding grounds for future literary agents. Other agents have come from academia, magazines, or the movie or television industry; while still others succeeded their fathers or other relatives.

We do not think that most agents enter the profession because of monetary incentives. It is difficult to estimate average salaries, because they depend not on seniority or other clear-cut objective standards but on the volume of business of a particular agent and the number of books signed up in a given year. One agent may sign up only some ten or fifteen books and make between $15,000 and $20,000. Another may sign up twenty or thirty books and gross between $30,000 and $50,000. Presidents or vice-presidents of major agencies usually have incomes well above $50,000, whether or not they sign up many books themselves. All in all, this is not a calling in which any but a very few are likely to make much money. In the following section we shall describe one of the superstars in the agency world.

NEW DEVELOPMENTS

At present, many agents and agencies handle relatively few clients and operate on a shoestring; while a few very large agencies handle a great many. Scott Meredith deals with 6,000 to 7,000 "properties" a year—not all of them books, to be sure; some are articles or movie and television scripts. By contrast, a medium-sized agency may handle between 250 or 300 authors; while small, solo practitioners may deal only with 15 or 20 writers a year. It is hard to predict whether this diversity of scale is likely to diminish in the future.

To be sure, certain large-scale buccaneers in the agency business have recently attracted a great deal of attention. Scott Meredith, perhaps the best known among them, hardly resembles the gentleman types, such as Harold Ober, who previously dominated the world of literary agencies. Meredith merchandises many literary works as if they were toothpaste, and he deals with editors in a highly charged atmosphere of intense competition.[21] He may not have invented the literary auction, where a book is sold to the highest bidder, but he certainly perfected it. He handles politicians as well as hookers, Norman Mailer as well as the former paramours of the high and mighty. His agency does not employ independent agents working on a commission basis, but has "editors" who work for a salary. While most agencies do not have a fee for reading manuscripts, Meredith charges $50 for a short story or an article, $100 for short novels or works of nonfiction, and $150 for longer books. Fellow agents speculate that Meredith's reading services produce a major portion of his firm's total income. Meredith represents some three thousand authors—with such success that his yearly net income is on the order of $300,000. "I love my work," he told a reporter. "It's Las Vegas every day."

Such agents are still relatively rare, however. Most literary agencies must survive on a considerably leaner diet. All of them are, after all, small businesses; and in this day, small business, compared with its corporate counterpart, does not flourish. There is no trend toward merger and consolidation as in the publishing business, mainly because relatively little capital is required for entry into the agency business. Yet it is conceivable that the increasing emphasis on blockbusters and best sellers in the publishing industry will one day be reflected in the world of agencies, with more firms like Meredith's. In the immediate future, agencies will attempt to enlarge commissions from 10 percent to 15 percent, as some have already begun to do; they may generally begin to charge fees for reading manuscripts; they may cut corners to lower expenses; and they surely will resist attempts of publishers to cut them out of profitable deals in subsidiary rights.

Literary agencies have been rapidly proliferating in recent years. There were 118 agents or agencies listed in the 1965 *Literary Market Place*. By 1980 the number had increased to 242; and the 1981 *Literary Market Place* lists 269, a 10 percent gain.[22] With this increase, there has come increasing specialization.

There are agents and agencies that continue to cultivate close relations with their authors, do a fair amount of editorial work on manuscripts submitted, and carefully select the specific house or houses that they deem most suitable for a particular book. Such agencies are selective when it comes to signing up new clients, in order to give personal service to all their authors.

Yet, as we have discussed, there are agents and agencies that, while providing personal services for a few enormously successful authors, continue to sign up as many clients as they can. These agents provide few editorial or personal services and pride themselves on the fact that they submit a manuscript simultaneously to several houses in order to get the highest bid for their "product." As one such agent remarked, "[Multiple submissions] serve two functions . . . the competition may bring a higher price, and if the response is negative, you don't have to wait a year and a half to find out."[23] Such agents and agencies have also followed Scott Meredith's practice of auctioning off manuscripts to the highest bidder—thus indicating that they care not about the specific fit between a book, its author, and a particular house but only about the "bottom line." They try to justify this practice by claiming that the amount of cash paid is an indication of a house's commitment. As Morton Janklow put it, "By creating a financial risk on the part of publishers, [we] force the houses to take a more aggressive posture." "Make them pregnant," he adds, "and they'll work harder."[24]

There have emerged several new types of agents, one of which we have already discussed in chapter 10. These are the "packagers," who do not limit themselves to literary products but choose instead to shuttle between New York and Hollywood, building bridges between the film and the book industries. Packagers attempt finely orchestrated deals in which film rights, hardcover rights and paperback or film rights, and soft cover novelizations are contracted for all together in one neat bundle. As one of the most successful packagers, Irving Paul ("Swifty") Lazar, has noted, "Publishing is no longer the Max Perkins/Liveright world it used to be but pure show biz."[25]*

In addition to the literary agent, there is another intermediary between author and publisher. In the last decade, a few specialized lawyers, whether within agencies or as independent practitioners, have come to occupy prominent positions in the publishing world. As contracts have become more complex, as subsidiary rights often become more important than book rights, as front money and ancilliary income mushroom, the larger agencies have found it necessary to hire specialized lawyers. What is more, some millionaire writers have found it cheaper to employ an independent lawyer for a high one-time fee, instead of an agent with a continuing 10 percent commission. Morton J. Janklow, the best-known among this new breed of lawyers, seems to have been phenomenally successful in recent years. Operating with the brio of Scott Meredith and the flair of Barnum, he has managed to extract fabulous sums from several publishing houses. William Safire's *Full Disclosure* (Doubleday, 1977), for which the Literary Guild had offered $75,000, was finally auctioned off to it for $275,-000. This price, in turn, led to the sale of the paperback rights to Ballantine for $1,375,000. When asked what type of book he preferred to handle, Janklow replied, "Big books. Renowned authors or renowned subjects," and then added disarmingly, "Of course, we are not averse to getting some serious writers who need our kind of talent."[26]

In the next decade or so, we expect that, for their big deals, celebrity authors will increasingly rely on lawyers, but that other authors will stick to agents with some literary sense and some respect for relationships based on firmer foundations than the cash nexus and legal expertise.

ACADEMIC MIDDLEMEN

Although some agents represent academic authors, literary agencies have made only small inroads in the field of scholarly and text publishing, as they commonly lack the necessary specialized knowledge. In these areas, where editors are even more dependent on others to screen manuscripts than they are in trade publishing, the middlemen come from the academic world and act as readers, advisors, or patrons.

* The reference is to the eminent Scribner's editor Maxwell Perkins (see page 89) and to the enterprising publisher Horace Liveright (1886–1933), who with Albert Boni founded the firm of Boni & Liveright in 1918.

The common academic intermediary is consulted by editors more or less regularly but does not have a permanent relation with one publishing house, nor does he or she initiate book projects. Few editors, whether in university presses or professional/scholarly houses, will sign a contract for a serious nonfiction book without having consulted with one or several academic "readers." Such readers are customarily paid low fees for their services—usually between $50 and $150 per manuscript; yet publishers seem never to have found it difficult to secure eager recruits. The element of power and influence may be as important in such cases as in relatively permanent advisory positions. Where one may not have the depth of relations with a single house, one may be compensated by having a hand in the decision making of many, or at least of several, houses.

Unlike text publishing, professional and scholarly publishing operates without the benefit of formal market research. Academic readers can thus be viewed as agents of market research as well as of quality control. They are supposed to be familiar with trends in their fields and to be able to judge the quality, as well as the appeal, of a manuscript. Any editor in the scholarly and monograph field has a regular stable of readers and informal advisors. Some houses prefer to appeal to readers from different regions of the country and from different types of academic institution; others are likely to concentrate on a set of readers associated with a few major universities, or only one, or with one particular theoretical orientation. In the latter case, there is the danger that a house will miss out on significant new developments of which its advisors are not aware; but this disadvantage may be compensated for by a particular house's becoming the major avenue of publication for members of a special school of thought. A wide net of heterogeneous advisors or readers may, on the other hand, lead to uncertainty in decision making and to a tendency to publish works that appeal to the lowest common denominator among them.

Certain houses come to be perceived by knowledgeable potential authors as dealing mainly with, say, behavioral psychology or functional analysis in sociology and—according to the gossip of insiders—as relying upon scholars of a particular persuasion for editorial decisions. Such insiders' views often become self-fulfilling prophecies[27] in that once a house is seen to be dominated by a set of advisors or readers with a specific theoretical bias, writers who do not share it tend not to submit their manuscripts there, and that house's publishing program will come to be confined by that bias. (See page 83 on "invisible colleges.")

Experienced editors in academic and scholarly houses naturally attempt to avoid the danger of serving as the tools of a reader or an advisor pursuing his or her own academic or extra-academic purposes. They attempt not to depend too much on a clique, and they know how to offset adverse judgment of one advisor or reader for the favorable judgment of another. In fact, they may appeal to an advisor or reader only for cosmetic reasons. Having already decided to publish a certain book, the editor may send it to an advisor or a reader in order to enhance its appeal when he proposes it to the editor in chief or the publication committee.

Sometimes, academic middlemen are professors who are recruited by scholarly or professional houses to serve as series editors or as general advisory editors. Such editors receive a small proportion of the sum set aside for royalties, usually 2 percent or 3 percent; and some are paid annual retainers. Series editors or general advisors are supposed to act as brokers and attract interested colleagues in a specific field or subfield. They are deemed to be knowledgeable about up-and-coming young scholars, about those oldtimers who have yet another book or two to write, and about those who are played out. These academic advisors sniff out the trends in the profession by going to professional meetings and following the journal literature. They are supposed to know what is in and what is out; they are the truffle hounds of the academic world.

Though they may at times derive some substantial income from their work with publishing houses, one suspects that monetary incentives are unimportant, as most receive relatively little money for the amount of time and effort involved. The quest for a measure of influence and power is a more important incentive. Professors have relatively few bases for acquiring power. To be sure, the senior faculty has considerable power over untenured juniors on the lower steps of their careers; but such power is a local affair and has little significance in the larger academic community.[28] This kind of power hardly interests those cosmopolitan academics who strive for eminence in the wider world of their profession. Some power and influence may come from serving on prestigious editorial or advisory boards of professional journals or on review boards of granting agencies and foundation panels, but such positions are usually temporary and subject to rotation. Successful advisory and series editors may serve for many years and may hence have the power significantly to influence publishing trends in their field of interest—at least in one house. We have even encountered highly influential scholars who advise several houses. Two examples will suffice. One well-known historian has a series with a university press, is an advisor to a small text house, and has another series with a commercial monograph publisher. A major sociologist has long advised a large text firm, an eminent university press, and a well-known scholarly house. In addition, he has edited several series for several different houses and regularly reviews manuscripts for many houses.

From editors points of view, as we have said, editorial advisors are a necessity since the former are rarely trained in the discipline whose books they publish. This dependence may lead them to be ambivalent about the advisors on whom they depend. We found that editors were not averse to joking about the foibles of their advisors and especially about the latter's alleged huge egos and "lack of business sense." Editors know that they must "stroke" and flatter advisors, invite them to lunches at fine restaurants, and ply them with liquor at academic conventions in order to retain their services, but once they have left the room, they may well be transformed into scapegoats by the editors.

Motivations stemming from power and the desire to have influence may be especially strong in those disciplines that have not yet reached what the historian of science Thomas Kuhn has called the stage of normal science. Where many approaches, methodologies, and theoretical directions compete, it can be an important asset to have a corner on a series of books published by a particular house. A few advisory and series editors may use their positions to enhance their personal power; most of them, it seems, use their positions to defend the "ideal interests" of the particular "invisible college" to which they belong. It is the power and influence to shape a field's development that motivates many academic people to accept such tasks. A sense of having a hand on the tiller in guiding academic goods from the scholar's desk to the marketplace may be both exhilarating and part of the obligation one owes to the discipline that has accorded one a position of prominence. And to be able to refer a colleague to a new, as yet unpublished work may enhance one's own academic reputation. Only a very few scholars, however, are involved in these more or less permanent advisory positions.

There is still another type of broker, the "patron," who like the series and advisory editor, is actively engaged in bringing new manuscripts or projects to the attention of editors. Such a patron is a senior professor who brings junior academic clients to the attention of editors and hence serves, much like a literary agent, to screen intellectual products. Anthropologists talk about patron-client relationships as relations between two people, one of whom is in some way superior to or in a more favorable position than the other. The first dispenses favors, rewards, and protection; and the second is supposed to reciprocate by loyalty or support.[29]

Much of academic life resembles a feudal state where some power holders protect their dependents against rival feudal dignitaries. Senior people enhance their power to the extent that they manage to acquire many younger dependents who, in turn for their favors, pledge loyalty and fealty to them or to the particular intellectual orientation they represent. Such feudal relations are most pronounced when it comes to small sectarian circles that wish to push their younger members into eminence in order to gather strength, but these relations seem to exist in somewhat attenuated forms throughout academic life. It is widely believed that for a group of scholars to perpetuate their orientation over a long period, new academic cohorts must be consciously recruited and fostered. A major means to this end is to facilitate publication of the work of younger members. This is difficult to do in the case of academic journals, since manuscripts are usually referred anonymously (an author's name is deleted before a manuscript is sent to an academic referee to be read); and journal referees usually do not know which manuscripts they will be called upon to evaluate. Matters are very different, however, in regard to books.

The academic patron in scholarly and monograph publishing writes a note to or calls an editor and tells him or her about the manuscript that a protégé has sent or is about to send to the editor, and thereby assures, at least in most cases, that the manuscript will be evaluated quickly and with real attention. In other words, the patron ensures that it moves into a priority queue from what otherwise might remain a pile of low-priority manuscripts.

The young academic author attached to a great university has less need of a patron's sponsorship, as editors are likely to visit such universities in search of authors; but such sponsorship is crucial for an author who teaches in a less well known university—even after having received a degree from a major one. Nothing concentrates an editor's attention like a strong supportive letter from a major scholar whom the editor respects. To be sure, almost every editor has encountered the patron who indiscriminately praises the work of every one of his or her students and followers; but such injudicious advisors are soon spotted, and their recommendations neglected. The patron must, hence, cultivate a judicious and tactful style when making recommendations; and if skillful, will note the weaknesses of a manuscript even while extolling its overall merit. It can be said that an author has been among the two or three best students it has been the patron's pleasure to teach in the last few years—but not that this author is the most brilliant student the patron has ever had. The patron can praise the writing style of a client but not call him or her a new Gibbon. A patron can stress that a manuscript breaks new ground, without suggesting that its writer ranks with Max Weber or Joseph Schumpeter. An experienced patron will be moderate in assessing merit; excess leads to disbelief on the part of an editor.

It is probably impossible to discover how many academic books have benefited from the efforts of patrons; but—on the basis of our field observations in half a dozen scholarly and monograph houses and university presses, as well as of our general knowledge of the academic world and its ways—we believe that the number would be high. Not that letters of recommendation assure that a manuscript will be accepted—there are too many other criteria involved in an editor's decision. One of us has shown elsewhere that only a minority of recommended manuscripts eventually were published at one well-known scholarly house; however, the intervention of a patron increased an author's chances from approximately one out of one hundred to one out of ten.[30] Here, as in many aspects of social life, the weaker one's own resources, the more one needs to appeal to people with stronger resources if one's voice is to be heard in the land. And if a patron is willing to write an introduction to a protégé's book, thus publicly anointing it, this will be an additional stimulus for an editor to risk publishing it, and for colleagues to purchase it. Thus, for the aspiring academic author, the patron-broker, like the literary agent, is a friend at court.

Chapter 12

Book Reviewers

PEOPLE unfamiliar with the book business, including many authors, simply assume that after a book appears in print it will be reviewed. However, of the over forty thousand titles published in the United States every year, we estimate that only some six thousand are reviewed. Book reviews thus affect the success or the failure of a relatively small percentage of books released annually. Few original paperback releases are reviewed; their success depends on mass advertising. The modern blockbuster, as has been seen in an earlier chapter, depends on ballyhoo, radio or television talk shows, and author tours rather than on serious reviews. This discussion of book reviewing applies, then, to a relatively small proportion of books. However, for those books with pretensions to intellectual or literary merit, reviews are of major consequence.

A long-standing literary myth, found in older textbooks, has it that Keats was killed by an unfavorable book review, that he gave up the struggle against tuberculosis because of despair and hopelessness over a reviewer's scorn. Goethe, himself by no means a stranger to writing book reviews, nevertheless wrote, *"Schlagt ihn tot, den Hund! Er ist ein Rezensent"* ("Beat him to death, the dog! He is a book reviewer"). And in our own day, in somewhat milder tones, Carlos Baker, the critic and literary historian, wrote, "Among those who distrust the critic as an intrusive middleman, edging his vast . . . bulk between author and audience, it is not

308

uncommon to wish him away out of the direct line of vision."[1] Thus, even though a writer may at times be author and at others reviewer, the roles tend to involve unconscious ambivalence, if not outright hostility.

This situation is not hard to understand. For book reviewers—who may be appraisers of the fruits of intellectual labor, or diviners of trends in popular culture, or mere drudges dutifully reporting plot and setting—are above all among a select group who provide the first public response to a book. Hence, authors and editors stand in considerable awe of those reviewers who have a reputation of critical independence, and await their reviews with an anxiety similar to that of students during exams. Most exams, however, are geared to fairly predictable objective criteria; such criteria—at least according to many authors—are largely absent from book reviewing. The book reviewer, authors often complain, is guided by personal bias when assessing the merits of a book, or is like the person who writes a cookbook without ever having entered a kitchen.

It is misleading to speak of book reviewers in general, because they range from hacks—direct descendants of the Grub Street tradition, who provide plot summaries or short descriptions served up in a sauce of flowery adjectives ("exciting," "masterful," "brilliant")—to literary craftsmen of distinction such as Edmund Wilson, Lionel Trilling, Alfred Kazin, or Irving Howe, who render serious critical judgments—however much some of their reviews seem to have been written with the left hand. The latter reviewers typically write for a limited audience, while the former are forever conscious of mass taste or the publisher's eye.

Hack reviewers have often relied on the publicity handouts supplied by publishers rather than read the books themselves. In his characteristically pungent way, the English novelist and essayist George Orwell once noted:

> The truly shameful feature of literary life before the [First World] War was the blurring of the distinction between advertisement and criticism. A number of the so-called reviewers ... were simply blurb writers.... These wretches churned forth their praise ... like so many mechanical pianos. A book coming from the right publishers ... could be absolutely certain of favorable reviews.[2]

A hallmark of hack reviewers in Orwell's England as in contemporary America is that they rarely write an unfavorable review. Not only do they lack critical standards against which to measure a book, but they are also afraid of retaliation by authors, publishers, or editors. Moreover, many editors of book review sections in newspapers and journals seem to agree that if a book is bad, it is not worthy of a review. As one such editor said in an interview, "Why tell anyone about a book he has never heard of if only to say it stinks?"[3] Nonetheless, however apt Orwell's lament may be about reviewing in the United States today, we are also blessed with sophisticated critical writers who, like Orwell himself, take their cultural responsibilities seriously—that is, they consider a book in terms of contemporary taste and literature as well as, particulary in the case of scholarly books, in light of the past.

WHAT BOOK REVIEWERS AND THEIR EDITORS DO

Book review editors are in somewhat the same position as the unhappy orange sorter in the well-known joke who suffered an anxiety neurosis because all through the day he had to make crucial decisions about which oranges fell into small, medium, and large categories. Book reviewers must, day in and day out, try to cope with the huge stacks of books that land on their desks with inexorable regularity. However they screen newly released books, they can still review only a few. Doris Grumbach, after serving for roughly two years as book editor of the *New Republic*, wrote that she read about 450 books during that period, assigned about 500 others for review after having scanned them, edited hundreds of manuscripts, and read "enough galleys to paper the main reading room of the Library of Congress."[4]

The choice by the individual book review editor of books to be reviewed depends on a complicated mix of information received through various informal grapevines, on pre-publication publicity, on an editor's previous assessment of an author's work, on information supplied by the publishing house, and finally on the editor's scanning, if not actually reading, the book. Thus, one can understand why, even though major authors are reviewed by most newspapers and journals, there is widespread variation in the coverage of less established authors.

Publishers are only too eager to help book reviewers and their editors decide which books to review and in what light to judge them. People who feel great anxiety about the future, anthropologists tell us, engage in ritual to propitiate the spirits and to make them more amenable to human wishes. Likewise, publishers engage in a variety of social rituals to propitiate professional reviewers, including wining and dining them and inviting them to cocktail parties, and in various other ways making them more receptive to the new crop of books that is to appear in the literary marketplace. Such gestures of conciliation are likely to be ineffective: the gods are mainly silent before they render judgment.

Editors or directors of publicity at publishing houses may meet with the editors in chief of important newspapers and journals to apprise them of forthcoming lists and to suggest that particular books are deserving of major reviews. Although publishers may in this way help direct the interest of book review editors to their offerings, etiquette forbids that the former try to influence reviews even though they may suggest a specific reviewer. Book review editors are likely to remain as inscrutable after such lunches as they were before them. With the possible exception of authors with established reputations, the critical reception of a book tends to be as unpredictable as local weather. Publishers may also call reviewers and ask them to pay attention to books that have been overlooked. A reviewer's response to such a request depends on his or her assessment, developed over time, of the particular publisher's judgment. Furthermore publishers are not alone in their efforts to push for reviews of books; many authors spend a great deal of time lobbying for their books and the books of their friends.

It is not uncommon for book-publishing editors—perhaps in order to reduce the uncertainty about the reception of their books—to create a circle of friends and acquaintances among reviewers, entertaining them, sometimes at home, on a regular or an occasional basis. One veteran of the book trade has written of the impact of this "work" on social relations: "It is perhaps the mark of the successful higher-up editor that he or she combines his or her professional and private life in such settings to the point that it is no longer easy to say when, if ever, the work week ends."[5]

From time to time, the head of a prestigious house will invite key reviewers or book review editors to his home when the other guests are among his most eminent authors. Such high-level contacts in a congenial and convivial atmosphere, it is hoped, will smooth relations between authors and reviewers and reduce friction. Mutual flattery and ingratiation, so we were told, are not uncommon at such occasions. Nevertheless no major reviewer's critical integrity seems to be unduly compromised under such circumstances. That integrity is among his or her chief assets, and serious reviewers are not likely to risk it just because they have enjoyed a publisher's hospitality and had the chance to eat a well-catered meal in the company of a few literary personalities. It may well be that the suggestions of a major publisher—say, Robert Gottlieb of Knopf or Roger Straus, Jr., of Farrar, Straus & Giroux—are listened to carefully and with respect by book editors and reviewers—not because they are conspiring but because, as in other areas of life, such interaction leads to mutual liking.

Our research into the networks of editors suggests that their contacts with reviewers fit into a systematic social as well as commercial circle. The editors who are in touch with major reviewers are also in touch with one another and with top literary agents. Thus, there exists a circle of agents, reviewers, and editors at such trade houses as Viking, Random House, Simon & Schuster, and Knopf, who, if they do not interact directly or on a regular basis, see the same third persons. Though agents do not call directly upon reviewers, for example, key agents, key reviewers, and key editors all are linked in triple chains. Thus, agent X is regularly in touch with editor Y who sees reviewers S and N. The circle includes a relatively small élite set of editors, agents, and reviewers who are linked through a network of intermediaries.

Keeping in touch with reviewers is more typical of editors of trade books than of their colleagues in scholarly or monograph houses. For obvious reasons there is little need for such contacts on the part of textbook editors. Of the seventeen editors of trade books who responded specifically about their contacts with reviewers, all but three mentioned the names of at least one reviewer with whom they were in regular contact. The editors at prestigious or high-powered houses such as Knopf, Atheneum, or Simon & Schuster mentioned several reviewers—as many as nine or ten, in one case. A handful of non-trade book editors also gave the names of reviewers with whom they keep in touch. These editors tend to have had a background in trade publishing or to head large university presses or major scholarly houses that often garner page 1 reviews in such journals as the *New York Times Book Review*.

To return to the book review editor who, having decided which of the daily pile of books on his or her desk are worthy of attention, must then decide whom to ask to review each. Editorial policies in this regard seem to vary widely. Doris Grumbach feels the readers are indifferent to a reviewer's name, and that an editor can cultivate new and young reviewers and hence avoid the predictable responses of old hands.[6] Our experience, however, does not back up her opinion. It appears to us that many readers, at least knowledgeable ones, will turn to a review by Alfred Kazin or C. Vann Woodward regardless of the book either happens to review. The current book review editor of the *New Republic* pursues a policy that confirms this view: Jack Beatty selects reviewers who help "sell magazines."

Be that as it may, a book review editor, especially for a magazine such as the *New Republic*, who is not in a position to lure reviewers with money, must assess the field of potential reviewers and their incentive to engage in book reviewing. Here Doris Grumbach is on sure ground when she says that academics will often gladly review for nothing "to see their names in print or to add to their list of publications."[7] There are also many academics who still welcome the opportunity to break out of their habitual disciplinary confines to have a wider audience for their views than scholarly journals offer. It is also true that even colleagues in one's discipline are often more impressed by a review in a journal for the general public than in one for scholars. It has been the experience of at least one of us that a writer receives more kudos from his colleagues for his reviews in *Science* or the *New Republic* than for those in the *American Journal of Sociology*.

Many book reviews are assigned to reviewers who have no academic affiliation. They may be free-lancers, poets, novelists, journalists, or old-fashioned men or women of letters; it is impossible to generalize about so diverse a group. They may write reviews that run the gamut from the illuminating to the inept. The previous track record of most such reviewers is all a book editor can rely on when making assignments.

In making a choice, the book review editor may do best to keep in mind what an old pro, Carlos Baker, has called the seven deadly sins of criticism. He is worth quoting at length:

> The seven deadly sins of criticism, if we are to avoid them, and not one of us completely does, require of us a constant reassessment of our motives. There is, for example, the critical sin of covetousness, which may cause the critic to seek fame at the expense of the author whose work he exploits. The closely associated sin of envy leads to the denigration of the works of others for the hidden purpose of self-aggrandizement. To indulge the sin of gluttony is to bite off more than one is prepared to digest, denying others the right to partake. To be lustful is to indulge in inordinate desire for the gratification of one's sense of power. The deadly sin of anger leads to the loss of one's composure and sense of balance during the inevitable exchanges of differing opinions. The deadly sin of sloth is to repeat accepted lies about an author or a body of work because one is too lazy to dig out the truth. The critical sin of pride is to hand down judgments from on high with a godlike assumption of infallibility, and to assume, along with the robes of the judge, the axe of the executioner.[8]

What makes a good book reviewer is, of course, not only the personal ability to avoid the sins that Carlos Baker enumerates. A reviewer must also have the ability to adapt the review to the style and the level of the medium. One is likely to come a cropper if one writes for a popular journal in a style appropriate to the *New York Review of Books*. As the sociologist Kurt Lang put it in a study of book reviewing, "The reviewer's role is partially defined by his relation to the publication which employs him or solicits his review. Each publication has a slant to which every contributor adapts."[9] Lang noted in particular that when it comes to daily and weekly publications, the function of the book critic has metamorphosed with the changing times. He cannot assume that the book-reading public has the homogeneity of interests it once had. The reading public does not share a uniform conception of the importance of books, and this is due primarily to the variety of offerings. . . . As a consequence, the book reviewer cannot just report a personal reaction. Because he seems more impelled to document them [*sic*], a much larger proportion of the total space is given over to mere outlining, even lengthy quotations, of the book content.[10]

In other words, unlike the nineteenth-century reviewer who could assume that he shared standards and tastes with an élite audience, the contemporary reviewer for the non-élite media must fill reviews with information that his predecessors could safely dispense with. The media are surely not the message, but they powerfully condition its character.

BLURBS

Perhaps even more necessary to publishers and their directors of publicity than attention for their books and favorable reviews, are quotable phrases or sentences that can be used as blurbs on the jacket of a book or in advertising. Thus, major reviewers and authors are repeatedly sought out by editors and publicity directors in quest of favorable reviews to provide such quotes. The author Jessica Mitford tells about a director of publicity who did not find her blurb sufficiently flashy and flowery. She suggested to him, tongue in cheek, that editors and reviewers compile a checklist of appropriate adjectives for praise that could then simply be checked off, saving reviewers a lot of tine. Whether such quotes are really effective is doubtful. The plethora of such encomiums in book advertising, in particular, seems to suggest that inflation has set in, that the sheer number of such endorsements has lessened their value.

REVIEW MEDIA

We asked editors to tell us which reviewers and which review media they were likely to cultivate. Only a very few journals or newspapers were mentioned. The *New York Times* overwhelmed all others with fourteen mentions of its reviewers. The rest ran poor seconds and thirds: the *Chicago Sun Times*, the *New Republic*, and *Newsweek* received three mentions each; the *San Francisco Chronicle*, the *Chicago Tribune*, the *Washington Post*, the *New York Post*, and *Publishers Weekly* all received a couple of mentions. The *Boston Globe*, the *Saturday Review*, the *Nation*, *Partisan Review*, and the *Village Voice* each had a reviewer mentioned but once. Our sample of trade editors is small, but the general picture of sought-after reviewers coming from the leading newspapers of the most cosmopolitan cities, a scatter of major magazines, and, above all, the *New York Times*, is probably accurate. Thus, a few reviews may well make or break a book—even though on occasion a "sleeper" (a book that gets little review attention but turns out to sell well) may capture a sizable audience.

PRE-PUBLICATION ATTENTION

Pre-publication reviews in magazines primarily addressed to booksellers and librarians play a considerably more important part in the reception of a book, especially a trade book, than is generally realized. A favorable review in *Publishers Weekly* and, to a somewhat lesser extent, in *Library Journal, Booklist, Choice,* and *Kirkus Reviews* will generate substantial bookstore and library orders. Librarians, in particular, swear by reviews in the first three journals. Pre-publication reviews are crucial to the fate of a trade book, but they are usually written by people who have a fine sense for market appeal rather than impressive literary or intellectual credentials.

Publishers Weekly is the major pre-publication review, each issue covering approximately one hundred books. Although *PW* prints only some thirty thousand copies, it is read by everybody in the book trade; and through it a book will receive the attention of insiders in the publishing, the bookselling, and the library fraternities. Several months before a book is released, a short paragraph will appear in the "PW Forecasts" column, edited by Barbara A. Bannon, the senior editor in charge of pre-publication reviews. As "Forecasts" editor, she supervises all reviews, including fiction, nonfiction, paperback, and juveniles; she also is in charge of fiction and reviews many books herself. All this makes her one of the few king makers in the world of publishing. Of course, not all books are reviewed in *PW*. Textbooks never are, nor are most scientific monographs. *Publishers Weekly* does pay attention to scholarly books that speak to more than a single scholarly discipline; although there are frequent, and justifiable, complaints that these books are not accessible to the general educated reader. *PW* reviews trade books of all varieties, from serious political biographies to the latest "schlocky" historical (or hysterical) romances.

Bannon came to *Publishers Weekly* in 1945 right out of Manhattan College, where she had majored in English. She first worked on classified ads and promotion and joined the editorial staff in the late 1950s. Later she handled "Trade News" and, in 1967, became editor in chief of "PW Forecasts." She has held this position ever since. Although there have been changes and promotions among her staff, she currently runs the weekly review section with a staff of five, including a nonfiction reviewer, a paperback reviewer, a children's book reviewer, an associate editor, and an editorial assistant. She also uses free-lance reviewers.

Given her training and career, it comes as no surprise that Bannon is concerned primarily with spotting potential commercial successes. "Some books have commercial success written all over them," she has stated. "Others are harder to judge. One of my biggest problems is trying to find outside reviewers who can spot a commercial success before publication."[11] When books are appraised by Bannon's staff, purely intellectual or literary considerations must take a backseat to commercial potential, although *PW* does not completely neglect such considerations. For example, Walker Percy's *The Second Coming* (Farrar, Straus, & Giroux, 1980) received high praise from *PW*. Yet, in the end, the eyes of reviewers at *PW* and other pre-publication media are peeled for future best sellers. Pre-publication reviews serve to sift the more salable wheat of publishing commodities from the commercial chaff of books that may have considerable merit but are judged to have only limited sales appeal. Not that *Publishers Weekly*'s judgment is infallible. Some books are successful in spite of its inattention or even unfavorable reviews. Douglas Hofstadter's *Gödel, Escher, Bach* (Basic Books, 1979) was judged to be too demanding and difficult for a wide audience. Yet it sold well in hardcover, was nominated for several major book awards, won a Pulitzer Prize, and received one of the highest bids ever for a serious academic book in a paperback auction (won by Vintage). On the other hand, even Bannon's personal favorites sometimes fail. She loved Mary McCarthy's *Birds of America* (Harcourt Brace, 1971), pronouncing it "a complete success [that] is going to sell and sell."[12] It didn't.

Indeed, while it is clear that pre-publication reviews can and do affect a book's ultimate fate, there are other means through which a book attracts even more attention prior to publication, including the vast publicity and "hoopla" that may accompany book-club selection, paperback-rights sales, movie or television sales, and excerpts of the book in magazines and newspapers. Some editors have suggested that, even more important than the actual review in *Publishers Weekly*, is the information printed in italics beneath the review: such tidbits as paperback rights sold for $1,200,000 to

Dell, 40,000-copy first printing, Book-of-the-Month Club alternate, or excerpt to appear in *Redbook*. Booksellers and librarians notice these corroborating signs of a book's commercial potential. Often included in italics is information about the size of the publisher's advertising campaign for the book and about whether an author's tour is planned. These data are evidence of a publisher's commitment to a specific book. They are also part of an effort to create an impression of success prior to publication.

Pre-publication reviews are only one facet, albeit an important one, of a general screening process that takes place in advance of publication. Here it is clear that there is a dual market for books: serious readers and those who buy books because they are highly visible commodities. The pre-publication phase is vital for the big commercial book, which is tied in with a Hollywood movie or a television series or has a million-dollar or larger paperback sale, and to whose fate reviews appearing after its release are likely to be irrelevant. Moreover, as we have noted, some of these books are not reviewed after publication. Books with a smaller market, including most of those with pretensions to literary or intellectual merit, receive little attention before publication; their fate in the marketplace is determined by the major review media.

THE *NEW YORK TIMES*

Once a serious book is published, its author and publisher are likely to look first for a review in the daily and Sunday *New York Times*. Of the 15,000 to 20,000 books the *New York Times* receives for review each year, only some 2,000 can be reviewed. As one editor in chief put it, "I greatly welcome a review in the *Times* no matter whether it is favorable or not; any review [in the *New York Times*] sells books." (He made this remark in connection with an adverse Sunday *New York Times* book review of a scholarly book that nevertheless led to three bids from paperback houses; he sold the book for thirty thousand dollars.) Not only do booksellers and librarians eagerly scan the pages of the *Times* for books that are likely to have appeal, but editors in other book review media use the *Times* as a guide to what they ought to consider for review. As relatively few daily newspapers outside New York City have regular book sections, their harassed editors often assign books to outside reviewers based on what the *Times* reviews. These *Times* reviews thus screen books to be reviewed elsewhere. In addition, the daily *Times* book reviews are syndicated and run in papers throughout this country and in English-language newspapers abroad.

Criticism of the harshness of the *Times* book reviews has long been a favorite indoor sport among individual writers; but there have also been critics of the newspaper's blandness, especially during the 1950s and the 1960s. In a widely discussed article at that time—"The Decline of Book Reviewing"—the renowned critic Elizabeth Hardwick remarked on the *Times*'s reviews among others: "A book is born into a puddle of treacle; the brine of hostile criticism is only a memory. Everyone is found to have 'filled a need,' and is to be 'thanked' for something. . . . 'A thoroughly mature artist' appears many times a week and often daily."[13] In the initial parts of her assessment, she seems to be ascribing uncritical reviews and excessive praise to the pressure of publishers:

> The publishers needed favorable reviews to use for display of their product, as an Easter basket needs shredded green paper under the eggs. No one thought the pressure was simple and direct; it was imagined to be subtle, practical, basic, that is, having to do with the fact that the advertisements of the publishing business keep the book review sections going financially.[14]

But later in her essay she found that this explanation had, in fact, "an exaggerated acceptance." The basic reason for the *Times*'s low standards of reviewing, as she finally came to see it, was that "simple 'coverage' seems to have won out over the drama of opinion. . . . All differences of excellence . . . are blurred by the slumberous acceptance."[15] Hardwick backed up her opinion by reference to a study of book reviewing, conducted at Wayne State University in Detroit, that found that 51 percent of the reviews summarized in *Book Review Digest* in 1956 were favorable, that 44.3 percent were noncommittal, and that unfavorable reviews amounted to only 4.7 percent.[16] She concluded, "In the end it is publicity that sells books, and book reviews are only, at their most, the great toe of the giant."[17] Moreover, the *Times* is acutely aware that it is read by an audience of well over one and one-half million, many of whom would lose interest if the *Times* were to adhere to the high critical standards of, say, the (London) *Times Literary Supplement*, with its élite audience of some fifty thousand.

Hardwick was supported by other highly critical commentators. The poet and book reviewer John Hollander wrote in 1963 that "The defects of the *New York Times Book Review* are table talk even among those who write for it."[18]

> The Sunday *Times* book section seems to assign space and relative prominence to reviews of books on the basis of their expected circulation. . . . Very often . . . this coincides rather embarrassingly with the amount of advertisement space purchased by the publisher of the book.[19]

John Hollander, in turn, was echoed by the literary critic and historian Henri Peyre who believes that many reviews in the *Times* and elsewhere

> are too lenient or else noncommittal. The reviewer is reluctant to say outright that a book is bad or mediocre, either from fear of a publisher who is also an advertiser or from excessive kindness. The general editor's proverbial iron hand in a velvet glove is probably deficient in iron.[20]

Many critics contend that the quality of the *Times*'s reviewing improved considerably during the 1970s—an improvement that can be attributed to several causes in addition to the criticism we have cited. As the *Times*'s near monopoly for early reviews was challenged first by the (now defunct) *Herald Tribune Sunday Book Review* and then by the highbrow *New York Review of Books* (see pages 325–326) it tended to meet the competition by raising its critical standards. Its recent editors, John Leonard and Harvey Shapiro, men of letters themselves, have been more demanding and exacting in their judgments than was their predecessor, Francis Brown, whose background was in general magazine editing rather than in book reviewing. These recent editors are also not immune to the requirements of certain best sellers, established reputations, respectable authors, and respected reviewers, but they have shown time and again the courage of their convictions by featuring reviews of offbeat books that are unlikely to land on the best-seller list. Harvey Shapiro, the current *Times Book Review* editor, commented at a 1980 symposium on book reviewing:

> There are books that the culture determines we should review and there are books I am interested in even if few others are. We look to find books by unknown authors, by little known publishers, and we try not to penalize Simon and Schuster for being so commercial.[21]

In our interviews with book editors and authors we heard the complaint that the amount of advertising a publisher buys in the *Times Book Review* influences the choice of books for review. Indeed, as one goes through the *Times Book Review*, there does appear to be a relationship— but not a strong one—between the amount of advertisement space bought and the space given to a review. Then there is the charge that the *Times Book Review* is inclined to review books by its corporate sibling, Times Books. "Our junk," complained a rival publisher to us, "never gets reviewed, theirs does." Even so, the relationship again does not seem strong. The *Times* publishes advertisements by certain houses—say, Lyle

Stuart—whose books it rarely, if ever, reviews. It will carry ads for sex manuals or marriage counseling books that are seldom reviewed. On the other hand, the *Times* seems to make a deliberate effort to review books by as many houses as possible. True, its purpose may be to avoid alienating potential sources of advertising revenue; but it is also a sign of the newspaper's search for new sources of talent. While the *Times* may relax its standards for widely advertised blockbusters by authors such as Gay Talese or Erica Jong, it will also lend its front-page review to critical appraisals of books that have little mass appeal. The *Times* is also known to run lengthy reviews of books from publishers who rarely advertise. The claim that advertising dollars affect reviews, while superficially plausible, has yet to be substantiated.

The Sunday *New York Times Book Review,* as it is now, is likely to run certain high-level reviews on its first few pages. The back pages are given to short reviews of popular books and regular columns that discuss the latest mysteries and children's books. The Sunday *Times* employs a staff of outside reviewers who provide brief summaries of both fiction and nonfiction in a uniformly bland manner. The tension between culture and commerce that the Sunday *Times* book editors may well feel is illustrated by the contrast between their weekly publication of a list of best-selling books ranked according to the (often none too accurate) reports of booksellers across the country and the list of books they judge to be outstanding, regardless of sales appeal. Needless to say, the books on these two lists rarely coincide. When books by art historian Meyer Schapiro and historian Christopher Lasch made both lists, the Sunday *Times* editors themselves expressed surprise.

Few reviews in the Sunday *Times* are written by members of the newspaper's staff. Major reviews are usually assigned to well-known writers who belong to the circle of acquaintances of the book review editor and his staff. Major reviewers seem to change when a new book review editor takes over. In recent years, for example, the name of Irving Howe has appeared with some frequency in the *Sunday Times Book Review;* whereas it was absent under Francis Brown's regime.

Each editor seems to have a fairly regular "stable" of reviewers on whom to rely for reviews that come up to his or her standards. For books that for one reason or another cannot be adequately judged by the inner circle, the editor will appeal to reviewers outside it—frequently to well-known scholars, largely on the Eastern seaboard, but sometimes elsewhere in America, or even abroad. Such academic or highbrow reviewers, though they may not always write at the top of their form, appear much more frequently in the *New York Times Book Review* than was the case a decade or two ago. In addition to major reviews, however, each issue has to cover a great variety of other books in a somewhat shorter space. Here the criteria of selection, as well as the standards of excellence, seem less clear-cut. Often an author who has published in a related field, or is perceived as having done somewhat similar work, will be asked to review a book. The author of a book that has been favorably reviewed may soon thereafter be asked to review a related book. Then again, someone may be asked to review for a certain period, only to be dropped thereafter. For these reviews, which continue for the most part to be bland, the book review editor seems to function somewhat like the God of Calvinism. All of a sudden an author may receive a telephone call or a telegram indicating that he or she has been "chosen," but there seems little assurance that the state of grace will be maintained for any length of time. Such is the prestige of the *New York Times Book Review* that, even though it pays its reviewers very little, few refuse when it calls on them.

The review editors at the *Times* and other review media have over the years been accused of cliquishness. We believe this charge to be somewhat exaggerated. To be sure, review editors have their friends and acquaintances, and would not be human were they not to prefer them at times over outsiders. Furthermore, it is quicker and more efficient to call on reviewers who have already proved their worth. It is, therefore, entirely believable— and we are aware of such cases—that review editors not only select reviewers whom they believe will favor or will not favor a particular book, but also, on occasion, ask a reviewer to soften a critical appraisal if he or she wants the review to appear. Moreover, while commissioned reviews must be paid for upon delivery, they need not be printed.

A book review editor is likely to be indifferent to most books he receives; but when it comes to a book he cares about positively or negatively, his choice of reviewer is, in the last analysis, a political act. He usually knows which reviewers can be counted upon to praise or to slam, as the case may be, a particular book—and he chooses accordingly. As John Leonard, former editor of the *New York Times Book Review* and a current daily *Times* reviewer, once put it, most disarmingly, when talking about reviewing a book written by a friend, "I try to give it a good review. If I don't like the way his mind works, why is he my friend?" Later he added, "That was before I had any friends. An experienced reviewer has to learn to hide. The French critic and Justice of the Peace, Joseph Joubert, said it best, 'When my friends have only one eye, I look at them in profile.' "[22]

A book review editor, knowing the job has a social-control function, exercises it according to his or her own standards. One may do this by giving a prospective reviewer one's explicit assessment of a book in a phone call or a note, but the far more usual way is simply by specifying the length of the review and thus suggesting to a reviewer the importance one attaches to the work. At the *New York Times Book Review*, for example, a request for 400 to 800 words usually means that the book just qualifies for a notice; whereas 1,000 words or more indicate that the editor or a screening reader was impressed. In this way, as the literary critic Benjamin DeMott says, "space allocation tends to prestructure opinion."[23]

When the *Times*'s recent book editors made a determined effort to raise its critical level and to abandon the bland style of their predecessors, they were, in their turn, attacked by publishers who complained of their élitism and insensitivity to the concern of ordinary readers. Thus, William Targ, a former editor in chief of G. P. Putnam's, a large trade house, ended his memoir, *Indecent Pleasures* (1975), with a full blast against the "new" *New York Times Book Review*: "It has become tribal, with strong in-group concerns and an élitism complex. . . . Many reviews are written out of personal pique." To Targ—and to others who expressed similar sentiments to us—the *New York Times Book Review* "indulges in too many bizarre, marginal exercises on books not even of remote interest to the general reader and the book profession." Believing that it is the mandate of the *Times Book Review* "to present book news," Targ was perturbed to find lengthy critical reviews and essays that are "a disservice to the majority of the readers, writers, publishers, and booksellers,"[24] and would prefer, apparently, cut-and-dried lists of books and their subjects with a minimum of critical comment.

Reviews in the daily *Times* are almost exclusively written by in-house reviewers; and three men—John Leonard, Anatole Broyard, and Christopher Lehmann-Haupt—write the large majority of the approximately 350 book reviews that appear yearly. These men apply stringent standards of merit, even though it is rare to find a really negative review penned by Lehmann-Haupt. The daily *Times* frequently contains a page or two of book advertising; however, the majority of the books that are promoted are never reviewed in the daily columns.

Lehmann-Haupt has remarked that "the reviewers for the *Times* function with the knowledge that they are a newspaper and that certain books are news"[25]; and that, thus, the *Times* has a responsibility to review books that make headlines, "including publications by ex-presidents or someone else of questionable legal status, a major book club main selection, or a book that had a $3.5 million reprint sale."[26] He went on to say that the selection of other books for review is done according to the reviewer's interests, and some are a way of indulging his or her own whims. The latter may include "discovering" books that have been lost in the shuffle. In a review early in 1981, John Leonard described Faye Levine's *Solomon and Sheba* as a book that "was published last fall, when some of us weren't paying attention, for which we should be thrashed."[27] He went on to proclaim: "What a splendid first novel and how nice it is to have stayed in print long enough to be noticed by someone who didn't do his job the first time around."[28] We should also note that the daily reviewers write two, sometimes three, reviews a week. They face limits of both time and space (750 words). It is no surprise that they may complain—as John Leonard did on the Dick Cavett show in 1980—"that they do not have the time to be a critic."[29]

There is disagreement within the publishing community on whether a *Times* review, or an advertisement in its daily or Sunday pages, is a major factor in selling books. While a favorable film review in, say, the *New Yorker*, may affect hundreds of thousands of filmgoers, there is rarely anything comparable in book reviewing, whether in the *Times* or elsewhere. Most review editors find that the correlation between reviews and sales is complicated by the fact that reviews can be crucial for certain books and have no effect on others. We have already noted that big best sellers do not depend on reviews; unfortunately, it appears page 1 reviews of poetry are not always helpful for sales either, or so Harvey Shapiro has lamented.[30]

A well-known publisher, Sol Stein of Stein & Day, has estimated that a *Times* front-page review automatically increases sales by several thousand copies.[31] Irving Howe disagrees. He believes that in all his years of writing reviews for the *Times Book Review* there was only one instance in which a review of his had an appreciable effect on a book's fate. (His front-page review of the paperback reissue of Henry Roth's *Call It Sleep* [Avon, 1976; originally published, 1934] was mainly responsible for the book's sale of close to half a million copies.) In most cases, Howe surmises, even a front-page review only increases sales by a few hundred copies.[32] On the other hand, it is true that a review of Erving Goffman's *Relations in Public* (1971), which appeared in the *Times* after a long delay, led a paperback house to offer forty-five thousand dollars for it, only to learn that the paperback rights had already been sold by Basic Books, the hardcover publisher, for seven thousand dollars.[33] Similarly, the *Times* mystery critic praised a series of mysteries imported from England by a small Chicago house, and then—as its president said—"The roof caved in."[34] Fewer than three thousand copies of the British hardcover edition were in stock at the time, and after only two weeks the two leading titles were sold out. Paperback editions soon followed.

We do know that major reviews in the *Times* are likely to lead to orders of ten or more copies by the leading bookstores in the country, but whether the books will be sold is another matter. In sum, we are inclined to concur with the comments of the London *Times Literary Supplement*'s John Gross, who remarked at a 1980 Yale University symposium, "I've always felt reviews are far more important for authors' and reviewers' careers and reputations than they are for the sales of a book."

As to advertisement, even though a publisher may put as much as 60 percent to 80 percent of its advertising budget into the *New York Times Book Review*, many publishers tell us that they do so partly as a means of "showing the flag"—of telling authors, booksellers, and agents that the house believes in the book, rather than in the expectation of increasing sales. Moreover, there is some consensus in the publishing community that, with the development of new methods of promotion, the value of the *New York Times Book Review* as a sales tool has declined. But when all is said and done, the *New York Times Book Review* remains a prime showcase for advertising prestigious books.

OTHER NEWSPAPERS

Most other newspapers that review books are well below the *Times* in terms of critical standards and influence on booksellers and the book-buying public. The vast majority of daily newspapers give little attention to book reviews, either ignoring books altogether or running a series of syndicated or "canned" reviews more or less sporadically. Many of these "canned" reviews, such as those by Miles Smith of the Associated Press, are more like book reports than critical accounts. John Barkham's syndicated review column, which runs in some thirty-five papers, is somewhat more discerning.

Dailies that run regular reviews are few and far between. The *Washington Post*, the *Boston Globe*, the *Miami Herald*, the *Los Angeles Times*, *Newsday*, and the *Wall Street Journal* pay more than perfunctory attention to books. The *Washington Post*, the *Los Angeles Times*, and the *Chicago Tribune* as well as its competitor, the *Chicago Sun-Times*, run Sunday book sections of some distinction; and there are numerous papers across the country that have at least a page or two of book reviews in their Sunday editions. Some of the dailies cater to special audiences: *Newsday*, to affluent Long Island professionals; the *Boston Globe*, to Cambridge academics and technical intelligentsia in the Boston area; the *Miami Herald*, to the large community of retired New York Jews; and the *Washington Post*, to politicians and journalists chiefly interested in politically influential books.

On the whole, the record of newspaper reviewing is not particularly impressive. In many European countries—Germany, France, and Switzerland, for example—one can usually find distinguished book reviews in all the leading daily newspapers; and important books are brought to the attention of the reading public not only in the cities but across the provinces. In the United States, however, readers outside of New York and of a few other metropolitan communities have to turn to media other than newspapers if they wish to keep abreast of the publication and critical assessment of books of potential interest.

THE *NEW YORK REVIEW OF BOOKS*

In our judgment, next to the *Times*, the most significant review medium for books of scholarly and literary merit is the *New York Review of Books*. A biweekly, it was founded in the early 1960s during a newspaper strike, partly in conscious reaction against the perceived blandness of *Times* reviews; and its standards are considerably more exacting than, and its intellectual level is most of the time above that of, *Times* reviews. The *New York Review of Books* does not have the problem of appealing to the mass audience, since it addresses itself to an intellectual élite, largely academic in nature, and has a paid circulation of around 115,000 copies. It is known for its acerbity. Its founding editor, Robert Silvers, is an expert at sniffing the latest twists and turns of the *Zeitgeist*, so that the orientation of the *New York Review* has changed considerably over the years. It was in the vanguard of radical chic in the 1960s—one of its memorable issues at that time carried a diagram of a "Molotov cocktail" on its front cover. In those heady days, it provided an open forum for the linguist Noam Chomsky and other opponents of American imperialism and the Vietnam war. Nowadays, however, the radical writers appear to have been largely replaced by writers more in tune with the conservative temper of the times even though this review's general orientation is still somewhat left of center. What has not changed through the years is the *New York Review*'s high level of critical intelligence. Its reviews tend to be interminable, and it is especially receptive to the writings of Oxbridge dons who may not always be fully in touch with American intellectual styles; but it has maintained a level of excellence unsurpassed in any other nonspecialized review in this country.

What accounts for the success of the *New York Review* is the discovery by its editors of a relatively large new public that had not previously been addressed by the existing reviews. This public is not the élite that used to be guided by *Partisan Review* or similar publications; yet it is certainly not middlebrow either. It is a serious but somewhat culturally inert public that has largely come into existence as a result of the expansion of mass university education after the Second World War. By means of radical chic, or of serious cultural criticism, or of anglophile snobbery, the *New York Review of Books* has managed to appeal to this new public as liberal weeklies or literary quarterlies have not. Sensing the decline of the earlier restricted highbrow community, the *New York Review* both capitalized on that community and helped disintegrate it.

The *New York Review of Books* can be much more selective in its coverage than can the *Times;* the former is under no obligation to cover the whole world of books. Accordingly, coverage of books in sociology, for instance, has been spotty; whereas it is especially strong in history and the fine arts. In any case, almost invariably, its book reviews testify to the reviewers' high seriousness. The *New York Review*, it seems to us, performs an invaluable task in contemporary American intellectual life. Whether it sells books is, again, open to debate. The publishers we interviewed were divided on that score. A full-scale review of an offbeat book has sometimes helped significantly to increase sales; yet, in other cases it has not. Be this as it may, hardly an editor or editor in chief in trade houses that publish books with some intellectual pretensions, or in the scholarly houses or university presses, does not look toward the *New York Review* with some fear and trembling when publishing a serious book. Similarly, owners of the better independent bookstores and buyers for major university libraries tend to look to the *New York Review* for guidance. What is more, even if one of its reviews does not boost sales directly, a favorable one raises an author's standing and so makes him or her able to bargain for more money when negotiating a new contract.

Since the *New York Review* is able to be selective in its attention to new books and to take positions on political or literary controversies that the *Times* can ill afford, accusations of bias and cliquishness have swirled around the review since its inception.[35] It has been accused of being unduly inclined to review books by Random House because of personal ties between their editors.[36] The literary and political wars between Robert Silvers, one of the *New York Review*'s editors, and Norman Podhoretz, editor of *Commentary,* has provided much entertaining gossip among New York intellectuals. Writers beyond the Eastern seaboard have complained that the *New York Review* is excessively ingrown, exhibits the parochialism of the metropolis, and pays insufficient attention to non-metropolitan talent, while overvaluing the work of élite Oxbridge intellectuals. While books published by Eastern university presses receive considerable attention, editors from such distinguished presses as those at the universities of Chicago or California complain that their books are infrequently reviewed.

To pursue such matters would lead us far afield. Suffice it to say that the *New York Review* ranks with the *Times*, and sometimes above it, in establishing the critical reputation of both the reviewer and the book under review.

WEEKLY MAGAZINES

Our treatment of other review media must be briefer. Among weeklies, the *New Republic* has a distinguished record of printing thoughtful reviews of books of intellectual and literary import; it averages six book reviews an issue. For Jack Beatty, book review editor at the *New Republic* since 1978, deciding which books to review and who will review them is both an intellectual and an economic problem. He has stated, "We are journalists, we're in the magazine business and we want people to buy our magazine."[37] As a result, the *New Republic* chooses people "who have visibility, who have a public. . . . Our prejudice is not only for talent but also for people who are well-known."[38] Beatty has also noted that his weekly appeals to a particular audience. It is a magazine with "a responsible, liberal attitude to questions of politics and society."[39]

The *New Republic* receives "a great flood of books that are not worth looking at, only a small number deserve reviews."[40] Sometimes Jack Beatty will deliberately select a reviewer who will disagree with a book's argument: "I want a hostile review, one that is provoking and tendentious." The *New Republic* also may turn down a review it has solicited; although, as Beatty says, then "the book gets lost in the flood and is not reviewed. Some of the reviews are very good but they are not for our audience."[41]

Sometimes, though not frequently, political criteria in liberal weeklies such as the *New Republic* or the *Nation* will carry weight when it comes to the choice of a reviewer, as is true, of course, of conservative publications. The editor in chief of the *New Republic*, Martin Peretz, explained in a column that he had intended to write a sharply critical review of *Naming Names* (Viking, 1980), which Victor Navasky—the editor of the *Nation*—had written about the "Hollywood Ten" and the House Committee on Un-American Activities hearings, but that he had not done so partly out of "sloth" but also partly because Jack Beatty had warned him that such an adverse review might be taken as implying personal rivalry, a political vendetta, or journalistic competition.

Neither the *New Republic* nor the *Nation*, whose reviews carry less weight, are as influential or as uniformly excellent as they were in the past under such powerful editors as Edmund Wilson, Walter Lippmann, and Malcolm Cowley. Nevertheless, the standards of these journals are such that a major review, especially in the *New Republic*, may have as much influence on the educated public and the world of bookselling and libraries as does the *New York Review of Books*. The *Village Voice*, no longer the pace-setter it was in the 1960s and early 1970s, still has some importance, since it is read by many highly educated young professionals who can afford to buy books that are not best sellers. But, under its present editors, the *Voice* is no longer known for its critical stance on cultural and political issues.

Book reviews in weekly mass-circulation magazines such as *Time* and *Newsweek* seemed until recently characterized by the fact that they were made to be read as news rather than as criticism. This may be the reason that publishers feel these reviews did not influence book buyers as much as reviews in the *New York Times* or in more élite media. As Elizabeth Hardwick has shrewdly observed, "Some publishers have concluded that *Time* readers, having learned *Time*'s opinion of a book, feel that they have somehow already read the book, or if not quite that, if not read, at least taken it in, *experienced* it as a 'fact of our time.' They feel no need to buy the thing itself."[42] In recent years, however, these two weeklies have given up their previous policy of running only unsigned reviews; and, as a consequence, the seriousness of their reviews has noticeably increased. No longer protected by the cover of anonymity that allowed them, when not simply reporting a book's content, to indulge in wisecracking comments at the expense of an author, reviewers for these magazines now turn out serious reviews of relatively few books. With circulations of more than twenty million, both these weekly newsmagazines can bring books to the attention of vast numbers of potential readers.

On occasion, *Time* or *Newsweek* will use recently published books as springboards for a wider discussion in sections other than the book section. Such mention of books in other parts of these magazines is especially welcomed by publishers, since it attracts the attention of people who would not ordinarily look at the book section but may nevertheless be interested in a book's subject. A publicity director at a leading trade house commented to us: "A favorable review in *Time* or *Newsweek* gets the action started, particularly on a thoughtful book that doesn't have a mass audience waiting for it. . . . It can make it a lot easier to book an author onto the *Today* show."

The *New Yorker* stands in a class by itself. Read by a sophisticated audience that has the wherewithal to buy books, and meticulously edited by a distinguished staff, its book reviews should carry considerable weight. But the fact is that it devotes major reviews or review essays to very few books and, otherwise, limits itself to brief and innocuous notices. Its major reviews, especially when written by Edmund Wilson or Dwight Macdonald in the past, or by John Updike at the present, may have a great deal of impact; but, on the whole, the magazine is not as important for the critical reception of consequential books as one might expect. There is a certain tone that the *New Yorker* encourages in its reviews: a tone of gentlemanly insiders, highly sophisticated, yet eschewing the scruffiness and quarrelsomeness of most literary journals. It makes its educated readers feel that it is all right not to have to strain too much. As a result, however, its cultivated voice is so muted that its overall impact remains faint.

OTHER JOURNALS

Among the monthlies, both *Harper's* and the *Atlantic Monthly* have less importance in book reviewing now than they had in the 1930s. They provide balanced and well-reasoned assessments, usually on the mild side, for their predominantly middle-of-the-road reading public; but they review relatively few books. Their circulation is certainly less than it was before the Second World War, and is largely confined to the genteel strata of the Eastern seaboard's world of professionals and academics. It is doubtful that these journals are still major arbiters of taste and culture.

The *Saturday Review* was once a major review for a largely middle-brow audience; but it has undergone so many reorganizations in recent years that it is hard to see where it is headed.

Such journals of opinion as *Commonweal, Commentary, Dissent,* the *New Leader,* and the *National Review* run relatively few reviews; but those they do run are often of high quality, and their influence is likely to be more pervasive in small intellectual circles than in the public at large. These circles do, however, contain people who read many more books than does the general public, and these journals tend to reach opinion makers inside the intellectual and political world, so that their influence is considerably higher than their relatively low circulation figures would indicate.

One of us has shown in a previous study that, among a sample of élite intellectuals, 75 percent claimed to read the *New York Review of Books* and the *New York Times Book Review* on a regular basis. Over half of them claimed to read the *New Yorker,* the *New Republic, Commentary,* and *Harper's;* while around 40 percent read journals such as *Daedalus* and *Dissent.*[43]

The various scholarly review media, from the many disciplinary journals to such general academic ones as *Science* or the *American Scholar,* are central in the assessment of scholarly merit. But, except for the two mentioned, their reviews tend to appear one, two, and even three years after a book's publication and so have no impact on its immediate sales. These reviews may, in the long run, be decisive when it comes to an editorial decision to keep a book on the backlist or to remainder it; they may establish or destroy reputations; they may be major guides to promotion decisions in the academic world and determine the relative status of authors in the hierarchies of science and scholarship; but they are largely irrelevant when it comes to the initial assessment of a book's merit.

What distinguishes the scholarly journal from the other review media is that its reviews are written not by professional book reviewers but by members of the particular scholarly discipline. Scholarly reviews are typically written by peers of the author and, for this reason, may carry considerable weight. The fact is, however, that editors of scholarly journals differ about whom they will ask to review. Some editors make it a policy to keep a stable of lesser-known members of the discipline who, not publishing much themselves, are given an occasion to see their names in print—and hence to attract the attention of their department heads. Some of these lesser lights, to be sure, make special efforts to assess a book on its own merits; but others seize the opportunity to vent their spleen at a particular scholarly "establishment." Other scholarly journals, while receptive to newcomers, nevertheless make an effort to get respected central figures in the profession to take on the task of assessing the new crop of scholarly contributions.

Since the members of a discipline are likely to know about the varied standards of book review editors, it is not surprising that certain scholarly reviews are more influential than others. Assessing the alleged biases of book review editors and their reviewers is, as one might expect, a favorite sport in academia. Since scholars can read only a limited number of books but many more reviews, it is not surprising to find that all too often when academics gather in the common room or at conferences, they will talk more about reviews than about books.

Finally, there are the literary reviews—such as *Partisan Review*, *Kenyon Review*, and *Hudson Review*—which, though addressed to relatively small audiences and focused mainly on works of literature and criticism, have a significant impact in the intellectual world and in critically aware sections of trade publishing. They can make or break literary reputations, and they can constitute a showcase for seminal ideas which set critical styles in literary milieux and in the world of serious trade publishing and slowly filter down to the general public. *Partisan Review*, in particular, affected the style of a whole generation of intellectuals, in the 1940s and 1950s. Even though the journal is no longer so influential today, younger critics still look back on its earlier issues with a mixture of awe and nostalgia. It helped give birth to an acerbic, quick, elliptical, and bold style of critical writing and book reviewing that has left its mark on the best of current criticism.

CONCLUSION

Attempting to assess the drift of changes in book reviewing, and in the relationship between book reviewing and the publishing industry, in the last three or four decades, a few conclusions are warranted:

1. Many trade books, even highly successful best sellers, may nowadays not be reviewed by the major review media. Thus, for a trade book there may be no connection between reviews and sales. On the other hand, even review media that cater to a large audience pay close attention to serious books that seemingly lack mass appeal.

2. The impact of reviews depends on the kind of book being reviewed, and on where the review appears. Different review media are appropriate for different publishing markets. A favorable review of a demanding new science book in the Sunday *Times Book Review* may not affect sales, but a rave review in *Science can make a tremendous difference.*

3. Perhaps in part because blockbusters are no longer sure of automatic attention in the review media, their publishers have developed techniques to get around the book-reviewing fraternity altogether and to address themselves to booksellers directly. Currently, advance publicity for potential blockbusters will reach booksellers, and the major chains in particular, long before any reviews have appeared. Relying on pre-publication quotes to stimulate appeal, their publishers will attempt to solicit large book orders in advance of publication. We have even seen many large-scale advertising mailings that reach booksellers long before the advertised book was written!

4. Sophisticated critical reviewing in the *New York Review of Books* or, to considerably lesser extent, in media such as *Time* or *Newsweek* has made modest advances; and there have sprung up regional review media, such as the *West Coast Review of Books* or the *Los Angeles Times Sunday Book Review*, which have attempted to break the near monopoly of the Eastern seaboard for critical assessments of serious books.

5. The review media continue, for the most part, to refuse to review original paperback books. Thus, not only does a great deal of trash never get reviewed at all, but also hardcover publishing is sustained, since a book with any serious pretensions must first appear in a hardcover edition if it is to get review attention.

All in all, one might say about the state of book reviewing what used to be said about general conditions in the Hapsburg monarchy: "The situation is desperate but not serious." In some journals the hacks dominate the field and grind out their predictable reports, to repeat Orwell's telling phrase, "like so many mechanical pianos";[44] yet a number of first-rate reviewers continue to write and to uphold critical standards. Like the book industry as a whole, the book review media continue to navigate a course between the pressures of commerce and the responsibility to our common culture.

Chapter 13

Channels of Distribution

THERE are more than 450,000 books in print. Given this wealth of choice, imagine the reader in search of one particular title. A recently published best seller will be fairly easy to find: independent bookstores, chain bookstores, and book clubs will provide ready access. A best seller of five years ago may be found on a remainder table in hardcover or on a drugstore rack with other mass-market paperbacks; but chances are that it will be out of print and available, if at all, in a second-hand bookstore or a library. The reader in search of perennial sellers like the Bible, a dictionary, or the *Joy of Cooking* should have little trouble locating one or another edition. The sophisticated and selective book buyer will know that a scholarly monograph, if it is not to be found in a college or university bookstore, can be ordered directly from the publisher. Regular book buyers come to know the fare—meager or rich—of their local retail book outlets, from the single rack of paperbacks in the general store of a small resort town to specialized bookstores dealing only in mysteries, the occult, or science fiction in larger metropolitan areas. But the sad fact is that there is always a reader unsuccessfully searching for a particular book—and five thousand copies of that book somewhere in a publisher's warehouse.

This is the dilemma of distribution: how to get a particular book in the hands of the one who wants to read it (the purposeful reader) or of the one who would be likely to buy it given the chance to browse (the impulse buyer)? This complex process, which we examine in detail in this chapter, involves the efforts of booksellers to select and shelve those volumes that both customers and browsers are likely to want; of salespersons to place as many of their books as possible without losing credibility with the bookstores; and of publishers to see the current season's list, along with consistent sellers from their backlist, displayed in every bookstore. The interests of the various participants in distribution are seldom the same and their efforts are not necessarily mutually supportive. All of these complex efforts are further compounded by returns policies, by differences between chains and independent bookstores, and by varying rates of discount for different types of book. Before turning to the details of book distribution, let us look at some of the central features of this process.

For decades the distribution of books in this country has been criticized as cumbersome, costly, and woefully inefficient. John Tebbel, publishing industry historian, argues that distribution problems are a two hundred-year-old bottleneck resulting from the unique nature of book publishing:

> No other business puts out some 40,000 products on the market every year, each one of them different from the other, places them in retail outlets by the most haphazard means, compels most of them to make their way without benefit of any but the most minimal advertising or promotion, does little if anything to help the retail outlets with their problems of overcrowding and mostly inferior management—and then agrees to accept all the books the retailer has bought which it hasn't been able to sell. These books are then either destroyed or remaindered in a final process from which the author, who keeps everybody alive by producing the product in the first place gets nothing.[1]

The shortcomings of the distribution system are partly a consequence of the industry's strength and diversity in issuing new titles. With the exception of best-selling authors and widely promoted media tie-ins, however, books are unknown and uncertain properties. To encourage booksellers to sell untested new "products," publishers allow them to return unsold books. But such returns are not free; both bookseller and publisher pay a price. Booksellers have capital invested in their stock: books are paid for within thirty to sixty days; returns can be reimbursed or credited against future purchases from a publisher. Thus, money can be tied up for months. In addition, shelf space is taken up, and postage and paperwork must be paid for. Returns can be just as vexing and unprofitable. Publishers rarely have an accurate account of how many copies of a book have sold or, equally important, of how many remain to be sold. An extreme example of the problem is a story that William Jovanovich, president of Harcourt Brace Jovanovich, tells of a new novel with an initial printing of 50,000 copies. With the receipt of reorders, a second printing of 7,500 followed. To the company's dismay, 21,000 copies were returned over an eight-month period.[2]

The returns policy not only makes it difficult for publishers to know how a title is selling, it also discourages clearance sales at the retail outlet and involves the cumbersome return of unsold books, which the publisher will ultimately destroy or remainder at far below the original price. Estimates for hardcover trade return rates range from 25 percent to 40 percent; for mass-market paperbacks, the figure is as high as 60 percent. On a routine basis almost half of the mass-market paperbacks shipped out have their covers stripped and returned for credit. The books themselves are then destroyed—to the tune of one hundred million paperbacks a year![3] Chain store return rates are typically higher than the average. Few other enterprises routinely rely on the destruction of half their products to clear the market.

Given these drawbacks, why does publishing continue with a policy that would be intolerable in any other manufacturing industry? One answer lies in the publishing "truism" that there is no brand-name loyalty. We were constantly told in our interviews that each book is unique and must make its own way. Hence it is thought that booksellers choose individual titles without regard for the "brand name" of a particular publishing house and its reputation. We dissent from this view. Many instances of loyalty to particular publishers cropped up in our informal conversations with librarians and booksellers, who told us that a publisher's editorial and promotional reputation was an important factor in their ordering policies. In academia, too, there is keen awareness of the quality and content of a publisher's list. This informal evaluation of a publisher may extend to tenure decisions where a candidate's promotion sometimes rests upon the quality and standards of his or her publisher. In the world of trade publishing, John Schulz, of the B. Dalton chain, says that, when deciding on new fiction, he relies on his knowledge of a publisher's reputation: "Certain publishers put out certain types of books, and that gives an idea of what kind of book the new one will be."[4] We think publishers considerably underestimate the extent to which key intermediaries, such as booksellers as well as certain consumers, evaluate publishers' lists. Over time these evaluations become reputations and form the basis for book-buying decisions.

Another factor affecting distribution is the discount rates at which books are sold. College texts carry a discount of 20 percent to 25 percent, and most scholarly monographs are also sold at a 20 percent discount.

Some scholarly publishers sell their books at a 33 percent discount, and a few even offer trade discounts. The discount for hardcover books usually begins at 40 percent and escalates with the size of an order. The more books purchased from one publisher, the higher the discount. Mass-market paperbacks typically have a 45 percent discount, which also increases with large orders. Since chain bookstores order books in great quantity, they routinely receive better discounts than do independent bookstores.

The distribution of books involves a wide range of bookstores: between the small local ones and the national chains are college bookstores, religious bookstores, second-hand dealers, and an array of paperback outlets. In recent years, book retailing has grown considerably. In 1963 the United States Census listed 2,845 bookstore establishments; by 1977 their ranks had swelled to 12,718. Despite this dramatic increase, there are fewer bookstores per capita in the United States than in Japan and many European countries. Furthermore, as John Dessauer, publishing industry analyst argues, "most bookstores do not maintain a sufficiently varied inventory to satisfy their customer demands."[5] Traditionally, bookstores have been small single-unit businesses. However, recent growth has been most pronounced among chain stores, and the independents' share of the market has declined. In 1958, 90 percent of all bookstores and 72 percent of all bookstore sales were made by stores that were not members of chains. In 1977 the proportion of non-chain stores had dropped to approximately 80 percent, and their share of total sales had fallen to 51.6 percent. The bookstore chains have stimulated major changes in bookstore selling practices. The two most visible chains—Walden Books and B. Dalton, both subsidiaries of large retailing corporations—are the book industry's first national retailing organizations. Along with the proliferation of national chains, there has been growth in the number of smaller regional multi-store companies such as Kroch's & Brentano's in the Chicago area and Barnes & Noble in the northeast. Chains are not the only new entrants into book retailing: department stores, drug stores, and supermarkets have moved into it in a big way.

The expanding retail outlets have been supplied by a growing number of book wholesalers and distributors. In the 1970s a number of national distributors and book wholesalers either formed or expanded existing operations in order to service the increasing number of bookstores and book outlets. Wholesalers and distributors have been a central fixture in library book acquisition for decades, but until the 1970s they did not play a key role in distributing books to bookstores. National wholesalers are now bringing prompter service to bookstores and adding efficiency to the distribution process. Eleven major paperback national distributors are the pri-

mary conduits between paperback publishers and hundreds of regional independent wholesalers that stock non-bookstore outlets with paperbacks
and magazines. With the book chains and wholesalers has come increasing
usage of computer technology for accounting, inventory control, and in-
voicing. Large national operations, either retailers or distributors, no longer
regard bookselling as a unique enterprise. They are very much concerned
with the use of management-control systems to measure and analyze their
operations, innovations to which we will return later in this chapter.

Any analysis of book distribution must begin with a basic point: the
hundreds of book-publishing firms use a wide variety of marketing channels to reach their consumers. Some books, particularly scholarly ones, are
sold directly by publishers to the consumer. Most trade books reach buyers
through intermediaries, such as wholesalers, and different types of bookstore. Some customers are supplied by book clubs. A sizable portion of the
industry's output goes to a host of libraries and then reaches the public.
Not all books use every distribution channel. Certain types of book usually
reach their consumers through certain channels. The economist Fritz
Machlup has calculated the different distribution channels for trade books,
college texts, and professional books (a somewhat narrower definition of
our category of scholarly books).[6] According to 1975 industry data from
twenty-seven trade publishers, sixteen professional publishers, and ten
college text publishers, trade and text sales rely on one or two main channels, while sales of professional books are far more varied. Thirty-seven
percent of trade books are sold by general bookstores; another 33.6 percent
are handled by wholesalers; domestic libraries account for 9 percent of
trade sales. With college texts, college bookstores predominate; 69.4 percent of text sales are by college stores. Foreign sales are a distant second,
with 11.8 percent of text sales. Professional publishers are unique in the
range of their marketing strategies. Direct mail, which we have already discussed in chapter 8, is their primary method, accounting for 29.7 percent of
sales. This is followed by wholesalers, 20.2 percent; foreign sales, 13.4 percent; college bookstores, 12.3 percent; domestic libraries, 10.6 percent; and
general bookstores, 10.1 percent.[7] Of course, these statistics can be misleading. They tell us where publishers ship their books, not where the
books eventually are acquired by consumers. For example, wholesalers sell
to bookstores, college stores, and libraries. Since distribution patterns vary
for different types of book, we will discuss them separately beginning with
college texts, then turning to scholarly books and finally trade books.

COLLEGE TEXTBOOKS

College textbooks are sold and distributed in a very different way from trade or scholarly books. College textbooks are ordered not by their ultimate consumers, the students, but by the teachers for a particular course. Publishers can easily ascertain which instructors are potential buyers for their books. Unlike trade publishing, market research is both economically and practically feasible and has become a powerful tool in the development, design, and distribution of texts. Major text houses know which texts have leading positions in the market and which lag behind: that X has 6 percent of the relevant market, and that Y has only 2 percent. Close analysis of the successful texts and the laggards alerts the publishers to the topics and styles currently in or out of fashion. Then instructors are polled about any changes they would like to see in a particular text. These data are supplemented by information gathered by college travelers. The final result is a text that is usually bland and "safe," but profitable since it has been tailored to the demands of the market.

Once a textbook is published, the sales force of college travelers takes over, having been lectured by the text's editor and the sales department manager about the book's uniqueness. Since dozens of texts compete for the same market, each one must have some characteristics that set it apart from competing texts. As the sales force hits the campuses, dropping off examination copies and touting the book to the appropriate faculty member, the publisher begins a supporting advertising blitz, relying on direct mailings and ads in academic journals. If things go according to plan, professors will adopt the book for their classes.

When a faculty member adopts a book, the campus bookstore orders copies from the publisher. College bookstores are the primary channel through which college texts are sold. Traditionally they simply ordered the number of copies a professor recommended, shelved the texts by course number, and sold them to students once classes started. This routine has been changing in recent years.

Selling textbooks is not retailing in the usual sense of the term. College stores have no choice about which texts they will sell. They must cope with professors who order books long after deadlines (texts must be ordered by a certain early date, so that students can have books the first day of class), and with students who do not always purchase required texts.

Professors also commonly request that supplementary books on their reading lists be ordered, even though few students purchase them. In the past, college stores had no bargaining power in the price they paid for textbooks. The stores were, in essence, performing the last step in the distribution system for text publishers.

For years, textbook publishers sold texts to college stores at a discount of 20 percent. The stores paid shipping and handling charges, with the result that their income from sales was less than 20 percent. However, with the inflation of the past decade, the typical operating costs of college bookstores ran over 20 percent. Textbook publishers, in contrast, are among the publishing industry's most profitable and strongest performing divisions. College bookstores have charged that publishers' profits are excessive and realized at a store's expense.[8] These bookstores not only point to unfavorable discounts but assert that when a trade book (40 percent or higher discount) on a multi-departmental publisher's list is adopted as a text for a course, the discount is changed to 20 percent, the textbook rate. The latter charge is a bone of contention between publisher and bookseller.

College bookstore managers claim that their textbook sections are not likely to be profitable and take time for paperwork and floor space and tie up money in inventory. College stores are now stocking general merchandise on which they can make a larger profit. In addition to diversifying their offerings, they have intensified their practice of buying used books, are charging higher than the publisher's suggested list price, are not routinely ordering the number of copies a professor suggests, and are pressuring publishers for more favorable discounts.

The sale of used textbooks has become a big business. Traditionally, college stores offered students 50 percent of the original list price of a used text and then resold it for 75 percent of the list price. There are now several national companies that specialize in marketing used texts and professor's complimentary desk copies. Text publishers send out thousands of free examination copies. In the past, professors who did not want these books would give them to graduate students, the library, or a departmental fund. But in recent years, several companies began to send buyers from campus to campus, often going door to door, purchasing "freebies" from professors and reselling them to used-book wholesalers. Many of the used-book wholesalers themselves now buy back used and complimentary books on campuses. These books are then sold to college bookstores at reduced rates. The Association of American Publishers estimates the wholesale business in used college texts has doubled or tripled in the past four years.[9]

These buy-back practices have raised considerable controversy. Although professors, wholesalers, students, and college bookstores appear to benefit from "recycling" exam copies, book publishers most definitely do not benefit. Publishers call the practice unethical and charge that their profits and authors' royalties are being seriously eroded. A professor who receives ten to fifty complimentary copies a year may see nothing wrong with selling books he or she never requested; recycling the books seems infinitely better than throwing them in the garbage.

Now when a college bookstore receives an order for 120 copies of an introductory economics text, it no longer simply orders that quantity from the publisher. First, it will check and see if past records reveal whether students had purchased all the copies that were ordered. If there were sizable returns, the bookstore will reduce the order number to, say, 100. Next, it will see how many used copies it bought back from last year's students: suppose there were 25 buy-backs. The third step will be to contact a used-book wholesaler and find out how many used copies are available: another 30 copies can be procured from the wholesaler. The bookstore owner is thus left with an order for 45 copies, which will then be sent to the publishing house. By following these various strategies, college stores have been able to reduce their operating costs.

Text publishers are worried by these developments.[10] They have begun to plan new editions of successful texts as soon as one year after publication, so as to obviate used-book orders. Text houses are also including, with the royalty checks they send to authors, statements that are sharply critical of used-book wholesalers who resell examination copies.* Perhaps the text houses' most effective response has been to change their discount policies, which have been upped in some houses to 23 percent or 24 percent. John Wiley & Sons has raised its discount on texts to 25 percent and added a stiff penalty for excessive returns. Other publishers, such as Harper & Row, have discontinued traditional discount pricing and adopted net pricing arrangements in which the campus bookstore now decides how much to charge students. Bookstore operators seem to prefer a higher discount rate to net pricing.[11]

---

* One such letter from a large text publisher goes as follows:

It is a pleasure to send your royalty statement for the second half of 1978. May I take this opportunity to call your attention to a growing problem that may have had an effect on the amount of your royalties.

One of the principal methods of promotion used by all college publishers is to send sample copies to Professors to consider for adoption. Few Professors will adopt books they have not seen. In the past, relatively few Professor samples were offered for sale, even when they were no longer needed.

In the last two years, however, a large number of "independent" agents, encouraged and supported by used book wholesalers, have canvassed college campuses

The relationship between college textbook publishers and college bookstores is likely to remain acrimonious. College bookstores resent being dependent upon publishers. On the other hand, text publishers do not want to write up one hundred invoices and ship one hundred separate packages to one hundred different students. They rely on college bookstores for distribution but would prefer that relations with them remain as they were. However, with the entry into the field of aggressive used-book wholesalers, things are unlikely ever to be the same again.

Textbook publishers have been unsympathetic to the concerns of college stores. Textbooks, they point out, are pre-sold; and if college operations are unprofitable, it is due to poor management. Publishers should beware, however, because more efficient management is likely to appear in the guise of college bookstore chains. In the 1970s, several chains, among them Barnes & Noble, Nebraska Book Company, and the Follett Corporation, grew rapidly. The college chains are open about their policy of selling significantly more used copies than do independent stores.

The approximately two thousand eight hundred college bookstores, ranging from small-scale operations to large businesses like the Harvard Coop, sell many other kinds of books besides textbooks. They sell general trade books and are much more likely than is a regular bookstore to carry university press books and professional monographs. College bookstore sales are an important outlet for scholarly publishers in general. Many university presses have begun paperback lines to tap into course adoptions. Nor are scholarly presses alone; many trade publishers also have quality paperback lines—such as Doubleday's Anchor Press, New American Library's Mentor Books, Simon & Schuster's Touchstone imprint, and Random House's Vintage Books—that sell a considerable portion of their books as either course adoptions or non-curriculum sales in college stores.

---

systematically, offering Professors cash for sample books. The agent pays a small fraction of the book's value and resells it to a used book wholesaler at double the purchase price. . . . The used book wholesaler is the big winner, reselling the book to a College Store at double or triple his purchase price. . . . The College Store makes a little more profit on the sale of this book compared with one purchased from the publisher. . . . The Student pays the *same* price. . . . The agent and the wholesaler rake in outrageous profits without sharing any of the risk. . . . The author and publisher are the big losers, having invested time, talent and money and been cheated out of the original sale and royalty.

Used book wholesalers have been around for a long time. Publishers may not like them very much, but they have learned to live with the used book business—as long as publisher and author benefit from the original sale. The sale of sample copies, however, deprives the publisher of *any* return on his investment and the author of *any* royalties. These sales threaten the economic well-being of our industry at a time when markets are shrinking, competition is increasing, and inflation challenges us relentlessly.

SCHOLARLY PUBLISHING

Scholarly publishers use a wide variety of distribution methods. They may have a small sales force of their own that visits selected bookstores in major metropolitan areas and college towns. Or they may join together with several houses to contract for the services of commission men. Several of the commercial scholarly publishers we studied were subsidiaries of large publishing corporations. When the scholarly house published a book with potential broad appeal, the trade sales force of the parent company was responsible for placing the book in the bookstores. As can be expected, such arrangements did not always work well. A trade sales force is not well prepared to handle academic or professional books, and the performance of its salesmen and saleswomen is usually evaluated according to their success in selling the parent company's list. Bookstores do not get much out of an order for one or two copies of an academic book. Nevertheless, through a variety of means, some scholarly books do receive a limited distribution and are available in discriminating bookstores. Of course, some scholarly houses and university presses have a reputation for publishing books that are, at the same time, accessible to the average intelligent reader and deal with a topic of interest or importance. A publisher with such a track record will have more success placing its books in bookstores than will a house with a reputation for highly specialized, academic books.

Aside from subject matter and style of presentation, another barrier to bookstore sales of scholarly books is a publisher's discount policies. In general, most hardcover scholarly books carry a discount of 20 percent. If a scholarly house has one or two books with trade potential, books may be discounted at 40 percent for a period of six or twelve months, and then revert to 20 percent. Some scholarly houses are exploring the use of intermediate discounts of 33 percent in an attempt to increase bookstore sales. However, it is unlikely that scholarly books will ever carry discounts that are as favorable to booksellers as trade book discounts are.

Many academics are accustomed to ordering scholarly books directly from a publisher. Scholarly houses also advertise widely in journals like the *New York Review of Books* or the *American Scholar*. If the reader cannot obtain an advertised book in a local bookstore, he or she can write the publisher directly. A scholarly publisher may sell several thousand copies of a book individually, filling one order at a time. Scholarly publishers do a considerable amount of their promotion and sales through direct mailings to academics and other professionals. Publishers either maintain up-to-date mailing lists of academics and professionals in a particular field or lease appropriate lists from professional societies, journal subscription lists, or list brokers. The mailing lists enable them to pinpoint the professionals in a field who are likely to be interested in their recent publications. Even if after receiving a catalogue or a mailing one does not purchase a book for one's personal library, one may recommend purchase to the university library. Direct mailings permit flexibility in the design and format of advertising copy. Mail-order responses can also be charted and analyzed for effectiveness, so that a publisher can build a data base by which to estimate print runs and audience size for future comparable books.

The more specialized a book's topic, the more the publisher will rely on direct mailings rather than on other sales methods. When it comes to specialized monographs that are addressed not to a whole academic discipline—say, sociology—but to a narrower field within a discipline—such as demography—total sales will be comparatively modest, but knowledge of who is likely to buy such a book is quite high. The publisher, or the academic editor of a specialized series, knows with some accuracy who will be inclined to acquire a particular book. This is why monographs, though usually priced high, have a relatively certain market and can be profitable even with modest print runs.

Finally, scholarly books have another important outlet in library sales. A publishing house may have its own library sales force or rely on wholesalers. Whatever the means, library sales for serious scholarly books provide a floor on which a second level of sales through bookstores or direct mailings may be safely built. Several editors at scholarly publishing houses told us that if they did their job right and acquired important books of real substance, they could be assured of anywhere from one thousand to two thousand library-copy sales. For some books, this sale alone would put them into the black. Here again, a publishing house's reputation is important. With declining library budgets, libraries must become more selective and will rely on publishers with a reputation for, and a tradition of, publishing good scholarship.

HARDCOVER TRADE PUBLISHING

Large trade publishers usually maintain their own sales force of men and women (see chapter 4). Smaller trade houses arrange to have their books distributed either by larger houses or by commission men. The latter are salesmen who may represent a dozen or more publishing houses and cover a specific geographic territory. It is our impression that at the present time small houses are more likely to turn to larger houses than to commission men for the selling and distribution of their books.[12] Several corporate families, such as Knopf and Random House, began their relationships with distribution arrangements. Larger houses provide warehousing, selling, and billing services in return for approximately 30 percent of the sales generated by the smaller publishers' lists, after deducting charges for returned books. The smaller house can focus on editorial, design, and promotional matters; it need not hire a sales representative, rent a square foot of warehouse space, or send a single invoice. All this is done by the larger house. Among the more well-known houses who distribute other publishers' lists are Random House, Harper & Row, Simon & Schuster, E. P. Dutton, Scribner's, and W. W. Norton.

The advantage of this arrangement for large publishers is that it adds sales volume without increasing their investment. Added distribution enables the large publisher to have a big sales force and to use it fully. Moreover, any hit book that a small house has adds to the attractiveness of the overall list. From a small publisher's point of view, there are advantages and disadvantages. Larger houses are able to collect bills from wholesalers and bookstores more quickly than are small houses, particularly new small houses. This is a major plus. The distribution arrangement also provides the small house with better access to bookstores. A bookstore can combine and order from an entire list and receive a larger discount. If a small publisher were selling its titles individually, the bookstore would not receive as favorable a discount. It is also easier for a bookstore to deal with one large distributing source as opposed to dozens of small houses.

There is debate over whether the sales force treats equally all books that it distributes. When salespersons are presenting books to booksellers, the small publisher tends to think that its list is brought up last, sometimes as an afterthought. Another criticism is that the sales staff is usually not well informed about the books of the small house it is distributing. Yet whatever their relative merits—as small publishers continue to sprout, and as co-publishing arrangements flourish—we expect to see more of these distribution arrangements in the future.

Whether a publishing house has its own sales force, or is distributed by another house or by commission men, the key event for presenting the new list to the people who must sell it is the time-honored ritual, the sales conference. Held at least twice a year—in May for the fall list and in November or December for the spring list—the main purpose is to prepare the sales staff by informing them of next season's books and attempting to fire their enthusiasm for selling them. The sales force will be supplied with dust jackets, catalogues, and all sorts of other paraphernalia. The conference may last anywhere from one to four days and takes place, if not in New York City, in a sunny location such as San Diego or Sarasota, Florida, or in the Bahamas or Puerto Rico.

We were able to attend several of these conferences. They are fascinating to watch because editors present their new books, often discussing them in considerable detail, to an audience that is usually skeptical. "Pep talks" are the order of the day, as are the efforts after hours to fortify oneself with spirits. The dynamics of the occasion lie in differing expectations. Editors have high hopes for each of the titles. Members of the sales staff, in contrast, know that when they visit a store they have only a few minutes to cover a book. Moreover, they know their sales accounts and are aware that they themselves are effective only if they recommend books that the store will actually sell. A veteran salesman will highlight certain books and skip others altogether. Salespersons go to the sales conference looking for clues to which books will move or, in publisher's parlance, will have "legs" to get up and walk out of the store. The major clues they receive are the sales quota and the advertising budget for specific titles. These figures influence how much attention a salesman will devote to a specific title. Obviously, there is an element of self-fulfilling prophecy involved—higher expectations, more attention, and more time spent selling the book can influence how many copies a bookseller will order.

A seasoned sales staff, however, is quick to spot unrealistic print runs or inflated advertising budgets. At the conferences we attended, the sales force was often critical of cover designs, made many comments and suggestions about publicity plans, and pointed out the shortcomings of many titles. Sales conferences are marked by frequent questions, comments, and jokes. Some editors presented their titles with long detailed stories; others were lively and short. Experienced editors are skilled in deftly summarizing a book and explaining why it is worth publishing. They provide the sales staff with a "handle," a succinct sentence or two that captures the book's virtues. Editors make frequent comparisons to well-known authors or best-selling books. A few examples of "handles" follow:

- This is an extremely commercial book with the potential of *The Hite Report*. It's sort of a "sexual *Passages*."

- This book is the equivalent of *All the President's Men* in country X. We need to help orchestrate the revelations—it could be a "biggie."

A more candid approach by one editor was:

- This book will be hard to sell. I'll be the first to concede that, but it has a marvelous jacket, it's very well-written. It's been selectively but favorably reviewed. It reminds me of *Let Us Now Praise Famous Men*.

Members of the sales staff are quick to react to editors' presentations. Typical of their comments are the following:

- What's the use of a title that no one can understand?

- I think we are scraping the bottom of the barrel to publish the laundry of our backlist authors.

- Who are the authors? I never heard of them.

- If the book is aimed at the youth market, why not a paperback edition?

- No way I can sell many copies of a book that radical in the Southwest.

Once the sales conference is over, the salespersons return to their territories. The size of their sales area depends on the overall size of the sales force and the volume of sales in a specific region. These traveling salespersons, often called book travelers, may visit several hundred stores at least twice a year. They may call on libraries and wholesalers, but their primary accounts are independent bookstores and small, local chain stores. They travel through their territory equiped with the list of books they sell, perhaps galleys for a few especially important books, and the jackets and advertising copy for the rest. They will also check on a store's inventory of perennial backlist titles. Bookstore managers and owners are busy people, and stores are usually understaffed, so that a book traveler has only a few minutes to make the sales pitch for his wares. Hence he cultivates the ability to outline the content of his books in a pithy and succinct manner. If he is to be successful, he must know as much as possible about his various bookstore clients and about the customers they serve. Science fiction, say, is likely to do well in Palo Alto or in Cambridge, where scientists abound, but to have much less appeal in Chattanooga. Saul Bellow is likely to do well in Chicago and New York but will do poorly in Arkansas. Romances will find ready markets in suburbia and in areas frequented by women office workers and housewives, but will not do nearly as well in male-dominated industrial areas, where spy thrillers and westerns are snapped up. University towns differ from the suburbs. Affluent suburbs have a different reading clientele from that of aging cities or small towns.

Travelers not only serve their bookstore clients by offering and characterizing their new wares, they also serve as links between the small world of the bookseller and the large world of the publishing industry. They convey news as well as gossip; they describe trends as well as fads and fashions. Booksellers, to be sure, read pre-publication reviews as well as advertising brochures and trade publications; but they get much information about intangible aspects of the publishing business through word of mouth. When it comes to selling Norman Mailer's books, knowledge about his latest love affair may be more potent than a review assessing his literary merits.

In an especially good portrait of a young sales representative for William Morrow, a trade publishing house, N. R. Kleinfield points out that book travelers have a lot of sympathy for the plight of independent booksellers.[13] Today's traveler avoids high-pressure tactics and levels with the buyer. The salesman that Kleinfield followed on his rounds noted:

> There are three books on this list that I will not sell to any of my retail accounts. That's because they have no redeeming value. They're not good pieces of trash. They're not good pieces of literature. I could sell some of them if I wanted to, but they would just come back and it would ruin my credibility. I think that it's psychologically important to have a few skips on a list. It builds trust. It's something you can giggle over with the buyer. "Hey, look at this dud!"[14]

Old-fashioned book travelers frequently were cultivated people who loved books and were willing to forgo high incomes in exchange for the sheer pleasure of handling books. They found excitement and gratification in pushing a particular work to which they had taken a fancy. Bruce Bliven's lovely biography of a traveler who covered the American South is a fine example of the old tradition of bookselling.[15] These book travelers frequently had chosen their vocation after attempting careers as book reviewers or authors or in other branches of the book world. Bliven's account illustrates many of the tensions faced by book travelers. His informant,

347

George Fabian Scheer, points out, "Like all salesmen, I'm under constant pressure. . . . If my returns are low, my publishers suspect me of underselling. If I sell too hard and returns are high, my accounts turn me off. It's a tightrope."[16] Bliven describes a wonderful set of strong and long-lasting friendships between his book traveler and many bookstore owners. However, it is our impression, based on interviews with sales staff and bookstore owners, that traditional book travelers are increasingly less common. In their place is a new type of traveler, one who gives the impression that it was just by accident that one is selling books rather than pharmaceuticals. The reasons for this change are not altogether clear. Nevertheless, there is still a mixture of traditional and newer people among book travelers. Not so long ago one of us met the two regional sales representatives of a major house, both of whom were published poets.

One possible explanation for the change in the role of book traveler is the precarious state of many independent bookstores. In today's book industry, travelers do not call upon the large book chains, which buy their wares through their national offices. Contacts between the chains and the publishing houses are usually maintained by top sales executives. Chain bookstores are now responsible for the majority of bookstore sales; hence, relations with small bookstores are less important. Support for this view is found in a recent survey of independent bookstores by the American Booksellers Association, which reported, "Half of the . . . members' stores reporting in this survey are not profitable when judged by a reasonable standard of financial performance."[17] In 1977, adjusted net profit for the average bookstore amounted to 2.5 percent, while bookstores considered moderately profitable showed an adjusted net profit of 2.8 percent. This is a strong decline from 1968 when a similar survey showed an average adjusted net profit of 5.5 percent. Figures such as these suggest that, in order to operate an independent bookstore today, one needs either to be a compulsive book lover or to have a strong masochistic bent. Book travelers not only call upon independent bookstores, but they also contact the smaller chains, national book wholesalers, and regional independent distributors. Once a book leaves the publishing house, there are a number of distribution channels through which it may pass before it arrives on the shelves of a bookstore. And, even more significant is the fact that bookstores vary widely in their policies as to what type of books they will stock.

THE BOOK CHAINS

While independently owned bookstores have become increasingly unprofitable, the book chains enjoy a thriving business and impressive profits.
They manage to do so because they have been able to move away from
cottage industry practices to highly rationalized procedures. The chains
enjoy the same advantages over individual booksellers that McDonald's or
Howard Johnson's enjoy over a "mom and pop" café. This is not because
they have directly moved into territory formerly controlled by the independents. They have, for the most part, opened entirely new territory,
mainly in suburban shopping malls. Chain stores sell large quantities of
best sellers and pay little attention to the diversity of their book offerings.
The chain stores keep strict inventory control with the help of sophisticated computers.

The rise of bookstore chains in the 1970s has been nothing less than
phenomenal. The fastest growth has come from the expansion of two large
retail chains: Walden Books, a subsidiary of Carter-Hawley-Hale, and B.
Dalton, a subsidiary of Dayton-Hudson.* Both parent companies are large
diversified national retailers. Carter-Hawley-Hale also owns several up-
scale department stores—Neiman-Marcus, Bergdorf Goodman, and the
Broadway stores in California. Estimates of the sales of these two bookstore chains vary slightly, but it can be safely assumed that they account
for about 20 percent of all bookstore sales in the United States, and their
percentage of new book sales is considerably higher. B. Dalton, which was
founded in 1966, had revenues of $255,600,000 from 526 stores in 1980.
Walden Books had sales of $255,000,000 to $260,000,000 from 704 outlets
in 1980 and are reportedly considering opening another 400 stores in the
next five years.[19]†

The other large chains are considerably smaller, but with the exception of Brentano's, they are also growing. In order of 1980 sales revenues,
the other large chains are Barnes & Noble (52 outlets),‡ Kroch's & Brentano's (18 outlets), Zondervan (57 outlets), Coles (61 U.S. outlets, 220 in

* In business circles, Dayton-Hudson is well regarded. Mobil Oil recently chose the
chief executive officer of Dayton-Hudson, Stephen L. Pistner, to repair the sagging fortunes
of its retail chain, Montgomery Ward & Company.[18]

† A *New York Times* news article on the book chains reports that Dalton now has 540
stores nationwide. In 1980 it opened 100 stores, up from 64 in 1979. Walden Books currently
has 703 stores after opening 89 in 1980.[20]

‡ Barnes & Noble has expanded particularly fast in the New York City metropolitan
area. It acquired four Bookmasters outlets and converted them to cut-rate retail book stores in
the spring of 1979. More recently, Barnes & Noble has bought the assets of Marboro Book

Canada), Brentano's (31 outlets), Doubleday (26 outlets), and Cokesbury (34 outlets).[21] Their combined revenues do not approach that of either of the two large chains. Figures from the 1977 Census of Retail Trade, released in March 1980, give further indication of the rise of multi-unit bookstore chains. However, Census data on bookstores are not entirely satisfactory. For 1977, the Census lists 12,718 retail book establishments, owned by 10,688 firms; but these figures and their accompanying sales estimates do not include college bookstores, religious bookstores, or retail outlets like department stores, drug stores, and supermarkets. One other source, Knowledge Industry Publications, estimates that supermarkets alone account for 25 percent of paperback book sales.[22] Nevertheless, some useful information can be gleaned from comparing the 1972 Census with the 1977 Census: book sales by companies that own 25 or more stores rose 194 percent in this five-year period; the rate of expansion for all bookstores, including chains, was 101 percent.

The advantages enjoyed by the chains are many, including highly efficient computerized operations that keep track of their stock on a daily basis, register the sales record of every volume, and alert their buyers when a book begins to take off and new orders need to be placed. Sales records for each store are sent to corporate headquarters on a weekly, monthly, and year-to-year basis. Current and past rates of sales are available on computer; titles can be automatically reordered on the basis of their recent sales history, current customer request, and future sales projections. Thus, chain stores can promptly sweep slow-selling books from their shelves. The computer not only keeps records of total sales trends of a chain but also provides local information, so that the buyers can learn that a book that does well in Cleveland, say, may lag in Boston. The computer can produce profiles of local book-buying preferences and can even provide information on what particular category of buyer is attracted to a particular type of book.* One chain, Kroch's & Brentano's, continues to keep track of sales records manually and does not seem to be suffering from lack of computer technology.

While bookstores have traditionally been located on side streets and not in expensive central locations, the chains are where the action is. Lo-

---

Stores, the country's largest retailer of remainder books, former best sellers, and overstocked titles retailed at a fraction of their list price. Barnes & Noble operates approximately twenty college bookstores. It has pioneered the "supermarket" style of bookstore with shopping carts and checkout counters.

* Dalton uses demographic studies of 36,000 cities, with information broken down into census tracts. They find "the heaviest readers are between 21 and 49 years old. Most have a high school education and some college, a third have incomes over $20,000 and they're generally in managerial or professional positions. They're also predominately female."[23]

cated in affluent suburbs, the chains attract clients with money. They provide convenient parking and are open on evenings and weekends. Chain
ownership helps finance the purchase of prime real estate that an independent bookseller could not afford. A housewife buying groceries in a local
supermarket will often find a nicely furnished, brightly lit chain store right
around the corner. She may have listened to a talk show before going
shopping and heard about a new best seller. That best seller is prominently
displayed in the chain store and lures her in. The merchandising style of
the chain matches that of the supermarket. The sales personnel in chain
stores are not likely to be knowledgeable about books in general or about
the operation of the industry in particular, but they can certainly direct the
customer to the best sellers and to books recently discussed on television.
Just as in the supermarket, the sales personnel are unobtrusive. The product, usually wrapped in glossy covers, is made to sell itself. Chain stores
have certainly expanded the book-buying audience, particularly in areas
like the South, the Southwest, and the Midwest, where historically there
have been fewer bookstores.

With their un-bookish flair for merchandising, the chains are leaving
their mark on the book industry. In an annual column, "Year in Review,"
Publishers Weekly prints a list of the year's best-selling books. These lists
are often hotly debated, some publishers suggesting that the sales are arti-
ficial. In the 1980 review, *Publishers Weekly* took the unusual step of also
printing B. Dalton's best-selling list, and thus testified to the confidence
that *PW* has in Dalton's computerized record keeping. We quote *PW*:

> Publishers continue to question the veracity of the figures that some of their
> colleagues quote for these lists, often suggesting that sales figures in some
> houses are exaggerated to get an author on an annual list (while at the same
> time, all publishers attest to the correctness of their own figures). *PW* is still
> open to ideas for a workable, foolproof method for collecting sales figures for
> these lists that would be acceptable to all publishers. Short of attaining that
> ideal, we decided to reprint B. Dalton's 1980 best-sellers.[24]

In the past, the relation between publishers and booksellers was
largely a traditioinal market relationship where the bookseller chose the
books he wished to acquire but otherwise had no significant impact on the
publisher. With the coming of the chain stores, their book buyers have acquired new powers over the destiny of books and the fortunes of publishers. Chain stores and publishers are now linked in a complex network of
reciprocal dependency. Once a chain orders a book, it will classify it in a
particular category. Sales of each category are then added up, and the
weekly best-seller lists in hardcover fiction, trade paperbacks, mass-market

paperbacks, and so on are compiled. These lists also include bargain books, juvenile paperbacks, and many other specialized categories. Armed with this mass of knowledge, which is totally new to book publishing, a chain buyer can influence a publisher's promotion plans for particular books and encourage specific directions within the overall publishing program of a particular house. If the Dalton or Walden buyer is convinced, on the basis of either store's computerized lists, that a certain book is likely to take off, he will order a large number of copies. Having made a major investment in the book, the chain will then promote the book heavily and thus enhance its chances of making the best-seller lists. Success then feeds upon success, and sales increase. In this way the major chains help determine which books achieve best-sellerdom. Mass sales can now result from the conscious planning and decision making of the chain stores. The impersonal market of individual consumer choices has been replaced. It is no surprise that publishers' representatives now show key chain buyers manuscripts of forthcoming books even before they are set in type. Editors have told us that, for a book with a first printing of fifty thousand copies, the two large chains may order more than 10 percent of the publisher's total stock.

The chain store buyer is an important new figure on the publishing scene. In a similiar fashion, the chain store's advertising manager, who arranges for cooperative newspaper ads with the publisher, and its publicity person, who is in charge of all in-store ballyhoo, are becoming major figures in the book business, rivaling in importance the publisher's publicity and advertising departments. Judson Hand, who writes on the book world for the *New York Daily News*, describes all this with considerable acumen:

> As for the new show biz aspects of bookselling, it is nowhere so apparent as in Dalton's giant store near 52nd Street in Manhattan. There, movies are projected in store windows. On festive occasions, cookbook authors carve turkeys in the cookbook section. In the children's section, cubes on which the books are displayed are decorated with paintings by children, and overhead in the children's department hang replicas of the space ships in the movie *Star Wars*. In the store, there is a sunken auditorium where authors speak to an audience of more than two hundred people. Promotions have been mounted or planned which involve such unbookish pop culture figures as Spider Man and Superman.[25]

Chain store buyers and publicity people have become major nodal points in the making of best sellers, and must be stroked and cultivated by trade publishers since the latter's success or failure may well depend on the decisions and activities of the chains. Some publishers are worried that the chains have too much clout. In 1974, Harold McGraw, Jr., president of McGraw-Hill, stated what has since become a prevalent view: "Mass retailing will hopefully make the industry more profitable and efficient, and we certainly need it, but I worry about the standardization of book buying and a concentration only on books with mass appeal."[26] A weekly memorandum, the *B. Dalton Merchandise Bulletin*, sent out to all Dalton stores and many publishers, is carefully scrutinized at most trade houses. The bulletin lists current best sellers, hot titles, and promotion plans. Publishers are quick to alert the chains about author tours and broadcast appearances.

Of course, not every chain store is alike. The manager of Dalton's Fifth Avenue store in Manhattan says, "We try to be as eclectic as we can. We have chamber music and poetry readings. We want to change the image that we are a bookstore run by a computer."[27] A new Dalton store planned for New York's Greenwich Village will have later hours and more philosophy titles. But there is no question that chains emphasize books with fast turnover. Many wholesalers note that chains are restrictive in title selection, favoring best sellers and category titles to the exclusion of backlist books.[28]

INDEPENDENT STORES

The evidence seems mixed on whether the spread of chain stores has affected independent bookstores' chances for survival. The Book Industry Trends survey for 1978 states:

> There is increasing evidence, such as the survey of booksellers reported in *Publishers Weekly* on July 31, 1978, that the expansion of retail outlets has cut heavily into the sales of existing stores and that, in many communities, a larger number of outlets now competes for, on the whole, the same consumer dollars.[29]

Ethel Cross, manager of the Andover (Mass.) Bookstore, expresses concern: "Chains sell only the best-sellers—the cream—while we sell quite a few books that sit on the shelf a half-year or more. That's expensive. And we've definitely experienced a certain drain of customers to the chains."[30] A *PW* study suggests that, when a chain store opens near an independent store, the latter initially experiences a drop in sales, but then sales usually bounce back.[31]

Independent booksellers are much more united in their perception that publishers give chains preferential treatment in shipping new books and in discount rates. At the June 1980 American Booksellers Association convention in Chicago, discontents that had been festering among many smaller independent booksellers finally erupted. In a letter later circulated to publishers, they complained of discrimination against them in discount policies favoring the large chains. Booksellers have decided to undertake a class action suit against publishers, because they claim that publishers offer better discounts and co-op advertising to the larger chains.

The continued ascendancy of both book chains and discount stores over independently owned bookstores does not mean that the latter are likely to disappear. In an effort to survive, they are resorting to two tactics: increasing specialization and greater attention to personal service for customers. Specialization as a marketing strategy for independent bookstores is widespread. In a manner similar to magazine publishing—where specialized magazines catering to the young, women, the middle-aged, photographers, sports fans, pornography fanciers, and so on have replaced general interest magazines—or to the radio industry and cable television—where narrowcasting aimed at specific audiences is increasingly profitable—so in the bookstore business, differentiation is growing rapidly. In the Boston-Cambridge area, for example, where four Barnes & Noble discount stores have been opened in the last few years, and where the company plans to open another five by the end of 1981, many of the 115 bookstores are turning to specialization. Some now deal exclusively in used books, science fiction, women's literature, rare editions, or Asian literature. There is even one store that handles only cookbooks.[32] However such diversification can only be attempted in large metropolitan areas. In smaller places, which hardly sustain one or two general stores, such a strategy cannot possibly work.

Providing customers with better personal service may include opening individual charge accounts for regular customers and creating a warm comfortable setting. Many independent stores are making sure they have a diversity of titles and a good backlist stock. They carry more trade and academic paperbacks, small-press titles, and books of local and regional interests. And, perhaps most important of all, they welcome special orders. One of the reasons special ordering is feasible for independent stores is the presence of the large national and regional book wholesalers. Wholesalers have expanded considerably in the 1970s. A national firm, such as Baker & Taylor, may carry an inventory of one hundred thousand different titles. Smaller regional wholesalers have smaller inventories but provide rapid service, sometimes delivering a special order in less than a week. This compares most favorably to the four to six weeks it takes to order directly from a publishing house. Wholesalers function as middlemen and can promptly supply either a wide range of backlist titles or offer restock of successful titles. Since wholesalers handle a variety of publishers, they minimize processing and handling costs. Wholesalers are given favorable discounts by publishers because they generate large sales volume; retailers accept lower discounts in return for rapid service and less expensive transportation costs.

For years, intermediate distributors have supplied books for many types of libraries. Over 75 percent of book sales to libraries are channeled through wholesalers, which simplify and consolidate ordering, processing, and paying for thousands of books from hundreds of publishers. They perform other services for libraries as well, including cataloging, supplying checkout cards, and marking shelf numbers. Finally, wholesalers give higher discounts to libraries than publishing houses do. With most libraries facing severe financial shortages and cutbacks in operation, wholesalers will likely perform even more services for libraries in the future. Libraries purchase a significantly larger proportion of books that are published in print runs of less than five thousand copies.

POPULAR PAPERBACKS

When it comes to mass-market paperbacks, a wholly different system of distribution comes into play. Mass-market paperbacks are those ubiquitous soft-bound books found in supermarkets, drugstores, newsstands, transportation centers, and bookstores. It was once possible to distinguish them from other types of paperback by their price; but with inflation, some mass-market paperbacks now cost more than three dollars. They are best characterized by their size (4 inches by 7 inches), their design for easy display on book racks, their glossy covers, their mode of distribution, and—unless they are extremely successful—their short lifespan. If the books do not sell promptly, they are removed from the display racks and replaced by a new crop. The distribution system for mass-market paperbacks is largely ancillary to the distribution network for magazines and is hence geared to rapid turnover. Last week's romance may be almost as dated as last week's *Newsweek*. Since mass-market paperbacks are sold through a wide variety of outlets, both independent and chain bookstores are less significant forces in comparison with their central role in the sales of hardcover books and quality paperbacks. Discounts are higher in mass-market publishing than in other industry branches; for large orders to wholesalers discounts may be as high as 50 percent. As we mentioned earlier, return rates for paperbacks are also exceptionally high.

Since rapid distribution of new titles is of the essence, mass-market paperback publishers cannot rely on the U.S. mail. These paperbacks are shipped by truck along with magazines and newspapers. Many major paperback publishers own or control national distributing companies that, in turn, service independent distributors in a given territory.[33] The independent distributors cover different locales and carry the paperback offerings of most, if not all, major houses.

Mass-market paperback publishers and their national distributors are closely linked through exclusive national distribution contracts. Such contracts typically forbid distributors from carrying competing lines of paperbacks. These ties between paperback publishers and distributors make entry of new publishers into the field most difficult. The high degree of concentration in the paperback industry is partly explained by these exclusive contracts. The hardcover book field, where no such arrangements prevail, does not have such considerable barriers to new entrants.

What may be seen, from one perspective, as a barrier to entry can, from another, be seen as a justifiable strategy to minimize uncertainty. Paperback firms are wont to argue that without such ties to national distributors they would operate in so fickle a market that economic survival would be precarious. Because of both the enormous number of paperback titles released monthly (200 to 300 titles each month) and the consequent fierce competition for space on retail display racks, national distributors play a major role in stabilizing the flow of new releases to independent distributors and retailers.

Before releasing a book, a paperback publisher must make a decision on the print run. Such a decision requires some advance knowledge about the probable reaction of national distributors, which will in turn affect independent distributors and retail outlets. Because a national distributor is owned by a publisher or tied to one through exclusive contractual arrangements, the latter is able to influence the distributor's decisions and hence to decrease its, the publisher's, own uncertainties. The reverse may also happen, and there are cases where distributors affect publishers' decisions by providing them with estimates of the market for a particular title. In any case, as economists Michael Robinson and Ray Olszewski have argued, "The need to coordinate distributors' decisions with mass market publishers' planning provides an incentive derived from efficient market considerations to integrate either through joint ownership or other mechanisms that affect a long-run joining of interests."[34]

National paperback distributors do not deal with individual outlets. This is the function of independent distributors who are essentially wholesalers with a regional monopoly on magazines and paperbacks in retail outlets. The standard practice until most recently has been for IDs to enjoy regional monopoly franchises and for national distributors to have exclusive contracts with publishers or to be owned outright by them. These arrangements are no longer as exclusive as they once were. The tranquil world of tidy monopolies appears to be in the process of transformation.[35] Some paperback publishers have established direct sales departments. Book jobbers, who used to handle hardcover titles alone, have moved into the paperback market. Increasingly, independent distributors are poaching on one another's territory. Some independent distributors are moving into retail sales themselves. An estimated 200 of the some 500 or so IDs now operate their own retail stores. As a result, retailers complain about the unfair competition of ID-owned stores, and IDs complain about the invasion of jobbers into their territory. Jobbers distribute books through the mails, not through company-owned trucks, and are hence not tied to specific geographic regions. Finally, chain bookstores are buying directly from publishers and not through intermediaries and are facing the united opposition of national distributors, independent distributors, and jobbers.

Nevertheless, for most publishers, the majority of mass-market paperbacks are still handled by national distributors working with regional independent distributors who stock innumerable retail outlets throughout the country. The IDs are the agents who select the titles for retail display in their areas. As distinct from hardcover bookstores, paperback outlets exercise little control over the titles they display. They are shipped their quota of new titles from the IDs, and the only significant decisions most retail outlets make is whether to display the books prominently, or whether to return the many unsold items sooner or later. There is a German expression that wonderfully characterizes such an economic arrangement, *Friss Vogel oder Stirb* ("Eat bird, or die"). Given such methods of stocking paperback outlets, it is little wonder that the latest romances, mysteries, or popular blockbusters crowd the display racks, and that serious classic works of fiction and nonfiction are rarely found in newsstands, drugstores, or airports.

There are various degrees of force-feeding. Independent book stores have the privilege of ordering only the titles they desire, but drugstores have no such privileges and probably do not even wish to have to make

357

such decisions. In these stores, the book department may consist of, say, 350 pockets on a display rack, and the delivery man from the IDs who serves the store is in charge of what goes into them and what goes out. The prime space is on the top tiers of the racks. Here the newest releases will be displayed. The older ones move down a tier each week, until they reach the bottom tier and are then eliminated. It can take a typical book up to sixty days to move from top to bottom, but it often may only take four weeks. In paperback marketing, the route from glamour and glory to oblivion and destruction is very short. If you are stubborn and wish to buy a mass-market paperback that was published six months ago, you will probably have to write the publisher.[36]

The struggle for prime rack space is intense. Each month every paperback publisher has a lead book which receives the most advertising and promotion. A best-selling lead book can attract attention to the whole line of monthly releases and result in better rack space for all of them. This is why paperback publishers are willing to spend immense sums for the paperback rights to potential blockbusters. The bidding for these rights is well described in Thomas Whiteside's three-part series on publishing in the *New Yorker* (now a book published by Wesleyan University Press, 1981), and in several portraits of subsidiary rights directors.[37] Recently, several top publishers have pointed out the suicidal elements inherent in the bidding process.[38] After paying out huge sums for paperback rights, publishers must pump money into promotion to generate awareness of their titles. As one paperback editor in chief told us, "You pay tremendous sums at the top of your list just to get rack space for your lower titles. Then you'll spend at least $25,000 a month to create some attention. It's a crazy and costly game."

RETURNS

We have tried to give the reader a basic understanding of the distribution channels used in various sectors of the publishing industry. An exhaustive survey of book distribution would be a book in itself and would discuss a number of channels we have passed over, including international sales, remainders, book clubs, and reprint publishers. Nor did we go into detail about an important technological tool—the use of computers in the management of book distribution. Before closing our brief survey, we want to touch upon a controversial current development—the reform of the policy of permitting returns of unsold copies.

Speaking at the Library of Congress in 1980, the president of the Chicago bookstores, Kroch's & Brentano's, suggested that changes in the bookseller-publisher relationship must soon take place. Carl Kroch, noting that some of his recommendations were not necessarily in the best interest of his firm, nevertheless offered the following:

> The first, and probably most revolutionary, is that books be sold on an outright, not a returnable basis. Discounts would have to be adjusted to enable the bookseller to absorb the cost of unsold books. However, disposing of these books would enable the bookseller to have an honest clearance sale which would attract customers to the store.[39]

Harcourt Brace Jovanovich has decided to test the feasibility of a no-returns, high discount policy. As of 1 January 1981, Harcourt discontinued its policy of accepting returns and raised its wholesale discount to as high as 60 percent for orders over five hundred copies. The move has been characterized by some members of the industry as "brave"; while others see it as too radical. "Revision of returns policy is long overdue," says G. Roysce Smith, executive director of the American Booksellers Association, "but it would be quite traumatic to go from current wasteful practices to the opposite extreme."[40]

Book wholesalers are cutting back on Harcourt Brace Jovanovich titles because of the no-returns policy it has instituted. Phil Pfeffer, president of Ingram Book Company, has stated, "We don't feel the discount available to wholesalers from HBJ is commensurate with the risk of buying on a non-protected basis."[41] The booksellers' sentiment seems to be that a no-return policy makes sense for backlist titles, but few seem willing to risk ordering a new author without return privileges.

A number of other publishers—among them Atheneum, Crown, New American Library, Oxford University Press, and Scribner's—have instituted more moderate reforms. They offer new higher discount policies that include a penalty for returns. Many other publishers are currently considering revamping traditional discount, returns, and freight charge policies. We are surprised that more firms have not adopted the optional 50 percent discount, no-returns policy followed by David Godine, a quality small house in Boston. Such a policy should encourage bookstores that can buy efficiently to forgo the returns option. Other stores who want the return option must pay for the privilege by receiving books at a lower discount.

Publishers are also changing their freight charge policy: some are adopting free freight policies, while others are passing the costs through to customers in the form of higher prices.

Perhaps these reforms will bring some order to the chaos of book distribution. Despite changes and improvements in the marketing and distribution of books, it seems to us that much more effort is spent trying to get books into retail outlets and less attention is paid by publishers and distributors to actually selling books to consumers.

SUMMARY

College texts, scholarly books, hardcover trade books, and mass-market paperbacks each have their own distribution arrangements, and each sector currently faces significant obstacles. Textbook sales are being challenged by the burgeoning market of used texts. Scholarly publishers are threatened by library budget crises and government cutbacks in the funding of educational programs and scientific research. No doubt many trade publishers are envious of the textbook people's market research and the pinpoint use of direct mail by scholarly firms. Trade publishers continue to grapple with the difficult problem of how to market untested products without permitting returns, and are beset by rising postal rates. The furious scramble for rack space in the paperback field continues unabated. There were rumbles that paperback houses would turn to publishing more original works to avoid competing in costly paperback auctions for successful hardcover books; but now New American Library has forked over $850,000 for a first novel that it plans to publish as a paperback original. Competition for paperback originals will escalate, all in an effort to have a lead title that will attract attention to the rest of the paperback list.

Publishers bemoan current distribution practices. They also fear that the large book chains may exert their growing power to influence the publishing process. However, the reason that chains have so much influence is that they have found one means for simplifying and standardizing the distribution process. Unless trade publishers find their own way out of this quandry, the industry will be ever more likely to adopt the computerized retail practices of the chain bookstores. The retailing strategy of chain stores is simple and successful: focus on books that turn over quickly. Books that sell more slowly do not fit into their plans. An axiom of bookselling is that the greater the number of outlets controlled by one company, the narrower the selection of titles; otherwise, the economies of chain ownership will not be realized. Publishers often complained to us about the policies of the chains, but few among the former have attempted to improve or develop other channels of distribution.

Much change is currently afoot in book distribution. Whether it will be to the benefit or the detriment of diversity and pluralism in publishing policies is not yet clear. We have a strong feeling, however, that the decade of the 1980s will be crucial in determining the future of distribution policies, and that indirectly these decisions will have a pronounced effect on the editorial decision-making process.

Epilogue

Publishers as Gatekeepers
of Ideas

BOOKS are carriers and disseminators of ideas. More than any other means of communication, they are the most permanent, reasoned, and extensive repository of the thoughts of civilized man. Although the publishing industry may hold a more mundane view of itself, the book trade is, in fact, both the guardian and the constant creator of our written culture. With these sublime thoughts in mind, we began our study of publishing as a natural and inevitable outcome of our interests in men and women of ideas and in the organizations that support the production and dissemination of ideas. Yet compare our view of publishing with the statement recently made by Richard Snyder, president of Simon & Schuster, one of America's most successful publishers: "Any book, no matter how bad, is better than no book."[1] The policy of "any book" seems hardly consistent with the notion of publishers as "gatekeepers of ideas." This epilogue takes us back to where we began: the quest to understand the role of publishing in the production and marketing of ideas. This quest confronted our naïve fantasies about publishing—as we suspect it has the reader's—with hard, irresistible facts.

It has been our intention to analyze the structure of American

362

publishing, its organization, politics, and economics. We do not wish to tell publishers how to publish books, nor have we attempted to advise writers how to cope with developments in the industry. We do believe, however, that an understanding of the way book publishing operates as a gatekeeping enterprise will be useful to authors, publishers, and all those involved in the complex chain of producing and distributing books in ways that we as observers and analysts of this process cannot now imagine.

To begin with, publishing in capitalist countries has always been a matter of commerce: even subsidized presses must sell some books at a profit if they are to indulge their tastes in worthwhile but unprofitable books. The tension between commerce and culture, one of the themes of this study, has been shown to be a constant in American publishing, at least since the beginning of the last century. Thus, criticism of overcommercialization has been common at almost every phase of the book industry's history. Writing in the *Atlantic Monthly* in 1913, George P. Brett, then president of Macmillan, reflected on the industry's "present tendencies":

> Some years ago the publisher's task was a happier and easier one, for then there were, in considerable numbers, among the general public, book-lovers whose chief delight consisted in the discovery of the new author and the new book of merit.... The life of a best-seller is now little longer than a month.... The publication of books of general literature is by far the most interesting part of the publishing business, and the fact that our miscellaneous publishers are taking up other branches of work can only mean that the publication of works in general literature has become the less profitable branch of the business.[2]

Brett went on to list what have become perennial complaints of book people: the reading public is not expanding, book prices are too high, postal rates are too high, and distribution does not work.

Publishers seem to have had much in common with the ancient Greeks: they, too, look back to a golden age in the past when heroes and gods laid the foundations for our current derivative and decadent culture. There probably was a community of "gentle bookmen" (*sic*) in the past—just as there was a real Troy. But this community of bookmen existed also to make money; publishing has never been a benevolent eleemosynary institution. The differences between the present and the mythological past lie in the nature of the social structures and communities that comprise publishers, editors, authors, and their publics. These structures have indeed changed, and we have talked about the forces that produced and continue to produce some of these changes. Before reviewing how these changes have affected the gatekeeping role in publishing, we have to emphasize that there are major differences between types of house—differences that overshadow their common characteristics.

The first lesson we learned in our study was that one cannot talk reliably about *the* book-publishing industry as an entity. The publishing industry is composed of a great variety of entities, each having its particular characteristics. A large trade publishing house that is controlled by a multi-media corporation and strives to get as many books as possible on the best-seller list has precious little in common with a small regional house that publishes a few volumes of poetry a year. A textbook house offering introductory texts to college freshmen differs so much from a trade house in terms of operations, markets, and even characteristics of its editorial staff that the two seem to be in different industries altogether. Scholarly and university presses can successfully publish a few thousand copies of a book needed by scientists, scholars, or professionals to keep abreast of a field—a book that will rarely be found by the general public in any bookstore. Mass-market paperbacks with their drug-store display racks and movie tie-ins are still another sector of the industry. All these types of house operate in sharply divergent social atmospheres and in separate economic markets. What might be a successful publishing strategy for Bantam Books, a paperback firm, could spell disaster for Academic Press, a monograph house.

It now seems commonplace to us that publishing is a highly segmented industry, but this fact seems not to have been absorbed by either critics or defenders of the industry, or by authors.[3] A recent picture of the publishing industry by Thomas Whiteside—published by Wesleyan University Press as a book because, as we understand it, no commercial publisher expressed an interest in it—emphasizes almost exclusively the promotional ballyhoo, hype, and Hollywood tie-ins which, Whiteside suggests, pervade the industry. Whiteside is correct in his description and analysis as far as it goes, but he covers only a portion of the trade sector of the industry. Ironically, professional monograph publishing regularly returns a higher profit on investment than the circus-like world that he describes. On the other hand, reports that are periodically released by the Association of American Publishers assure us that the industry has never been more open or competitive. This is true if one looks only at the growth and proliferation of small, geographically dispersed houses. Most of these new houses have a marginal existence and can never hope to make it into the Big Leagues. Some of these small houses are flourishing within the cracks and fissures left unutilized by the major houses. However, as with most small businesses, their financial condition will be precarious, and there will be as many deaths as births among them. The view that the industry is open is disingenuous, because the rise of small houses does not offset the increased rate of concentration among large, vertically integrated publishing conglomerates. However, not all sectors of the industry have been equally affected. Certain branches of book publishing are highly concentrated, while others continue to be competitive. For example, it is difficult for any but the largest firms to compete in the introductory college textbook market because such a text nowadays requires, prior to publication, the outlay of several hundred thousand dollars. In contrast, ten or more scholarly monographs can be published for this amount; as a result, this sector of the industry has few barriers to new entrants.

Few authors are aware of the complicated chain of decisions through which a book must pass as it makes its way from author's desk to publishing house to bookstore shelf. The authors we interviewed were largely ignorant of the publishing process and probably have suffered as a result of their ignorance. Authors were also uniformly optimistic about the prospects of their books. As Samuel Johnson once said, "No place affords a more striking conviction of the variety of human hopes than a public library." Many authors, especially those writing for the trade sector of the industry, found their hopes dashed. What authors do not fully understand is that most manuscripts proceed through a filtering, or winnowing, process that consists of many complex stages. Promotion and distribution, the areas that most disappointed trade authors, are also complex processes. The key steps in publishing differ from house to house. There may be idiosyncratic factors peculiar to a particular editor or house; other factors are structural and depend on the size and organization of the house. Most important, however, is the sector of the industry. The gatekeeping function differs considerably from one branch of the industry to another and is also exercised by people not in the industry itself. If the industry itself has a hard time grasping the significance of gatekeeping, then authors who are the objects of this filtering process have an even less coherent view.

Far be it from us to dispute the fact that so much junk flows from the presses each year as to cast doubt on publishers' efficiency as gatekeepers. Some people might wonder whether the gates are so open that we are subject to censorship by deluge. In fact, many critics as well as some industry spokesmen have periodically insisted that a reduction in the more than forty thousand books published each year would allow firms to concentrate on really worthwhile books. Aside from the fact that the criteria for judging a worthwhile textbook are totally different from those for an entertaining novel or a timely political analysis, we have seen that the inability of publishers to agree upon or even to discern what will be commercially successful makes publishing an enterprise akin to horse racing. So the suggestion that book production should be reduced has never gotten very far. Even so, the central fact is that published books represent only a very small proportion of all manuscripts written. However it occurs—by literary agent or academic broker, or by an editorial assistant reading through the slush pile—gatekeeping is an organizational necessity.

The key actors in college textbook publishing are college professors, publishers' sales representatives (college travelers), acquisitions editors, book packagers, and market research departments. The latter two are new on the scene, and the relations between the first three have changed dramatically in the past ten years. College textbooks are ordered by professors, not by the students who are supposed to read them; and thus, the professors themselves act as gatekeepers. Publishers "road-test" book manuscripts and projects, even while they are being written and revised, by sending them for evaluation to outside readers, who are experts in particular fields. Thus, the content of textbooks is, in principle, controlled by an author's peers.

Recent attempts to rationalize textbook production has resulted in publishing houses becoming much more active at an early stage in the writing process. Instead of relying on travelers to report the needs of major professors, market research questionnaires are now used to assess the preferences of a large number of assistant professors who teach sections of introductory courses. Book packagers or the staff of a text house then oversee the production of a new text written to meet the demands suggested by the market research. The result is usually a bland text and one very similar to all the other texts on the market. Like many producers of mass consumer goods, text houses, on the one hand, claim to have abdicated all gatekeeping responsibility to the market researchers and hence to "consumer democracy," and, on the other hand, are themselves directly responsible for producing a homogenized product usually devoid of genuine intellectual excitement. Even in houses that do not publish managed texts, authors are told they must pay close attention to market research findings. Though rationalization of the textbook process was initially begun by small independent companies, the large amounts of capital involved in modern textbook production have made this approach attractive to larger houses.

Despite the resounding failure of some managed texts, the promise of greater control over the writing and publishing process seems difficult for most text houses to resist; and we expect to see in the coming years an even greater homogenization of texts at the college level. Authors who submit unorthodox or innovative proposals for new textbooks are usually rebuffed. Any interest at all from a publisher is likely first to be in the form of a suggestion that the author should read and attempt to emulate the current leading money-making texts in his or her field.

Of the three types of publishing we studied, scholarly publishing—which includes university presses, professional monograph houses, and commercial houses that aim at a broader audience—is the most closely tied to both the creators and the consumers of their books. In this sense, scholarly publishing retains some of the features of the "golden age" when authors and editors were closely connected in the common pursuit of excellence. In scholarly publishing, the academic system of "invisible colleges" plays a crucial gatekeeping role. The would-be author who ignores this system and sends a manuscript to an editor without an imprimatur from the appropriate "invisible college" does so at his or her peril.

A typical scholarly house makes more money by producing books that set trends and chart new waters, rather than ones that merely reflect currently accepted science or scholarship. It is absolutely crucial for an editor to select the significant "invisible colleges" and the central figures in these colleges. Thus, the scholarly book editor must be something of both individualist and gambler, willing to run the risk of error. There is an important difference between the world of intellectual-literary salons which regulated quality publishing in the past and today's system of "invisible colleges." The former aimed at integration and unity; the "invisible college" system is constantly splitting and reorganizing existing fields of research into more specialized subfields. The increase in scientific and scholarly circles has two important consequences. First, the potential audience for any book is limited, although competent publishers know how to reach it. Profits can be made on small print runs, but each editor will work on many more books per year than editors in text or trade publishing. Second, constant change in scholarly and scientific circles means that editors cannot long rest on their laurels. They cannot rely on their accumulated contacts but must always be making new ones. Some houses in the scholarly field remain successful year after year. Yet there are also many failures and many new entries as editors move from one house and take with them to a newly formed house the scientific or scholarly circle they had cultivated at their former house.

In such a system, the imaginative editor who locates a new area of research and a new "invisible college" working on a topic that has important implications for a broad audience can quickly capitalize on his or her discovery. The scholar and the editor are often closely intertwined: careers, reputations, and ideas may rise and fall with the fortunes of commercial scholarly houses and university presses.

Although the rise and fall of "invisible colleges" is an inevitable hazard of scholarly publishing, there are new challenges—rising production costs of books, declining real incomes for academics, drastic cuts in federal research dollars, and declining library budgets. Each of these threats may mean fewer sales and higher prices. One consequence will be that new knowledge will be disseminated less widely and less rapidly. We expect more turmoil in scholarly and university press publishing as a result, but this field is one of the few that seems to us more or less immune from the pressures of corporate enterprise. As yet, no one has found a way to simplify the scholarly publishing process. The key to profitability and success will not be to sign more books or to rely on market research—pressures commonly associated with corporate ownership—but will remain editorial discretion and imagination.

The majority of scholarly and text editors whom we spoke with were cognizant of their position in a decision chain that selects ideas for distribution. Editors of managed texts were proud of their creative efforts and frequently noted that they had taken the development of textbooks away from incompetent professors and had transformed for the better the education of college students. Many scholarly editors commented that they resented the role they play in university tenure decisions. Some scholarly editors boasted of helping to "make" a new scientific field. Scholarly and text editors occasionally questioned the extent of their influence and sometimes asserted that other forces, such as enrollment trends or federal funding policies for research, are considerably more important in determining the content of a field. Nonetheless, the majority of editors were aware of the central role that they played.

In sharp contrast to scholarly and text editors, editors in trade houses felt less important. The fate of a trade book is influenced by different individuals and organizations, many of which are located outside of publishing houses. Influence seems to be so diffused that many trade editors were uncomfortable with the gatekeeper label. They asserted that they were only publishing books that booksellers would stock and the public would buy.

Several factors help explain these sentiments on the part of trade editors. Many of them implicitly subscribed to the following contradiction: (1) editorial selection reflects the needs of the marketplace; (2) no one can regularly predict in advance of publication which particular book will sell. The contradiction is this: if editors are trying to cater to the market's demands for books, they must have certain criteria to guide their choice of particular books and their rejection of others. A major publisher can say "any book is better than no book," and trade editors can consistently deny that theirs is a gatekeeping role; but the simple fact is that not every manuscript submitted is published. Even the majority of manuscripts submitted by literary agents are not accepted for publication.

One of the reasons for the different perceptions of trade editors and editors in other fields is that, as we discussed in chapter 3, trade editors have become systematically disconnected from literary and intellectual circles that help determine standards and tastes. Since the 1940s there has been a continuing dispersal of literary and intellectual talent away from a few major metropolitan centers. American literary and intellectual life is diverse, pluralistic, and geographically scattered. Trade publishing has suffered from this growing lack of coherence, as sustained contact between writers and editors has declined. It is much harder for trade editors to discover new talent these days. Several editors told us that they no longer spend time searching for new writers; instead, they wait until a writer is noticed by other media, wins a prestigious fellowship from a foundation, or is sponsored by successful writers.

Another key difference in perception between trade and non-trade editors lies in the size of the market for their respective books. As we have pointed out, the audience for texts and scholarly books is highly targeted. Editors know largely who their readers are. Selling targeted books is much easier than selling books intended for "everyone" in a mass society. If a trade editor does not have a clear image of the potential readers for a particular book, then it is much harder to view oneself as an arbiter of taste.

Perhaps the major reason why trade editors disclaim the gatekeeper label is that a majority of trade books, as compared with scholarly books or texts, are not commercially successful. Many books fail at various points in the publishing process. Within the publishing house, a book may fail to generate subsidiary rights income and, as a consequence, is likely to receive less attention from the sales and advertising departments. In recent years, new book-promotion strategies have burgeoned, as publishing houses try to influence book buyers and, we might add, book reviewers with tightly organized author tours and broadcast interviews, with multicolored promotional brochures, and with broadcast advertising for multi-media tie-ins. Aside from blockbusters, most publishers produce more titles than they can effectively promote: and advertising budgets for most books are on the lean side. Only when a book takes off in spite of minimal publicity and advertising does the publishing house increase the budget for promotion.

Once a trade book leaves a publishing house, it encounters another set of gatekeepers. Traditionally book reviewers played a crucial role in deciding a book's fate. For serious books they still do; but for books with mass appeal, television talk shows have replaced book reviewers. For a book to succeed, its author must become a "media personality." This is but one aspect of the continuing integration of part of trade publishing into the entertainment industry. Even though the trend toward tie-ins between Hollywood, television, and publishing has recently somewhat abated, largely owing to a number of rather spectacular failures, we nevertheless expect that these ties will continue. Hence, many trade houses may concentrate on blockbuster media tie-ins even more than they do today, and close the gates—or at least keep them only slightly ajar—for, say, first novels or serious political studies that cannot expect large print runs or spectacular subsidiary sales. Granted that the fabulous sums paid by paperback publishers for hardcover successes may well decline in the future, the ubiquitous quest for bestsellers on the part of many houses will still make it exceedingly difficult to market books that do not appeal to a mass audience. Further mergers, acquisitions, or consolidations of existing medium or large houses by media conglomerates will further exacerbate these tendencies.

We have so far largely dealt with present trends and have seldom projected future trends that may affect the gatekeeping process. As any forecaster will unhappily concede, extrapolating present trends onto future scenarios is likely to be upset by entirely unpredictable events. We shall exemplify this by reference to two recent legal decisions that have affected the publishing community over the last few years: the Thor Power Tool Company Supreme Court decision and the U.S. Justice Department's decision ending a cozy, long-time agreement between British and American publishers not to invade each other's exclusive share of major world markets. The first decision may well have deleterious consequences for quality publishing in general and for monograph publishing in particular; the second has had a more favorable impact on all of book publishing and has led to the establishment of American offices by a number of British publishers.

In January 1979, the U.S. Supreme Court ruled—in a case brought by the Thor Power Tool Company against the Internal Revenue Service—that, contrary to what the plaintiff claimed, warehouse stocks of tools could not be depreciated for tax purposes unless they had left warehouse inventory. This meant that the tool industry had to discontinue its practice of carrying inventories at reduced prices for tax purposes. Soon thereafter, the Internal Revenue Service ruled that this decision not only was binding on the power tool industry but also applied, *inter alia*, to the publishing industry. To the I.R.S., books are products just like tools, toilet paper, or detergents.

As a result of the Thor ruling, some publishers have had to change their accounting procedures and the value of their backlist books in stock. Other publishers had already followed new accounting procedures; for still

others who publish few backlist titles the Thor decision is of little consequence; and university presses, as non-profit organizations, are tax-exempt
and hence not affected. But for many high-quality commercial firms, both
scholarly and trade, the backlist provided the backbone of their operations
through thick and thin, and they depended on being able to depreciate the
value of their backlist inventory. Now it is no longer economically feasible
to maintain stock on many titles and sell them gradually through backlist
orders, and now a house that formerly kept titles in print may decide to remainder one, or to destroy all copies of it entirely, rather than to bear the
cost of maintaining it in print. Such destruction will be especially harmful
for research monographs which are slow to sell. It will also penalize those
houses that, out of a sense of cultural responsibility, have pursued the strategy of building "symbolic capital" in books, rather than relying exclusively
on books that turn over quickly and provide an immediate return. In sum,
the Thor ruling—which, by the way, also affects booksellers even though
they are largely protected by their privilege to return unsold books—will
inflict harm. What is more, it strikes hardest, and disproportionately, at
quality houses, while the mass-product houses remain largely unaffected
since they maintain only minimal backlists. Senator Daniel Patrick Moyni-
han and others in Congress have attempted to pass legislation that would
exempt the book business from the Thor ruling, but they have been unsuccessful so far. As matters stand, the Thor ruling is a major impediment
to quality publishing, while it favors those in the industry who are out to
make a quick buck.[4]

While the I.R.S. and the Supreme Court's inane ruling will be detri-
mental to quality publishing, another ruling, in 1976, has been beneficial to
American publishing. For many years Britain and America carved up between themselves the world market for English-language books, much as
the imperialist powers agreed in the nineteenth century to cut up the rest
of the world for colonial domination. This exclusive arrangement, known
as the British Traditional Market Agreement, was upset by a U.S. Justice
Department consent decree in an antitrust suit against twenty-one U.S.
publishers. As a result, British and American publishers consented to cease
this practice, and agreed that the British could enter the American market
while Americans could now freely sell their books throughout the British
Commonwealth. British entry in the American market has so far not had a
major impact. Though a number of British houses have recently made
their appearance here, some of them seem not to be doing well, and several
have already abandoned this venture. In contrast, the sales of American
publishers—not only in Britain, but above all in Australia, New Zealand,
and the former British colonies in Africa, particularly Nigeria, and Asia—

have significantly increased. As a consequence, the export of American books, until recently a fairly minor item for most houses, has shot upward. In particular, textbooks and professional books published in America can now be found in Hong Kong, Sydney, and Nairobi. In addition, genuine co-publishing agreements between U.S. and British publishers have become more common.[5]

Among other portents of the future, it seems quite possible that the Chinese market for scientific and technical monographs from America will increase considerably if the present leadership of China maintains its current course of learning from the West instead of relying on home-grown technology. It is equally likely that those countries in the Third World—such as Taiwan, Singapore, South Korea, or Brazil—whose economic development has "taken off" will increase their consumption of technical and scientific books from America over even its already high rate. Developments such as these bode well for the publication of technical books. A consequence, however, is that these research reports will be less encompassing and less integrative; their emphasis will be on speed and data, not on broad-ranging ideas.

Recent trends in book retailing also influence what does and does not get published. The changes in bookselling are equally, perhaps even more, important when it comes to assessing the shape of things to come. If the long-term projections of the two largest book chains are correct, they will account for 50 percent of all new general-interest bookstore sales by 1983.[6] This revolution in the selling of books—and it is truly a revolution—is bound to have significant consequences on the decision-making and gate-keeping functions of publishers. Book chains, as distinct from individual booksellers, are geared to the buying of books in large quantities. The greater the quantity bought, the higher the discount the chains receive from publishers. Such discounts are often up to 17 percent higher than for individual bookstores. It does not pay for chains to clutter their shelves with books that can only be expected to reach a limited public. Hence, as the present symbiotic relation between trade publishers and book chains is further strengthened, publishers have an additional incentive to neglect books that are not likely to have mass appeal.

Trade editors also point to the strict financial controls that now circumscribe them. While close attention to the costs involved in publishing particular titles may make editors more selective, it has also meant that many trade editors spend less time with writers and their manuscripts and more time on internal organizational matters.

A 1981 *Forbes* magazine report on American industry begins its entry on book publishing with, "It's hard to find an industry that has been picked cleaner by the conglomerates than book publishing."[7] In the conglomerate-owned trade house, an editor feels like a cog in a large system which begins with agent prescreening, market evaluations, financial considerations, sub-rights negotiations, media tie-ins, and other such matters, rather than like a person with the opportunity to discover new ideas. As we have argued, the spending of large sums on potential best sellers is a conservative strategy, since the greater the financial risk, the larger the audience must be; hence, the subject matter must be safe and tried and true, not innovative. Under such circumstances, it is easy to see why many trade editors do not see themselves as gatekeepers but feel constrained by economic and organizational factors. Still, their location at the start of the publishing process remains crucial, and we hope that they are not forced to abdicate their responsibility to writers.

Where does all this leave writers? We have shown that most writers have never been on an equal footing with publishers, and that despite the enormous advances now paid to a few writers, they are still junior partners in the book business—partners whose financial rewards are on the average much less than the most poorly paid employee of a publishing house. Writing books is a part-time activity for most writers and thus subsidized by other activities or sources of income. Writing serves many functions other than directly earning a living. Writers often seem to be helpless by default; careful attention to the publishing process and to such matters as distribution and promotion—which writers often feel to be a publisher's prerogative—and above all, a clear understanding of the gatekeeping methods of the segment of the industry for which one is writing, can go a long way toward making writers more powerful partners in the publishing enterprise than most of them are now.

It is a common observation that whenever groups of publishers or writers gather, long faces and gloomy laments for the fate of book publishing are the order of the day. There are fears that gimmick books or nonbooks will overwhelm good literature and serious nonfiction and perhaps even swamp books that are just pleasant entertainment. In the past few years these fears have become even more pronounced, although at the same time many good books are published and most publishing houses remain profitable. While publishers may believe their problems are unique, they are in fact endemic in modern industrial societies, which are plagued with a basic contradiction: while the logic of mass production homogenizes tastes, the relative affluence of the society and the complex division of labor gives rise to specialization and differentiated tastes. There are numerous communities in American society with their own tastes and cultural preferences, many of them quite sophisticated. Publishers are not alone in having difficulty trying to reach these communities in an economically viable manner. In the record business, there is a sizable audience for jazz and classical music, but neither of these musical traditions is currently as profitable as middle-of-the road pop music. Television has long had the same problem. The commercial networks program for the lowest common denominator of taste; cable technology may finally offer opportunities to program for specialized interests.

The differences between books and most media born in the twentieth century, however, cannot be overstated: books are, for the most part, a medium for limited, select audiences, while movies and the broadcast media are inherently dependent on mass appeal. Of course, books can be marketed as mass-consumer goods, and some movies and television shows can be designed for segmented audiences. But there remain major differences in production costs: a book can be successfully produced and marketed for a sum well below one hundred thousand dollars—even for as little as ten thousand dollars. There is nothing comparable in the mass media where costs are often measured in the millions. While scholarly book publishers have long known how to publish successfully for small, specialized audiences of academics and professionals, trade publishers have yet to find fully satisfactory methods for publishing quality "mid-list" books—those that are valuable, enriching, or entertaining but have a limited audience.

While many of the problems currently facing book publishing are common to other culture-producing industries and, in fact, to most businesses producing high-quality consumer goods, we believe book publishing is different. Books provide more opportunities for the communication of complex ideas than any other medium. Books still carry a measure of respect and dignity, and they are reused more than the products of any other medium. Equally significant is the fact that publishing has long been one of the nation's most open and competitive industries. Efforts to establish one large, monolithic "media business" or to make book publishing a more rational endeavor would surely eliminate many of publishing's arcane and outdated practices, yet it would destroy the individualistic spirit that has made publishing such a major contributor to American literary, cultural, and scientific development.

Appendix on Methods

THIS APPENDIX discusses the methods used in sampling editors and others in publishing whom we interviewed and observed. Some account is given of the rules of thumb we used in the analysis of the data as well as the principles used in selecting houses for participant observation.

SAMPLE DESIGN

For reasons given in chapter 2, we decided that our study had to address the differences between larger and smaller houses, between independent and dependent houses, and between trade, college text, scholarly-monograph, and university press houses. Our major interest was, at first, in the publication of psychology and social science. We made no attempt to cover houses that exclusively published atlases, maps, encyclopedias, engineering, science, technical, religious, fiction, or children's books; nor elementary, junior high school or senior high school books; nor reprints or government publications. Of the over one thousand publishing houses listed in the 1975 *Literary Market Place,* 571 seemed to publish material in the social and behavioral sciences, history, and philosophy. This was our bible for constructing a sample of publishing houses that would be of interest to us. We proceeded to construct a computer-readable file of information on each of these houses, including material found in *LMP* and what we could collect ourselves. This file was analyzed prior to our selection of our sample.

As explained in chapter 2, we made an extraordinary effort to discover how many titles each house published in 1975. We discovered that 45 percent of all publishing houses in the United States in the fields we chose were located in the New York metropolitan area, and that they published over 60 percent of all titles released during 1975. By contrast, the West Coast had 4 percent of the houses, and these published one half of 1 percent of all titles. Because of our location, we decided to concentrate on New York, since it was of easy access to us and loomed so important. We also decided to interview on the West Coast in order to be able to learn something about what we were told was a very different publishing milieu from New York. (By subtraction, it is obvious that in 1975 just over half the publishing houses in the country were located neither on the West Coast nor in New York, and that they published fewer than 40 percent of all titles.)

We were also interested in which houses were independent and which were owned by either other houses or by non-publishing firms. Despite the move toward conglomerate ownership of publishing houses, only 30 percent of the houses in our file were owned by other corporations; and they produced fewer than 20 percent of the total number of titles. Moreover, a few large independent houses produced many more titles than the few large dependent ones. Of course, most of these large independent houses are conglomerates themselves. The large independent houses account for most of American publishing: the thirty-three publishing houses that in 1975 were not owned by other organizations accounted for almost 60 percent of all titles published in the United States that year; yet they comprised only 6 percent of the total number of houses publishing in literature, psychology, and the social sciences. Size was vindicated as something we needed to take into account in our research design.

Though we were committed to studying at least one university press, and while university presses are an important part of scholarly publishing, we discovered that they are trivial in number and in number of titles published. In 1975—of all the publishing houses in the United States publishing in the social sciences, psychology, history, and philosophy—fewer than

15 percent were university presses, and these published only 5 percent of the total number of titles. Almost 90 percent of the university presses published 75 or fewer titles per year. Only two published more than 225 titles per year, and these two presses accounted for 20 percent of all university press titles. University presses were also not a New York phenomenon: about 85 percent are located out of the New York metropolitan region.

The file we developed formed the basis for our sampling of editors for interviewing and publishing houses for observation. We decided to rule out all houses that published fewer than twenty books in 1975, on the grounds that they (1): were likely to be too idiosyncratic, (2) were not influential in the total picture of publishing, and (3) did not have the organizational diversity to justify either observation or interview. Surprisingly, only forty-five non-university press publishers in the New York metropolitan region and seventeen on the West Coast met our criteria for both subject matter and size. For each of these houses that was a scholarly or a text house, we attempted to locate the editor who handled social science and to interview him or her. We soon discovered that in trade houses, the notion of a specialist in social science was fairly meaningless, and we drew at random from the list of editors given in *LMP*. Once an editor's name was drawn, we tried to find someone who knew him or her to arrange for an introduction. Failing that, we simply wrote, explaining our purpose, and then called to arrange an appointment. These methods resulted in thirty-two interviews.

In addition to this systematic sample of social science editors (in non-trade houses) and to a random set of editors we drew in trade houses, we made a special effort to interview editors of psychology books. An eighteen-month period of *American Book Publishing Record, 1974* (plus the January through June 1975 issues) was searched for all books published in psychology. Psychology was defined as including: popular, general, applied, clinical and abnormal psychology, self-help, sex, drug abuse, alcoholism, and community mental health. The following was not included: social work; the family; cognitive, physiological, and most experimental psychology. A machine-readable record was prepared. All houses that published five or more books in psychology were listed; and the name of the psychology editor, if any, for such houses in the metropolitan New York area was ascertained. This procedure resulted in fifteen interviews in the New York area. In addition, four psychology editors on the West Coast were located and interviewed.

In the course of our interviews, a number of different persons were mentioned either as editors who were especially admired, or as persons we "just had to talk to." These editors were also interviewed as a "snowball" sample. Eighteen of the eighty-five complete interviews were "snowball" interviews. They form a large proportion of our interviews because (1) we wished to interview the more important editors, as nominated by a representative sample of editors; and (2) we discovered early in the study that in trade houses it was almost useless to distinguish among psychology editors, social science editors, and general editors. A good trade editor may have a specialty or two but, during the course of a year, often handles a wide variety of books. In order to understand the publication of trade books in psychology and social science, our original goal, we had to expand our concerns to cover trade publishing as a whole. The best way to add general trade publishing to our study, we reasoned, was to interview editors nominated as important by other editors. Several editors whom we got to know during our field work, and whom we extensively interviewed informally, also agreed to respond to a formal interview. To cover what we thought would be a different kind of publishing, we interviewed seven California editors in trade or text who were not already sampled as psychology or sociology editors.

In sum, we conducted eighty-five complete formal interviews. An additional thirteen interviews were incomplete, though parts could be used in the analysis. Finally, there were thirty-five editors whom we interviewed informally but who are not included in our formal statistical analysis.

The table below shows the number of editors interviewed according to type of house—trade, college text, monograph-scholarly, and university publishing. All respondents were promised anonymity, so that the names of the houses themselves cannot be listed. Those familiar with publishing can perhaps, relatively accurately, supply the appropriate names of the houses.

Table 1
Completed Formal Interviews

Type of Publishing	Number of Interviews	Number of Different Houses*
College Text	27	17
Monograph-Scholarly	17	16
University Press	7	5
Trade	34	18
Total	85	56

*If a publishing house had several divisions—for example, college text and trade—each is counted as a separate house.

The interviews were tape-recorded and lasted for at least one hour and a half, usually longer. The interview guide was developed after extensive pretesting and was revised six times. In addition to the interview, a vita and background form were given to editors to fill out. Responses from this form were naturally not quite as good as the responses to our in-person interview, but the form did save us from wasting valuable interview time in picking up material that could just as well have been answered in a questionnaire.

DATA COLLECTION AND ANALYSIS

The interviews were coded and transferred to machine-readable form and analyzed by Charles Kadushin with the assistance of Laurie Michael Roth, using the SPSS® (Statistical Package for the Social Sciences) and SCSS® (Conversational System) programs.[1] The sample as described is systematic and representative but can hardly be considered a true "random" sample, though we believe it to be the best sample of editors that could be obtained, given our objectives. The usual tests of significance are therefore of questionable value. Instead, given the small sample and the extensive amount of qualitative material available to back up all our statements, results were not reported unless they reached the .1 level of significance. Most of the results reported, however, were significant at the .05 level; though we stress that levels of statistical significance are to be taken merely as a guide. Since the tables are almost always only two or three variable tables, we decided not to encumber the book with them, thus allowing non-statistically oriented readers—as we assume are most of those interested in publishing—access to our analysis. Readers interested in technical details or the original data can obtain them from the authors.

Formal interviews, we felt, were not much more useful for understanding publishing than are interviews with athletic stars for explaining how to play ball. Next to actually playing, the best thing would be to watch and occasionally participate in some practice session. To this end, we negotiated agreements with ten different houses or subdivisions of houses to let us observe them at work, to participate in their meetings, to interview personnel informally, and generally just to hang around. Again, we worked with the division into larger and smaller, independent and dependent, and trade, text, scholarly, and university press. All observations were of houses in the New York metropolitan area. Among the independents we observed were one large trade house, one medium-sized trade house, and one small one. Also included were one medium-sized college text house and one small scholarly-monograph house. Among the dependent houses were observed one large scholarly-monograph house and one small one, as well as one medium-sized trade house. One medium-sized and one small university press were also observed. These studies, one of which resulted in a book,[2] utilized traditional field-work methods and diarylike note taking. Each observation of a house resulted in a detailed report.[3] That report, along with daily field notes, became part of our data files. The word "participant" in the participant-observer formula is a fair one, since each of our observers was also used by the press we were observing as an informal consultant—an unavoidable participation. To prove that we learned the business of publishing well, three of our six observers were offered a job in publishing as editors! An additional observer already had a job in publishing. The other two, not formally offered a job, were sounded out. None of our observers accepted the offers, partly for ethical reasons and partly because they had other commitments.

Several other data-gathering methods were used. To draw a sample of authors, we used lists of recent authors of the houses we had been studying. An additional sample of psychology writers was drawn from our file of psychology books. A mail questionnaire was sent to the list of authors developed in this way, and the returns were coded and punched and analyzed statistically by Laurie Michael Roth. In two publishing houses, a questionnaire about work and work satisfaction was distributed to all employees, including clerical and production workers. Charles Fombrun and Mary Ann Devanna analyzed the returns from one house,[4] and Michele Caplette analyzed the returns from another house in connection with her Ph.D. dissertation.[5] Caplette also sent a questionnaire to a special sample of 117 men and 200 women in small, medium, and large college textbook, general trade, and mass-market paperback houses as described in chapter 6 of this book. Arthur Samuelson designed and conducted lengthy interviews with ten agents who had been most frequently mentioned by the editors we interviewed. Since many agents are women, Michele Caplette supplemented these interviews with additional interviews with agents. Charles Kadushin and Selma Lenihan conducted a number of interviews about college texts, with editors, lawyers, packagers, and authors. Finally, we interviewed a variety of other persons in publishing, including subsidiary rights editors, booksellers, production people, and almost anyone we came across socially who seemed to have anything to do with publishing.

The authors of this book utilized all this material as well as the publishing and scholarly literature acknowledged in the footnotes. All of us conducted interviews with editors and authors, and all of us in one way or another were participant observers in publishing. In addition to formal interviewing and informal observation, it must be added that New York publishing circles are, after all, relatively known and circumscribed. At one point or another, all of our friends in publishing were interviewed informally, and all helped to supply stories and anecdotes. Such sources one always take for granted whenever a book is written. What should not be taken for granted is our formal observational and survey apparatus, which underlie the conclusions we have drawn in this book.

Notes

INTRODUCTION

1. Cf. David Manning White, "The Gatekeeper: A Case Study in the Selection of News," *Journalism Quarterly* 27(4 [fall 1950]): 383–90.
2. Cf. Marcia Bystryn, "Art Galleries as Gatekeepers: The Case of the Abstract Expressionists," *Social Research* 45 (2 [summer 1978]): 392–408.
3. Cf. Lewis A. Coser, *Men of Ideas* (New York: Free Press, 1965).
4. Arthur Stinchcombe, "Bureaucratic and Craft Administration of Production: A Comparative Study," *Administrative Science Quarterly* 4 (September 1959): 168–87.
5. Everett Hughes, "Work and Self," in Hughes, *The Sociological Eye* (Chicago: Aldine, 1971), pp. 338–47.

CHAPTER 1. COMMERCE AND CULTURE: A HISTORICAL SURVEY OF BOOK PUBLISHING IN AMERICA

1. E. L. Doctorow, "Words into Rhinestones," *New York Times*, 19 March 1980.
2. Bernard Malamud, quoted in John Y. Cole, ed., *Responsibilities of the American Book Community* (Washington, D.C.: Library of Congress, 1981), pp. 24–25.

3. Quoted from Michael Wendroff, "Should We Do the Book?" *Publishers Weekly*, 15 August 1980, p. 28.

4. Ibid., p. 27.

5. Alfred Kazin, "American Writing Now," *New Republic*, 18 October 1980, p. 27.

6. Ibid.

7. José Ortega y Gasset, *Obras Completas*, (Madrid, 1966), vol. III, p. 38, as quoted by Robert Wohl in *The Generation of 1914* (Cambridge: Harvard University Press, 1979), p. 3.

8. *North American Review* 56 (1843): 110, as quoted in Ann Douglas, *The Feminization of American Literature* (New York: Alfred A. Knopf, 1977), p. 82.

9. Q. D. Leavis, *Fiction and the Reading Public*, reprinted (New York: Russell and Russell, 1965); originally published in London (Chatto, 1932).

10. Henry Holt, "The Commercialization of Literature," *Atlantic Monthly*, November 1905, pp. 578–600.

11. Alfred R. McIntyre, "The Crisis in Book Publishing," *Atlantic Monthly*, October 1947, pp. 107–10.

12. James T. Farrell, "The Fate of Writing in America," *New Directions*, vol. 9 (1946).

13. Frank L. Mott, *Golden Multitudes: The Story of Best Sellers in the United States* (New York: R. R. Bowker, 1947).

14. Charles A. Madison, *Book Publishing in America* (New York: McGraw-Hill, 1966), p. 51. We have relied heavily on this fine volume in the next few pages.

15. *Publishers Weekly*, quoted in ibid., p. 54.

16. Ibid.

17. Ibid., pp. 563–64.

18. T. B. Lawler, quoted in J. Kendrick Noble, Jr., "Assessing the Merger Trend," *Publishers Weekly*, 31 July 1978 (special issue on the "Question of Size in the Book Industry Today"), pp. 35–42.

19. Committee on Report to the Public, "Textbooks in Education," American Textbook Publishers Institute, 1949.

20. Richard A. Peterson and David Berger, "Cycles in Symbol Production: The Case of Popular Music," *American Sociological Review* 40 (April 1975): 158–73.

21. Richard Cyert and James G. March, *A Behavioral Theory of the Firm* (Englewood Cliffs, N.J.: Prentice-Hall, 1963).

22. Frederick M. Scherer, *Industrial Market Structure and Economic Performance* (Chicago: Rand McNally, 1970), p. 354.

23. For a variety of viewpoints on this issue, see "Concentration and Conglomeration in Book Publishing" in the *Proceedings of the Symposium on Media Concentration*, vol. II (14 and 15 December 1978), Bureau of Competition, Federal Trade Commission, pp. 549–648. The publishing industry is represented by the papers of Townsend Hoopes and Winthrop Knowlton; John Brooks and Irwin Karp speak for the Authors Guild. More analytic and dispassionate assessments are provided by Walter W. Powell, Frank J. Sirianni, Michael Robinson, and Ray Olszewski.

24. Townsend Hoopes, "The Book Publishing Industry," FTC Symposium [23].

25. Angele A. Gilroy, "An Economic Analysis of the U.S. Domestic Book Publishing Industry: 1972–Present," Congressional Research Service Report no. 80–79E, 7 January 1980.

26. O. H. Cheyney, *Economic Survey of the Book Industry 1930–1931* (New York: R. R. Bowker, 1931).

27. Cheyney, ibid., as quoted in J. K. Noble, "Books," in B. Compaine, *Who Owns the Media?* (White Plains, N.Y.: Knowledge Industry Publications, 1979), p. 258.

28. This section borrows freely from Walter W. Powell, "Competition versus Concentration in the Book Trade," *Journal of Communication*, spring 1980, pp. 89–97.

29. Frank J. Sirianni, "Patterns of Change within the Publishing Industry," FTC Symposium [23].

30. For a more detailed analysis of this development, see Walter W. Powell, "The Blockbuster Decade: The Media as Big Business," *Working Papers for a New Society*, July/August 1979, pp. 26–36.

31. John Brooks, "Remarks," FTC Symposium [23].

32. Madalynne Reuter, "The Trade Market: How Bad Is It? How Bad Is It Going to Be?" *Publishers Weekly*, 2 May 1980, p. 36.

33. Robert K. Merton, *Social Theory and Social Structure* (New York: Free Press, 1968).

383

34. See Donald Sheehan, *This Was Publishing: A Chronicle of the Book Trade in the Gilded Age* (Bloomington: Indiana University Press, 1952); Walker Gilmer, *Horace Liveright: Publisher of the Twenties* (New York: David Lewis, 1970); Hiram Haydn, *Words and Faces* (New York: Harcourt Brace Jovanovich, 1974); and Dorothy Commins, *What Is an Editor? Saxe Commins at Work* (Chicago: University of Chicago Press, 1978).

35. Lucian K. Truscott IV, "A Variety of Publishers' Perspectives," *Publishers Weekly*, 31 July 1978, p. 50.

36. Liz Roman Gallese, "Houghton Mifflin's New Trade-Book Boss Expands Lines, Cuts Costs, Manages Ideas," *Wall Street Journal*, 5 December 1980, p. B1.

37. John Leonard, "More Fact Than Fiction," *New York Times Book Review*, 28 December 1980, p. 18.

CHAPTER 2. PUBLISHING WORLDS: SECTORS WITHIN THE INDUSTRY

1. "Book Publishing," *U.S. Industrial Outlook 1980* (U.S. Dept. of Commerce, 1980), p. 96.

2. Angele A. Gilroy, "An Economic Analysis of the U.S. Domestic Book Publishing Industry: 1972–Present," Congressional Research Service Report no. 80–79E, January 1980, p. 3.

3. For more discussion of the problems involved, see J. Kendrick Noble, "Books," in Benjamin Compaine, ed., *Who Owns the Media?* (White Plains, N.Y.: Knowledge Industry Publications, 1979), pp. 251–92. For an exhaustive attempt at data collection on book publishing, see Fritz Machlup and Kenneth Leeson, *Information through the Printed Word* (New York: Praeger, 1978), especially pp. 85–103.

4. Lewis A. Coser, "Publishers as Gatekeepers of Ideas," *The Annals* 421 (September 1975): 14–22.

5. Walter W. Powell, "Control and Conflict in Publishing," presented at the IXth World Congress of Sociology, Uppsala, Sweden, August 1978. Later published in *Society* 17 (1 [November–December 1979]): 48–53.

6. See David M. Gordon, *Theories of Poverty and Underemployment* (Lexington, Mass.: D. C. Heath, 1972).

7. Richard C. Edwards, Michael Reich, and David M. Gordon, eds., *Labor Market Segmentation* (Lexington, Mass.: D. C. Heath, 1975), p. 4.

8. See Charles Tolbert, Patrick M. Horan, and E. M. Beck, "The Structure of Economic Segmentation: A Dual Economy Approach," *American Journal of Sociology* 85 (5 [March 1980]): 1095–1116; and Robert T. Averitt, *The Dual Economy: The Dynamics of American Industry Structure* (New York: Horton, 1968).

9. Paul M. Hirsch, "Production and Distribution Roles among Cultural Organizations: On the Division of Labor across Intellectual Disciplines," *Social Research* 45 (2 [summer 1978]): 315–30.

10. N. R. Kleinfield, "Problems and a Few Solutions," *New York Times Book Review*, 28 December 1980, p. 3.

11. Don Fine, quoted in Kleinfield, "Problems" [10].

12. Judith Krantz, quoted in Thomas Whiteside, "Onward and Upward with the Arts: The Blockbuster Complex," third installment, *New Yorker*, 13 October 1980, p. 110.

13. Edwin McDowell, "The Loyalty of Authors to Publishers Has New Name: It's Spelled M-O-N-E-Y," *New York Times*, 22 January 1981, p. C12.

14. Herbert K. Schnall, quoted in "The Book Boom: Action in Paperbacks," *Business Week*, 4 July 1977, p. 50.

15. Pierre Bourdieu, "La Production de la croyance: contribution à une économie des biens symboliques," *Actes de la Recherche en Sciences Sociales*, 13 (February 1977), especially pp. 23–24.

16. Paul M. Hirsch, "Public Policy towards Television: Mass Media and Education in American Society," *School Review* 84 (summer 1977): 481–512.

17. Michael T. Hannan and John Freeman, "The Population Ecology of Organizations," *American Journal of Sociology* 82 (5 [March 1977]): 929–63.

18. Ray Walters, "Paperback Talk," *New York Times Book Review*, 9 November 1980, p. 41.

19. John P. Dessauer, "An Authors' Holy War," *Publishers Weekly*, 11 July 1980, p. 30; Publicity Release, "AAP Responds to Charges of Concentration," 15 March 1978.

20. "California Corner," *BP Report*, 16 March 1981, p. 8.

21. Herman Wouk and the Authors Guild, Inc., "Statement before the Antitrust and Monopoly Subcommittee, U.S. Senate," 12 May 1978, p. 9.

22. Winthrop Knowlton, "Statement before Federal Trade Commission Symposium on Media Concentration," 15 December 1978, p. 9.

23. Ibid., pp. 7–8.

24. Madalynne Reuter, "The Trade Market," *Publishers Weekly*, 2 May 1980, pp. 36–37.

25. *Publishers Weekly*, 31 October 1980, p. 18.

26. Oscar Dystel, speech to the Mid-America Periodical Distributors Association, Chicago, Ill., 1977, reported in *Publishers Weekly*, 14 November 1977, pp. 31–33.

27. Oscar Dystel, Eighth Annual Bowker Memorial Lecture, "Mass Market Publishing: More Observations, Speculations and Provocations," reported in *Publishers Weekly*, 12 December 1980, pp. 18–25.

28. Richard Peterson and David Berger, "Cycles in Symbol Production," *American Sociological Review*, April 1975, p. 169.

29. Interview with Richard Snyder, *Publishers Weekly*, 11 April 1977, pp. 35–36.

30. Larry Freundlich, quoted in N. R. Kleinfield, "The Shifting Paperback Market," *New York Times*, 10 October 1980, p. D4.

31. Charles Perrow, "A Framework for the Comparative Analysis of Organizations," *American Sociological Review* 32 (4 [April 1967], pp. 194–208; and *Organizational Analysis: A Sociological View* (Belmont, Calif.: Wadsworth, 1970).

32. Thomas Williamson, quoted in Karen J. Winkler, "Competition Brings Changes to College Textbook Industry," *Chronicle of Higher Education*, 23 May 1977, p. 7.

33. Donald Farnsworth, quoted in Beverly T. Watkins, "Textbook Publishers See Higher-Education Slowdown Affecting Their Growth," *Chronicle of Higher Education*, 17 September 1979, p. 3.

34. Dantia Quirk, *The College Publishing Market*, 1977–1982 (White Plains, N.Y.: Knowledge Industry Publications, 1977), p. 16.

35. Ibid., p. 20.

36. *Publishers Weekly*, 4 July 1977, p. 43.

37. J. K. Noble, "Books," in Compaine, *Who Owns The Media?* [3], p. 277.

38. Frances FitzGerald, *America Revised* (Boston: Atlantic Little, Brown, 1979).

39. *U.S. Book Publishing Yearbook and Directory, 1980–1981* (White Plains, N.Y.: Knowledge Industry Publications), p. 29.

CHAPTER 3. NETWORKS, CONNECTIONS, AND CIRCLES

1. Charles Kadushin, *The American Intellectual Elite* (Boston: Little, Brown, 1974).

2. Mark S. Granovetter, *Getting a Job: A Study of Contacts and Careers* (Cambridge: Harvard University Press, 1974).

3. Stanley Milgram, "The Small World Problem," *Psychology Today* 22(1967): 61–67. See also Nan Lin, Paul W. Dayton, and Peter Greenwald, "Analysing the Instrumental Use

of Relations in the Context of Social Structure," *Sociological Methods and Research* 7 (1978): 149–66.

4. Ithiel de Sola Pool and Manfred Kochen, "Contacts and Influence," *Social Networks* 1 (1978): 5–51.

5. The first statement of the theory of social circles is found in Georg Simmel, *The Web of Group Affiliations*, translated by Kurt H. Wolff and Reinhard Bendix (New York: Free Press, 1964); originally published in 1922. For more recent work, see Claude Fischer, "Toward a Subcultural Theory of Urbanism," *American Journal of Sociology* 80 (1975): 1319–41; Charles Kadushin, "Networks and Circles in the Production of Culture," *American Behavioral Scientist* 19 (1976): 769–85.

6. Richard D. Alba and Myron P. Gutmann, "SOCK: A Sociometric Analysis System," *Behavioral Science* 17 (1972): 326. For an extended example explaining how the program is used, see Richard D. Alba and Gwen Moore, "Elite Social Circles," *Sociological Methods and Research* 7 (1978): 167–88.

7. Kadushin, *American Intellectual Elite* [1].

8. Allen H. Barton, Bogdan Denitch, and Kadushin, *Opinion Making Elites in Yugoslavia* (New York: Praeger, 1973).

9. John Higley and Gwen Moore, "Elite Integration in the United States and Australia," *American Political Science Review*, 1981.

10. Andrew McGill, Barbara Young, and Charles Kadushin, "A Study of Power," *Detroit News*, 17, 20, 24, and 27 September/1, 4, 8, and 15 October 1978.

11. Sociologists have long been interested in theories of social exchange. For classic examples see, Peter Blau, *Exchange and Power in Social Life* (New York: John Wiley, 1964); and George C. Homans, *Social Behavior: Its Elementary Forms* (New York: Harcourt Brace & Jovanovich, 1961). A critical review is found in Peter Ekeh, *Social Exchange Theory: The Two Traditions* (Cambridge: Harvard University Press, 1974).

12. Diana Crane, *Invisible Colleges: Diffusion of Knowledge in Scientific Communities* (Chicago: University of Chicago Press, 1974).

13. Kadushin, *American Intellectual Elite* [1], chap. 1.

14. Lewis A. Coser, *Men of Ideas* (New York: Free Press, 1965).

15. Peter Steinfels, *The Neoconservatives: The Men Who Are Changing America's Politics* (New York: Simon & Schuster, 1979).

16. Kadushin, *American Intellectual Elite* [1].

17. Lewis A. Coser, *Men of Ideas* [14], chap. 10, "Literary Bohemia."

18. Kadushin, *American Intellectual Elite* [1], p. 22.

19. A point suggested by Paul DiMaggio, personal communication.

CHAPTER 4. CLIMBING THE EDITORIAL LADDER

1. This chapter draws upon Michele Caplette, "Editorial Career Paths in College Textbook Publishing," which was presented at the 74th Annual Meeting of the American Sociological Association, Boston, Massachusetts, August 1979.

2. The Association of American Publishers, *The Accidental Profession: Education, Training and the People of Publishing* (New York: AAP Education for Publishing Committee, March 1977).

3. Thomas Wehr, "Getting Into Publishing," *Publishers Weekly*, 24 March 1975, p. 23.

4. Ibid.

5. Ibid., p. 24.

6. Ibid.

7. James Lardner, "The Slush Piles: Where Authors' Hopes Abide," *New York Post*, 28 October 1978, p. 13.

8. Rosabeth Moss Kanter, *Men and Women of the Corporation* (New York: Basic Books, 1977), pp. 69–103.

9. Stella Dong, "Publishing's Revolving Door," *Publishers Weekly,* 19 December 1980, pp. 20–23.

10. Ibid., p. 21.

11. Ibid., p. 22.

12. "Employment and Salaries in Book Publishing," *The U.S. Book Publishing Yearbook and Directory, 1979–80* (White Plains, N.Y.: Knowledge Industry Publications, 1980), p. 56.

13. B. S. Dong, "Revolving Door," [9].

14. Allen Barton, et al., "Background Attitudes and Activities of American Elites," in Bogdan Denitch, ed., *The International Study of Opinionmakers* (London: Sage, forthcoming); Robert D. Putnam, *The Comparative Study of Political Elders* (Englewood Cliffs, N.J.: Prentice-Hall, 1976).

CHAPTER 5. TO SIGN OR NOT TO SIGN

1. For a good summary of this work, see Henry Mintzberg, *The Structuring of Organizations* (Englewood Cliffs, N.J.: Prentice-Hall, 1979), pp. 227–40.

2. Tony Schwartz, "A Publisher Who Sells Books," *New York Times Book Review,* 9 December 1979, p. 9.

3. Richard Balkin, *A Writer's Guide to Book Publishing* (New York: Hawthorn Books, 1977), p. 6.

4. For an excellent introduction to the sociology of access and delay, see Barry Schwartz, *Queuing and Waiting* (Chicago: University of Chicago Press, 1975); for an application of the importance of queuing in book publishing, see Walter W. Powell, "Publisher's Decision-Making: What Criteria Do They Use in Deciding Which Books to Publish?" *Social Research* 45 (2[summer 1978]): 227–52.

5. Daniel Menaker, "Unsolicited, Unloved MSS.," *New York Times Book Review,* 1 March 1981, pp. 3, 22.

6. For a more detailed discussion of decision making in scholarly publishing, both commercial houses and university presses, see Walter W. Powell, *Getting Into Print* (Chicago: University of Chicago Press, 1982).

7. N. R. Kleinfield, "Congdon: 'Cottage Industry' in Publishing," *New York Times,* 8 July 1978, p. 25.

8. "Interview with Nat Wartels of Crown," *Publishers Weekly,* 15 May 1978, p. 71.

9. T. Schwartz, "A Publisher" [2], p. 9.

10. Michael Wendroff, "Should We Do The Book? A Study of How Publishers Handle Acquisition Decisions," *Publishers Weekly,* 15 August 1980, p. 26.

11. Ibid., p. 25.

12. Ibid., p. 28.

13. Ibid., p. 27.

CHAPTER 6. WOMEN IN BOOK PUBLISHING: A QUALIFIED SUCCESS STORY

1. "Employees on Payrolls by Industry," in *Employee and Earnings Publication* (Bureau of Labor Statistics, December 1980), table B–2.

2. Women in Publishing, 9 to 5 Organization. *Women in the Boston Area Publishing Industry: A Status Report* (March 1973).

3. Charles Madison, *Book Publishing in America* (New York: McGraw-Hill, 1966), p. 70.

4. Ibid., pp. 277, 284.

5. John Tebbel, *A History of Book Publishing in the United States*, vol. III: *The Golden Age Between Two Wars 1920–1940* (New York: R. R. Bowker, 1978), p. 147.

6. *Publishers Weekly*, 19 May 1928, p. 2035.

7. John Tebbel, *A History of Book Publishing in the United States*, vol. II: *The Expansion of an Industry 1865–1919* (New York: R. R. Bowker, 1975), p. 177.

8. Margery Davies, "Woman's Place Is at the Typewriter: The Feminization of the Clerical Labor Force," in Richard C. Edwards, Michael Reich, and David M. Gordon, eds., *Labor Market Segmentation* (Lexington, Mass.: D. C. Heath, 1975), p. 284.

9. Donald Sheehan, *This Was Publishing: A Chronicle of the Book Trade in the Gilded Age* (Bloomington, Ind.: Indiana University Press, 1952), p. 5.

10. See Dee Garrison, "The Tender Technicians: The Feminization of Public Librarianship, 1876–1905," *Journal of Social History*, (winter 1972–73), pp. 131–59.

11. Interview with Beulah Hagen, Columbia University Oral History Collection, 1976. She has provided a wealth of information regarding authors, publishing, publishers, and her own experiences in publishing.

12. Tebbel, vol. II [7], p. 8.

13. Ibid., p. 176.

14. Ann Geracimos, "Women in Publishing: Where Do They Feel They're Going?" *Publishers Weekly*, 11 November 1974, p. 22.

15. Tebbel, vol. III [5], p. 169.

16. Ibid., p. 259.

17. Ibid., p. 133.

18. Hagen, interview [11].

19. Cynthia Fuchs Epstein, *Woman's Place: Options and Limits in Professional Careers* (Berkeley: University of California Press, 1970), p. 152.

20. See Peter B. Doeringer and Michael J. Piore, *Internal Labor Markets and Manpower Analysis* (Lexington, Mass.: D. C. Heath, 1971) for an explication of the dual labor market (primary and secondary) model. See Francine Blau and Carol Jusenius, "Economists Approaches to Sex Segregation in the Labor Market: An Appraisal," in Martha Blaxall and Barbara Reagan, eds., *Women and the Workplace* (Chicago: University of Chicago Press), pp. 181–200, for a review of the different economic approaches to discrimination against women in the labor market and the applicability of the dual labor market approach.

21. Jessie Bernard, *Academic Women* (University Park: Pennsylvania State University Press, 1964); Caroline Bird, *Born Female: The High Cost of Keeping Women Down* (New York: David McKay, 1968).

22. "Up the Ladder: The Corporate Woman," *Business Week*, 24 November 1975, p. 58.

23. Aljean Harmetz, "Women in Film Industry: Room at the Top," *New York Times* 28 January 1980, p. D10.

24. *The 1980 Media Encyclopedia Working Press of the Nation* (Burlington, Iowa: National Research Bureau, Inc., 1980) lists top executives in the three major networks.

25. Rosabeth Moss Kanter, *Men and Women of the Corporation* (New York: Basic Books, 1977).

26. Lewis A. Coser, *Greedy Institutions* (New York: Free Press, 1974).

27. Daniel Levinson, *The Seasons of a Man's Life* (New York: Alfred A. Knopf, 1978).

28. Michael Korda, *Success! How Every Man and Woman Can Achieve It* (New York: Random House, 1977), p. 169.

29. Geracimos, "Women in Publishing" [14], p. 23.

30. Patricia Holt, "Women and the Job Ladder," in "ABA: Low Key and No-Nonsense," *Publishers Weekly*, 4 July 1980, p. 66.

31. Interview with Elisabeth Geiser, director of the University of Denver Publishing Institute, 30 May 1978.

32. Holt, "Women and the Job Ladder" [30], p. 63.

33. Thomas Whiteside, "Onward and Upward with the Arts: The Blockbuster Complex," first installment, *New Yorker*, 27 September 1980, p. 60.

34. Geracimos, "Women in Publishing" [14], p. 5.

CHAPTER 7. CRAFT AND CORPORATION: THE ORGANIZATION OF PUBLISHING HOUSES

1. George P. Brett, "Book Publishing and Its Present Tendencies," *Atlantic Monthly,* April 1913, p. 455.
2. Kenneth McCormick, "Editors Today" (Bowker Memorial Lecture), quoted in William Miller, *The Book Industry* (New York: Columbia University Press, 1949).
3. Miller, *Book Industry* [2], p. 32.
4. Ibid., p. 33.
5. Ibid.
6. Bennett Cerf, *At Random* (New York: Random House, 1977), p. 278.
7. Ibid.
8. Ibid., p. 281.
9. *Publishers Weekly*, 19 June 1981, p. 18.
10. Edwin McDowell, "Book Publisher Quits, Attacks New Mentality," *New York Times*, 18 June 1981, p. C32.
11. Patricia Holt, "The Hollywood Agent: As Book and Movie Industries Merge, the Agent Turns Packager," *Publishers Weekly*, 14 May 1979, pp. 134–38.
12. Corwin Edwards, "Conglomerate Bigness as a Source of Power," in *Business Concentration Price Policy* (Princeton, N.J.: Princeton University Press, Conference of National Bureau of Economic Research, 1955), pp. 334–35.
13. Henry Mintzberg, "The Manager's Job: Folklore and Fact," *Harvard Business Review*, July/August 1975, pp. 49–61.
14. Charles Perrow, *Complex Organizations: A Critical Essay* (Chicago: Scott, Foresman, 1979), pp. 146–53; Herbert Simon, *Administrative Behavior*, 3rd ed. (New York: Free Press, 1976), pp. 79, 98–103: James March and Herbert Simon, *Organizations* (New York: John Wiley, 1958), pp. 127, 165, 169.
15. Cf. Willard F. Mueller, "Conglomerates: A 'Nonindustry,' " in Walter Adams, *The Structure of American Industry*, 5th ed. (New York: Macmillan, 1977), pp. 461–71.
16. Henry Mintzberg, *The Structuring of Organizations* (Englewood Cliffs, N.J.: Prentice-Hall, 1979), p. 5.

CHAPTER 8. THE MANUFACTURE OF APPEAL

1. *Wall Street Journal*, 31 October 1979.
2. Benjamin M. Compaine, *The Book Industry in Transition: An Economic Study of Book Distribution and Marketing* (White Plains, N.Y.: Knowledge Industry Publications, Inc., 1978).
3. Ibid.
4. Daisy Maryles, "Harlequin to Launch Mystique Books via Tested Market Strategies," *Publishers Weekly*, 28 August 1978, pp. 375–76.
5. Compaine, *Book Industry* [2], p. 146.
6. Elihu Katz and Paul F. Lazarsfeld, *Personal Influence* (Glencoe, Ill.: Free Press, 1955); Elihu Katz, "The Two-step Flow of Communications: An Up-to-date Report on an Hypothesis," *Public Opinion Quarterly* 21 (1957): 67–78. For an application of these theories to publishing, see Leonard Felder, "A Business School Master Plan for Marketing Books," *Publishers Weekly*, 29 January 1979, pp. 76–80.

7. James Coleman, Elihu Katz, and Herbert Menzel, *Medical Innovation: A Diffusion Study* (Indianapolis: Bobbs-Merrill, 1966).

8. Study conducted by Charles Kadushin. For attributes of innovators, see Everett M. Rogers and F. Floyd Shoemaker, *Communication of Innovations: A Cross-Cultural Approach* (New York: Free Press, 1971).

9. Richard Balkin, *A Writer's Guide to Book Publishing* (New York: Hawthorn Books, 1977).

10. Bronislaw Malinowski, *Argonauts of the Western Pacific* (London: Routledge & Kegan Paul, 1922).

11. Nancy Evans, "Marketing Philosophies Are as Diverse as the People Who Make the Decisions," *Publishers Weekly*, 3 July 1978, p. 30–35.

12. Barry Siegel, "Talk Shows Selling Books—TV Often Writes Story," *Los Angeles Times*, 17 October 1979, Part I, p. 1.

13. Thomas Whiteside, "Onward and Upward with the Arts: The Blockbuster Complex," third installment, *New Yorker*, 13 October 1980, pp. 96 and 101.

14. Ibid., p. 102.

15. Hillary S. Kayle, "Booking Authors on the 'Today' Program," *Publishers Weekly*, 5 February 1979.

16. Ibid.

17. Patricia Holt, "Turning Best Sellers into Movies," *Publishers Weekly*, 22 October 1979, pp. 36–40.

18. Robert Dahlin, "Bantam and Its Film Development Subsidiary Find Box Office in Book-Movie Projects," *Publishers Weekly*, 4 April 1980, p. 38–39.

19. See also Nacy Hardin, "For Paperback Houses, There's No Business like Show Tie-in Business," *Publishers Weekly*, 17 February 1975, pp. 46–51; Aljean Harmetz, "Courtship of Hollywood and Novelists Moves Closer to Marriage," *New York Times*, 26 November 1979, p. 15.

20. Avery Hunt, "The Lure of the Cover," *Newsday*, 28 March 1976.

21. Ibid.

22. Nancy Evans, "Publicists: Ingenuity Lights the Fire; Perseverance Fans the Flames," *Publishers Weekly*, 14 March 1980, pp. 28–36.

23. *Publishers Weekly*, 13 August 1979, p. 36.

24. *New York Times*, 28 May 1975.

25. "Where the Book Money Goes," *Publishers Weekly*, 31 October 1980, p. 36.

26. Joyce Bermal, "Feeding News to the Public," *Publishers Weekly*, 8 February 1980, pp. 24–28.

27. Daniel Boorstin, *The Image* (New York: Atheneum, 1962), p. 57.

28. *The Living Talmud: The Wisdom of the Fathers*, trans. and ed. by Judah Goldin (New York: New American Library, Mentor, 1957), chap. II, p. 115.

CHAPTER 9. AUTHORS: A WORM'S-EYE VIEW

1. Disraeli and Longman as cited in Annabell Jones, "Disraeli's *Endymion*: A Case Study," in Asa Briggs, ed., *Essays in the History of Publishing in Celebration of the 250th Anniversary of the House of Longman* (London: Longman, 1974), pp. 141–86.

2. Cass Canfield, *Up and Down and Around* (New York: Harper Colophon, 1973), p. 69.

3. Eugene Exman, *The House of Harper* (New York: Harper & Row, 1967), p. 145.

4. Rebekah Jordan (pseudonym), "The Tangled Truth about Authors' Atrocity Stories," *Publishers Weekly*, 21 May 1979, p. 36.

5. Lewis A. Coser, *Men of Ideas* (New York; Free Press, 1965).

6. Oliver Goldsmith, *An Inquiry into the Present State of Polite Learning in Europe* (1759), in *The Works of Oliver Goldsmith*, vol. II of four vols., ed. Peter Cunningham (New York: Harper, 1881), pp. 56–57; quoted in Leo Lowenthal, *Literature, Popular Culture and Societies* (Englewood Cliffs, N.J.: Prentice-Hall, 1961), pp. 61–62.

7. Henry Nash Smith, *Democracy and the Novel* (New York: Oxford University Press, 1978).

8. Marvin S. Rosen, "Authors and Publishers: 1759–1830," *Science and Society* 32 (2 [spring 1968]): 218–32.

9. See Charles A. Madison, *Irving to Irving: Author-Publisher Relations 1800–1974* (New York: R. R. Bowker, 1974).

10. Henry Holt, "The Commercialization of Literature," *Atlantic Monthly* 96 (5 [November 1905]): 600.

11. Charles E. Smith, "Defining the Economics of Publishing," *Society* 17 (1 [November/December 1979]): 32–33.

12. Paul Kingston, Jonathan R. Cole, and Robert K. Merton, *The Columbia University Survey of American Authors: A Summary of Findings* (New York: Author's Guild, Inc., 1981).

13. Ibid.

14. Ibid.

15. Ibid.

16. Gaye Tuchman and Nina Fortin, "Edging Women Out: Some Suggestions about the Structure of Opportunities and the Victorian Novel," *Signs: Journal of Women in Culture and Society* 6 (2 [winter 1980]): 308–25.

17. Ibid.

18. Ann Douglas *The Feminization of American Culture*, New York: Knopf, 1977.

19. Barron's Profiles of American Colleges, 10th ed. (Woodbury, N.J.: Barron's Educational Series, Inc., 1976).

20. Lowell Hargens and Warren Hagstrom, "Sponsored and Contest Mobility of American Academic Scientists," *Sociology of Education* 40 (1967): 24–38.

21. Robert K. Merton, "The Matthew Effect in Science," *Science* 159 (1968): 56–63.

22. Jonathan Cole and Steven Cole, *Social Stratification in Science* (Chicago: University of Chicago Press, 1973).

23. Harriet Zuckerman, "Stratification in American Science," *Sociological Inquiry* 40 (1970): 235–57.

24. Walter W. Powell, *Getting Into Print: The Decision-Making Process in Scholarly Publishing* (Chicago: University of Chicago Press, 1982).

25. David Caplovitz, *The Poor Pay More* (New York: Free Press, 1963).

26. Authors Guild Bulletin, "Bulletin Second Front: Guild Releases vii, ciii in Series of Semi-Annual Contract Surveys," *Authors Guild Bulletin*, April–May 1979, pp. 15–18.

27. Reginald Stuart, *New York Times*, 15 April 1981, p. 14.

28. The following account is drawn from reports in *Publishers Weekly*, *The BP Report on the Business of Book Publishing*, and the *New York Times*.

29. Madalynne Reuter, "Shere Hite Sues Macmillan Over Limitation Clause," *Publishers Weekly*, 11 June 1979, p. 16.

30. A. E. Hotchner, "A Fool for a Client," *More*, April 1978, pp. 24–29.

31. Herbert Mitgang, "Book Ends: The Satisfactory Clause," *New York Times*, 28 December 1980.

32. *Authors Guild Bulletin*, January/February 1979, p. 1.

33. John F. Baker, "The Year 1980 in Review," *Publishers Weekly*, 13 March 1981, p. 28.

34. Judith Appelbaum and Nancy Evans, *How to Get Happily Published*, (New York: Harper & Row, 1978).

CHAPTER 10. BOOKS WITHOUT AUTHORS

1. Cf. Hans H. Gerth and C. Wright Mills, eds., *From Max Weber: Essays in Sociology* (New York: Oxford University Press, 1948), p. 50.

2. Stephen Grover, "How An Ex-Secretary Climbed to the Top in the Publishing Field," *Wall Street Journal*, 17 September 1979, p.1.

3. For more on subscription publishing, see pp. 111–120 in Benjamin M. Compaine, *The*

Book Industry in Transition: An Economic Study of Book Distribution and Marketing (White Plains, N.Y.: Knowledge Industry Publications, 1978).

4. On the Engel factory, see *New York Times Book Review*, 18 March 1979, pp. 37–38; *New York Times*, 22 May 1979, pp. D1, D13.

5. "Trade News," *Publishers Weekly*, 16 January 1981, p. 45.

6. Ibid., p. 43.

7. Ibid., p. 45.

8. Thomas Whiteside, "Onward and Upward with the Arts: The Blockbuster Complex," second installment, *New Yorker*, 6 October 1980.

9. Ibid., pp. 104–7.

10. For an interesting pen portrait of several writers of movie novelizations, see Darcy O'Brien, "No, but I Wrote the Book," *New York Magazine*, 15 October 1979, pp. 54–59.

11. "Stanley Newman to Move to Head New MCA Publishing Group," *Publishers Weekly*, 3 July 1978, p.23.

12. Ray Walters, "Paperback Talk," *New York Times Book Review*, 3 December 1978, p. 105.

13. Ibid., p. 106.

14. Walter W. Powell, "The Blockbuster Decade: The Media as Big Business," *Working Papers*, July–August 1979, pp. 26–36.

15. Barry Siegel, "Talk Shows Selling Books—TV Often Writes Story," *Los Angeles Times*, 17 October 1979, Part I, p. 1.

16. Phillip Whitten, "An Analysis of the Development and Interaction of Two Innovations in Educational Publishing: the 'Managed' Book and the 'Structured' Book," unpublished doctoral dissertation, Harvard University Graduate School of Education, 1976, pages 36ff. Whitten was associated with CRM and later with the Dushkin Publishing Group (as an editor).

17. Irving Louis Horowitz, "Packaging a Sociological Monsterpiece," *Society*, June 1972.

18. Whitten, "An Analysis" [16], p. 7.

19. Dantia Quirk, *The College Publishing Market*, 1977–1982 (White Plains, N.Y.: Knowledge Industry Publications, 1976).

20. Whitten, "An Analysis" [16], p. 39.

CHAPTER 11. MIDDLEMEN IN PUBLISHING

1. Cf. John Tebbel, *A History of Book Publishing in the United States*, vol. II: *The Expansion of an Industry* 1865–1919 (New York: R. R. Bowker, 1975), pp. 141–147.

2. Ibid., p.15.

3. Quoted in William Targ, *Indecent Pleasures* (New York: Macmillan, 1975), p. 217.

4. Ibid., pp. 51–52.

5. Lewis A. Coser, *Greedy Institutions* (New York: Free Press, 1974).

6. Cf. Hubert M. Blalock, Jr., "Middleman Minorities," in his *Toward a Theory of Minority-Group Relations* (New York: John Wiley, 1967), pp. 79–84.

7. Cf. Robert E. Park, "The Nature of Race Relations" in Edgar T. Thompson, ed., *Race Relations and the Race Problem* (Durham, N.C.: Duke University Press, 1939), pp. 18ff. See also Georg Simmel, "The Stranger," in *The Sociology of Georg Simmel*, ed. and trans. by Kurt H. Wolff (New York: Free Press, 1950), pp. 402–8; and Everett Stonequist, *The Marginal Man* (New York: Russell & Russell, 1961).

8. Cf. Edna Bonacich, "A Theory of Middleman Minorities," *American Sociological Review* 38 (1973): 583–94.

9. On the twin notions of psychological and sociological ambivalence, see Robert K. Merton, *Sociological Ambivalence and Other Essays* (New York: Free Press, 1976).

10. Thomas Weyr, "Midwives, Middlemen and Auctioneers," in *The Business of Publishing* (New York: R. R. Bowker, 1976), p. 52.

11. Ibid.

12. Ibid.

13. Thomas Weyr, "Midwives" [10], p. 52.

14. Thomas Weyr, "Matters of Taste—and Tax Shelters," in *The Business of Publishing* [10], p. 60.

15. Ibid., p. 60.

16. Targ, *Indecent Pleasures* [3], p. 218.

17. Ibid., p. 219.

18. Robert K. Merton, "The Self-Fulfilling Prophecy," in his *Social Theory and Social Structure,* enlarged ed. (New York: Free Press, 1968), pp. 475–90.

19. Lewis A. Coser, *The Functions of Social Conflict* (New York: Free Press, 1956).

20. Rose Laub Coser, *Life in the Ward* (East Lansing: Michigan State University Press, 1962).

21. Linda Wolfe, "Scott Meredith Runs the Lit Biz Like a Crap Game," *More,* November 1976, pp. 38–43.

22. Robert Dahlin, "Agents 1980," *Publishers Weekly,* 28 November 1980, pp. 20–24.

23. Ibid.

24. Ibid.

25. Patricia Holt, "The Hollywood Agent: As Book and Movie Industries Merge, the Agent Turns Packager," *Publishers Weekly,* 14 May 1979, pp. 134–38. Also see N. R. Kleinfeld, "The Literary Agent," *New York Times Book Review,* 7 December 1980.

26. Linda Wolfe, "Mort Janklow: Friends Make the Man," *New York,* 13 February 1978, pp. 41–44.

27. Merton, "Self-Fulfilling Prophecy" [18].

28. Cf. Alvin W. Gouldner, "Cosmopolitans and Locals," in *Administrative Science Quarterly* 2 (December 1957 and March 1958): 281–306 and 444–80, respectively.

29. Cf. Ernest Gellner and John Waterbury, eds., *Patrons and Clients in Mediterranean Societies* (London: Duckworth, 1977), passim.

30. Walter W. Powell, *Getting Into Print: The Decision-Making Process in Scholarly Publishing* (Chicago: University of Chicago Press, 1982).

CHAPTER 12. BOOK REVIEWERS

1. Carlos Baker, "What are Critics Good For?" in Francis Brown, ed., *Opinions and Perspectives* (Boston: Houghton Mifflin, 1964), p. 5.

2. George Orwell, "As I Please," in *The Collected Essays, Journalism and Letters of George Orwell* (New York: Harcourt Brace, 1968), vol. III, pp. 168–69.

3. Quoted in Herbert Gans, *Deciding What's News* (New York: Pantheon, 1979), p. 163.

4. Doris Grumbach, "An Editor's Report," *New York Times Book Review,* 17 August 1975, p. 31.

5. Richard Kluger, "Such Good Friends," *American Libraries,* January 1973, p. 21. We have relied on this most informative essay in several places.

6. Grumbach, "An Editor's Report" [4], p. 31.

7. Ibid.

8. Carlos Baker, "What Are Critics Good For" [1], pp. 7–8.

9. Kurt Lang, "Mass, Class, and the Reader," in Milton Albrecht, James Barnett, and Mason Griff, eds., *The Sociology of Art and Literature* (New York, Praeger, 1970), p. 457.

10. Ibid., p. 464.

11. Robert Lasson, "The Power of the First Word," *New York,* January 1973, p. 67.

12. Ibid.

13. Elizabeth Hardwick, "The Decline of Book Reviewing," in John Fischer and Robert Silvers, eds., *Writing in America* (New Brunswick, N. J.: Rutgers University Press, 1960), pp. 61–72.

14. Ibid., p. 62.

15. Ibid., p. 64.

16. Ibid., p. 68.

17. Ibid., p. 71.

18. John Hollander, "Some Animadversions on Current Reviewing," *Daedalus* 92 (winter 1963): 147.

19. Ibid., p. 149.

20. Henri Peyre, "What Is Wrong with American Book-Reviewing," *Daedalus* 92 (winter 1963): 138–39.

21. Symposium on the Art and Politics of Book Reviewing, Yale University, 11 November 1980, remarks by Harvey Shapiro reported in *Yale Daily News*, 12 November 1980.

22. John Leonard, "Critic's Notebook," *New York Times*, 11 September 1980.

23. Benjamin DeMott, "How to Read Book Reviews," *Atlantic Monthly*, February 1975.

24. William Targ, *Indecent Pleasures* (New York, Macmillan, 1975), pp. 407–9.

25. Symposium on the Art and Politics of Book Reviewing, Yale University, 11 November 1980, remarks by Christopher Lehmann-Haupt reported in *New Haven Register*, 12 November 1980.

26. Ibid.

27. John Leonard, "Books of the Times," *New York Times*, 27 January 1981, p. C9.

28. Ibid.

29. John Leonard, appearing on Dick Cavett's "Literary Panel," 19–20 November 1980 WNET-TV, N.Y., N.Y.

30. Shapiro, Symposium [21].

31. Thomas Weyr, "The Making of the New York Times Book Review," *Publishers Weekly*, 31 July 1972.

32. Irving Howe, personal communication.

33. Weyr, "Making" [31].

34. Robert Dahlin, "Trade News," *Publishers Weekly*, 4 July 1980, p. 43.

35. Philip Nobile, "A Review of the New York Review of Books," *Esquire*, April 1972; and Dennis Wrong, "The Case of the New York Review," *Commentary*, November 1970.

36. Richard Kostelanetz, *The End of Intelligent Writing, Literary Politics in America* (New York: Sheed & Ward, 1974). This is, however, a most partisan source.

37. Symposium on the Art and Politics of Book Reviewing, Yale University, 11 November 1980, remarks by Jack Beatty reported in *Yale Daily News*, 12 November 1980.

38. Ibid.

39. Ibid.

40. Ibid.

41. Ibid.

42. Elizabeth Hardwick, "Decline" [13], p. 72.

43. Charles Kadushin, *The American Intellectual Elite* (Boston: Little Brown, 1974), p. 41.

44. Orwell, "As I Please" [2].

CHAPTER 13. CHANNELS OF DISTRIBUTION

1. John Tebbel, "A 200-Year-Old Bottleneck," paper presented at the Center for the Book in the Library of Congress, excerpt printed in *Publishers Weekly*, 19 September 1980, pp. 139–40.

2. William Jovanovich, "Businesses Catering to Popular Culture Are Suffering Many Unhappy Returns," *New York Times*, 26 December 1980.

3. Ibid.

4. Roy Hanson, "From Sales Pitch to Discount Pile," *Newsday*, 4 October 1978, p. 5A.

5. John Dessauer, *Book Publishing: What It Is, What It Does* (New York: R. R. Bowker, 1974), p. 104.

6. Fritz Machlup and Kenneth Leeson, *Information through the Printed Word*, vol. I: *Book Publishing* (New York: Praeger, 1978).

7. Ibid.

8. Beverly T. Watkins, "College Stores Say They Lose Money Selling Textbooks," *Chronicle of Higher Education*, 23 April 1979, p. 13.

9. *Wall Street Journal*, 14 May 1981, p. 1.

10. Charles W. Stevens, "Textbook 'Freebies' Are Very Expensive, Publishers Complain," *Wall Street Journal*, 10 November 1978.

11. Beverly T. Watkins, "Some Publishers to Relax Pricing Rules for Textbooks," *Chronicle of Higher Education*, 5 May 1980, p. 10.

12. Mike Shatzkin, "Distribution Deals," *Publishers Weekly*, 23 June 1980, pp. 31–36.

13. N. R. Kleinfield, "On the Road with a Book Salesman," *New York Times Book Review*, 24 August 1980, pp. 3, 20, 21.

14. Ibid., p. 20.

15. Bruce Bliven, Jr., "Profiles: Book Traveller," *The New Yorker*, 12 November 1973, pp. 51–108; also published as *Book Traveller* (New York: Dodd, Mead, 1975).

16. Ibid., p. 100.

17. "ABA Membership Profile Links Control of Expenses to Profitability," *Publishers Weekly*, 20 February 1978, pp. 98–102.

18. For more information on Dayton-Hudson, see Harvey D. Shapiro, "The Daytons of Dayton-Hudson," *New York Times*, 17 June 1979, Sunday Business Section, pp. 1 and 9.

19. The data are from *BP Report on the Business of Book Publishing*, 8 June 1981, vol. 6, no. 27, pp. 1–2.

20. See Edwin McDowell, "B. Dalton Opening Two Stores," *New York Times*, 28 April 1981, p. C9.

21. *BP Report* [19].

22. *U.S. Book Publishing Yearbook and Directory, 1980–81* (White Plains, N.Y.: Knowledge Industry Publications), p. 96.

23. Quoted in John Mutter, "B. Dalton Bookseller: A Novel Approach to Retailing," *Sales and Marketing Management*, 14 May 1979, pp. 49–51.

24. Daisy Maryles, "The Year's Bestselling Books," *Publishers Weekly*, 13 March 1981, pp. 31–36.

25. Judson Hand, "The Big Business of Bookselling," *Flightime*, December, 1978.

26. "Mass Merchandising Hits the Bookstores," *Business Week*, 9 February 1974, p. 80.

27. Quoted in "B. Dalton Marks a Year in its Fifth Avenue Store," *New York Times*, 14 November 1979.

28. See the many similar comments of wholesalers in "Wholesalers Assess Chain Business: Chains Becoming More Restrictive," *BP Report on the Business of Book Publishing*, 23 January 1978.

29. Book Industry Study Group, *Book Industry Trends 1978* (Darien, Conn.: 1979), p. 163.

30. Mutter, "B. Dalton Bookseller" [23].

31. Daisy Maryles, "How Chains Impact on Independent Retailers," *Publishers Weekly*, 31 July 1978, pp. 52–54.

32. Maureen Taylor, "Boston—A Lot of Literacy," *Publishers Weekly*, 31 October 1980, pp. 38–39.

33. Michael Robinson and Ray Olszewski, "The Economics of Book Publishing," Federal Trade Commission Symposium on Media Concentration, 14–15 December 1978, Washington, D.C., vol. II, pp. 604–44.

34. Ibid., p. 638.

35. Roger H. Smith, "Independent Distributors," parts I and II, *Publishers Weekly*, 27 November and 4 December 1978.

36. Roger H. Smith, "How Mr. Zinna Fills the Racks in Wilmington, Delaware," *Publishers Weekly*, 2 April 1975.

37. Thomas Whiteside, "Onward and Upward with the Arts—The Blockbuster Complex," *The New Yorker*, 29 September, 6 October, and 13 October 1980; Susan Braudy,

"Paperback Auction: What Price a 'Hot' Book?," *New York Times Sunday Magazine*, 21 May 1978, pp. 18, 91–95, 106–8.

38. In particular see Oscar Dystel's annual Bowker Memorial Lecture, reprinted in *Publishers Weekly*, 12 December 1980, pp. 18–25.

39. Carl A. Kroch, "A Need for Fundamental Change," *Publishers Weekly*, 19 September 1980, pp. 140–41.

40. Daniel Machalaba, "Harcourt Brace to Ban Return of Books," *Wall Street Journal*, 3 November 1980.

41. Quoted in *BP Report on Business of Book Publishing*, 4 May 1981, p. 2.

EPILOGUE: PUBLISHERS AS GATEKEEPERS OF IDEAS

1. Quoted in Hugh Seidman, "Can Books Survive the Book Business?," in John Y. Cole, *Responsibilities of the American Book Community* (Washington, D.C.: The Center for the Book, Library of Congress, 1981), p. 27.

2. George P. Brett, "Book Publishing and Its Present Tendencies," *Atlantic Monthly*, April 1913, pp. 454–62.

3. For example, see the divergent testimony before the Subcommittee on Antitrust, Monopoly, and Business Rights, U.S. Senate, 13 March 1980, by Townsend W. Hoopes, president of the Association of American Publishers, and Irwin Karp, counsel for the Authors Guild. Their comments are printed in Cole, *Responsibilities* [1].

4. See, in particular, "Endangered List," *The Nation* 231 (12 [October 1980]); and Daniel Machalaba, "Controversial Tax Ruling Perils Stock of Spare Parts, Other Items," *Wall Street Journal*, 11 December 1980.

5. See Gordon Graham, "After the Consent Decree: A New Era in the Marketing of English-Language Books," *Publishers Weekly*, 31 January 1977, pp. 38–40; Roger Berthond, "Publishing 1: Confidence Tinged with Anxiety over U.S. Challenge," London *Times*, 1 November 1976, p. 4; and Herbert Mitgang, "Publishing: A New Atlantic Alliance," *New York Times*, 25 March 1977.

6. Maxwell J. Lillienstein, General Counsel, American Booksellers Association, in Cole, *Responsibilities* [1], pp. 34–35.

7. Richard Phalon, "Publishing," *Forbes*, 5 January 1981, pp. 253–54.

APPENDIX ON METHODS

1. Norman H. Nie, et. al., *SPSS: Statistical Package for the Social Sciences* (New York: McGraw-Hill, 1975); Norman H. Nie, et. al., *SCSS: A User's Guide to the SCSS Conversational System* (New York; McGraw-Hill, 1980).

2. Walter W. Powell, *Getting Into Print* (Chicago: University of Chicago Press, 1982).

3. Observers were: Walter Powell, Laurie Michael Roth, Michele Caplette, Frank Sirianni, Mary Ann Devanna, and Annabelle Sreberny.

4. Mary Anne Devanna and Charles Fombrun, "Dominance and Social Structure," paper prepared for the 39th Academy of Management Meetings, Atlanta, Georgia, August 1979.

5. Michele Caplette, *Women in Publishing: A Study of Careers in Organizations*, Ph.D. dissertation, SUNY at Stony Brook, May 1981.

Index

Index

Film industry: acquisitions of publishing houses by, 28; and book packaging, 265–66; and commercialization, 19; diversification in, 25; inside trading with, 182; and marketing of blockbusters, 217–18; and novelizations, 266–69; sale of rights to, 212, 213; tie-ins with, see Tie-ins

Filmways Pictures, 28, 268
Final Payments (Gordon), 222
Financial department, 186
Fine, Don, 42–43
Fitzgerald, F. Scott, 89
FitzGerald, Frances, 56
Flaubert, Gustave, 3
Focus groups, 205
Follett Corporation, 341
Fombrun, Charles, 380
Forbes magazine, 372
Foreign Affairs, 88
Foreign Policy, 88
Foreign sales, 337, 371–72
Fortin, Nina, 233
Fortune magazine, 32, 36, 108
Free Lance Newsletter, 274
Free-lance services, 25, 40, 123, 186–87, 189; and author relations, 250; and managed texts, 273
Free Press, 49, 64
Freedgood, Ann, 50
Freeman, John, 46
Freight charges, policies on, 359–60
Freundlich, Larry, 53
Friede, Donald, 149
Full Disclosure (Safire), 302

Gartenberg, Max, 287
Gatekeeping, 4–5, 6–7, 62, 97–98, 362, 365, 369, 372
General Electric (GE), 26, 56
General Learning, 56
General Telephone, 26
Geoghegan, John J., 182
Gissing, George, 18
Gödel, Escher, Bach (Hofstadter), 316

Godine, David, Company, 47, 359
Goethe, Johann Wolfgang von, 308
Goffman, Erving, 323
Goldberg, Lynn, 222
Goldsmith, Oliver, 226
Gordon, Mary, 222
Gosse, Edmund, 22
Gothic romances, 264
Gottlieb, Robert, 105, 253, 294, 298, 311
Gran, Phyllis, 148
Great Los Angeles Fire, The, 266
Green, Dan, 138
Green, Gerald, 218
Griffin, Merv, 217
Gross, John, 324
Grosset & Dunlap, 23, 28, 268
Growth, pressures for, 32
Grumbach, Doris, 310, 312
Guber, Peter, 266
Guest, Judith, 107
Gulf & Western, 28, 34, 51

Hagel, Raymond, 28
Hagen, Beulah, 151–54
Haley, Alex, 218, 219
Hamilton, Elisabeth, 152
Hand, Judson, 352
Hannan, Michael T., 46
Harcourt, Alfred, 152
Harcourt Brace Jovanovich, 25, 28, 55, 65, 68, 267, 335, 359
Hardcover trade books, see Trade houses
Hardwick, Elizabeth, 317, 328
Harlequin Books, 201, 264
Harper & Brothers, 21, 149, 151–53, 225
Harper & Row, 27, 28, 47–49, 56, 99, 140, 152, 182, 204, 219, 256, 267, 273, 278–79, 340, 344
Harper's magazine, 114, 329
Harvard Coop, 341
Harvard University, 235, 237, 294
Harvard University Press, 68

402